DISMANTLING COMMUNISM

DISMANTLING COMMUNISM
Common Causes and Regional Variations

Edited by
Gilbert Rozman
with Seizaburo Sato and Gerald Segal

The Woodrow Wilson Center Press
Washington, D.C.

The Johns Hopkins University Press
Baltimore and London

Editorial Offices:
The Woodrow Wilson Center Press
370 L'Enfant Promenade, S.W., Suite 704
Washington, D.C. 20024-2518
Telephone 202-287-3000, ext. 218

Order from:
The Johns Hopkins University Press
701 W. 40th St., Suite 275
Baltimore, Md. 21211-2190
Telephone 1-800-537-5487

Printed in the United States of America
∞ Printed on acid-free paper

9 8 7 6 5 4 3 2 1

Library of Congress Cataloging-in-Publication Data

Dismantling communism : common causes and regional variations / edited
  by Gilbert Rozman with Seizaburo Sato and Gerald Segal.
        p.   cm.
    Includes bibliographical references and index.
    ISBN 0-943875-35-8
    1. Communist countries—Politics and government. 2. Communist
countries—Economic policy. 3. Post-communism. 4. World
politics—1985–1995. I. Rozman, Gilbert. II. Satō, Seizaburō,
1932–   . III. Segal, Gerald, 1935–
D860.D58   1992
320.947—dc20   92-15892
                                                                     CIP

The Center is the "living memorial" of the United States of America to the
nation's twenty-eighth president, Woodrow Wilson. The U.S. Congress
established the Woodrow Wilson Center in 1968 as an international institute
for advanced study, "symbolizing and strengthening the fruitful relationship
between the world of learning and the world of public affairs." The Center
opened in 1970 under its own presidentially appointed board of directors.

In all its activities the Woodrow Wilson Center is a nonprofit, nonpartisan
organization, supported financially by annual appropriations from the U.S.
Congress, and by the contributions of foundations, corporations, and
individuals. Conclusions or opinions expressed in Center publications and
programs are those of the authors and speakers and do not necessarily reflect
the views of the Center staff, fellows, trustees, advisory groups, or any
individuals or organizations that provide financial support to the Center.

Woodrow Wilson International Center for Scholars
1000 Jefferson Drive, S.W.
Washington, D.C. 20560
(202) 357-2429

CONTENTS

FIGURE

TABLES

PREFACE

This international study of "dismantling communism" had its origins in Oiso, Japan, shortly after China's 1989 Tiananmen tragedy. The occasion was a conference on the reform process in China convened by the Asia Pacific Association of Japan and the Royal Institute of International Affairs of the United Kingdom. This timely and lively meeting was the second in a series of British-Japanese conferences on the socialist world funded by the Sasakawa Peace Foundation. In an effort to broaden the scope of future collaborative research, the Oiso convenors, led by Seizaburo Sato, invited the Woodrow Wilson International Center for Scholars to participate, with a view towards creating a tri-regional intellectual forum. The challenge was not just to involve American, Japanese, and European scholars, but to think comparatively about the reform process across the Leninist systems of Asia, Eastern Europe, and the Soviet Union.

The rapidity with which the Tiananmen events changed the prognosis for China was harbinger of the rapidity with which change, very different kinds of change, was coming to the socialist world. These rapid changes were uppermost in the minds of scholars from the United Kingdom, Japan, and the United States who met together and in separate national groups numerous times during 1990 and 1991. Yet their task was to think historically and comparatively in an effort to probe the deeper commonalities and differences of the socialist world. These seminars in Britain, the United States, and Japan resulted in two international workshops held at the Woodrow Wilson Center in Washington, D.C., in October 1990 and January 1991. The chapters that constitute this volume were initially presented at those workshops.

They were presented, but not finalized. Perhaps more than most such international projects, this has been a truly dynamic, integrative, and ongoing process. Authors were asked, whenever possible, to stretch beyond their own regional or disciplinary context. The views and critiques of colleagues with different perspectives became essential. And as Eastern Europe and the Soviet Union underwent systemic change in 1990, 1991, and 1992, new questions were asked and new answers sought.

This project benefited from a remarkable continuity of participants at conferences, planning meetings, and workshops convened in Tokyo, London, and Washington. Although not all are represented in the volume, all made substantive contributions. Participants from Japan included Shigeki Hakamada, Tsuyoshi Hasegawa, Etsuro Hondo, Takayuki Ito, Hiroshi Kimura, Tatsumi Okabe, Seizaburo Sato, and Akihiko Tanaka. Participants from the United Kingdom included: Judy Batt, Barry Buzan, Peter Ferdinand, Paul Lewis, Neil Malcolm, Edwina Moreton, John Phipps, and Gerald Segal. Participants from the United States included Thomas Bernstein, Nicholas Lardy, Daniel Nelson, Thomas Remington, Gilbert Rozman, and Brantly Womack.

This widely scattered group became an intellectual community due to the leadership of the three co-chairmen: Seizaburo Sato, Gerald Segal, and Gilbert Rozman. Seizaburo Sato's international experience and full participation contributed greatly to the collegial spirit and success of this complex project. All who were involved owe a special debt of gratitude to Gilbert Rozman, who served as primary editor of this volume. He carefully read, re-read, edited, and re-edited each of the chapters. His persistence in urging all writers to think comparatively, to reach beyond China or the Soviet Union or East Europe, stretched the comparative reach of each chapter.

The Woodrow Wilson International Center for Scholars provided central coordination and hospitality during this two-year project. We benefited as an institution and as individuals. In exploring common and uncommon themes in socialist countries, my colleagues Blair Ruble, Director, Kennan Institute for Advanced Russian Studies, John Lampe, Director, East European Studies, and I initiated cross-regional comparative enquiries, which are continuing. Kirsti Hastings, Asia Program Assistant, provided administrative support.

This book brings together chapters resulting from the first phase of this comparative study of socialist reform. A second phase, the study of the global impact of changes in the socialist world, will be forthcoming.

The Sasakawa Peace Foundation provided generous financial support both for the international workshops and for research in Britain, Japan, and the United States. Kazuo Takahashi, Program Director of the Sasakawa Peace Foundation, initiated this project and attended most of the sessions. Toshihiko Okoshi, Program Officer, provided helpful administrative suggestions and likewise attended most sessions. Their encouragement and confidence is deeply appreciated by all who were involved.

Mary Brown Bullock
Director, Asia Program
Woodrow Wilson Center

INTRODUCTION

Gilbert Rozman

By the end of the 1980s, the world community had become convinced
that communism, as it had been practiced for more than half a century,
could not survive. It was in crisis. At the same time, capitalism continued to advance, not only in the West but also in East Asia, the recent
hothouse environment of industrialization. Whatever its problems, capitalism had moved forward into a new era of regional and global integration characterized by high hopes for technological progress and
lively and invigorating competition. The conclusion based on this stark
contrast seemed unmistakable: communist-led countries one by one
would succumb by shedding their outdated system and joining the world
capitalist one. What had begun with Soviet de-Stalinization in 1956 and
had been given new life with China's Four Modernizations in 1978
accelerated under the impact of the open door, the responsibility system,
glasnost, perestroika, "new thinking," informal associations, popular
movements, free elections, and the "new world order." In short, communism began to crumble before our eyes. Reform of communism
promised a radiant future, even if the path of transition looked rocky.

In the first months of 1991, with Chinese intellectuals on trial and
mounting Soviet pressure on the secession-minded republics, the mood
of optimism about establishing a harmonious global community faded.
The glow of easy victory in the Persian Gulf War was shadowed by the
uncertainty of further cooperation with the two communist members
of the U.N. Security Council. Where communism had not quickly collapsed as a transplant imposed by foreign armies, the three-way alliance
of the Communist Party, the military, and the security forces narrowed
the scope of reform at home and raised military concerns abroad. Would
Chinese troops threaten to reunite Taiwan by force despite the opposition of the United States and all of capitalist East Asia? Would Soviet
armed forces refuse to settle for a military budget commensurate with
the country's weak economy and insist on a union of fifteen republics

in the face of secessionist tendencies spreading across national frontiers nearly as fast as the radioactivity from Chernobyl had spread five years earlier? Or, no less alarming to those eager for a single world order, would Moscow and Beijing revive their special relationship of the 1950s to ward off capitalist pressures? Li Peng, China's Premier, suggested as much during the Gulf War in January 1991. With old-style communists well entrenched in the inner circles of the Kremlin and Zhongnanhai, reforms appeared to be stymied; dismantling the old order seemed to have turned into a halting process with an insurmountable core of opposition.

Early in 1991 the fate of the transformation hung precariously in the balance. The heroes of reform had left the center stage, and Deng Xiaoping and Mikhail Gorbachev readily countenanced harsh critics of the West and the market. Hu Yaobang, Zhao Ziyang, Eduard Shevardnadze, and Aleksandr Yakovlev—the unabashed champions of reform— had suddenly fallen victim to the skeptics. In China the momentum of earlier economic reform continued, leaving a time bomb ticking beneath the closed political and ideological environment the leaders were rushing to create. In the Soviet Union Gorbachev's retreat from a reform platform was more ambiguous, and at the level of the republics the forces of both separatism and reform retained a strong base of operation. Nonetheless, in August, on the eve of the formal signing of the agreement first reached in late April between Gorbachev, Boris Yeltsin, and the leaders of eight other republics on creating a smaller, decentralized union, a three-day "palace coup," placing Gorbachev under house arrest, sounded a new alarm. As in Beijing, hard-liners were prepared to turn loose their awesome forces to subdue the reform activists, and for a few worrisome days observers understandably reacted with pronounced skepticism about the prospects for continued reforms. After the coup failed a headlong rush began to demolish the old structure, but worrisome possibilities remained: The collapse of the economy might prompt another coup by forces that could not quickly be dispersed or political separatism matched by independent militaries could engulf the dismembered Soviet Union, now called the Commonwealth of Independent States, in internecine conflict. Under Boris Yeltsin Russia took the lead in assaulting the remaining structure of the communist system, arousing a public backlash due to rampant inflation and insecurity.

This book steps back from both the giddy optimism anticipating unconditional surrender by communism to capitalism and the alarmist pessimism warning that communism might somehow get back on its feet. The pressures of the 1980s and the constellation of pro-reform forces, internal and external, were not sufficient to produce a quick capitulation of the strongholds of communism in Moscow and, especially, in Beijing, whatever the enthusiasm for radical reform may have been at the periphery in Berlin, Riga, and Shenzhen or among the most Westernized intellectuals physically close to the center but mentally never part of it. Indeed, even when the miscalculations of hard-liners produced a debacle (China's antispiritual pollution campaign in 1983–84 and especially the Soviet Union's failed coup of August 1991), remnants of the old order remained entrenched in ways that could still shape the future. Neither the backlash mood in China from mid-1989 and in the Soviet Union for a time in early 1991 nor the residual power of the surviving coalition of antireform forces offered convincing proof that the momentum of dismantling could be fully arrested. If communism with its outdated technology cannot muster the brute force needed to seize the assets of its rival, and if the people refuse to watch from the sidelines as the already huge gap in modernization widens, then the reforms will proceed. Moreover, the old order will continue to be disassembled, even if the hybrid between the surviving elements of communism—including those embedded in the remnants of the Soviet Union—and the emerging shifts toward a market economy and democracy does not closely resemble what we regard as capitalism. Short-term ups and downs must not keep us from seeing where the long-term forces are leading.

Pressures to dismantle the past are gathering force, but we should avoid the temptation of assuming that short-term political struggles must be resolved in favor of the genuine reformers. After all, Hu Yaobang and Zhao Ziyang dared to risk their high posts in an uphill struggle to sustain the reform momentum, and both Shevardnadze and Yakovlev raised their voices in dramatic warnings against the danger of dictatorship before their worst fears were confirmed for a short time. Sometimes in the open and sometimes out of sight, a continuous confrontation ensues between those for accelerated reform and those wary of anything but minimal adjustment. From time to time this clash bursts into the limelight, producing the decisive turning points of our contemporary era. In this book we point to factors that led to different outcomes at Tiananmen in June 1989 and before the Russian parliament building in August 1991. We also take care to view these events within the context of the long-term processes that are deteriorating the old system. We also recognize where a threshold has been crossed, turning reform into full-scale dismantling. This occurred quickly under popular pressure in

Eastern Europe and fortuitously in most of the Soviet Union after the August coup further discredited the Communist Party. By early 1992 it still had not occurred in China, Vietnam, or North Korea.

Our book takes a comparative, interregional approach to the transition from communism. This is needed precisely because the old order, established according to a common blueprint, remains a formidable force in shaping the emerging, but ill-defined, new order. In one of the two giants of communism, China, as in Vietnam, the old order is so strongly represented in the management of reform that it inevitably remains at the center of attention in building anew. In the other giant, now fractured into fifteen pieces, hurried privatization as well as political instability is likely to favor the forces of old, however they may be renamed. Even in the postsocialist societies of Eastern Europe, the legacy of the deeply rooted communist order cannot be denied. Disentangling the clinging vines of the once omnipresent party from the fragile shoots of the emergent civil society poses a common problem across Eurasia from Poland to Vietnam. To properly appreciate the problem and the prospects for a solution, a comparative and inter-regional approach offers special promise.

The dismantling of communism, whether at once or piece by piece, is a process unlike any that has preceded it. Of course, there have been many cases of decentralization and democratization by discredited authoritarian states. Purges of old leaders and their followers, elections of new parliaments, property redistribution to stimulate material incentives, and renewed openness to the outside world often followed, bringing a new order on the heels of the old. The fate of communism is qualitatively different for at least three reasons. First, its apparatus for imposing order is enormous, combining the resources of the military, the security forces, and the party cells. This apparatus assumes a dual role. It is the instrument responsible for "reform from above," and it is the shield against "chaos from below" as reform unfolds. Second, communism is closely identified in several countries with great-power nationalism. As the reform process heightens ethnic rivalries or fear about the subversive influx of foreign ways, communism simultaneously presents itself as amenable to some degree of openness and as the defender of the national essence. Third, the entire welfare system, based on job security, suppressed inflation, and a perverse kind of economic predictability, is inextricably associated with the communist order.

A changing order is supposed to sacrifice these sacred cows in the name of efficiency, but communism harbors claims to both agendas at the same time. Whether initiated in the name of socialism or in the hope of replacing it, reforms threaten the maintenance of public order, the claims to great-power nationalism, and the minimal guarantee of popular welfare. Sooner or later, communism responds to the frustrations aroused by reform and capitalizes on its role as defender of these deep-seated values. Given these circumstances, we must avoid the temptation of simply predicting its speedy and total collapse, with no lingering impact on the shape of the future. Instead, we must search for new patterns of interaction between forces new and old.

Especially for the Soviet Union and China, it is simplistic to expect convergence with Western capitalism without, at the very least, a mixed system of indefinite duration. In place of central plans and ministerial powers, local and regional authorities gain considerable power. Monopolies thrive during shortages and when dependency on authorities is high. Small and weak firms often must seek permits, protection, supplies, and other favors in a nonmarket environment. Bartering has spread in the Soviet Union as the ruble and state allocations of materials and funds have become unreliable. In China there has been no collapse of the center nor of the currency, but price controls, enterprise subsidies, and other artificial barriers to market competition still distort the forces of capitalism. There is no direct transition from socialism to capitalism.

This study of the transformation of socialism ends with mid-winter 1992: From this vantage point it is possible to look back to the changes from 1978 to 1991 that reveal the striking similarity in the deep-seated causes of reform. At the same time it is also possible to discern sharp regional variations in the path of transformation. We can trace the domino effects in Eastern Europe after the opening of the Berlin Wall, Russia's transition from Gorbachev's era of reforms to the start of a Yeltsin era of full-scale dismantling, and the post-Tiananmen era in Asia when China's economic gains continued to propel the area into the international economy while party elders whose leadership dated back to the pre-communist era resisted a broadening of reforms. Where communism and nationalism most obviously worked at cross purposes, the shift from low-keyed moderate reform to full-scale reform brought, without delay, a rush to remove the Communist Party from power. Where the relationship was more ambiguous, the party could play the champion of reform for a time. This lengthened the stage when reform was inconsistent and hesitant.

The terms "reform," "revolution," and "dismantling" all figure in the analysis that follows. Obviously, communist leaders offer different definitions of reform depending on their immediate objectives. Sometimes the reforms were no more than narrow accommodations to change, not intended to sidetrack the building of communism or to challenge its fundamental principles. At other times the changes were far-reaching.

For example, Deng at the start of the 1980s accepted the breakup of collective farming, and Gorbachev in the first months of 1990 ended the Communist Party's constitutional monopoly over power. We review the whole range of reform and, by comparing the setbacks of June 1989 in China and of August 1991 in the Soviet Union, we also assess the limits of reform and how domestic forces work to reverse them. Then, by looking at Russia's accelerated dismantling after August and the overall momentum of the collapse across most of Eurasia, we consider the pressures still mounting on Asian communism.

Our treatment of reform does not have a particular endpoint in mind (for example, complete convergence with some Western model). Reform includes any major changes toward a market economy, decentralized authority, democracy, freedom of information, openness to the outside world, meritocracy, material incentives, demilitarization, and elimination of the special status of the Communist Party. This is not an exhaustive list, but it conveys our interdisciplinary interest in politics, international relations, economics, and sociology. Tentative reforms nibble away at the command economy, at centralization, at censorship, and at a closed society. Radical reforms shake the very pillars of the communist system, even if damage control by the leadership limits, for a time, how much might be swept away.

Definitions of socialism have varied widely over the years and across countries. Sometimes the term is used to refer to "social democracy" and to distinguish Western European "welfare states" from communist states. At other times the term differentiates the current condition of countries led by Marxist-Leninist parties from the promised, but still distant, communist future. We follow this second usage by labeling the countries we study, at least prior to a transfer of power through elections to another political party, as "socialist." Since they are led by Communist parties, we also identify them, especially when we are highlighting political or ideological features, as communist. The two labels are often used interchangeably. Even though the transformation can have many outcomes, including a greater similarity with the social democracies, we call the process of change the "transition from socialism" or the "dismantling of communism." We say this well aware that aspects of communism will continue to shape these countries. Indeed, the party's power is not easily transferred unless a full onslaught is directed against its role in the workplace, in social organizations, and in the control of public order and information.

The contributors to this volume are at least of two minds on the use of the term "revolution." On the one hand, the term seems eminently suitable because of the gravity of the transformation in political institutions, economic systems, and social structures. If the cataclysms that gave rise to communism in Russia, China, Vietnam, and elsewhere are properly referred to as revolutions, the no less momentous reversals of many of those changes are revolutions as well. On the other hand, if the hallmark of a revolution is mass violence on a vast scale, then how should we characterize the festival atmosphere and popular celebrations in many of the nations we examine? At least in Eastern Europe, what was imposed by Stalin's armed forces might best be called a form of imperialism rather than revolution and what was achieved at the end of the 1980s might be termed a form of national liberation. Yet communism created its own full-fledged domestic machinery; many of the same ingredients are present in one country after another in the struggle for reforming and then dismantling the weight of communism that pressed heavily upon these nations for four decades.

"Dismantling" suggests the depths to which reform has been driven and the revolutionary consequences of change, however much it has been directed from above. Within the once formidable communist bloc of nations, an irrepressible force is taking apart a structure built to serve a command economy, a mobilized and sheltered society, and a single-minded, all-powerful dictatorship. What starts as a careful release of selected elements in the structure accelerates into a tumble-down collapse. The possible outcomes of dismantling are still far from clear in the countries themselves, and we must concentrate on the process itself and variations in it.

Self-definitions of socialism in communist-led countries have highlighted class power (the proletariat), the social class system (no antagonistic classes), the distribution system (to each according to his work), and the ownership system (the means of production are held by the people as represented by the state and collectives). All fail to present an adequate image of reality. What we observe is not power in the hands of the working class; a two-class system of workers and peasants with a so-called stratum of intelligentsia; distribution that measures a worker's contribution to national well-being or ownership on behalf of the entire people. These were ideological misrepresentations of reality.

Deng Xiaoping's four cardinal principles, first articulated in March 1979, come closer to the essence of socialism. First, China must keep to the socialist road (that is, identify itself as socialist and reject criticisms that question this principle). Second, it must uphold the dictatorship of the proletariat (that is, reject an open political process based on multiparty pluralism). Third, it must support the leadership of the Communist Party (that is, limit control within the society to those acting under the leadership of the party). Finally, China must adhere to Marxism–Leninism–Mao Zedong thought (that is, retain ideology as a guide to action). When one or more of these principles is relaxed, as occurred under Gorbachev, we should not jump to the conclusion that socialism is gone. The ideology may be ridiculed and downplayed, even by some who favor continued rule by the Communist Party. The party may accept open elections for some offices or even entire parliaments. The trappings of democracy may obscure the pillars of dictatorship. As a result, we can speak of "reform of socialism," but communism itself is replaced only when the Communist Party and those representing it lose their privileged position in the society.

A number of Eastern European countries made a break with socialism in 1989–1990, and Moscow in early 1990 eliminated article 6 guaranteeing a monopoly to the Communist Party and recognized free elections for some parliaments, including the democratic election of mayors in the largest Soviet cities. Yet even this was not tantamount to ending the socialist system. Additional changes in the Supreme Soviet, in the property system, and in democratic controls over the military, the KGB, and the Communist party are all necessary in the transition from socialism. Communism endures as long as the party and the nomenklatura remain rather isolated from reform. Only in the late summer of 1991 was the political stalemate in Moscow broken, followed by initiatives in all of these areas. At last communism had fallen in its first and most important stronghold.

Reform of a communist-led system is not an unusual occurrence. A social system prone to radical experimentation cannot escape the necessity of a periodic cooling off. Leaders who resort to War Communism, the Great Purges, the Great Leap Forward, the Great Proletarian Cultural Revolution, and other experiments and outrages against humanity must allow their exhausted nation occasional respite. Reform in its broadest sense is a retreat from communist policies—from a system defined differently by various leaders and national movements, but retaining many shared elements from the Leninist, and especially the Stalinist, course that established the common starting point.

Since reforms proceed at varying rates in different sectors, it is no easy task to find a composite score for the degree of reform in a particular country. For example, a severe setback to political reform may not seriously disrupt microlevel liberalization of the economy. Inconsistencies can exist, but through comparison we also can identify tendencies to overcome them and characteristic sequences in the reform process. These regularities should not be surprising. The causes of reform are much the same from country to country. The history of socialism over at least several decades unfolded in a similar manner.

Looking at the stages of socialism from its inception and at its successive, usually abortive, attempts to reform, we discern many reasons for the timing and the intensity of the reform impulses. The dynamics of communism can be traced to generational change at the top in the leadership and the party, to internal developments in the society related to modernization and popular mood, and to external developments in the international communist system and the world economy. Relatively weak impulses stemming exclusively from exhaustion of the internal society and domestic economic collapse produce tentative reforms. Stronger impulses aroused by changes in leadership heighten the will to undertake lasting reforms. When these factors are in sync—a major change in leadership, a desperate society, and an inviting international arena—fundamental reforms can be achieved.

This constellation of favorable factors formed after Mao's death. The Deng leadership rose to power disassociated from the policies of the Cultural Revolution, aware of the utter exhaustion of a completely dissatisfied people, and allied with capitalist countries eager to make China a close economic partner. In the Soviet Union some favorable factors operated after Stalin's death, but the greater continuity of leadership, the lesser panic about domestic conditions, and the deeper sense of superpower rivalry made full-fledged reforms unlikely. Only when Gorbachev took office did a true reform constellation emerge. An abrupt generational change occurred, worries abounded about domestic stagnation, and there was hopelessness over the high-technology advances by rivals, who, after all, could be persuaded to share their knowledge and investments with Moscow as they had done with Beijing. In Eastern Europe the removal of Moscow's external constraint was sufficient to jolt the populace into welcoming what promised to be the warm embrace of Western Europe. In Vietnam, close to the dazzle of ASEAN's upsurge, and, even more, in Mongolia, with no particular foreign constraints, reform forces also made notable gains.

Even among countries with strong impulses to pursue reform, the intensity of the stimuli varied as did the expectations about what might be achieved. Leaders, driven by different immediate priorities, opted for different approaches to reform. The following chapters single out four of the priorities for separate treatment: sustaining economic development, especially seen in China's reform strategy; achieving political legitimacy, a focal point of reform in Poland and elsewhere in Eastern Europe; coping with an increasingly modern society, seen in its purest form in the large and relatively autonomous countries of the Soviet Union and China; and integrating into the world division of labor and the world order, a problem faced in socialist countries large and small. These goals could not be pursued in isolation; it is necessary also to examine the reform process as a whole, particularly the combination of economic and political change that often takes the center stage.

Part I explores the stages of reform. The first chapter by Gilbert Rozman reviews the history of reform in China and the Soviet Union and discusses reform stages as measured by five determinants: leadership, the public mood, modernization, the world environment, and ideology. After the stage of transition to socialism and the stage of radical socialism, both of which contained forces building toward reform, a stage of tentative socialist reform began. The last stage is radical reform. It is fraught with uncertainty and resistance, and it leads to the dismantling of socialism. In Chapter 2 Tsuyoshi Hasegawa offers a framework for identifying the relationship between political and economic reform. He explores alternative sequences when either political or economic reform is given priority. Through the histories of four countries, Hasegawa shows the similarities and differences in the transition from socialism.

Parts II and III cover regional variations in China, the Soviet Union, Asia, and Eastern Europe. As would be expected, the Soviet Union and China figure most prominently. The future of communism depends on the fate of their Communist parties. From the rise of Deng and Gorbachev more than six years apart to the attempted crackdown against the full-fledged reformers more than two years apart, the Soviet and Chinese cases present stunning parallels as well as clear-cut differences. One difference in late 1991 was the assault on the party in the republics of the fragmenting Soviet Union, interpreted by Thomas Remington in Chapter 3, and the propping up of the party in China, discussed by Tatsumi Okabe in Chapter 5. The comparative chapter by Shigeki Hakamada and Rozman treats the two countries together.

Other Asian socialist countries—Vietnam, Mongolia, and North Korea—occupy the center of attention in Akihiko Tanaka's chapter. Both Gerald Segal and Tsuyoshi Hasegawa also include Vietnam in their substantial overviews cutting across regional boundaries. Asian communism, except in China, has not been in the forefront of reform and, apart from Mongolia, has placed the greatest barriers in the path of dismantling.

The treatment of Eastern Europe stresses developments leading to the turning points of 1989 and then the first, comparatively bold steps that followed. Judy Batt's comparative analysis covers Poland, Hungary, Czechoslovakia, and the German Democratic Republic. She distinguishes two paths to systematic crisis and breakdown: the path of intransigent resistance to reform and the path of failed reform. She then covers the transfer of power and the reconstruction of politics. Takayuki Ito focuses specifically on the problem of legitimacy. He questions the legitimacy of the old regime, especially in Poland. Diverse sources of stability other than legitimacy and efforts to build legitimacy under pluralistic democracy also are discussed.

Part IV is concerned with the linkage between domestic and foreign policy. Paul Lewis approaches East European reforms from the point of view of Soviet relations. He proposes an imperial framework, outlining the imperial concept in relations and then documenting developments in the Soviet imperial perspective under Gorbachev. Although his chapter and the two earlier ones on Eastern Europe do not say much about Romania and Bulgaria, German unification, or economic reforms in 1990–91—themes that might be best treated as postsocialism—they present complementary perspectives with broad application to the Eastern European regimes and to other outposts of socialism.

Among the contributors who wrote about China there were differences of opinion. Rozman and Hasegawa stress the tension between substantial economic reform and meager political reform. They believe pressures are rapidly mounting for an acceleration of the reform process in China. Tatsumi Okabe and Nicholas Lardy, for somewhat different reasons, foresee a longer fuse before the flame of Chinese political reforms is likely to be relit. Lardy challenges the idea that China's economic strategy is approaching a dead end and can be reinvigorated only by political reforms. In his view China is continuing to advance in economic reforms without any pressing need to launch political reforms. As for Okabe, he discerns a source of stability in a kind of subject culture found among Chinese peasants, and he forecasts, not an outpouring of discontent, but a corporatist type of gradual change if the reform succeeds.

The second clash of opinions, related to the first, concerns the balance between what is common to all socialist transformation and what is unique to particular individual countries. Stressing common stages and sequences of reform, Rozman sees various dimensions of reform marching in tandem, although, like Hasegawa, he concedes the existence of periods of imbalance. In contrast, Gerald Segal argues that external policy is largely independent of domestic policy. The various aspects of reform may emerge quite independently of each other.

The currents of reform and dismantling continue to move rapidly. Many uncertainties and differences of opinion will ultimately be resolved by events. Of all matters worthy of attentive observation, perhaps the two themes treated by Hasegawa and Segal are most crucial for determining the course of reform: the relationship between political and economic reforms and the relationship between openness to the outside world and domestic reforms. To those two themes we devote our fullest coverage. Supported by examples of many socialist countries in Eastern Europe and Asia, we search for generalizations about what occurred between the fall of 1978 and the winter of 1991–1992 and seek to clarify factors that will shape the fate of the world's most pervasive social movement and most far-reaching experiment in planned reconstruction of human existence.

After the failure of the Soviet coup of August 1991, communism in its long-time world center was on the run. This could only accelerate its collapse elsewhere. Without being able to carry the story forward to the continuing developments in China and North Korea as old leaders pass from the scene or to trace the breakup of the Soviet Union to the point of resolving how Russia and its suspicious neighbors will coexist and find a cooperative way to rebuild their economies, we must stress a process set in motion. What we can find in our overview of Eurasia are common causes of a system on its way out and regional variations reflecting a progression: first Eastern Europe, next the Soviet Union (more decisively among its Western than its Moslem nationalities), and, it appears, last East and Southeast Asia would cross the threshold of abandoning the communist system. By 1992 while a few communist regimes still struggled to retain their foothold, the goal of integration into the economies of Europe and the Asia-Pacific region and into the emerging global order had become the driving force for a new era.

I

STAGES OF REFORM

1

Stages in the Reform and Dismantling of Communism in China and the Soviet Union

Gilbert Rozman

Descriptions of the first stages of a communist society have long projected vivid images of socialist construction—both physical and organizational. There was the concrete imagery of the proletariat working with brute strength to erect the massive edifice of the industrial structure. There was also the abstract imagery of unending organizational progress: Following the revolution each victorious Communist Party claimed first to be laying the foundation for and then to be building socialism, incrementally reaching higher and higher through reorganization of the society toward the tower of communism.[1] By extending the cells of the Communist Party deeper and deeper into the formal and informal structure of society, it was thought that the blueprint of the new community could be realized. By the start of the 1990s, the hopes for climbing up through the clouds in stages had died; down-to-earth concerns are now provoking plans to restructure and even to take apart the existing edifice. As events sporadically outrace the compromise formulas adopted by leaders, parts of the edifice go tumbling down.

The old imagery should now be turned upside down. The vast complex that was communist society is now being disassembled. As shoddy as the original construction was, a functioning, partially modernized society must somehow utilize the remnants of the dismantled structure at the very time a new one is being put in its place. "Decommunization," whether fast or slow, for a long time must make do with the shell of the old order. Just as there were stages of construction, there must be stages of dismantling, which follow stages of reform that make dismantling possible. Symbolic milestones in tearing down the old order—such as taking apart the Berlin Wall, assaulting statues of Vladimir Lenin, and removing monuments and placards to a pantheon of less exalted figures—represent a small fraction of the work under way.

The original plans for restructuring (perestroika) and reform failed at the end of the 1980s. Communist countries appear to be left with no autonomous course of development. The strategy of China's supreme leader, Deng Xiaoping, of limited, primarily economic, reforms floundered before the outpouring of urban discontent in the spring of 1989 and the impasse in economic initiatives reached even earlier. The outrage against the state's brutal crackdown adds to the pressure for change. Soviet leader Mikhail Gorbachev's perestroika produced a spiraling economic downturn as well as parliamentary opposition led in the Russian Republic by Boris Yeltsin, who was impatient to push ahead whatever the cost to socialist principles. In September 1990 a 500-day economic program, credited more to Yeltsin than to Gorbachev, challenged the very existence of socialism in the Soviet Union. Even when this plan was set aside in favor of vesting more power in Gorbachev, no alternative to the eventual dismantling of the system was seriously proposed. After a coup in August 1991 came close to undoing the reforms, the process resumed with a vengeance as territorial separation accelerated alongside the demise of Communist Party cells in all nooks and crannies of the society.

Both the Soviet Union and China are discovering that their outdated, centralized, and labor-intensive factories and shops, their rigid multilayered planning system and overgrown ministries, their top-heavy agricultural collectives and state farms, and especially their hierarchical communist networks have no place in a truly modernized society. Reforms can be postponed, but they cannot be contained. Either they are abandoned for a time at an enormous cost, or they gather more and more momentum. Despite the many twists and turns along the way, the eventual outcome appears to be the end of the old system of communism. In 1991 the Chinese leadership was still trying to halt this explosive process. To bolster its case it cited selective economic successes and the tumultuous effects of dismantling communism in the Soviet Union. Chinese communism, however, could do little more than buy time before the next wave of reform swept over it.

I am not alone in proposing stages of reform as a way to interpret recent events. When asked to explain why he had chosen as his closest aides the very men who had plotted against him, Gorbachev answered,

> I think that there are stages in the development of perestroika, we should never forget what kind of society we are trying to

reform and how extensive these reforms are. . . . I prefer stages. . . . So at this stage, it is a totally different situation and there's a powerful democratic movement, a powerful public opinion . . . and new values have emerged, the values of those who established perestroika. People have a different position.[2]

A day later, under pressure from Yeltsin, Gorbachev appointed an entirely new cast of leaders, men who had stood against the coup. The coup failed, Gorbachev said, "because we have reached such a stage in the development of our society when it has only become clearer that everything has got to change—the authority, the federation, the economy, our attitude, our relationship with property, and the position of the individual. And we are already a different society where there is no place for those reactionary forces."[3]

Those, who are impatient for change, or who fear a reversal of reform, view a theory of stages as a barrier to change. The notion of stages can become an excuse for inaction, they insist. Readily they point to the case of China. Chinese leaders are more extreme than Gorbachev was in arguing that democratization and other political reforms need to be delayed because the country is not now at the right stage for them. Yet those who press for reform can advocate stages. China's critics counter with stage theories of their own. As early as 1979 they argued that underdevelopment necessitates, at this stage, borrowing heavily from capitalism or that reform, at this stage, requires political reform to succeed. Stage theories, explicitly or implicitly, play a large role in the debates about reform and even in reform policies.

This chapter recognizes the validity of identifying stages and using them for comparisons. Rather than repeating what advocates and critics of reform policies have to say about stages, it introduces an independent perspective drawn from observations of Chinese and Soviet communism. Through comparisons the stages emerge.

POSTCOMMUNISM IN CHINA AND THE SOVIET UNION

The existing structures of socialism closely resemble one another, and the international requirements for modernization are widely shared. In the transition into which the socialist countries have entered, there are many common elements. Each country may seem to be groping on its own, but discovering what works and, at least on occasion, learning from each other are likely to lead in similar directions. Over the long run the price of failure is too high for a country to stop at half measures.

The dismantling process now under way in the Soviet Union and in China has much in common, as did these countries' efforts to contain the process without eliminating some of the most resistant vested interests until Gorbachev gave way to Yeltsin. Stalling and even some backtracking do not negate the basic course of transition.

Only in the two giants of communism are we likely to find the purest evolution of the socialist system. Formed through indigenous revolutions, reliant on their own political and economic resources, and the product of their own ideological twists and turns, the Soviet Union and China epitomize the internally directed path of socialism. They differ from satellite or externally guided socialist states, especially in Eastern Europe, where the system depended heavily on outside pressure and then collapsed at the first opportunity. They also differ from smaller, largely internally directed socialist states, such as North Korea and Cuba; at the beginning of the 1990s only a longstanding socialist autocrat made possible there the temporary retention of a high degree of political independence despite a fairly large degree of economic dependence. Of the three types of socialist systems, the large-scale, internally directed type is most significant, both theoretically as the purest case and strategically as the source of two of the world's great powers.

Whereas North Korea, Cuba, and parts of Eastern Europe could anticipate relatively quick absorption into a regional capitalist economy once the dikes burst and the dismantling begins in earnest (although there is no "quick fix," as the former East Germany reveals), the Soviet Union and China face an uncertain and presumably lengthy transition away from socialism. Reordering their huge internal economies will take time as they expand links to the outside. Through their struggles to combine the old and the new, we can see the outlines of a partially reformed interregnum and eventually of postcommunism—an intermediate system, which, for the foreseeable future, does not mean a direct convergence with capitalism. The age of postcommunism is only beginning. By looking back at the forces that have produced it, we can begin to appreciate how it is likely to unfold.

Of course, the challenge of reforming a socialist system has resurfaced at intervals throughout the history of communist-led states The brusque methods of building socialism inevitably produced economic crises followed by reform programs to set things back on track. What is different about the 1980s is the total exhaustion of the traditional model of socialism on which each country had relied. This dead end resulted from at least two new circumstances. First, the two countries (the Soviet Union because of relentless administrative measures and China in part because of the fanatic campaign methods of the Cultural Revolution) had used virtually their entire resource base—human resources, natural resources, and capital resources. Extensive development was no longer an option.[4] Modernization had reached an impasse.

Second, computerization, high-technology electronics and information services, and other intensive uses of intellectual resources made the wasteful socialist economies patently obsolete.[5] After the world oil crisis in 1973, this technology gap, especially between the two giants of communism and capitalist East Asia, widened precipitously.[6] To forsake isolation meant to plunge forward into a rapidly changing global economy. For Soviet and Chinese communism, there was no longer any possibility of cosmetic renewal, even in the short term. At the very least, a fundamental reform was required. Without planning it, leaders started the process of dismantling socialism.

In the interest of integration into the world economy, leaders sought to improve expertise and efficiency. They reached for appointments beyond the nomenklatura system and turned to market forces to make the most of scarce resources. Reform socialism's tolerance of such threatening changes is limited, but postcommunism represents in Eastern Europe, Russia, and elsewhere a transformation from the existing "partocracy" toward full-fledged achievement orientation once a civil service reform and privatization are carried forward as proposed. This means a degree of convergence with capitalism rarely anticipated, but not an end to the role of both traditional and socialist legacies in shaping the next stages of development. China and the Soviet Union long remained in the era of reform socialism; yet by looking backward and forward we can discern factors that appear to lead these countries toward a postcommunist era. Indeed, the earth-shattering events of August 1991 propelled the Soviet republics into a new era when the eradication of Communist Party central committees, newspapers, and property appeared to presage the transition to a market-oriented society, although rival claims of sovereignty and independence threatened to mar the economic cooperation and military stability necessary for such a transition.

FIVE DETERMINANTS OF THE STAGES OF SOCIALISM

When revolutionary movements swept into power in Russia in 1917 and in China in 1949, they started a chain reaction they could scarcely have anticipated. Looking back at the long-term consequences of their actions, we can discern at least five forces at work: the leadership in each country, the public mood, the level of modernization, the world environment and ideology. Each will be discussed in turn.

First, there was a natural progression of leadership, produced by the gradual aging and eventual replacement of the revolutionary generation as well as by the winnowing of initially diverse elements and the conscious recruiting of successors to suit the purposes of the power-hungry victors in this struggle. The relative youth of the revolutionaries and those they recruited once in power ensured that the process of succession leading beyond these first circles would continue for many decades. Leadership and elite succession would last at least fifty to one hundred years, including decades of reform and dismantling, before normalcy for a modernized society could come into sight. With a normal circulation of elites, educational and entrepreneurial criteria for office strongly predominate over political and ascriptive criteria despite actual deviations from equality of opportunity ideals. Once a young generation raised in an atmosphere of normalcy or reform reached maturity, the pressures mounted fast for revamping the system through sustained reform.

Second, there was an evolution of the public mood as the socialist system aged. Incentives and interests that possess popular appeal in the uncertain and, to some degree, buoyant times soon after the revolution give way to a different psychology. Of course, the degree of success of the earlier policies, as well as the changing character of the society, influences the pace of this transition. Revolutionary zeal abates, bureaucratized normalcy spreads, and, sooner or later, privatized concerns prevail.[7] Traditional, national ways of thinking were no doubt influential in shaping popular expectations and the degree to which socialist policies satisfied them. Unlike the leadership transition, the evolution of public mood has no foreordained time limitation. It is likely, however, to occur more rapidly (in fewer decades) and to create a gap in synchronization. Mass mobilization may motivate some in the early days, but new generations cannot long be galvanized by the political goals of the old order. The public is ready for a reform program well before the nucleus of the leadership, even if narrow vision associated with vested interests may lead to a divided response when a reform leader does take the helm.[8] Furthermore, mass psychology is subject to sudden arousal. This occurred in China in the spring of 1989 and in the republics of the Soviet Union in the summer of 1991. The emotionally charged situation left leaders Deng and Gorbachev trailing far behind.

Third, the stages of socialism were determined by the initial level of modernization in each country and by the subsequent advances and imbalances in this process. The Soviet Union and China used socialism as a means to achieve a modernized society with a large industrial sector, while countenancing elements of severe backwardness. The course of modernization, placing demands on other elements of the society, inevitably resulted in far-reaching consequences for the entire package of socialist policies. A more complex, modernized society grew more interdependent, heightening the effects of imbalance.[9] This process became cumulative, rising in intensity as the decades passed and affecting the popular mood especially when the leadership proved slow to respond. Unmet requirements of modernization often raced ahead of popular awareness of the severity of the situation; this force often took the lead in raising the need for reform. An economic slowdown could signal that the system could not continue, whatever the preference of the leadership and the consciousness of the public. It was not just the universal forces of modernization that were at work; communism evolved its own approach, arousing distinctive pressures to sustain the process or to realize some of its fruits.

Fourth, even in the two most self-sufficient large countries in the world there was fallout from the world environment. Socialism in one country could not advance indefinitely without adjusting to the state of the world.[10] The competition between China and the Soviet Union played a role in this international context. No country wanted to fall farther and farther behind. As in the case of internal modernization, external demonstration effects exerted a cumulative and increasingly powerful influence. Nonetheless, filtered through censorship and isolation, the external factor could not play as decisive a leading role as it did in some other parts of the world. Over time the external effect tended to grow, particularly as the technology gap and the efficiency gap in the most modern sectors widened. As capitalist powers, especially the United States, became partners in international cooperation, they were better trusted and more successful in communicating an alternative vision, including an appealing lifestyle.

Fifth, and by no means least important, was the built-in ideological blueprint, as articulated by Joseph Stalin and Mao Zedong, for reaching successively higher stages of socialism. Although this dogma failed to correspond to reality, it did much to shape the unfolding scenarios.[11] The ideology identified a sequence toward which the society was to be headed—one which more and more clashed with the requirements of modernization and the opportunities available in the world environment. Of all the forces, this and leadership represented the most formidable barriers to reform. Yet within the ideology as within the leadership there were forces for reform that helped to keep this possibility alive. Once reform began in earnest, the sudden flowering of a multicolored reform ideology of changes attracted swarms of followers.

The character of these five determinants of socialist stages was substantially the same in the Soviet Union and China. To be sure, significant differences existed. For example, the leadership of Mao but not of

Lenin continued for a quarter century, and China's closest neighbors thirty years after its revolution included some of the world's most dynamic countries, while the Soviet Union's neighbors in the late 1940s were either prostrate victims of war or bitterly divided states in the grips of civil turmoil. Despite these differences we should keep in mind that in each country young revolutionaries took power in still not very modernized settings and largely closed their countries to what were perceived as hostile developed countries. Moreover, Mao's program for building socialism drew heavily on Stalin's program developed in the second decade of Soviet power. This explains a high degree of ideological similarity despite later protestations to the contrary.[12] These circumstances help to account for great overlap in the duration, sequence, and character of the stages in the two countries. The forces of leadership and ideology set the pace for a time. Then the public mood, made more restive by the forces of modernization and the world environment, took the lead for change.

THE STAGE OF TRANSITION TO SOCIALISM

This transitional period beings with the first jolt of the revolution and ends with the climactic mobilization of virtually the entire society. The end is not strictly when the leader proclaimed that socialism at last exists. (Such a proclamation was made by Stalin in 1936, about seven years later than the "revolution from above," and by Mao in 1956, one year before our cutoff for the start of an all-out, forced mobilization.) Rather, the end of the stage of transition to socialism occurs when the society suddenly plunges into an irreversible spin into an unseen abyss—1929 in the Soviet Union and 1957 in China. Until then the potential for reform remained substantial; afterwards it would take a huge effort from the top to revive. Once this line had been crossed—frenetic development approved, dissent of any kind branded counterrevolution, humanity callously moved about without regard for its welfare—socialism, as we usually understand it in communist-led countries, was in place.

Reform forces are eager to tug even a communist-led society toward a market economy and a pluralist democracy. But when modernization is not yet far along and traditional forces are little prepared to support changes, the reform forces are likely to be overwhelmed. Even so, their early efforts can inspire later generations. The memory of Lenin's New Economic Plan and, thirty years later, of China's relatively stable reconstruction and First Five-Year Plan continued to flicker for a long time.

Beijing condensed into about eight years what required about twelve in Moscow. Putting the reform forces and customary restraints to rout proved to be an easier task for the orthodox ideologues in China's capital. We can find explanations for China's faster transition as well as for a common outcome by reviewing the five forces outlined in the previous section.

At the time of its revolution, China's leadership had evolved well beyond the loose, underground conspiratorial alliance of the Bolsheviks. Unlike Lenin, Mao had ruled his own territory and his own army for nearly two decades. He had conducted large-scale purges, launched thought rectification campaigns, and cemented relations with a huge network of revolutionaries, particularly the veterans of the perilous Long March in 1934–35. The rural, uneducated, and military predominance in these Chinese networks made it easier for a powerful leader, at the head of a band of secondary leaders each with his own network, to solidify lines of authority. In addition to this different background before the seizure of power, the contrast between Mao's survival for over a quarter century after 1949 to reign as the socialist autocrat and Lenin's early demise in 1924 before the era of radicalism and autocracy helps to explain the quicker consolidation of radical leadership in China. Starting in office with a far-flung organization and continuing at the helm, Mao could speed the leadership transition to radicalism. He enjoyed the cooperation of a whole echelon of leaders, many of whom were predisposed to this leap forward.

Selective radical policies could, of course, precede such a consolidation in the exercise of power, as seen in the extreme policies toward workers and peasants in Soviet War Communism of 1918–21. Yet at an early date they could not easily be sustained. Stalin relied on part of the leadership corps formed in this wartime context and then, around the time of Lenin's death, on the large-scale recruitment of a loyal following, mostly from worker ranks. As Mao did in the late 1920s and early 1930s and intermittently thereafter, Stalin simultaneously struggled against more cosmopolitan elements in the party and squeezed out his rivals. Moreover through six or seven years of the twists and turns of NEP gradualism, preceding by thirty years China's similar era of relative gradualism, he maneuvered through countless leadership debates, clashes and purges to form just the combination of subordinates he needed. Angered by enduring opposition, eager to accelerate a recently launched industrialization program, plagued by insufficient control over rural resources, Stalin and Mao both shifted abruptly to a more radical course.

The Soviet and Chinese people responded to the transition to socialism somewhat differently. In China there was a greater outpouring of revolutionary enthusiasm as well as a firmer base of support, at least cautious support. Certainly, traditional political culture played a role. Communists could avail themselves of Confucian assumptions about ebb and flow of dynastic cycles, the expected transfer of the Mandate of Heaven, and the importance of a self-proclaimed virtuous ruler championing a moral agenda. They also benefited from the more persuasive historical interlude of painful collapse through imperialist humiliations, internal anarchy and warlordism, and economic stagnation amid pockets of progress. In contrast to the eight-month interval between the fall of imperial Russia and the rise of the Bolsheviks, there was a thirty-eight-year hiatus after the fall of imperial China, somewhat ameliorated by the decade of relatively stable Guomindang power but then exacerbated by the even longer period of Japanese invasion and civil war. The Bolsheviks came to power after denouncing Russia's involvement in World War I, whereas the Chinese communists rode the nationalism of vigorous support for the war against Japan to prominence. Through these contrasting experiences, they elicited different types of support. The Chinese population, stirred by nationalism, was better prepared to accept communist authority, albeit a nonradical version. They greeted the revolution with considerable hope, as Soviet commentators on China's intelligentsia observed.[13]

The first years in power also found the Chinese leaders more successful in eliciting active support. Through a vigorous land reform campaign, Beijing managed to reach deeply into rural society, giving a material stake to a majority of the people and promoting millions of activists while alienating relatively few through needless violence. Moscow scarcely penetrated to the level of its rural population of 80 percent or so. China's party apparatus enveloped the factories just as they began to expand rapidly. It gained support by starting at the ground floor of industrialization. Russian factory traditions were more deeply entrenched. Not until the second half of the 1920s was recovery complete from the urban collapse resulting from civil war and War Communism. Yet the Soviets also organized worker activists, aroused an enthusiastic party and youth league corps, and reached the younger generation through a rapidly expanding educational system. When the meaning of socialism remained vague, many people pinned high hopes on high-sounding ideals despite some short-term evidence to the contrary. By the end of the transition era in both countries, a sizable corps of activists was ready to take charge of a radical program. One of the objectives of a new program would be to rekindle and make full use of such spirited support.

More modernized than China, the Soviet Union could compensate for its less extensive organizational roots when implanting socialism in the economy. Its broader urban infrastructure and better trained personnel made the shift to a planned economy under state ownership easier to manage, if still risky in the absence of any precedent. At the same time, the alternative of a market economy, building on the notable achievements of Russian modernization from the 1890s to World War I, retained considerable attractiveness. Chinese leaders had less ambivalence. The Soviet model of modernization promised just what was needed in their desperation to catch up by tugging the weak urban economy from the command posts of the state. Given the low level of modernization and the complete lack of confidence in past methods, China's communists were ready to push forward at the earliest opportunity. They had already completed one five-year plan and collectivization, using relatively moderate methods, before shifting to an extreme, radical program to maximize the potential economic benefits. Apart from rational reasons, leaders eager to complete the building of socialism before they died were driven by impatience and even a kind of religious zealotry.

The different international environment in the struggle between socialism and capitalism made the disinterest in moderation on the part of the Communist Party of China fully comprehensible. Soviet options in the late 1920s were varied, and they continued to be so with the onset of the Depression in capitalist countries and the spread of fascism. Chinese options three decades later appeared minimal as communist leaders saw, on the one side, a united socialist bloc under Stalin's radicalized control and, on the other, a united and by no means prosperous East Asian capitalist bloc under Washington's leadership, whose sympathies centered on the Guomindang still in power in Taiwan. Even if there was some hesitation by the Chinese to lean completely to one side, the Soviet side beckoned and the Korean War cemented the bond.

By 1956–57, however, China's options were wider. Before its leaders radicalized their policies, they could have taken note of the postwar rebound of capitalism and the Soviet shift to peaceful coexistence. As in the Soviet case in the late 1920s, a hostile international environment played some role, but it was not a determining factor.

Although the preceding forces heightened China's leaders' haste to put the transitional stage and its reform elements behind them, ideology may have supplied the strongest push along with leadership. During the 1920s, socialism as a force for constructing a new order remained vague and hotly debated. In the first half of the 1950s, it was as clear as it would ever be: Stalin's explanation for Soviet development transposed onto the international stage. Mao abandoned reform methods in part because this was the only course expected of a proper communist leader.[14]

Ideology took a new twist before China had completed its transition. Nikita Khrushchev's de-Stalinization speech at the Twentieth Party Congress in February 1956 set in motion within the international communist movement an ideological struggle and a leadership struggle. Mao insisted on proving that his country was more faithful to the cause. To be sure, during the Hundred Flowers Movement of 1956–57 his response acquired a populist streak to elicit feedback from the populace about how to improve the system. Mao was tempted by an alternative ideological framework of new democracy that had been grafted onto communist ideology to secure a united front in the years of revolution and civil war. Self-doubts in the Chinese leadership about early steps toward radicalism and the Chinese fright over Soviet leadership and especially over Hungary's mass rejection of Stalinism made it briefly appear possible that Mao and his associates would turn directly to reform socialism. But the momentum of the radicalization process, the anger against the many intellectuals who dared to expose the system's shortcomings, and the essence of the Chinese communist experience drove Mao and his associates to act in haste. By outdoing Moscow in radicalism, Beijing would prove its ideological superiority. Reform socialism stood little chance of victory when the revolutionaries of yesterday had not adequately tested their dreams.

THE STAGE OF RADICAL SOCIALISM

The essence of radical or dogmatic socialism is the nearly total mobilization of society from above. Partly because of the desire to prevent dissent or deviance, radical socialism paradoxically leads to a conservative approach to many social problems. Despite the insistence on conformity in various spheres, the term "radicalism" still applies because of the extreme policies that disrupted ordinary social existence. Circumstances differed in China and the Soviet Union. They led the CPC (Communist Party of China) in the 1950s to exercise control through intermediate organizations, especially rural people's communes, urban residential committees, and factory party organizations. The CPSU (Communist Party of the Soviet Union) primarily utilized secret police organizations to watch the heads of the intermediate bodies, such as state farm chairmen and one-man managers, as well as ordinary citizens. There was a horrifying sameness, however, to the consequences and the duration of this phase of socialism. Communization repeated the misery of collectivization nearly three decades earlier. Households were herded into organizations that tried to destroy their traditions, and millions were callously left to die from administratively induced rural famine. Roughly five years later in the Soviet Union and in China wholesale terror, packaged in purges, reigned. It affected political rivals at the top, most of the intellectual elite, and any ordinary citizen who stood out because of independent spirit, family background, or occupational sensitivity, or who merely happened to be in the wrong place at the wrong time.

Even after the worst of the purges had passed, a downtrodden society would be allowed little respite until its paranoid party dictator had died. Excluding the interruption of the Soviet Union's Great Patriotic War in 1941–45, each country spent about twenty years in this phase of radical socialism before it began to give way after the death of the socialist autocrat. First had come extreme experimentation with new social forms. Then had followed the zenith of the purges, and finally, as an exhausted population waited for relief, had come routinized radicalism in which dogmatism remained at a high pitch without a major shift in course. Leadership and ideology had pushed in the direction of radicalism, without any serious obstacles to that extreme course from other forces: Modernization could be based on extensive methods—therefore the mass mobilization of radical socialism seemed suitable to the leadership; popular activism could be incited among a vocal minority, while terror simultaneously applied to many others kept mass discontent largely out of sight; and little interaction occurred with the capitalist countries so that they could not become a model for change. This complex of radical approaches could be construed, for a time, as plausible for countries of the communist world to advance toward a developed economy, which could support a strong and militarized state.

On the whole, there was little prospect for reform during this stage of socialism, but in each country two exceptions arose. They can be traced, in large part, to the evolution of communist leadership. Before Stalin's great purges and Mao's Cultural Revolution the consolidation of personal authority faced limitations from a tradition, which, since the days of the revolutionary movement, required at least a semblance of collective leadership. The chaotic and tragic upheavals at the beginning of the 1930s in the Soviet Union and at the end of the 1950s in China inevitably aroused discontent within the veteran leadership still doubtful about the sudden abandonment of the earlier, more gradual methods of socialist transition. Stalin's grip was tighter. The underground, conspiratorial background of the Bolsheviks had made the center more powerful, while extensive purges of the main rivals in the second half of the 1920s left the top leader more firmly in charge. Stalin's ruthlessness and his early flexibility in rewarding the new breed who took charge with material incentives and power and privilege dispelled quickly the threat from the old guard.

Through the first half of the 1960s, Mao faced a much more serious threat to his power and to radicalism. Forced to make concessions to reform socialism for his survival, Mao cemented his power base in the army after ousting the defense minister, Peng Dehuai, who had courageously but unsuccessfully opposed the Great Leap Forward. Given both the nationwide guerrilla movement that had swept a broad coalition of revolutionaries into power and the decentralized operational management of Chinese society after 1949, Mao consolidated his authority differently than Stalin did. Unlike the Soviet case, a genuine partisan tradition secured an ongoing place in the Chinese communist world view, reducing the buildup of the state. When challenged by rivals, Mao chose ideology as a major weapon with which to reach down through the ranks of the party as far as youthful Red Guard activists. His considerable success as an inspiration did not produce any equivalent to Stalin's highly centralized apparatus of control. Mao was dependent on a faction-ridden military under old guard leadership and on Lin Biao, Peng's successor as defense minister. In three years this man went from the most abject Mao worshipper (he launched the 1969 campaign to make Mao's pithy sayings in the *Little Red Book* the source of all wisdom) to the villain in what was described as an attempted coup against Mao. Through the sword and the pen—carried by the army and susceptible youth—Mao turned aside the pressures for reform. Real reform would have to await the autocrat's death.

The second possibility of reform came in the emergency circumstances of a country torn apart and then starting its difficult recovery. In the Soviet Union World War II elicited some concessions from Stalin, such as tolerance for religion as a way to boost patriotism. Yet neither at a time of desperation when Hitler's armies advanced through the Soviet heartland taking millions of Soviet lives, nor at a time of relief, when the Soviet Union emerged victorious as one of two world superpowers, did Stalin take reform seriously. He was content with the radical methods of the 1930s and, adding more intense mobilization under party control, essentially reimposed them after the war for his remaining eight years. Radical socialism had fit the logic of his rise to power, and Stalin saw no leadership or ideological reason to change course.

Indeed, the extravagant claims about "scientific socialism's" responsibility for the triumphant victory in war and for the sudden and spectacular spread of communist rule to one-third of mankind seemed to offer proof that no change was necessary. They even breathed new life into the revolutionary zeal of some urban residents. Stalin's cynical exploitation of newfound confidence, without concessions to the desperate longings of his people for peace and better living conditions, would soon hasten the dissipation of zeal.

There was a similar and more abrupt falloff in zeal in China. After the Cultural Revolution lay in ruins, Mao's frantic efforts at sending youths to the countryside to tap further the frenetic energies of aspiring communists only hastened the collapse of enthusiasm. China had no success in war or superpower competition to explain, in retrospect, its interlude of destructive frenzy. More dispiriting than the underremunerated labor required of exhausted Soviet citizens after World War II was the plight of Chinese youths, sent by the millions to the impoverished countryside where they soon felt useless and unwanted. In urban offices in China the embittered enemies of struggles only a few years past now worked side by side after prolonged physical labor in May 7 cadre schools, which had been hastily established in barren rural locations to reeducate intellectuals and officials. Unlike Soviet families, Chinese families could not take satisfaction in material incentives, educational opportunities, or even a notable advance in their nation's industrial construction. To find an escape from the inconclusive collapse of what had amounted to a civil war, Mao turned to Deng Xiaoping and other reviled targets of the Cultural Revolution, but he and his close associates, later known as the Gang of Four, could not bring themselves to countenance reform measures. Despite appearances, and a program blatantly incompatible with reform, China hung on the brink of reversing its course and turning to the only possible escape—reform; leaders castigated reform but failed to find any other direction in which to turn.

Severe problems of modernization and a favorable international context made reform socialism an increasingly inviting alternative for China in the 1970s. Three decades earlier, different conditions faced the Soviet Union. Devastated by war, the Soviet leadership could assuredly apply mobilization methods that had, in its view, worked well enough during the building of a heavy industrial sector in the 1930s and again during the urgent demands of wartime. The modernization needs of the Soviet Union did not yet appear to have changed in the first years after 1945. The cold war and the prospect of extending the proven methods of five-year plans to the establishment of a unified military-industrial complex from Canton to Berlin diminished interest in accommodation with capitalist economies. In contrast, at the start of the 1970s China was isolated from most socialist countries and had become a kind of darling in the capitalist world for turning the Sino-Soviet conflict into a joint effort at restraining Moscow. Capitalist assistance was there for the taking. Furthermore, the greater radicalism of China's economic policies (they were more hostile to material incentives and the lucrative bonuses of "Stakhanovism") left prospects for modernization in shambles. The forces in favor of a reform course were building despite the refusal of China's leadership, to the last moment of Mao's life, to take action, which would have been tantamount to admitting two decades of monumental waste and needless destruction.

Both Stalin and Mao had committed themselves to an ideology. They, along with a whole chain of overseers and enforcers, could stay securely in power only by sustaining this commitment. Leaders trapped in the logical sequence of radical socialism do not seek an escape from the forces keeping the system going from within and without. To prevent others from doing so, they intensify the ideology of radicalism. For Stalin, who was often more cynically manipulative than ideological, the intensification of restrictions did not mean genuine use of ideology for finding answers to problems. For Mao it did. In both cases the system failed to respond to, or even to acknowledge, its problems. Beneath the surface, pressures for reform were rising. The objectives at first were limited, given the absence of information about the outside world and one's own country, communication with like-minded thinkers, and organizations through which to channel demands. Once the chain leading down from the charismatic leader acting as the final arbitrator of dogmatic ideology was broken, suppressed reforms could not long be postponed.

THE STAGE OF TENTATIVE SOCIALIST REFORM

However smudged its reputation, the Soviet NEP, as well as its short-lived analogue in China's recovery from the Great Leap Forward in 1961–62, represented an alternative conception of socialism. After all, the NEP had Lenin's blessing, and it had helped extricate socialism from an economic crisis. This does not mean that a direct appeal to this model might reasonably have been attempted in all situations, but that at least the outline of this alternative would remain not far out of sight. Strident Chinese criticisms of Soviet revisionism also helped to identify the alternative to the status quo of radical socialism.[15]

Leadership

A leadership struggle followed quickly after Stalin's death and, twenty-three years later, after Mao's as well. In both instances there was a consensus among the cautious forces of bureaucratic stability and the more adventurous forces favoring some systemic adjustment that destabilizing elements of terror and intimidation had to be quickly eliminated. Within several months of Stalin's death, Lavrentii Beria's arrest and execution signaled the assertion of bureaucratic authority over the terror of the secret police. Even more swiftly came the arrest and campaign against the Gang of Four in October 1976, which brought an end to the lingering Cultural Revolution with its threat of retribution against anyone who raised the specter of reform.

Once these major terrorizers of the people were subdued, the leadership struggle could center on policies as well as power and personalities. In each country the contestants were limited to a few top leaders who shared responsibility for the outrages of radical socialism. Inside the Kremlin this meant lieutenants who had displayed their fidelity to Stalin's megalomania for more than two decades. Inside Zhongnanhai, where rival factions not only had survived the height of the Cultural Revolution but had even seen some of their leaders return from oblivion in the early 1970s, the break with Maoism could move almost immediately to the vanguard of the struggle. In October 1976 Deng Xiaoping, having been purged for a second time earlier in 1976 and facing the recently promoted Hua Guofeng (whose claim to power largely consisted of Mao's blessing and the promise to follow Mao faithfully) benefited from the widespread desire among the Chinese people to turn socialism onto a different track. He also could count on a strong power base in the army.

Ironically, it was Stalin's faithful lieutenant Khrushchev who dramatically denounced his predecessor, while the oft-punished Deng arranged a compromise that weighed Mao's achievements more than twice as heavily as his mistakes. This outcome can be explained by five factors: (1) the Chinese tradition of respect for the founder of one's dynasty and for other ancestors from whom one's own authority derives; (2) the deep concern about legitimation and consensus in a collective leadership that was able to continue party rankings dating from the era of revolution and that was aware of the terrible costs of divisiveness in the preceding Cultural Revolution; (3) the availability of Lenin as a backup seer in the Soviet Union and the absence of an equivalent alternative source of legitimacy in China; (4) Khrushchev's de-Stalinization, much opposed in China at the time and interpreted later as causing Khrushchev's own ouster; and (5) the reluctance to break with many techniques of Maoism that were regarded as indispensable for the continuance of a communist regime.[16] The Chinese leadership sought to move forward in virtual unison toward reform firmly under its control, while the Soviet leadership failed for a time to agree on the ground rules for reform.

In the Khrushchev era a generational struggle occurred between the beneficiaries of Stalinism, whose dazzling upward mobility in the 1930s and 1940s gave them a strong stake in the party-dominated bureaucratic system, and the expanded postwar intelligentsia, mostly inclined to assume the role of an ordinary modernized elite at liberty to express its own interests as experts. Tentative reform encouraged the recent graduates of higher education to utilize their expertise in leadership posts; yet the senior bureaucrats, along with the huge military and security apparatus, could not easily be dislodged. Far from retirement and sufficiently educated and experienced to expect to be of continued service in the upper ranks of a command economy, the products of Stalin's limited technocracy would cling to their posts into the 1980s.[17] Their entrenchment made it difficult to push beyond tentative reforms. Only gradually was the balance at middle levels of leadership shifting to the side of expertise. Even seventy years after the revolution the leadership's relative success in blending "red and expert" had left a powerful corps of apparatchiki—factory and farm managers, institute directors, diplomats, party secretaries, and so on. It would take many more years to remove them, although some who were exposed in August 1991 as supporters of the coup soon were replaced. Nevertheless, the combination of the aging of the old guard and the substantial education and international experience of its successors drove the leadership transition forward. Gorbachev's generation started work in an era of reform and carried a reform perspective with it two or three decades later when power was shifting in its direction.

The stage of tentative reform in China beginning in 1978 did not initially witness a comparable generational struggle. Unable to consolidate their position during the Cultural Revolution, the bureaucratic successors in China remained in the shadows of the surviving revolutionary generation. Potential experts had been given little opportunity to gain education or experience. In the first years of reform, they could not easily vie for top leadership roles. For a time the revolutionary generation, the bureaucratic successors trained under socialism, and the new generation of experts worked together to oust many of Mao's uneducated postrevolutionary activists, a group with no close Soviet parallel. Eventually, however, their interests diverged. As in the Soviet Union, the leadership composition was too heavily weighted against modern elites to enable the forces of reform to prevail as early as a decade after the beginning of tentative reforms, unless there had occurred a failure of will at the top. The initial victory went to those dependent on the command administrative system. They set back the course of reform.

There are reasons to expect that China will not take seventy years to produce a full-fledged reform leadership. The bureaucratic forces remain less consolidated than those in Soviet history, having struggled with limited success against partisan traditions and still under the sway of an aged revolutionary generation that is likely to leave the scene in the 1990s. In the 1980s, reform-oriented leaders already played a larger role than they did in the Soviet Union at any time before the Gorbachev era; there seems to be no alternative but to turn to them again without great delay. Furthermore, the Confucian tradition of meritocracy based on demanding examinations strongly supports the new educated elite over the militarized and undereducated revolutionaries. Unlike the Soviets, the Chinese did little to create a hybrid of "red and expert."[18] As a result, the experts may not find such severe impediments, with the prominent exception of the People's Liberation Army, to their rise once the old guard is gone, but the experts remain few and not well organized. As in the remnants of the Soviet Union, it is primarily the threat of widespread violence that might cause the military to intercede. The scope of nationalistic separatism is less in China, but the military's triggerpoint at the behest of a still quite unified and powerful party may be considerably lower. The contrast between June 1989, when Chinese troops after some hesitation obeyed their old-guard leader Yang Shangkun, and August 1991, when defections and uncertainty resulted in Defense Minister Dimitryi Yazov failing to hold the Soviet military for the coup, is only somewhat instructive because in the first case Deng gave the order and in the second Gorbachev was under house arrest, casting doubt on the legitimacy of the order.

Tentative reforms in both countries increase the discretionary authority of regional and local bosses. Rather than formal bureaucratic lines of control, personalized forms of governance tend to fill the vacuum left by the decline of terror. Severe limits on open information about politics, together with tight restrictions on genuine interest-group articulation, clear the way for personal fiefdoms. In the Soviet Union ethnic cleavages reinforced these centrifugal tendencies. In China lingering factionalism from a regionally based revolutionary movement, coupled with traditional regionalism and localism, seem to provide fertile soil for such fiefdoms.[19] In the years since the Cultural Revolution, increased ethnic autonomy is also tolerated. Modern elites are strongest in the central cities of both countries, while fiefdoms readily occur on the periphery with the connivance of the weak bureaucratic stratum. Local networks under party leadership are more pronounced in China since the steeply vertical ministerial networks leading to the center were less developed and more quickly undercut through reforms. When the contradictory nature of the tentative reforms leads to leadership clashes and setbacks for the modernized elites, the personalized networks further solidify; this complicates the renewal of reform. To the extent that tentative reforms are halting and incomplete, the way is opened for local bosses more than for national bureaucrats.

There is always a large element of chance in leadership changes. Deaths are unpredictable. Succession battles are decided by many short-term considerations. There is no way to be precise in predictions. Yet the life cycle of leaders (usually seventy to ninety years), generational succession (every thirty or, at most, fifty years), and the formative experiences of differing stages of socialism set limits on what is possible. Forty years after its revolution, China is well along in a sequence that took seventy years to reach fruition in the Soviet Union. Prior to the outburst of nationalism that began to tear the Soviet Union apart in 1990 and 1991, there was also more autonomy for regional reform leadership to evolve in China beginning in 1978. Economic interests drive these Chinese leaders. The emergent republic-level Soviet leaders are driven by emotionally charged nationalistic causes. In part, the generational struggle pits the younger regional forces against the older central ones, and China has an advantage in the rise of a new economic elite. As can be seen in the early 1992 struggle between Ukraine and Russia over control of the Black Sea fleet, most Soviet regionalism is foremost a battle over power.

Popular Sentiment

At the beginning of the era of tentative reforms, the Soviet people were fearful of the unknown and depressed by the dreadful conditions of daily life. After Khrushchev had raised hopes with grandiose promises, adventurous programs, and eye-opening revelations, the Brezhnev leadership sought for roughly two decades to contain these stirrings. Its approach was fundamentally different. Despite the high-sounding rhetoric about a new era of developed socialism,[20] and some bombastic claims about the superiority of the socialist way of life,[21] promises in the new era were generally low key and vague. Although there was still the ballyhoo of five-year-plan statistics and even colossal plans to build the BAM railroad line through Siberia north of Lake Baikal and to divert the northern rivers to irrigate Central Asia, Brezhnev's initiatives were few and far between. Trying to cool expectations, Brezhnev intensified censorship but to little avail; news from the West increasingly drifted over the Iron Curtain.

For some time Soviet leaders succeeded in channeling discontent into private forms of expression. They did this by raising living standards quite steadily at first and by offering ample leisure, plentiful alcohol, and an unpressured existence.[22] Security for citizens with limited horizons abounded—in Soviet military might, in leadership stability under Brezhnev, in undemanding but guaranteed jobs, and in stable provision of basic necessities and minimalist welfare. Families well understood the rules of the society, including the opportunities for advancement through a mixture of achievement, patronage, and often bribery. But as the corruption worsened and the economic improvements slowed to a halt, the popular mood worsened. The Afghan War and leadership instability in the early 1980s, along with the increasingly brazen "telephone justice" by well-placed officials, who flexed their power through an informal call or two by which they dictated the outcome of court proceedings, undermined the people's feeling of security. Simultaneously, they became more aware of technological advances and political democracy elsewhere in the world. Accustomed to casual work attitudes and a private orientation toward life, many Soviets were slow to respond to Yuri Andropov's efforts to tighten discipline, even though, a few years later, Andropov was regarded by many with more respect than Gorbachev. The popular mood had shifted decisively to the side of genuine reform, although many did not yet appreciate the eventual implications for their own way of life.

China's popular mood at the start of reforms was more depressed by reality and more anxious for genuine changes than was the Soviet Union's. The Deng leadership tried to avoid the errors committed by Khrushchev.[23] Periodically, it sought to suppress the reform expectations by reiterating the four cardinal principles as firm limits to change and by stirring campaigns against those who ignored them. After initial excitement about the Four Modernizations and the promise of high levels of socialist democracy and legality, there were few bold promises, although leaders gained sufficient confidence to predict that a steady course would quadruple the GNP over two decades. Following a brief fling in the late 1970s at building huge industrial projects with a great infusion of foreign assistance, interest shifted to more modest programs emphasizing organizational reforms. Going beyond Khrushchev and taking advantage of the age of television, Chinese leaders opened the eyes of their citizens to the outside world. This gave a huge impetus to reform. Yet the leaders, worried about so-called spiritual pollution, from time to time tightened restrictions.

The Deng leadership tried to avoid the lurching caused by Khrushchev's rocky course. At an early date it veered toward the retrenchment of the Brezhnev aftermath. Nonetheless, the popular mood rose and fell to a more extreme degree than in the Soviet Union. The overall message citizens receive from this stage of socialism is not to expect consistency from their leaders or to count on the promises of reform. In the midst of resurgent frustration from unmet expectations, new safety valves serve to relieve some of the tensions.

Chinese leaders gained some respite through the satisfaction and escapism of private pursuits. The household responsibility system in agriculture—followed by the use of small-scale private enterprise in services, rural industries, urban repairs, and even urban manufacturing—opened a vast outlet for the energies of the people. With their earnings from long hours in these family-centered or collective enterprises, households spent lavishly on weddings as well as on consumer durables and, for a minority in the cities, education. In this way they turned away from the ideal communist values.[24] Rural entrepreneurs in China, as the second economy beneficiaries under Brezhnev, did not become activists on the national stage. It was the intellectuals—those who gained the least materially and found their technocratic or humanistic aspirations most frustrated—who became most impatient. In spite of hostility from China's small intelligentsia, Chinese communists were able to drape themselves in the garb of nationalism, at least prior to June 1989, because of the lower levels of education and of ethnic fragmentation among the people and the greater success of the leadership in improving living standards through reform.

Modernization

Economic modernization normally brings with it a civil society, but Stalin and Mao crushed the pre-existing institutions of a civil society and refused to permit new ones. After their deaths, the demand for such institutions quickly intensified. It was partially met by selected publications such as *Novyi Mir* and the *World Economic Herald*,[25] distinctive academic institutes such as Moscow's Institute of World Economies and International Relations or Beijing's Institute of Marxism–Leninism–Mao Zedong Thought, and the think tanks under Yuri Andropov or Aleksei Kosygin before 1968 or under Zhao Ziyang before June 1989. In China private think tanks also formed but were crushed in the 1989 crackdown. Adopting an international orientation, these forces for accelerated reform based heavily on capitalist models appealed to the logic of convergence theory and the requirements of the current stage of scientific and technological transformation.

The Soviet struggle over the logic of modernization came to a head in the second half of the 1960s. The Brezhnev-led forces arrayed against a civil society emerged victorious, even if they compromised by appropriating some of the symbols of modernization theory and by refraining from reversing most of the organizational advances of the previous decade. It was claimed that a new era of developed socialism signified the compatibility, and even the superior linkage, of socialism and modernization.[26] Socialist planning and ownership create a rational course for accelerating the scientific and technological revolution and forging a new way of life commensurate with higher economic development. Under the guise of the rosy rhetoric, there was little more than policy stagnation. The real meaning of the information age, the consumer revolution, and scientific management was lost on leaders whose primary purpose was to retain power and to offer security to loyal cadres regardless of their abilities. In the 1960s and 1970s Soviet economic growth could continue on the basis of a last large cohort of entrants into the labor force and a still available reserve of natural resources, including oil. The environmental implications of extracting raw materials and energy on a vast scale still seemed to be of minor consequence.

By the mid-1980s (and earlier for the intelligentsia), many Soviets had become aware that further modernization and socialism as it had been practiced were incompatible. Programs to reverse a worsening economic slide had, one after another, failed. Not only was the civilian economy being starved by the cost of sustaining a high-technology arms race from a weak economic base, but even the military sector was beginning to despair due to Washington's Star Wars initiative and the widening technological gap in micro-electronics. Disgust at rampant corruption and moral degeneration brought to the forefront voices of morality warning of a crisis. As Thomas Remington explains in Chapter 3, the result was "a peculiar and explosive combination of modernization and system decay." Under Andropov moral concepts internal to socialism were invoked; under Gorbachev it was universal human values.

The World Environment

The lessons of unparalleled East Asian dynamism and, for Soviets, of China's economic spurt of the early 1980s reinforced the message that a different course of modernization existed. Through capitalist organization combining state regulation and private entrepreneurship, some thriving economies were being established. International observers highlighted the intense export competition that promised to preoccupy a divided capitalist bloc for the foreseeable future and the readiness of Washington to lighten its military burden in order to become more competitive. The experts had originally become alerted by the "Japan shock," already in evidence in the early 1970s, and they grew more alarmed by the "NIES shock" caused by the newly industrialized economies from Singapore to South Korea that occurred in the mid-1980s. If Moscow had any hope of modernization, it too must develop its economy by the rules of modernized societies.

Beijing was, of course, less modernized in 1978 than Moscow was in 1985 or even in 1953.[27] Yet the combined pressures of its obvious modernization needs and of the most vivid international successes led its leaders to realize that a smattering of tentative economic reforms was not enough. Unlike the Soviet Union which boasted of its economic performance in 1953, 1964, and even the late 1970s, China at the end of the 1970s made few if any claims about its achievements. The international demonstration effect around its periphery was more convincing. Population pressure exacerbated agricultural poverty and unemployment in the cities, requiring radical policy changes. As a result, China's tentative reforms started with the ideologically sensitive areas of small-scale entrepreneurship through farm and shop management. This bold and successful beginning quickly heightened the interest in proceeding further. Having encouraged a new class quickly numbering in the millions of entrepreneurs, Beijing had started on a new course of modernization with a powerful logic of its own, but one still unwelcome to many state bureaucrats and managers and still somewhat frightening to much of the urban labor force accustomed to the security of guaranteed jobs and controlled prices.

Ideology

In the absence of the give-and-take of political pluralism, struggles over theories of socialism and world development became central battlegrounds. The reform forces seized every opening to broaden the meaning of socialism. Each minor victory added an element of convergence with capitalism: humanism symbolized universal human values; alienation represented social problems common to both social systems; developed socialism at first suggested common features of industrialized societies, but, after it was appropriated by the leadership trying, against all odds, to accentuate how far ahead socialism had raced, the language of reform shifted to references to the beginning or early stage of socialism as justification for borrowing from capitalism; other reform-oriented ideological undercurrents related to concepts of class (recognition of anything resembling the middle class raised positive implications for convergence), the state (as opposed to the party or the dictatorship of the proletariat), and peaceful coexistence (or an open door).

The Brezhnev and Deng leaderships took questions of ideology with utmost seriousness. Although at first they accepted some ideological challenges to conservatism as helpful to planned reforms, they soon grew wary of the ideology of reform. Of course, Deng challenged some basic concepts, especially those relating to the economy; yet he, too, wanted an ideological shield to protect the communist movement. Even if the West had become a welcome partner economically and, to a degree, politically, it remained an ideological threat. Ideological conservatism, asserted in China in March 1979 and in the Soviet Union in 1966 and reasserted intermittently and more stridently thereafter, exerted pressure that often led to other forms of conservatism. As long as the ideological course resisted genuine reform, pragmatic policies leading to substantial successes in economic reforms, détente with the West, and international trade did not have much hope of turning into a sustained reform course.

THE SHIFT FROM TENTATIVE TO FULL-FLEDGED REFORM

Communist leaderships turn to partial reforms to accomplish specific goals, while buttressing controls to limit perceived spillover effects. They undertake reform and simultaneously draw the line; from time to time when they fear that the line is being crossed, they pull back the reins on reform. Tentative reform periods are jerky: a reform initiative in one sphere is soon followed by retrenchment in another. At times the reforms seem to be going nowhere. Leadership anxieties about going forward result in a holding pattern. The early gains from reform programs no longer can be easily duplicated. Rulers become preoccupied with threats to their power caused by: arousing popular sentiment for further change, turning loose an uncontrollable momentum of market-oriented modernization, opening the country to unpredictable globalization, or replacing ideology with pragmatism. Unlike the turmoil that marks the era of radical socialism, stagnation is the eventual outcome of tentative reform. Pressures build for comprehensive reform. This leads, contrary to the wishes of party leaders, toward a desire to dismantle the system.

Leadership

Comparing the turn from the late 1970s to the early 1980s in the Soviet Union and from the late 1980s to the early 1990s in China, we find many similarities. An aged leadership temporized, no longer making even a semblance of reform, while a frustrated younger generation could do little besides wait. The architects and enthusiasts of the earlier reforms numbered among the most impatient supporters of a new wave, while many genuine technocrats, promoted to guide the economy, chafed at the incompetence and corruption around them. Purges racked the ranks of the most outspoken theorists and publicists of reform, but they scarcely slowed the buildup of closet (and sometimes quite daring) reformers in academia, the arts, and even the bureaucracy.

With some leadership change at or near the top, these reform forces could be activated. The deaths of Mikhail Suslov and then Brezhnev led to the relaxation of ideological controls. Soviet analysts grew bolder, for example in writing about the failures of Chinese socialism.[28] To curtail corruption, Andropov accepted the need for a widespread purge of local and regional officials and for replacements often more supportive of reform than were their predecessors. Even as Konstantin Chernenko, who took charge of ideology and raised the rallying cry of intensified ideological struggle against capitalism, was struggling against Andropov and then Gorbachev, the anticorruption drive after Brezhnev's death reinvigorated the reform forces. China's anticorruption drive of 1990 was too weak to produce similar consequences, but the momentum of its decentralized and outward-looking economic development added to the forces of reform.

A program for economic acceleration may damage genuine economic reform, but it also may activate the forces of reform. Such a program shifts the balance of power from the organization and propaganda departments of the Communist Party to the economic bureaucracies, which then are closely judged for their performance. As a result, cracks in the community of economic leaders and advisors quickly widen, increasing the likelihood of sober assessments and rival strategies. Chinese acceleration in 1977–80 and Soviet acceleration in 1985–87 (with elements of it earlier in 1982–84) changed the terms of debate, bringing reformers more fully into the policy-making process.

Serious reform brings a readiness to turn to experts rather than reds. There is a depoliticizing of leadership. This happened, to a substantial degree, in China as a reaction against the Cultural Revolution's denigration of expertise. Rehabilitation of the victims of radical socialism made a bigger impact on the Chinese than on the Soviet leadership.

With few potential successors in place in the late 1970s, China's top leaders also turned more decisively toward "better educated, more competent, and younger" cadres, while retiring many incumbents. Under the largely apolitical direction of Zhao Ziyang and Hu Yaobang, a third echelon of new leaders—100,000 at the county level, 30,000 at middle levels, and 1,000 at the center—entered the fast track for promotion.[29] College-educated mayors symbolized the new professionalism.[30] No comparable quick generational transition occurred in the Soviet Union, where the blending of reds and experts was much farther along.

Even as the third echelon rose rapidly in China, the limits on its climb remained firmly in place. The Communist Party, especially through its first secretaries and organizational and propaganda departments, retained a powerful grip on government. Legislative authority and independence were weak. Ostensibly retired officials continued to be influential. Even the highest officials lacked consistent support from the elderly advisors who had the final say and from the military and party hierarchies interlocking with them. As seen in January 1987 and June 1989, the reformers were in the vulnerable position of a caretaker government allowed to act only within prescribed limits.

Gorbachev quickly leapfrogged ahead of the Chinese in leadership reform. He did this by relegating the old organs of power to the periphery and by creating new organs, both his own presidential council for a time and the elected legislatures along with the local governments they formed. To be openly against the system became the best credential for election across most of the Soviet Union. Boris Yeltsin, the maverick evicted in late 1987 from the Politburo, was elected to Russia's highest post in the spring of 1990 and popularly elected by direct vote in June 1991. Oleg Kalugin, the KGB turncoat of June 1990, was elected to the Congress of People's Deputies in September. Ethnic nationalists rode the bandwagon of anti-Sovietism to victories in one republic after another. China, however, refused to give such open opponents any leadership platform. In 1990 it continued to arrest, and in some cases to keep incommunicado in prison, the most vocal political dissidents, while releasing, on condition of silence, some who had been arrested earlier. From October 1990 to August 1991, Gorbachev relied on old-line communists resistant to reform. Indeed, he surrounded himself with the very men who on August 19 almost succeeded in staging a military coup. But after being saved by Yeltsin and the reform forces, Gorbachev was obliged to rely on ardent reformers. Soon they did not need him any longer.

The new communist leaders in China from 1978 and in the Soviet Union from 1985 turned to public opinion as a major source of support.

The voice of the people now mattered. Rather fragile leaders, faced with opposition from entrenched political hardliners and bureaucrats, needed public support in order to make progress on their ambitious agendas and to keep their grip on power. Unleashing glasnost on their political opponents, they rallied the intellectual community behind them and raised popular expectations. Leadership legitimation became one of the driving forces behind reform.

Before this process was far along, the two countries diverged in their approach to legitimation. China's leaders decided to channel popular participation into micro-level elections, into limited glasnost regulated by frequent party documents, and into selective appointments to broaden representation. The hesitant and inconsistent government response was a throwback to the Khrushchev era's tinkering with superficial popular participation in place of genuine democracy. It left rising expectations, especially in educated circles, largely unsatisfied even as material conditions for the majority were noticeably improving.

Gorbachev did not draw such a firm line on public involvement. The Russian prewar tradition of political participation had evolved further than China's pre-1949 experience. The Soviet intelligentsia was a more powerful interest group than the Chinese intelligentsia. From the time of Khrushchev, it articulated many ideals of a new intellectual elite. Memories of the abortive reforms in the 1950s and 1960s led to intensified demands to push much farther ahead. Gorbachev lacked Deng's solid connections with veteran leaders. To solidify his hold on the top post, he needed to widen his appeal. These and other factors can be cited to explain the difference, but perhaps most important was Gorbachev's inability to provide any other type of legitimation than democratization within the context of worldwide concern for human rights in the Soviet Union. To be taken seriously, he had to present an entirely new approach and appear to guarantee a very different future.

In the first phase of the legitimation crisis, Gorbachev proved himself more willing than Deng has been since 1978 to let historical truth come out, regardless of cost to party pride. Having failed to respond to the Chernobyl nuclear accident with full candor, he was driven toward greater openness. In the second phase, Gorbachev accepted the existence of voluntary informal associations. Unlike Deng, who suppressed the democracy movement of 1979 and tried to avoid any semblance of chaos, such as had occurred in the Cultural Revolution, Gorbachev, apart from the interval of late 1990 and early 1991, encouraged democracy. He worried primarily about the viselike grip of the bureaucracy and the apathy of the people who had lost hope in combating it. Beginning with artists' protests against their bureaucratic masters and carried forward by environmental protests against the northern rivers project, the Soviet people showed that they were ready to pour into the streets to join together for countless causes.

The third phase of the search for new legitimation produced a shift to parliamentary power and multicandidate elections. Of the two countries, only the Soviet Union entered this phase. But it did so without offering the parliaments a clear mandate, and soon they were seen as ineffectual and not a stepping-stone to the type of strong leadership needed. Since the voting process at the all-union level was rigged to favor established organizations, the result fell well short of a genuine democracy. By 1991 the nations of the Soviet Union were insisting on further steps, granting the republics their own representative governments and sovereignty.

Chen Yizi's article on what happened in China after the Tiananmen Square repression of June 4, 1989, suggests many parallels with what happened in the Soviet Union twenty-one years earlier when the Red Army suppressed the Prague Spring.[31] The trend toward the free market—much more developed in China—was cautiously, but mostly unsuccessfully, supplanted by central planning; steps toward political reform or democratization were derailed by the centralization of power (indeed Mao's model was more openly invoked as a positive example than Stalin's had been); and buds of pluralism in cultural and intellectual life were squashed by authoritarianism. The people lost some of their hope in the Communist Party and its social system. Youth sought escape, while laborers grew spiritless. More decisively than in the Soviet Union, the intellectuals in China turned hostile. Even the cadres objected to the system. Local governments in China now receive 70 percent of total government revenues as opposed to 30 percent prior to reforms.[32] Their newfound power, Chen predicted, would thwart consolidation by the center. Chen foresaw a grand coalition of democratic reform elements in China, including elements within the party and within every sector of society, as well as Chinese in Taiwan, Hong Kong, and elsewhere. This vision was extreme in stating how much had been lost in 1989 and in anticipating how easily unity among the reformers would be achieved; overtaking Soviet democratization would be hard.

Economic retrenchment at the turn of the 1970s in the Soviet Union and in the 1990s in China took similar forms. Despite talk of a consumer emphasis, the military had first call on resources and was rewarded for its support. (Of course, in China not many years earlier it had been cut by one million men.) Old-style ideologues gained a louder voice, dampening policies that favored individual incentives such as China's policy of enabling a few people to get rich first. In the midst of wide inequalities resulting from the expanded private sector (the second economy in the Soviet Union and collusion between local authorities and favored traders), a new egalitarianism arose.[33] Ordinary worker families in major cities gained security (but not an incentive to work harder) from bonuses and a leveling of differences between mental and manual labor. Scientists, engineers, and other mental laborers, however, lost hope. The result under Brezhnev and later Deng was escapism, lethargy, and extreme neglect of positions, such as teaching, vital to the moral fiber of the society. Yet, there was also one enormous difference. China's earlier changes in economic structure remained largely intact, producing more and more vested interests learning how to operate in a non-centralized economy.

Popular Sentiment

Public opinion in the Soviet Union in the 1970s and in China in the early 1990s appeared to be apathetic, but was really fuming beneath the surface, ready to catch fire at the first sparks. While anticorruption and acceleration campaigns do not by themselves light the necessary fire, they scatter cinders of openness. As Brezhnev and Deng faded into a stupor of inactivity, initiators of reform realized that it was necessary at the start to expose the obstacles to success. Once given the opportunity, in a break with stagnation, new leaders would be tempted to shift the blame for their overwhelming problems to the past and to use such revelations to discredit their rivals. The bureaucracy itself became a primary target of Gorbachev.

Under these conditions, fewer topics remain off-limits in "zones without criticism." To some degree, criticism of the party and the state is permitted despite continued worries about the loss of prestige for these organizations. Lines of hierarchy are redrawn, reducing the stultifying role of the traditional democratic centralism in favor of interest group articulation on the basis of region, ethnicity, and economic specialization. Openness, both in print and in political organization and elections, introduces the most subversive force of all in a top-heavy system rife with gripes and grudges.

Tentative reforms in the Soviet Union of the 1950s and 1960s and in China beginning in 1978 succeeded in deradicalizing the society, sharply reducing terror and arbitrary rule while creating for many tolerable living conditions and opportunities for personal gain. These reforms removed barriers by making concessions; yet they did not build many of the institutions that are needed to sustain modernization over a long period. Because there was considerable slack in the micro-economy (where personal incentives were long ignored) and much room for improved efficiency through bureaucratic management of the macro-economy (higher agricultural purchase prices, better educated managers, less cronyism in departmental operations), the economy notably improved for a time. To follow these achievements China and the Soviet Union unsuccessfully attempted to rekindle growth through a new wave of tentative reforms. Presures for more thoroughgoing changes quickly mounted.

Konstantin Pleshakov and Dimitry Furman are among the few who have delineated the common stages of development in China and the Soviet Union. They argue that cultural traditions "very distant from each other" account for divergence in development.[34] The two authors outline three stages: (1) the beginning stage of enormous mass enthusiasm; (2) the mature dogmatic society, linked to the idea of an earthly heaven without private property (along with the idea of a richer and freer existence); and (3) the reform era, under many Soviet leaders from Khrushchev to Gorbachev and under Deng in China. Patterns of development differed, in part, because of different levels of socioeconomic development (levels of modernization). More backward, China had more peasants, which paradoxically permitted the faster restoration of normal economic activity in the third stage. Also the countries differed because of the distinctive world environment at the time of their revolutions. The Communist Party of China formed within the international communist movement headed by Stalin; therefore it lacked the democratic spirit of Lenin's party in 1917. Acknowledging these and other factors as minor sources of differences, Pleshakov and Furman stress culture as the most influential force affecting the rhythm of transition from stage to stage.

They compare the eclipse of Eastern Orthodoxy (de-Christianization) from the time of Peter I and the rapid loss of religiousness after 1917 with the continued vitality of the Confucian sense of social duty and rebelliousness against a sovereign who does not fulfill his duties. This was followed by mass activism in the Cultural Revolution and again at Tiananmen Square in 1976 as the forerunner to the ouster of the Gang of Four. Pleshakov and Furman insist that tradition or the loss thereof had much to do with the outbreak of revolutions in China and the Soviet Union and with the character of the later terror and the different reactions against it.

Unlike Russia's tradition of uncontrolled, tyrannical authority, the Confucian tradition limited autocracy. It could not be overturned even by Mao's campaign to rehabilitate Qin Shihuang, viewed by intellectuals as the arch-villain in Chinese history and the man closest to the Russian outlook. Mao manipulated the masses; Stalin took advantage of their uncertainty and fear to try to break them. The Soviet authors conclude that traditional modesty and fear operated to limit reforms in the post-Stalin decades, producing endless arguments at each step of the path to reform. Yet what threatens chaos simultaneously opens the way to a fully democratic society. The rich cultural life that continued in the period of "stagnation" and earlier, even under Stalin, has positive consequences today, while China's recent homogeneity of thinking and lack of new ideas—reflected in the moderation of demands by demonstrators in the spring of 1989—suggest that parliamentary democracy is still a distant prospect.

Pleshakov and Furman believe that the processes leading to a democratic society are likely to go forward in conditions of social catastrophe in China as they did in the period of stagnation in the Soviet Union. Continuation of China's economic and foreign policy successes, along with the healing after the Cultural Revolution, have sufficed for some democratization, even if the results were limited. Early plans for micro-level elections were quickly redesigned and mostly derailed. Only through defiant rallies led by college students did the Chinese people make their voice heard. The rallies were suppressed in January 1987 and in June 1989, when sympathetic leaders at Deng's side were toppled and campus activists and some intellectual supporters were silenced. In contrast, Gorbachev gained a majority for turning to parliamentary means to break an impasse in the top leadership. Even if he acted out of desperation as bureaucrats paralyzed one reform initiative after another, he also became an ardent critic of the structural inertia inherent in the existing centralized system, which could not energize the "human factor" without an outpouring of activism from below. Wavering about the desirability of such activism when nationality conflicts simmered, Gorbachev in the final analysis depended on it in resisting the opponents of reform.

The third phase of open parliamentary elections and televised sessions led inexorably to insistence on a fourth phase characterized by the end of the Communist Party's monopoly on power and the start of multiparty elections. Newly elected presidents of republics and mayors of big cities took the lead in bringing diversity to the Soviet Union. Having opened the agenda to decentralization away from the top-heavy system of the past sixty years, Gorbachev watched almost helplessly as claims for sovereignty or at least for control over local resources and developmental policies arose at every level. In just five years the Communist Party had become a fragmented debating society. Seen as an atavism, it had little appeal to voters or to the decision makers concerned with revising the Soviet economy. Soon parliaments also were sinking in popular esteem as the public became impatient for a strong hand to cope with severe problems. After many months of wavering, Gorbachev shifted to the right toward the end of 1990. His strong-arm approach, however, also was unpopular. In 1992 the prospects for democracy depended on the elected leaders of the fifteen new nations. Already in January the leader of Georgia was ousted by force amid charges that he had turned into a petty tyrant. It was Yeltsin more than any other leader who would decide the fate of democracy.

Modernization

Socialism offers one type of response to a particular stage of modernization. Its advocates defiantly challenge modernization theorists and believers in the universalism of capitalist development by insisting that the shift from being a largely rural, little educated country to being an industrialized modern power can be accomplished more efficiently through state planning, a centralized economy, and concentration on heavy industrial complexes. As a result of such innovations, socialist modernization deviates from the customary range of variation observed in countries that have been advancing through modernization. They are outliers, and as their economies grow more complex, the pressures mount to veer back toward the pack. If they are to escape from the confines of smokestack industrialization where authoritative bosses impose their demands on a proletariat with little personal responsibility, they must accept the logic of convergence or growing similarity between socialism and capitalism, as it turns out, on the basis of changes in the former.

The move toward convergence produces a snowball effect. Once barriers are dropped and pragmatism becomes the chief criterion for policy selection, the rush toward convergence becomes faster and faster. Approval of foreign investment leads to encouragement of joint ventures, then to special economic zones, and eventually to a convertible currency and foreign subsidiaries. Openness to the outside starts with a crack, widens to an open door, and, unless artificially blocked by costly barricades, eventually becomes an open house where foreigners are welcomed. China's attempt to place a screen in the open door to keep out "bourgeois liberalization" is a temporary interruption, which many foreign partners anticipate will be pushed aside as the holes in the screen widen and the logic of greater convergence more fully impresses itself on China's leaders and people.

Only when there is a clear notion of two paths of development—capitalist, based on exploitation and imperialism, and socialist, based on different principles—can ideas of convergence be dismissed lightly. Once reforms begin in earnest and profitability and productivity become the principal goals, there emerge new and more revealing measures of success and failure. China's modernization of 1979–89 produced many successes, changing the standards for juding performance. Without official acceptance, the reasoning of convergence theory had penetrated deeply. The same result occurred in the Soviet Union under glasnost. Eager for shedding the old order the all-union parliament granted Gorbachev the authority to take personal charge of sweeping policy changes, but he continued to hesitate on fundamental economic changes after accepting in September 1990 a bold 500-day program that might have produced accelerated convergence. Again in the summer of 1991, Gorbachev ventured to the edge of a strong economic reform package, then blinked and pulled back. It took the failed coup to push him over the edge into Boris Yeltsin's waiting arms. Regardless of intentions born of desperation, the goal of borrowing as much as possible did not mean that what was eventually introduced in local areas and individual organizations would be very similar to capitalism as it exists in the North Atlantic and the Pacific rim. The legacy of decades of communism ensures that convergence will be a gradual and incomplete process.

The World Environment

For a time Soviet and Chinese authorities let their citizens interact with foreigners through carefully cordoned contacts. Informants watched and listened, while those privileged to have the contacts were instructed on what to say and required to file reports. First Moscow realized that for technological transfer and superpower success it needed a large corps of internationalists. Then Beijing decided that it could narrow an enormous scientific chasm by sending large numbers of students as well as older scholars to centers of world scholarship. It was remarkable how quickly education bridged the cultural gap. The children of highly placed officials and academics were most apt to be educated, and their impressions soon resonated through influential circles.

Communist leaders long railed against the notion of universal human values. Yet those values quickly began to operate once educated and urban citizens discovered the arts and even the political culture of the West. Simultaneously, the youth culture of rock music, dance, and material possessions ranging from jeans to Walkmans penetrated the psyche of an entire generation. The citizens of communist-led countries were starved for culture and ready, in many cases, to embrace wholeheartedly the popular culture of the West.

Once the floodgates of foreign contact are opened, people grasp at every chance to travel and live abroad. This results not only from the enormous gap in living standards, but also from the spiritual emptiness produced by socialism. Together with convergence in modernization policies, internationalization of individual attitudes and behavior accelerates to the extent that exposure occurs. Beijing has tried to put the brakes on this process, only to find that its citizens refuse to return. To avoid a brain drain it is necessary to offer conditions and compensation appropriate to the acquired education and skills. Moscow has been slower than Beijing to send its students abroad. It is not yet clear how well returnees will be utilized and integrated into either society. Until this issue is resolved, internationalization will not be able to advance very far. By 1992 the desire to escape to the West in both China and Russia was intense, but willingness to return had become rare.

Ideology

At least three interrelated struggles occur in the transition from reform to dismantling. There is a leadership struggle, extending from backroom deals to street campaigning. There is a struggle over modernization policies, involving teams of economic advisors competing to win acceptance for their proposals and then, at the implementation stage, ministries and managers searching for loopholes and advantages to twist the reform to their benefit. And there is also a struggle over ideas. Researchers in the various academies of sciences, faculty in higher education, journalists, and even some officials search for a world view capable of swaying the political agenda. The primary aim of this search is dethroning communist ideology.

Each of the social science disciplines plays a role, often sequentially, in the struggle against past ideology. Philosophy, often equated with ideology, is likely to be first since there are many codewords and abstractions that must be removed as plugs in the dike restraining free discussion. Economic revisionism is not far behind, given the urgency of finding answers to the ongoing economic crisis. Ultimately, these two types of openness will appear strictly utilitarian unless they are grounded in history, which convinces the public of the need to escape from almost unimaginable sufferings. De-Stalinization and de-Maoization—the gateways to historical objectivity—were a true test for the leadership's commitment to openness; even when these struggles were in progress, the focus was shifting to the more demanding test of de-Leninization. Sociology is also a keen barometer of the regime's willingness to shift from ideological dogma to scholarly objectivity. Only by accurately exposing the very nature of the existing society and its severe social problems does the case for dismantling become clear. Political science is the discipline that offers the ultimate test of whether the regime is prepared to measure the public's attitudes toward authority and its objections to the Communist Party monopoly. One by one these disciplines develop and tread farther onto previously hallowed ground, making the once sacred ideology a profane target for all to attack.

In the 1980s China's de-ideologization had spread to all disciplines. Yet artificial limits operated in each and in the journalistic areas that complemented them. By drawing the line most clearly in the area of ideology, China's leaders kept reform from turning into dismantling. At the same time, they made it difficult for reform to continue. Conservative forces were not scattered in disarray as they were during the first five years of the Gorbachev era and again in the seventh year when they were further discredited by their failed coup. Instead, they were well organized, and during intermittent campaigns they became mobilized into crash offensives against ideological deviance. Ideological conservatism in China in the 1980s, as in the Soviet Union in the 1950s and 1960s, remained well entrenched even when permission was briefly given to men such as Liu Binyan or Su Shaozhi to stretch the limits of reform thought. By late 1989 Chinese ideological limits had tightened.

Soviet de-ideologization beginning in 1985 led the way to political and then economic reforms. China's refusal to allow similar glasnost, in spite of the December 1984 recognition by the leadership that it was wrong to bind present policy to the not altogether relevant interpretations of Marx and Lenin, constrained political and eventually economic reforms. Once the ideological gates are opened, the leaders of China will have to confront numerous sensitive questions ranging from Mao's handling of reeducation in the early years of communism to the Tiananmen brutality of June 1989. Raising these and other issues may dramatically accelerate the reform of socialism, as occurred in the age of glasnost in the Soviet Union.

STAGES IN DISMANTLING SOCIALISM

Leadership

At the level of leadership, socialism as practiced by Communist parties is over when multiparty elections bring to office popular leaders who contest for power and when the nomenklatura is abolished in favor of a normal pattern of elite mobility based largely on education and career performance. In the language adopted by Tsuyoshi Hasegawa in Chapter 2, this is the turn to polyarchy. China's reforms produced sponsored promotion of talented persons such as Zhao Ziyang and, in turn, his brain trust, and a shift toward a more meritocratic nomenklatura, often based on personal oversight one level higher in the administrative hierarchy rather than, as previously, impersonal criteria two levels higher.[35] Soviet reforms resulted in contested elections in which party reformers led by Yeltsin at first were victorious. Later, amid the embarrassment of the Twenty-Eighth Party Congress, they left the party. In late 1990 and early 1991 the Communist Party of the Soviet Union, fragmented as it was, still grasped many of the reins of power in shadowy alliance with the KGB and the military. The struggle over the survival of communism was not yet resolved. It came a giant step closer to resolution when the active and passive supporters of the coup were ousted later in 1991. Finally at the end of the year communism died along with the Soviet Union.

We can find in this process several stages of reform leadership. If in 1985–86 Gorbachev assumed the role of a pragmatic reformer (a role also assumed by Deng for a time) and in 1987–88 through tolerance of criticism and encouragement of openness he advanced to the status of an enlightened reformer, then in 1989–91 his position as president might be characterized as no longer that of a despot but increasingly that of an elder statesman presiding over his country as a systemic reformer. The first role signifies an intermittent or inconsistent commitment to transformation, the second a full-scale commitment but only to change managed from above, and the third a commitment so deep that it transcends concerns about keeping the process under personal control. Shifting from the old system to a new system takes precedence, no matter what the cost to personal authority and the power structure. It was also possible for a brief time to envision a fourth phase of the leadership transition. The parliamentary system might essentially replace the old authority structure as the principal arbiter of the country's fate. In this phase our labels would no longer identify a type of reformer but a degree of democratization in the system. In the fourth phase there would be a democratic system, perhaps modified by the weighted representation of vested organizations or ethnic groups or with some scope for spheres of influence only partially subject to democratic decision making.

At times Gorbachev backtracked from this transition and demanded extraordinary powers. His shift to the conservative side at the end of 1990 and the crackdown on Baltic separatism in January 1991 made a democratic system appear increasingly unlikely. At this point, however, three factors intervened to revitalize the democratization process. First, Gorbachev refused to turn the clock back very far, and the hardliners became more and more restless. Second, Yeltsin seized every possible opportunity to turn to the voters and build a popular consensus behind the electoral and parliamentary process. Third, by bungling their coup and adorning Yeltsin with heroic stature, the hard-liners accelerated democratization mixed with nationalism. There arose the danger of contradictions between democratization and nationalism, especially in the face of impending dismemberment of the union. Given Yeltsin's impatience with constitutional niceties, what seemed likely was that he, like Gorbachev, would operate as a systemic reformer. The shift from Gorbachev's rule based, at most, on indirect elections to Yeltsin's popularly elected presidency did not guarantee continued democratization.

Public Sentiment

The people become more opposed to socialism until an overwhelming majority are willing to pay the price (in loss of security and a further decline in living standards) of scuttling it. This reaction does not occur immediately. Historical myths must be exposed, fuller knowledge of the outside world must be disseminated, alternative interpretations of the forces of development must become convincing, and the early efforts at reform must reveal the limitations of half measures. The education of the public advances through phases that are also affected by the progress of the leadership transition.

In both countries the Deng and Gorbachev eras began with a mood of popular skepticism laced with apathy. People did not expect very much from a new leader's promises of reform. Yet, even a pragmatic reformer could rather quickly elicit a mood of narrowly channeled optimism marked by opportunism. Not expecting a radical change in the overall system, people became cautiously hopeful that some areas would continue to improve and they could seize the moment for personal benefit. With a shift to the ruling style of an enlightened reformer battling against great odds or with a pronounced gap between types of reform—asynchronic or unbalanced reform—the popular reaction could take the form of idealism (common among intellectuals) against a backdrop of short-term pessimism about the overall course of change. Motivated by a newfound sense of idealism, Chinese students in 1989 took to the streets because they were pessimistic that any other course would succeed. Soviet urban voters, although aroused by political campaigns with high ideals, angrily doubted that their newly vocal representatives would find a way to remedy the vices of their socialist system.

By 1990 more Soviets than Chinese had advanced to the phase of idealism mixed with pessimism. After June 4, 1989, the Chinese began to retreat to the mood of an earlier phase. Idealism was not easy to sustain, but the leadership could not simply count on apathy or opportunism as a means to turn the clock back to the easier days of the early and middle 1980s. Neither China nor Russia advanced to the point of hope that a system is emerging capable of changing reality. In the late summer of 1991, the main channel for hope in the Soviet Union was decentralization focused on national aspirations, but this appeared against the backdrop of alarm about the chaotic collapse of the union and the still deteriorating economy. In early 1992 national independence proved to be no solution to new strains of economic protectionism and struggles over control of the military.

Modernization

In the first phase of reform, leaders believe that modernization can be achieved by correcting imbalances. After a time it becomes clear that shifting investment funds to hard-pressed sectors and adjusting prices and incentives do not suffice. Then the need for organizational changes in the management of enterprises or farms is increasingly appreciated. In the second phase, leaders favor restructuring the system. In addition to changes in management, reform requires changes in the economic system (such as bankruptcy provisions). Chinese leaders resisted language that might acknowledge the necessity of changing the system (*zhidu*), but in October 1984 they began urban factory reforms that, coupled with earlier changes in rural areas and the urban service sector, could have made a great difference. The Soviet leadership agreed in principle by 1987 to proceed to perestroika. It entered the second phase of reforms to restructure the system with bold language despite more hesitant implementation.

Finally in 1990, after having accomplished little genuine restructuring apart from a loss of control over the economic levers that had kept the centralized economy functioning, both the parliamentary reformers and the Gorbachev leadership seemed to realize the need for a third phase. No longer groping to find their way, some reformers favored making a fast, clean break with the centralized economy. But Gorbachev gained sweeping powers and chose a different approach. Soviet rhetoric advanced well beyond official Chinese views at the peak of China's reform, but the country's economic behavior still lagged behind China's. Yeltsin and leaders of some other republics wanted to charge ahead, and when the center collapsed in August 1991 they had their chance. A team of committed reformers took charge of economic policy. Working with the International Monetary Fund and other world organizations, they were prepared to pursue shock therapy. This was the approach taken in 1992, with Russia in the lead. There were critics, however, who preferred the gradualism of China's undeclared restructuring of the system to the perilous effects of shock therapy. Nicholas Lardy's chapter in this volume explains some of the reasoning for gradualism.

The World Environment

Opening socialist countries to the world is an incremental process. In the first phase the advanced capitalist countries acquire new importance as the models of high technology and high living standards. Foreign relations must be normalized and, in important respects, open in order to capitalize on the superiority of the outsiders. To galvanize reform forces at home, the attractiveness of foreign achievements must be vividly presented. In the second phase foreign countries become models of economic organization. As restructuring the domestic system assumes a high priority, attention turns to borrowing from the organizational methods of capitalist states. Hesitantly in 1986 and again in 1988 China moved toward a third phase of discovering models of Western civilization. This means recognizing that the humanistic and democratic traditions of the West make a positive contribution to world development, contrasting with one's own country's abnormal or stunted development under communism of earlier decades. This third phase of openness was readily accepted by the Russian intellectual community already accustomed in the nineteenth century to praising the civilizing force of Westernization. The fundamentalist groups on the Russian right failed in 1990–91 to win elections on the basis of their opposition to Westernization. The people were siding with the intellectuals in borrowing more than economic organization from capitalism.

By the end of 1989, the Soviet Union was proceeding to a fourth phase of integration with the world community. The concept of the post–cold war era pointed to political coordination in pursuit of a model of a new world order. Soviet acceptance of NATO's stabilizing role in Europe was a good example of this. Soon thereafter the joint response to the Iraqi invasion of Kuwait suddenly made that world order more of a reality. Although China cooperated in the international quarantine of Iraq and, as a permanent member of the Security Council, condemned Iraqi aggression, it was reluctant to adopt the rhetoric of a world no longer divided between socialism and capitalism. Indeed, the intensified propaganda in 1989 warned of the threat from the bourgeois theory of peaceful evolution away from socialism. Capitalism and even imperialism continued to endanger China, it was argued. On January 31, 1992, when Yeltsin and Li Peng joined George Bush and other world leaders at the United Nations, there was a clear contrast between Yeltsin's strong advocacy of rapid change aimed at a new world order and Li's cautious resistance to imposing Western values on the world.

Ideology

In the first phase of deconstructing socialism, the model for reform reverts to late Lenin and the NEP. By dividing the history of socialism at home and abroad into good and bad periods (or aspects of a single period), spokespersons leave a portion of the ideology unchallenged. In the second phase there is an attempt to find an alternative strand of ideology, for example in the views of Bukharin to prove that there still exists a socialist path of some sort to be discovered and followed. In the third phase the world view turns against socialism in search of a model mixing national characteristics of development and the historical path of the West. Chinese leaders tried to allow a limited acceptance of both Bukharin and Chinese Confucianism, but they balked even at permitting the late Lenin model to displace more orthodox approaches. In 1990 they appealed again to Mao Zedong thought and the model of the self-sacrificing Lei Feng, a complete product of ideological education, to counteract dangerous liberalization. In this campaign leaders tried to halt the dismantling of socialism by moving all the way back to nonreform ideology along with some elements of the thinking of phase one.

The Soviets pushed relentlessly forward with new thinking. Ideology yielded on all fronts, despite temporary setbacks. For example, when it seemed as if the third phase was yielding to a fourth in which ideology might give way to pragmatism, censorship came creeping back early in 1991. When the popular television program "Vzgliad" tried to show a special on Shevardnadze's resignation in protest against Gorbachev's turn to the communists, the special was cancelled, and then the program went off the air. When Soviet troops took control of buildings in Vilnius in January 1991, the media centers constituted prime targets. The future of glasnost had grown cloudy. Like the Chinese reform process before it, glasnost seemed caught in the contradictions of reform with no exit in sight. In late August glasnost was again given a powerful boost. Yegor Yakovlev, the editor of the reformist *Moscow News*, was named to head the broadcasting company in charge of central television and radio. This cleared the path to the open flow of information, solidifying a post-communist worldview.

At the start of the 1990s, the Soviets still lagged behind the Chinese in implementing economic reforms and opening their economy to foreign penetration, but they largely agreed on the need to push forward, beyond China's reforms. In almost all noneconomic respects, the Soviet Union seemed to be ahead in efforts at dismantling. At last in 1992 the Soviet Union and its communist system were no more. Dismantling would now proceed in a post-communist environment under national leaders in a hurry for results.

China in 1991 was at an impasse, with an unbalanced pattern of reform. Initiatives in one area were out of phase with initiatives in other areas. It is unlikely that China can stay in this confused state for long. Having failed to develop a coherent blueprint for retaining the existing structure of socialism, China would, many observers expected, resume dismantling it in the foreseeable future. Of course, much depended on economic results. The private and collective sectors, aided by outside investment and foreign trade, continued to give vitality to parts of the economy, perhaps helping to delay the day of reckoning but making it all the more inevitable.

Despite their greater readiness to dismantle the tower of communism, the Soviets found that they had built it so high that they could not easily climb back down. Community roots and household entrepreneurship were difficult to locate. Above all, the union needed to be taken apart before suspicious nationalities could learn to work together again. The Chinese, however, had never destroyed the rural community and within it the farming household deeply embedded with Confucian traditions. Dismantling an edifice only works if at the bottom there exists a foundation on which to build. In China there seems little doubt that the foundation is there.

NOTES

1. According to official claims, socialism is a stage reached in the Soviet Union in the mid-1930s and in China in the mid-1950s, while communism represents the future once the material wants of society are satisfied and distribution is to each according to his needs.
2. "A Demand Was Made That I Resign. I Said You Will Never Live That Long," *New York Times*, August 23, 1991, p. A11.
3. "Gorbachev's Speech to Russians: 'A Major Regrouping of Political Forces,' " *New York Times*, August 24, 1991, p. A6.
4. This commonplace theme of the early Gorbachev years can be found in many of the Soviet leader's speeches. It was also a popular, though unrealized, slogan of the Leonid Brezhnev era. The same theme surfaced in China (for instance, in criticisms of the rigid, traditional model of socialism shared by the Soviet Union and China).

See Jiang Shengfu, "Luelun Sulian de jingji gaige," *Shijie jingji yu zhengzhi neican*, no. 1, 1985, pp. 22–25, 48.

5. "K novomy obliku sotsializmu," *Kommunist*, No. 13, September 1989, pp. 3–24.
6. Nodari Simoniia, "Mnogoobrazie mira i formatsionnoe razvitie chelovechestva," *Kommunist*, no. 16, November 1989, pp. 106–14; and V.K. Makarov and R.P. Povileiko, "Chem interesna Iaponiia," *EKO*, August 1989, pp. 176–77.
7. Vladimir Shlapentokh, *Soviet Ideologies in the Period of Glasnost: Responses to Brezhnev's Stagnation* (New York: Praeger, 1988), pp. 31–60.
8. Tatyana Zaslavskaia, *The Second Socialist Revolution: An Alternative Soviet Strategy* (London: I.B. Tauris & Co. Ltd., 1990), pp. 163–81.
9. S.L. Agaev, "Sovremennyi mir i raznymi puti k odnoi tseli," *Rabochii klass i sovremennyi mir*, No. 2, March-April 1990, pp. 30–43.
10. Zhou Xincheng and Li Jun, "Shiying woguo jiakuai chengshi tizhi gaige de xuyao jinyibu kaizhan Sulian, dongou guojia jingji tizhi gaige de yanjiu gongzuo," *Shijie jingji yu zhengzhi neican*, no. 11, November 1984, pp. 15–19.
11. Su Shaozhi and Feng Lanrui, "Wuchanjieji qude zhengquan hou de shehui fazhan jieduan wenti," *Jingji yanjiu*, no. 5, May 1979, pp. 14-19; Jin Hui, "Shilun zhengzhi tizhi he jingji tizhi de guanxi," *Sulian dongou wenti*, No. 4, April 1984, pp. 8–13.
12. Gilbert Rozman, *The Chinese Debate About Soviet Socialism, 1978–1985* (Princeton, N.J.: Princeton University Press, 1987), p. 39.
13. V. G. Gel'bras, *Sotsial'no-politicheskaia struktura KNR 50-60-e gody* (Moscow: Nauka, 1980), pp. 26–29.
14. "SSSR-KNR: ostavliaia proshloe v proshlom," *Argumenty i fakty*, No. 5, February 3-9, 1990, pp. 4–5.
15. Mao Tsetung, *A Critique of Soviet Economics* (New York: Monthly Review Press, 1977).
16. Rozman, *The Chinese Debate*, p. 261.
17. Constance Squires Meaney, *Stability and the Industrial Elite in China and the Soviet Union* (Berkeley: Center for Chinese Studies, University of California, 1988).
18. Gilbert Rozman, "Shades of Excellence: The Communist Party and Elites in China and the Soviet Union," in Mel Gurtov, ed., *The Transformation of Socialism: Perestroika and Reform in the Soviet Union and China* (Boulder: Westview Press, 1990), pp. 155–77.
19. N. Simoniya, "The State, Cooperatives, and Bureaucratic Capital," *Moscow News*, nos. 8–9, March 11–18, 1990, p. 19.
20. Terry L. Thompson, *Ideology and Policy: The Political Uses of Doctrine in the Soviet Union* (Boulder: Westview Press, 1989).
21. A. P. Butenko, *Sotsialisticheskii obraz zhizni: problemy i suzhdeniia* (Moscow: Nauka, 1978).
22. James R. Millar, "The Little Deal: Brezhnev's Contribution to Acquisitive Socialism," *Slavic Review* 43 (1985): 694–706.
23. Rozman, *The Chinese Debate*, p. 356.
24. Ezra F. Vogel, *One Step Ahead in China: Guangdong Under Reform* (Cambridge, Mass.: Harvard University Press, 1989), pp. 418–20.
25. Dina R. Spechler, *Permitted Dissent in the USSR: Novy Mir and the Soviet Regime* (New York: Praeger, 1982); and Li Cheng and Lynn T. White III, "China's Technocratic Movement and the *World Economic Herald*," *Modern China* 17 (1991): 342–88.
26. Donald R. Kelley, "Developments in Ideology," in Donald R. Kelley, ed., *Soviet Politics in the Brezhnev Era* (New York: Praeger, 1980), pp. 182–99.
27. Gilbert Rozman, ed., *The Modernization of China* (New York: The Free Press, 1980), pp. 493–99.
28. Fedor Burlatsky, "Mezhdutsarstvie, ili khronika vremen Den Siaopina," *Novyi Mir*, no. 4, April 1982, pp. 205–28.
29. Ding Wang, "An Analysis of the PRC's Future Elite: The Third Echelon," *Journal of Northeast Asian Studies* 4 (Summer 1985): 19–37.
30. David Bachman and Li Cheng, "Localism, Elitism, and Immobilism: Elite Formation and Social Change in Post-Mao China," *World Politics* 41 (October 1989): 64–91.
31. Chen Yizi, "Li Peng Regime in Dilemma," *Inside China Mainland*, trans. and excerpted from *Jiushi niandai yuekan*, no. 6, August 1990, pp. 1–2.

32. Ibid., pp. 1–2.
33. "Basic Features of the New Egalitarianism," *Inside China Mainland,* trans. and excerpted from *Jingji yu guanli yanjiu,* No. 2, 1990, pp. 10–11.
34. K. Pleshakov and D. Furman, "Obshchee i osobennoe v sotsial'no-politicheskom i ideologicheskom razvitii KNR i SSSR," *MEiMO,* December 1989, pp. 35–48.
35. John P. Burns, ed., *The Chinese Communist Party's Nomenklatura System* (Armonk, N.Y.: M.E.Sharpe, 1989), pp. xviii–xxiv.

2

The Connection Between Political and Economic Reform in Communist Regimes

Tsuyoshi Hasegawa

The crisis of communism stems from the economic, political, and ideological foundations of the system, foundations that transcend cultural and geographical differences, that are shared by all regimes of this character, and that make the communist system distinct from other types of regimes. To extricate itself fully from the crisis, a communist regime must create two preconditions: a market economy and a democracy. There are many possible connections between the two preconditions, as the following questions suggest. Can a market economy be introduced without, at some point, political reforms? Conversely, is political reform possible without changing the economic foundations? Will a transition to a market economy necessarily produce political forces that demand political change? Will a transition to democracy necessarily lead to the creation of a market economy? Is it better to start from economic reforms or from political reforms?

Creating both a market economy and a democracy requires a process that may vary in the order of priority, the level of synchronization between the two goals, the speed of transformation, and the degree of backtracking. This chapter attempts to answer the preceding questions by examining the reform process in Hungary, China, the Soviet Union, and Vietnam. Even more central than the observations themselves is the attempt to provide a theoretical framework for connections between political reform and economic reform in all communist regimes.

THE CRISIS IN THE COMMUNIST SYSTEM

To examine whether and how a transition from the communist system can be accomplished, one must first understand the nature of the crisis that confronts all regimes of this type. The crisis rots away all three foundations of a communist system: the command economy, the Communist Party dictatorship, and the communist ideology that once legitimated the command economy and the dictatorship.

A great paradox of Marxism is that its powerful reasoning for the inevitable demise of capitalism can be turned on its head and used devastatingly against the communist system itself. The economy is indeed the basis for the superstructure, and it is precisely in the economic performance that the communist system has proved to be a dismal failure. A revolutionary situation in all communist regimes is caused by fundamental contradiction between productive forces and productive relations in the communist system. The productive relations expressed by state monopolies serve as nothing but the fetters for further development of productive forces.[1] What has gone wrong?

Leaders in the underdeveloped world have viewed communism as an entry ticket to a promised land in which economic "efficiency," achieved by rapid industrialization, could be accomplished without sacrificing political "equality." Communism captured the imagination of these leaders since it seemed to offer an alternative path for modernization without relying on Western capitalism, the very source that condemned their countries to backwardness. The command economy is, therefore, not merely a developmental strategy designed to carry out industrialization of a backward country. It is above all a challenge to capitalism by offering not merely an alternative economic system that is superior to capitalism, but also an alternative civilization.[2]

The command economy initially succeeds in accomplishing industrialization. Nevertheless, this industrialization is carried out by means of "socialist primitive accumulation," in which low agricultural purchase prices and high consumer goods prices enable the state to accumulate and use revenues. In this process, the most productive elements of society are physically eliminated. The market mechanism that has ensured competition and the infrastructure associated with the market are systematically destroyed. Although variations exist, this process occurs in all communist regimes, and this is no accident. Once competition is abolished, the only alternative is control by state monopolies in all spheres of economic activity. If this control is to become more effective in an environment of countless complications, it must become progressively more complete and more detailed. The concomitant result of this process is the development of a ubiquitous bureaucracy that must fill the gaps and bottlenecks that inevitably result from planning. Thus, in the end, "the command-administrative system" replaces "the economy." The success of the command economy has inevitably led to its stagnation. Forced accumulation no longer works, even in raising gross indicators of production.

The success of the command economy is like the success that results from killing the goose that produces golden eggs. Once the initial "great leap" was accomplished, the command economy ceased to move "forward." Moreover, the more advanced is the economic structure, the more glaring the inadequacies of the command economy. Central planning and state monopolies are least equipped to adjust to the vicissitudes that govern the modern economy. In particular, the command economy is incapable of internally generating innovations fundamental for modern capitalism. Since communism is a challenge to capitalism, and since it is destined to measure its performance against that of capitalism, the failure of the command economy has devastating effects on the morale of the population, the confidence of the leadership, and the credibility of the ideology.[3]

A command economy is antithetical to democracy. Democracy bestows on individuals and groups in society the right to express their political opinions and to participate in the political process. The authority that directs all economic activities must have total control over the means of production and natural and human resources, and it must be able to allocate them at will for the goals it seeks to achieve. In a command economy, freedom to express political opinions that protect and enhance the interests of independent groups hinders the ultimate goals that the regime seeks to attain.[4] Moreover, in communist regimes the meaning of democracy is perversely changed. Not only are those who disagree with the regime's goals destroyed, repressed, and silenced, but people are mobilized to demonstrate their active commitment to such goals. Thus, mobilization becomes an important aspect of "people's democracy" under communism. Under communism a rule of law is impossible. There cannot be administrative law that binds the Communist Party, which transcends all laws. Neither should there be an independent judiciary. Thus, the command-administrative system devours not merely the economy, but also the state and the politics.

A market economy requires a rule of law, but a command economy inevitably leads to arbitrariness.[5] Competition in a market economy requires formal rules made in advance that determine the conditions under which individuals engage in competition, and these rules must be applied to everyone equally. Such rules fundamentally contradict the aim of a command economy since "the planning authority cannot confine itself to providing opportunities for unknown people to make whatever use of them they like" and since "it must constantly decide questions which cannot be answered by formal principles only, and in making these decisions it must set up distinctions of merit between the needs of different people."[6] A command economy does not eliminate conflicts in economic activities. On the contrary, it generates them because central planning cannot prescribe the minutiae of economic activities at the lowest level. Contingencies unforeseen by the plan arise. In the absence of legal norms, these contingencies must be solved by extralegal means such as deceptions, bribes, corruptions, and above all by intervention of the party apparatus. The functioning of a command economy thus breeds illegality. With this illegality grows the power of the Communist Party apparatus. Indeed, a command economy and a shadow economy are Siamese twins: The one without the other cannot exist.

There is an integral connection between the command economy and the Communist Party dictatorship. While the command economy has left communist regimes hopelessly behind global economic standards, their political system has lagged far behind civilized norms. It is precisely this relationship that poses a fundamental dilemma for transition from the communist system.

Transition from the communist system thus involves two interrelated and interdependent processes: transition from a command economy to a market economy and transition from Communist Party dictatorship to democracy. Three features are important in this twin transition. First, one without the other is impossible. A market economy presupposes decentralization, autonomous economic organizations that can make independent decisions without interference from the central authority, and a rule of law that governs every individual and group in society. A market economy and a communist dictatorship are thus incompatible. Likewise, democracy is incompatible with a command economy since the latter requires the highly centralized, omnipresent, and omniscient bureaucracy characterized by arbitrariness. Second, although the twin transitions go through stages, it is impossible to stop in the middle and create a stable regime somewhere between the communist system and a society governed by a democracy and a market economy. Third, transition from communism is a process of self-rejection.

The central question is, How to achieve these twin transitions? Timing, sequence, and stages become crucial factors in transitions from communism. The first question is timing. When is the opportune moment for transitions? Is it better to start transition from above, when the regime still has staying power? Or is the nature of the communist system such that it cannot transform itself unless it is pushed against the wall by pressure from below or from outside? Does timing affect the way transitions are carried out?

The second question concerns sequence and the relationship between political and economic transitions. Which transition must come first? Is economic transition possible before political transition begins? Or does the economic transition presuppose political reform? What problems arise when economic transition proceeds without political reform or when political transition precedes economic reforms? For extrication to be successful, must twin transitions be synchronized, and if so how? Is there an optimal transitional path?

The third question is concerned with stages of transitions since dismantling the communist system cannot be carried out overnight. What stages are there in twin transitions, and what criteria should we use to identify them? Timing and sequence are integrally related to this question since each transition from one stage to another poses the same questions raised earlier with regard to the general process of transition.

THEORETICAL FRAMEWORK

In sum, a communist system cannot make a sudden and single leap to a market economy and a democracy. Stages occur in the political transition and in the economic transition. Figure 2-1 shows how these two transitional sequences in the economy and politics are related. The simultaneous changes along two dimensions at differing stages are diagrammed. The remainder of the chapter explains the relevance and the limitation of this theoretical approach in view of the changes in Hungary, China, the Soviet Union, and Vietnam.

Political Transition

In Figure 2-1, the vertical line represents political transition to democracy.[7] The immediate cause that triggers the first move toward liberalization in a communist system varies from country to country. It could be a succession crisis in the top leadership, reaction to the preceding negative period, an acute economic crisis, international pressure, popular discontent manifested in mass protest movements, or some combination of these factors. But behind any reform in a communist regime is an economic crisis.

Facing economic crisis, a communist regime must carry out two reforms that set the liberalization process in motion. It must modify the decision-making mechanism by including a broader portion of the society in the political process, and it must modify the ideology to accommodate new economic measures. This leads to "redefining and extending rights" and tolerating "spaces" for free expression and collective

Figure 2-1
POLITICAL AND ECONOMIC TRANSITION IN THE
COMMUNIST SYSTEM

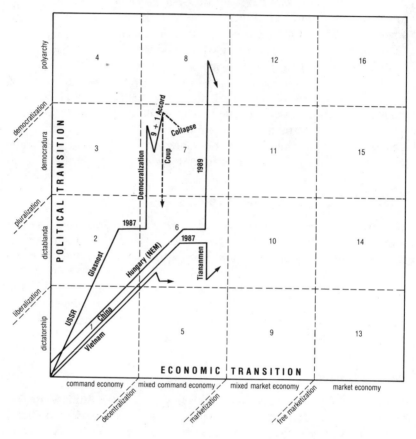

action for individuals and groups in society.[8] This is the stage called "consultative authoritarianism" by Lowenthal and "dictablanda" by O'Donnell and Schmitter.[9]

A dictablanda thus achieved opens the window ajar through which a civil society is resurrected. Eventually it leads to a limited democracy—what Lowenthal calls "democratizing and pluralistic authoritarianism" or what O'Donnell and Schmitter call a "democradura." A dictablanda is a noncompetitive dictatorship; a democradura is a competitive system, but competition is limited in three ways. As Di Palma states, "participation is restricted to usually conservative forces that exclude others; these forces share government offices according to consociational arrangements fairly independent from electoral verdicts; they also leave touchy issues out of the policy agenda."[10]

O'Donnell, Schmitter, and Di Palma distinguish liberalization, the first stage of political transition, and democratization, its next stage. Liberalization refers to the process of "making effective certain rights that protect both individuals and social groups from arbitrary or illegal acts committed by the state or third parties." Democratization is defined as "the processes whereby the rules and procedures of citizenship are either applied to political institutions previously governed by other principles . . . or expanded to include persons not previously enjoying such rights and obligations . . . , or extended to cover issues and institutions not previously subject to citizen participation. . . ."[11] As Di Palma points out, "liberalization mentally evokes democratization, and democratization is signaled by elections."[12] Democratization can be further divided into two processes: pluralization and democratization. Pluralization is the process that moves from a dictablanda to a democradura, and democratization in the narrow sense refers to the process that moves from a democradura to what Robert Dahl calls polyarchy, a pluralistic democracy, when a multiparty system is restored and a democratic election is held. In this chapter I use the term "democratization" in a narrower sense than do O'Donnell, Schmitter, and Di Palma.

A "pact" or "garantismo" may emerge at crucial moments for political transition. A pact is "an explicit, but not always publicly explicated or justified, agreement . . . which seeks to define . . . rules governing the exercise of power on the basis of mutual guarantees for the 'vital interests' of those entering into it."[13] A pact may be a temporary solution to avoid crisis. It is often a compromise among various political and social groups. No single group can impose an ideal project on others, and competing groups are interdependent. "[T]hey can neither do without each other nor unilaterally impose their preferred solution on each other if they are to satisfy their respective divergent interests."[14] A stalemate is a crucial moment for political transition. Political actors with conflicting interests have an incentive to accept such a pact because otherwise "their immediate prospect is a reciprocal stalemate, fed by recalcitrance and polarization, and without visible exit."[15] This pact, which creates a democradura, contributes to the emergence of new actors who desire to participate in the process from which they are excluded. As Di Palma writes, "Garantismo should often imply the formation—willy-nilly, formal or implicit—of broad and inclusive constitutional coalitions, reaching the outer peripheries of the political spectrum."[16] The mobilization that follows the establishment of democradura is thus likely to provoke the formation of quasi-political parties within the Communist Party or outside it (informal groups), although groups of neither kind are officially recognized as political parties. In such situations elections become an attractive means for conflict resolution.

The decision to hold a national election profoundly affects the transition since the regime and the opposition focus their energies on winning seats.[17] Through organization of election campaigns, diverse groups coalesce into quasi-political parties, and boundaries between the regime and the opposition (as well as those between the opposition parties with regard to policies and tactics) emerge clearly. Although political parties (or quasi political parties) play little part in the liberalization, the prospect of an election brings them to the center stage in the pluralization-democratization process. As O'Donnell and Schmitter state, "If there is ever a 'heroic' moment for political parties, it comes in their activity leading up to, during, and immediately following the 'founding elections,' when, for the first time after an authoritarian regime, elected positions of national significance are disputed under reasonably competitive conditions."[18]

During preparations for elections, the opposition parties are frequently divided over candidates and encounter difficulties in fund raising. They are the victim of covert and overt obstructions in their campaign efforts from the political machine still monopolized by the Communist Party. This situation often leads the Communist Party to overestimate its popularity since it expects the gratitude of the populace for liberalizing, pluralizing, and democratizing. What it does not understand, however, is that the first "founding election" is often turned into a plebiscite on the Communist Party itself. When people are given the first opportunity to vote by hands and not by feet (that is, to choose freely between genuine alternatives), they often reject candidates who represent the Communist Party and vote for any candidates who oppose it. One of the likely results of the founding election is the elimination of the article in the constitution that guarantees the Communist Party as the sole ruling party.

The election and the subsequent political arrangements enormously influence pluralization and democratization since they tend to shift the attention to rules and procedures. General rules of the game are agreed on by the ruling Communist Party and the opposition. Those radicals, both right and left, who refuse to participate in the new game are eliminated from the political process. Even the hard-liners who reject radical changes must begin to play by the new rules.

We must consider next why the transition from liberalization to democratization is a probable scenario in communist regimes. Di Palma offers an argument as to why democracy is a more attractive alternative to authoritarian dictatorship. First, democracy is generally associated with the idea of social progress.[19] Second, "if democracy is not the key to progress, neither were those alternative regimes that came to replace democracy, claiming superior performance and indeed a superior concept of man."[20] Third, democracy is superior to other regime types in its ability to curb oppression, to reassert the citizens' self-interest, to reconstitute community, and to re-establish a sense of personal worth and public dignity.[21] Fourth, democracy becomes an attractive choice when "the costs of mutual tolerance . . . are made to be smaller than those of maintaining a repressive system."[22] Di Palma describes "democracy's rules" as a "means for mutual coexistence," and he claims that they "need not be more than a second best for the parties that negotiate their adoption." Paraphrasing Dankwart Rustow, he writes that "acceptance of democracy's rules is not a prerequisite, since their elaboration may well be an integral part of the transition itself. It follows in sum that genuine democrats need not precede democracy, and that the transfer of loyalties from dictatorship to democracy does not require exceptionally favorable circumstances."[23]

Once democratization is set into motion, "the postponements and niggardly accommodations promised by a *democradura* should be a poor match for participation, representation, equality, popular accountability, and the other standards of democracy to which contemporary public opinion seems ever more alert." At this point the risk of not moving to full democracy is "the rapid waning of any limited credibility its political formula may have—in sum, no extrication, no exit."[24]

The Economic Transition

The horizontal axis of Figure 2-1 depicts the multistage transition from a command to a market economy. The first stage is a mixed command economy. While maintaining the basic structure of a command economy, the regime begins to chip away at it by decentralizing economic decisions and privatizing agriculture and the service sector. It may open the domestic market for foreign economic activities through joint ventures with foreign corporations, free economic zones, and foreign investments. I refer to the movement from a command economy to a mixed command economy as "decentralization," which here connotes not merely decentralization of economic decision making, but the broader spectrum of economic transformation described earlier. In this chapter the term "liberalization" refers exclusively to political liberalization.

One subjective condition and at least one of the following four objective conditions must be met for decentralization from a command economy to a mixed command economy. The subjective prerequisite is the existence of leadership prepared to introduce a partial form of a market economy in order to extricate its country from the economic crisis. As for the objective conditions, the first is that a significant change in property relations must take place not merely in theory but in reality. There must exist a legally recognized private sector, which occupies a significant share of total economic activities, although this share does not have to be predominant. The private sector thus created must form an island of a market economy in the sea of a command economy. Second, enterprises must be given a large sphere of decision-making authority with regard to production, sales, price setting, and wages. Third, the central authority must gradually shift economic decisions either to the local level or to the enterprise level. Fourth, the economy must be open to international capitalistic economic forces through joint ventures, free economic zones, or direct foreign investments. Nevertheless, at this stage the state sector continues to be predominant, particularly in crucial sectors of industry. The central planning organ continues to play an important role in the allocation of resources.

The next stage of transition is marketization. In this transition from a mixed command economy to a mixed market economy, the market economy becomes predominant. The commanding heights such as transportation and energy may still be controlled by the state. In general, the state assumes an assertive role in intervening in macroeconomic decisions and in protecting the interests of some segments of the population likely to be profoundly affected by marketization. Two crucial conditions must be met for a mixed command economy to move into a mixed market economy. The first is the price system. In a mixed market economy, price is determined by equilibrium in the market. It is not arbitrarily fixed by the central government or planning agency. Price reform represents the most important divide in the entire transitional process from a command economy to a market economy. The second condition is privatization of most state enterprises. Which of these conditions should be accomplished first is an important practical question. Implementation of a price reform without breaking the monopoly of state enterprises may create hyperinflation without accompanying competition. And yet without price reform it is impossible to set proper prices for state enterprises to be privatized. After stabilization during the third stage, even the commanding heights may be denationalized, and a full-fledged market economy can be established.

I call this process "free marketization," as distinguished from marketization. A genuine laissez-faire economy where the state does not intervene in the economy, particularly in macroeconomic policy, does not exist in the real world. One can, however, distinguish between a mixed market economy (where the state controls the market) and a genuine market economy (where the state merely regulates it). In a genuine market economy the role of the state is restricted only to ensure the proper function of market forces. The market then becomes the driving force of economic activities.

In three respects economic transition differs fundamentally from political transition. First, political transition can be evolutionary. Liberalization, pluralization, and democratization are stages, each one serving as a stepping-stone to the next. Evolutionary development does not fit well in economic transition since one cannot have an ambiguous stage, where a command economy and a market economy coexist in equal balance. Thus, a mixed economy that exists as a halfway house between a command economy and a market economy has to be guided either by the command principles or the market mechanism. Whereas liberalization tends to provoke momentum toward pluralization and pluralization toward democratization, decentralization does not in itself generate a momentum toward marketization in the economic transition. It seems almost impossible for pockets of privatized economic entities or decentralized economic decisions to develop spontaneously into a market economy. The roots of a command economy are so resilient that they are bound to stifle such incipient, fragile development from below. Thus, strong leadership from above is necessary for decentralization to lead to marketization. And yet strong leadership, buttressed by strong machinery to implement its decision, can be created only by the Communist Party apparatus, which is the greatest impediment to political transition.[25] Herein lies the first contradiction between economic reform and political reform.

The second fundamental difference between economic and political transition is that the techniques of democratization are less difficult to learn than those of marketization. In other words, the infrastructure needed for democratization is simpler than the infrastructure needed for marketization. A handful of like-minded people can get together, form a political association, disseminate its platform, appeal to the broader population for political action, and use the mass media to widen its political base. Models of democracy—such as competitive elections, electoral laws, a parliamentary or presidential system, checks and balances, and judiciary independence—can be borrowed and transplanted relatively easily even in an environment that is known to lack strong democratic antecedents and traditions,[26] although this transplantation in an indigenous political culture may create a system that does not conform to the classical definition of Western democracy.

A market economy, however, cannot be transplanted so easily. Associations of like-minded people, even with the blessing of the regime, will not immediately create a market. It has to be created from below, voluntarily and spontaneously, without the intervention of the state. The state may create the framework, but the contents within this framework must be filled from below. The mentality nurtured by the command economy is more difficult to break than is the political culture that developed under the communist dictatorship. A market economy also requires management skills, stock and commodity exchanges, a banking system, a taxation system, commercial laws, foreign trade, marketing, advertising, and information networks. The necessary expertise cannot be learned overnight. For the infrastructure to be developed, strong governmental programs backed up by state subsidies are required. Herein lies another contradiction—a contradiction between the need to dismantle the strong dictatorship required by political transition and the need to strengthen the central power to hasten economic transition.

The third difference is timing. Dismantling a command economy and replacing it with a market economy can take decades. By comparison, the political system can be dismantled relatively quickly. Synchronizing the two processes is a difficult but crucial factor for transition from communism.

The sixteen boxes in Figure 2-1 represent the sixteen possible combinations of political and economic transition. Even within each box there can be movement along the horizontal and the vertical lines. Whether the ultimate goal is Box 16 (liberal democracy) or Box 12 (social democracy), extrication from the communist system is not possible without marketization and democratization. Box 4 (democracy and a command economy) and Box 13 (a communist dictatorship and a market economy) are theoretically impossible.[27]

TWO TRANSITIONS

Recent reform and revolution in the communist regimes are fundamentally different from transitions from authoritarian regimes to democracy. The major difference between transitions from communist systems and transitions from authoritarianism is that while communism starts from Box 1, authoritarianism starts from Box 9 or Box 13. In other words, authoritarian transitions do not require an economic transition. Not only in the sense that transitions from the communist system must complete these dual tasks, but also in the sense that an economic transition is far more difficult than a political transition, immeasurably more difficult burdens are imposed on transitions from the communist system than on transitions from authoritarian regimes. In the communist economic transition, the most dramatic and traumatic moment is marketization; the central authority has to let go of the mechanism that has ensured its economic control, like letting go of a kite into the sky, to the uncontrollable forces of the market mechanism. In the political transition, the equivalent of the price reform is a multicandidate election. The regime lets loose its hold over power to the uncontrollable and unpredictable forces of popular will. The major task of both political and economic transition is to "regulate and institutionalize uncertainty of outcomes." Unlike a market economy and a democracy, a command economy and a dictatorship are designed for fixed outcomes. For a market economy and a democracy to function, "institutional dispersion and the removal of politico-institutional monopolies" are necessary. Political transition and economic transition inevitably merge since "legalization of equal access to institutional positions," and "deployment of these positions to countervailing socio-economic positions" are prerequisites for both. In a democracy and in a market economy, "no single social or institutional formation should determine outcomes by monopolizing and fusing institutions or by its sheer social position."[28]

The First Step: Decentralization-Liberalization

For a communist regime to extricate itself from economic crisis, it must initiate decentralization. To move in this direction, two requirements have to be met. The first is the initial step of de-sanctification of ideology. In communist regimes Marxism-Leninism must be turned on its head: To change the basis of society one must change the consciousness. The step of de-sanctification of ideology cannot be confined to the economic sphere. Decentralization must be accompanied by liberalization in the political transition. Liberalization can be achieved either by the regime's relaxation of its ideological straitjacket and/or by a change in leadership, in which more pragmatic, less ideological leaders assume top positions.

The second requirement for decentralization is an expansion in the decision-making process far wider than the traditional political process. Experts have to be brought in to map out the economic reform program, while foreign capital makes important inroads in the economy. Infrastructure, such as the financial system and management experts, must be created. This change in decision making can occur two ways: by inclusion of a broader segment of experts in the decision-making process itself or by a takeover of the traditional decision-making process by technocratic economic experts. Thus, the first logical transition is from

Box 1 to Box 6. This path can be achieved in a roundabout way from Box 1 to Box 2 and then from Box 2 to Box 6, but it seems doubtful to reach Box 6 via Box 5 without liberalization.

Hungary. The first communist country to achieve this step from liberalization to decentralization was Hungary. Before 1968, Hungary followed a Stalinist system of communism. Specifically, it had (1) established a dictatorship by the ruling Marxist-Leninist party, (2) nationalized industry, commerce, and agriculture and banned private business, (3) created a vast state bureaucracy that completely controlled the economy, (4) placed management of all enterprises under a command-administrative system of production and distribution of goods and resources through the central planning agency as well as a command-administrative system of finances through the State Bank.[29]

In the first liberalization-decentralization process, "settling past accounts" plays an important role.[30] It can serve as a catalyst that triggers the liberalization-decentralization process, or it can be an important outcome of de-ideologization that inevitably results from this process.

Khrushchev's de-Stalinization in 1956 touched off a mass revolt in Hungary. When reimposed, the Stalinist regime lacked legitimacy, which it attempted to regain by implementing economic reform. Thus, in Hungary the very purpose of economic reform was political; it was designed to "transform the basis of party rule from coercion to consent," and to achieve "moral legitimacy" through "economic efficiency." Economic reform was therefore "a form of substitute politics."[31]

In Hungary liberalization preceded the economic reform. Janos Kadar's famous statement, "Those who are not against us are with us," captures the essence of de-ideologization that provides "spaces" for free expression on limited subjects. Together with ideological relaxation, expanded inclusion of experts in decision making took place. In 1957 an economic commission was created. More than two hundred economists and managers took part, and they completed three reports for radical economic reform. Although their proposals were not immediately adopted, the economists came to enjoy freedom of expression unencumbered by the ideological straitjacket. The serious discussions they had on economic management did not remain academic. Practical proposals were made in a number of economic commissions organized by Rezso Nyers, then Central Committee secretary and later Politburo member.[32] A window was opened. Thus, in Hungary the transitional path went from Box 1 to Box 2 to Box 6.

The Hungarian economic reform (New Economic Mechanism or NEM) began in 1968. Its purpose was to create a regulated "socialist" market economy under the condition of the Communist Party dictatorship by combining a self-regulating market and a macroeconomic control from the central planning. In other words, its purpose was to move from Box 6 to Box 10. The economists who were responsible for the NEM believed that once the central economic control based on the obligatory planning indicators was abolished, and a more flexible price system, financial regulators, and incentives were efficiently coordinated, a "socialist market economy" that organically unified planning and a market would automatically emerge.[33] One of the most fundamental aims of the NEM was to eliminate the central control over productive goods (as opposed to consumer goods). Under the new system productive goods were to be sold freely through wholesale enterprises at the price agreed on by the buyer and the seller. The second important feature was the price reform. Nevertheless, this price reform should not be confused with the introduction of the equilibrium price system. Its purpose was to create a mixed price mechanism, where goods and services determined by a market (mostly productive goods) coexist with goods and services (mostly consumer goods) regulated by the government. The introduction of these two features explained the shift of governmental control from the planning agency to the price agency and the ministry of finance.[34]

The NEM shifted economic decision-making power about production from the central planning agency to enterprises. But it did not implement any structural reform of enterprises or any change in the investment-capital procurement system. The unitary banking system remained intact. The monopolistic position of large state enterprises became even stronger through subsequent mergers. The NEM did not encourage privatization in commerce and services, nor did it take any measures to develop private entrepreneurship. Thus, the marketization implemented by the NEM was limited to marketization of productive goods. It did not extend to the creation of a labor market or a capital market. Therefore, the market created by this reform was a quasi market at best and not a self-regulated market that functions in all spheres of the economy.[35]

Hungary satisfies the subjective condition I listed earlier as part of the criteria for decentralization. The regime intended to modify significantly the command economy by introducing a regulated market. As for the objective conditions, the NEM aimed at decentralization of economic decisions, eliminating the power of the central planning agency to dictate the details of production and distribution and giving enterprises the crucial decision-making power. In fact, in two respects the Hungarian economic reform went even farther than these objective conditions I set for decentralization. First, the planning agency's monopolistic control over the means of production was eliminated, and productive goods became subject to commercial transactions among enterprises. Second, the NEM implemented the price reform and created a mixed price system. Nevertheless, it did not go far in privatization. It did not alter property relations significantly or actively open the economy to Western capitalism. And it was precisely these negative factors that eventually nullified the positive aspects of the Hungarian reform.

Ironically, decentralization in Hungary not only did not achieve its purpose of gaining political legitimacy, but it also created a more severe economic crisis. The root cause was the absence of political reform. As Judy Batt states,

> The logic of market-type reform was undermined by the organizational system, which was left untouched and in which powerful conservative interests were entrenched. The branch ministries, which were superfluous once traditional directive planning was abolished, were left in place. Organizational reforms not only failed to break up the economically (and often also technologically) unjustified large industrial enterprises, but even promoted further mergers and concentration.[36]

In this situation the central government lost macroeconomic control, succumbing to decentralized economic forces that evaded central discipline. Nevertheless, these enterprises, unexposed to foreign competition under the heavy shield of protectionism, were unable to improve export performance. By the end of the 1970s, Hungary was confronted with "massive, unmanageable hard currency debts, inefficient and outdated production structures, budget deficits, and an inflationary excess of purchasing power in the hands of the population."[37]

Although the economic reform in Hungary was carried out to perpetuate the Communist Party dictatorship, it changed the structure of power. As a result of economic decentralization, "power was diffused to regional party apparatuses, sectoral ministries and large, industrial conglomerates, all of which were heavily represented on the Central Committee."[38] This was not an evolution of the political system, but, as Batt argues, "a highly imperfect form of political decentralization which transmitted social interests in a selective, distorted way, and which thus seriously weakened the ability of the central authorities to construct and implement coherent policies, and in particular, to maintain overall macroeconomic control."[39] Moreover, the conscious cadre policy to attract young able professionals into the party contributed to the decay of the monolithic unity of the ruling party itself. De-ideologization was the precondition for attracting such young professionals, but the failure of the economic reform inevitably disillusioned them. The young recruits "provided a substantial constituency in favor of radical change within the party itself."[40]

Dismantling the command economy does not immediately create a market economy. On the contrary, in Hungary dismantling the command economy without accompanying political reform led to a more serious economic and political crisis. The Hungarian experience thus clearly demonstrated that a socialist market economy was an illusion and that a market economy was impossible without dislodging the monopolistic Communist Party dictatorship.

China. The immediate factor that prompted China to embark upon the transition was the reaction to the catastrophic consequences of the Cultural Revolution. In 1978 the Central Committee Plenum, under Deng Xiaoping's leadership, decided to carry out the four modernizations. This decision signaled a sharp break with Mao Zedong's revolutionary legacy. It was China's first step in both the economic and the political transition.

Since the transition in China began as a reaction to the legacies of the Cultural Revolution, the liberalization process began with "settling the past accounts." In 1980 Liu Shaoqi and many other officials and intellectuals who were persecuted during the Cultural Revolution were rehabilitated, and those who were still alive regained their previous positions. In the following year the Central Committee passed a watered-down resolution criticizing Mao's mistakes, but insisting that he was 70 percent good and 30 percent bad. The resolution characterized the Cultural Revolution as a total error. Hua Guofeng was forced to resign as the head of the party and the state. He was replaced by the reform leaders of a younger generation, Hu Yaobang and Zhao Ziyang under the tutelage of Deng Xiaoping and other old leaders.[41]

In 1978 China launched radical economic reforms to revitalize the economy by decentralization and marketization. The economic reforms began with agriculture: the unit of production was transferred to the households, which meant that agriculture was virtually privatized. By 1984 household production encompassed 96.6 percent of all peasants in China, and agricultural production improved rapidly.[42] Together with agriculture, the rural firms classified as township and village enterprises (TVEs) developed. Their growth rate far outstripped the state-owned industry. At the end of 1988, the number of TVEs was more than 18.8 million.[43] Reforms in industry lagged behind those in agriculture.

Nevertheless, by 1987 a number of significant changes had taken place in industry as well. First, de-etatization of property had begun.

By 1987 property occupied by the state had been reduced from 80.8 percent to 69.7 percent, while collective and private property had increased from 19.2 percent to 27.1 percent and from zero to 2.4 percent respectively. Second, enterprises were given the expanded right of self-determination in economic decisions, including sales and prices of products (within 20 percent of the fixed price). Third, at least in principle, the market was recognized as the primary economic mechanism, and central planning was given a subordinate role. The Thirteenth Party Congress in 1987 adopted a resolution stating that "the state controls the market, and the market guides enterprises."[44] Fourth, the Chinese economy was opened to international capitalism through joint ventures, free economic zones, and foreign investments. Of the conditions for decentralization, China satisfied one subjective condition (the leadership was definitely committed to introduce the market mechanism) and four objective conditions. By 1987 China had accomplished decentralization, and the Chinese economy had entered the stage of a mixed command economy.

China's reform strategy sharply contrasted with Hungary's economic reform. The Hungarian reform attacked the core of the central command mechanism from the very beginning, but it failed to create a private sector. In China the central core of the command economy was maintained almost intact, but along with it a newly emerging private sector was created. The private sector developed at the encouragement of the leadership, so powerfully that the dynamic market forces began to affect the state sector.

The result of China's economic reform was impressive. An annual growth was as high as 9 percent. Nicholas Lardy states that "by the end of the 1980s resource allocation in the Chinese economy was probably more market driven than either in the Soviet Union or the states of Eastern Europe."[45] According to Lardy, the market forces that were allowed to develop led to the virtual accomplishment of convertibility of the yuan. In domestic financial markets, Chinese banks began offering longer-term savings deposits, and the government began issuing government and treasury bonds. By the end of the 1980s the share of output produced by the private sector reached almost 65 percent of China's national income.[46] As far as the economic transition is concerned, the Chinese economic reform has reached farther than any other reforms in communist regimes in decentralization. Nevertheless, the essential features of the command economy remain intact. De-nationalization of most state enterprises has not taken place. Price reform remains on the agenda for the future. For these reasons China still cannot cross the divide separating the mixed command economy and the mixed market economy.

Although it is often argued that China chose economic transition without political transition, in political reforms China was initially one step ahead of the Soviet Union. In fact, without liberalization it would have been impossible to start the economic transition.[47] The impetus for the transition was rejection of the Cultural Revolution. It is natural that scholars and intellectuals began to oppose the Maoist political system. In 1978 political scientist Wu Jialin pointed out the importance of the democratic procedures that had been criticized as "small democracy" and "bourgeois democracy." Others advocated the introduction of checks and balances to prevent abuse by the government. The most comprehensive political reform plan was presented by Liao Gailong, who insisted that democracy was not merely a means, as Mao Zedong had argued, but an end in itself. He advocated the separation of the state from the party, and he proposed that the Congress of People's Representatives be divided into bicameral organizations. He wanted it to become an organ where diverse interests in society were mediated.

In effect, scholars and other intellectuals argued that China should adopt a democradura by initiating pluralization. The fact that their opinions were allowed to be aired indicated that liberalization had begun in China. Moreover, liberalization was not limited to intellectual discussions. In the summer of 1980, Deng Xiaoping himself raised the possibility of political reform designed to eliminate the old political system characterized by "cult of personality," "fusion of party and state," and "the party's domination in all political processes." Deng's criticism was important because this was the first time that the communist leader in power pointed out the systemic defect of the Chinese political system.[48] Nevertheless, Deng's objective was to improve the guiding principles of the party, not to introduce democracy. Although he recognized the need for political reform, Deng Xiaoping believed that the communist dictatorship should be maintained without any concessions. The constitution adopted in 1982 reaffirmed China's commitment to the four fundamental principles: socialism, the guiding role of the party, the people's democratic dictatorship (at other times referred to as the dictatorship of the proletariat), and Marxism-Leninism and Mao Zedong's thoughts.[49]

Debate on political reform reemerged in 1986. This time the debate was prompted by the argument that economic reform by itself could not move further without political reform. In April 1986 the Academy of Social Sciences held discussions on political reform. The director of the

Political Science Institute, Yan Jiaqi, argued (1) that the central task of political reform is to prevent excessive concentration of power; (2) that the party's monopoly power should be replaced by separation of power among the legislature, executive, and judiciary; (3) that both in the party and the state decentralization should take place so that power should be transferred to lower organs; (4) that social organizations should be separated from the government; and (5) that popular participation in politics should be granted.[50] Some intellectuals also advocated freedom of speech.

Despite all of these arguments by reform-oriented intellectuals, few political reforms were acceptable to the older leaders. The liberalization process in China never progressed to pluralization. After successfully moving from Box 1 to Box 6, China was unable to go further.

The Soviet Union. To appreciate the significance of Mikhail Gorbachev's perestroika, one must examine the failed reforms that preceded it. The essence of perestroika is the attempt to revitalize the Soviet Union by revamping the Stalinist system. Nikita Khrushchev's de-Stalinization did not challenge the principle of the Communist Party dictatorship, although it contributed to the removal of terror as an ordinary political instrument. All economic reforms under Khrushchev and Leonid Brezhnev were designed to make the command economy more efficient—not to overhaul it. Real systemic reform had to await Gorbachev's perestroika.[51]

Perestroika is a clear case where the political transition moved ahead of the economic transition. The initial move in the transition was radically different in the Soviet Union than in China. The first economic measures taken by Gorbachev—the intensification (*uskorenie*) program, the anti-alcoholism campaign, recentralization, the introduction of *gospriemka* (state certification for quality control)—were all within-the-system reforms that actually made it more difficult to move the economic system in the direction of decentralization.[52] These economic measures were diametrically opposed to those bold steps by China toward decentralization, especially, the privatization of agriculture and the large-scale opening of the economy to foreign companies. And unlike the Hungarian reform, Soviet reform did not attack the central core of the command economy.

The intensification stage of economic reform in the Soviet Union failed to yield the economic dividends that the Chinese derived from their decentralization. There are at least three reasons for this dissimilarity between the Soviet Union and China at the initial stage of transition. First, their negative legacies differed. In China the transition began as an effort to overcome the legacy of the Cultural Revolution.

"Settling past accounts" in the Soviet Union, however, was initially limited to "the period of stagnation," thus making it almost impossible to attack the basic framework of the Stalinist command economy. Second, the leadership politics in the two countries differed. Gorbachev was elected general secretary by the narrowest possible margin in the Politburo. To establish his power base he had to eliminate the Brezhnevite holdovers, and to do this he had to make an alliance with the non-Brezhnevite hard-liners.

These two reasons also explain why the initial stage of economic reform in the Soviet Union was not as bold as in Hungary. The third difference between the Soviet Union and China was the economic structures within the command economy. These dissimilarities led to different strategies for transition at the initial stage. In the Soviet economy centralization was more thorough than in the Chinese economy. Even under the command economy, local authorities in China enjoyed considerably more decentralized power. In addition, in the Soviet Union the peasantry as a class was completely destroyed during the collectivization. In China the peasants, who retained the memory and know-how of private farming, still remained. These features of the Soviet economy made it impossible for Gorbachev to launch an economic reform similar to the Chinese reform. It is doubtful, therefore, that even if Gorbachev had initiated his economic reform with privatization of agriculture, he would have achieved the same gains as the Chinese did.[53] In any case, when Gorbachev decided to move perestroika to the next stage, he had to do it without the economic benefits of decentralization.

Perestroika began in earnest only in 1987, when Gorbachev began to talk about perestroika as revolution from above. In order to mobilize social forces for perestroika Gorbachev pursued the glasnost campaign seriously. Liberalization had begun. Under glasnost the Soviet Union moved from Box 1 to Box 2. In 1987 Gorbachev also attempted to move to Box 6 by adopting a series of economic reform measures. The laws of private business and of cooperatives were intended to create a private sector. The state enterprise law granted, in theory, the principles of self-financing, self-management, and self-accounting to state enterprises. The monopoly of foreign trade by the Ministry of Foreign Trade was abolished, and enterprises were given the right to trade with foreign partners. The law of joint ventures allowed Soviet enterprises to form joint ventures with foreign firms.[54] But these measures were met with conservative obstructions from the nomenklatura entrenched in the state and the party bureaucracies. Gorbachev was thus unable to move the economic system in a significant way to a mixed command economy. For instance, the state enterprise law that envisaged enterprises with autonomous decision-making power was nullified by the system of state orders that comprises more than 90 percent of enterprises' production. Nevertheless, it would be wrong to assume that these measures did not change the economic structure at all. In fact, the existence of cooperatives, liberalized foreign trade, joint ventures, and self-administered state enterprises helped the command economy beyond the threshold of a mixed command economy, although its advance lagged far behind advances in Hungary and China.

In sum, the Soviet Union moved rapidly from Box 1 to Box 2. As soon as it began to move to Box 6, however, the momentum of decentralization was stalled by the conservative opposition.

Vietnam. Three factors had a decisive impact on the communist system in Vietnam. First, Vietnamese communism was born out of wars that lasted for more than forty years. Second, the country was divided into the communist North and the capitalist South until 1975, when the Vietnamese Communist Party (CPV) hastened the socialist transformation in the South. Third, this hasty socialist transformation occurred at the same time that other communist countries began the process of reform.

The Fourth Congress of the CPV in December 1976 decided to carry out the immediate and speedy socialist transformation in the South, which meant the collectivization of agriculture. Despite resistance from peasants, the communists banned all private commercial activities in 1978. The campaign to eliminate capitalism in the South, known as the "X2 campaign," led to the brutal suppression of 40,000 "capitalist merchants" and to the mass exodus of the Chinese merchants who occupied one of the most vital sectors of economic activities in the South. Rice production declined sharply. The command economy was extended to the industry and handicrafts in the South. Almost 1,500 large and medium-sized private businesses were converted into state-run enterprises, and 150,000 workers (70 percent of the labor force in the South) became state employees. Thus, in addition to inefficient state enterprises in the North, the state began to support newly nationalized enterprises in the South, which quickly became unprofitable. Furthermore, the monetary reform in 1978 that introduced the new currency for the entire country wiped out the savings of private business people and merchants. What supported the socialized industry in Vietnam was massive state subsidies, which in turn were subsidized by foreign aid, mostly from the Soviet Union. Despite this dire economic crisis, Vietnam invaded Cambodia in 1978 and it had to carry on the war with China in 1979.[55] The standard of living fell dramatically. In May 1980 a Vietnamese cabinet minister told a foreign journalist that he was amazed at the Vietnamese people's "ability to suffer." He added, "In another country, the government would have been changed."[56] It was clear that if Soviet aid was withdrawn or even reduced, the bottom would fall out.

Eventually, the economic crisis pushed the reluctant CPV to take reform measures. The Central Committee Plenum in September 1979 adopted a partial (end-product) contract system in agriculture.[57] Peasants were allowed to dispose of surplus products at the free market after they delivered the amount contracted with production brigades. In addition, the government raised the procurement price by 500 percent. These measures contributed not only to revitalization of agricultural production, but also to marketization and privatization of agriculture. In industry the government attempted to decentralize economic decision making in 1981 by granting to enterprises more rights and by reforming the wage system. The production plan for state enterprises was divided into three parts: (1) obligatory production on the state order; (2) voluntary production with the use of resources from the state; and (3) independent, secondary production. Goods produced in the first two categories had to be delivered to the state, but enterprises were given the right to dispose of goods in the third category. Also enterprises were given a limited but expanded right to set the price for goods in the second and the third categories. Awareness that the egalitarian wage system had deprived the workers of incentives to work harder led to a new wage system. A contract system and piecework payment system were tried. These reform measures caused hyperinflation.[58] It became increasingly clear that the Soviet Union would not continue its generous subsidies to Vietnam.

The Sixth Party Congress in 1986 was a turning point in Vietnamese communism, signaling the first move in the transition from the communist system. General Secretary Truong Chinh, a staunch pro-Maoist hard-liner, admitted with amazing frankness the failure of the socialist transformation and resigned. The new leadership was taken over by Nguyen Van Linh from the South, who immediately proposed a policy of renovation (*doi moi*). Nguyen Van Linh openly criticized the X2 campaign, admitting that "our conception of socialism was simplistic and unrealistic" and that this led to mistakes of "subjectivism and voluntarism."[59] The new reform-minded leaders made three important agricultural decisions: the Law of Land (December 1987), Politburo Resolution No. 10 (a renovation of economic management in agriculture) and Politburo Directive No. 47 (which solved a number of urgent land-related problems). These three rulings virtually restored private agriculture.[60] For industry and handicrafts the new leadership decided to "exploit the potential of all economic sectors," and for this purpose, as Vo Van Kiet emphasized, "all narrow-minded prejudices and discriminatory regulations [against private sectors] must be abolished."[61]

The Central Committee plenum in 1987 shifted the operations of public enterprises from state subsidization to "economic accounting" and changed the mechanism of state economic management.[62] The new regulation was similar to the Soviet state enterprise law: state enterprises, which receive mandatory state orders, are free to use additional funds for developing their production and business after they meet state orders as well as to decide upon their labor and wage policy independently. Furthermore, the National Assembly in 1987 passed a new law on foreign investment, "the most liberal in all Southeast Asia."[63]

The *doi moi* policy introduced a market economy in Vietnam and opened the economy to foreign capital under the tutelage of the Communist Party. At least at its initial stage, the Vietnamese transitional path resembles the Chinese pattern. Rather than making a frontal attack on the command economic structure as in Hungary, the CPV adopted a strategy to expand the private sector first while maintaining the command economic structure. But the immediate task of Linh was stabilization of the economy by controlling runaway inflation. For this he was forced to adopt an austerity policy by charging the high interest rate of 12 percent a month.[64] This policy was partially effective in reducing inflation, but the shortage of capital forced enterprises to reduce production and lay off workers, thus increasing unemployment.[65]

Positive results of the *doi moi* policy did not appear until 1989, when the rice harvest exceeded domestic consumption for the first time, and Vietnam became the world's third largest rice exporter behind Thailand and the United States. Private business is flourishing as overseas Chinese seek joint ventures in Ho Chi Minh City. Coupled with contraband goods smuggled from China, Thailand, Cambodia, and Singapore, consumer goods flood the market as they did during the initial stage of economic reform in China. There is also a construction boom. After the withdrawal of troops from Cambodia in 1989, ordinary citizens began to believe that peace had finally arrived and rushed to build their homes by using their savings hidden under the bed.[66]

Nevertheless, the economic transition is not smooth sailing. The high interest rate, unaccompanied by an increase in productivity, is causing stagflation. Vietnam now must pay for oil and other commodities with foreign currency. It is turning to the outside world, particularly Japan, for foreign investment.[67]

The *doi moi* policy was not merely limited to economic reform, but extended to political reform. Its political aim was to extricate the Com-

munist Party from the affairs of state. For the economic success of the
doi moi policy it was considered imperative to ensure that the state can
conduct its business without constant interference from the party. In
addition, the National Assembly and the people's councils at every level
were encouraged to become more independent legislative bodies. Furthermore, the party itself was encouraged to adopt more democratic
inner-life in the decision-making process as well as in selection of cadres.
Nevertheless, these moves of liberalization were not to proceed too
rapidly, but to be carried out step by step.[68]

Where did the impetus for reform come from in Vietnam? Was it
accompanied by liberalization? It appears that the impetus came from
pragmatic party officials who pushed out of office the older generation
of leaders, who had held the leadership position in fighting the wars.
Van Nhan Tri, a Vietnamese emigré economist, reports that since the
Sixth Plenum in September 1979 heated discussions had been conducted at the top level of leadership, and by the Tenth Plenum in Oc-
tober-November 1981, the pragmatists had won.[69] Carlyle Thayers's
study also shows that by 1986 there was a sharp decline in the old
generation and the military in the central committee, and conversely a
marked increase of regional party officials.[70] Within two years after the
Sixth Party Congress, Linh replaced nearly all of the forty provincial
secretaries and 80 percent of some 400 district party heads.[71] Linh
brought with him his entourage of party officials from the South. This
leadership change was actually the equivalent of liberalization since it
was accompanied by de-ideologization and the takeover of the decision-
making process by more pragmatic party officials. Thus, Vietnam's *doi
moi* policy represents the transition from Box 1 to Box 6, although it
must be admitted that Vietnam has only barely crossed the boundary
to Box 6.

The Crucial Test: Extrication from Box 6

A mixed command economy is a destabilizing system in which decentralized elements tend to be absorbed into a command economy unless
it is pushed to the next stage: a mixed market economy. But marketization without political reform is an impossible task. Box 6, the most
crucial stage in the transitional process, is full of conflicts and contradictions. The transition from decentralization to marketization is impossible without strong tutelage from the central leadership committed
to this transition. Yet such a transition is likely to meet desperate resistance from forces that oppose marketization for ideological reasons or
because of their private interests and privileges. To ensure the success

of marketization, "iron hands" may be needed to silence the opposition. The transition from Box 6 also is impossible without an independent business class and the legal guarantee for its existence—a factor that basically contradicts the notion of "iron hands."

Thus, it is almost impossible to go straight from Box 6 to Box 11; the path to Box 11 is either through Box 7 or through Box 10. Either path is fraught with danger. If a transition is through Box 7, the political base of the leadership is necessarily weakened, and the central guidance needed for marketization may be hopelessly fragmented. On the other hand, the transition through Box 10 tends to frustrate demands for pluralization and democratization, the process necessary for the rule of law and an institutional guarantee of democracy. If the leadership knows what it intends to do and can convince the population that the continuation of a dictablanda is merely a temporary measure to accomplish marketization, the transitional path through Box 10 might be preferable. Nevertheless, the fact remains that marketization is a painful process that inevitably imposes tremendous hardships on a wide segment of the population, creates great social inequities, and thus intensifies social tensions. Thus, one might argue that to ensure a successful transition, the leadership that guides it must have a popular mandate that comes only from some form of consensus reached at least in a democradura, if not in complete democracy. Ultimately the legitimacy of a communist regime determines which course is better. These two approaches underscore the dilemma of the transition from the communist system.

Once a democradura and the initial step for marketization are accomplished, a move toward a pluralistic democracy seems inevitable (from Box 11 to Box 12). Some would argue that Box 12 (social democracy) and not Box 16 (liberal democracy) is the ultimate goal of the transition from the communist system. I would argue that the difference between Box 12 and Box 16 is a matter of degree and thus becomes irrelevant to the discussion that concerns us here.

Hungary. By the end of the 1970s it became clear that the Hungarian economic reform had failed. This failure contributed to the erosion of the rule of the Communist Party (officially called the Hungarian Socialist Workers' Party). The root cause for the failure of the New Economic Mechanism (NEM) can be sought in its inability to change property relations. Thus, the state sector not only continued but also expanded its dominant position. Moreover, unlike in China, the privatized sector was not promoted at all in Hungary until the early 1980s. Although the government encouraged market transactions among enterprises, it tightly controlled credit—in effect, whipping the horse while tightly holding its reins.[72] Enterprises were given decentralized decision-making power. They were controlled by the central government only indirectly, through economic regulations on prices, profits, tax rates, wages, and credits. Nevertheless, enterprises behaved, not according to the market mechanism, because a genuine market did not exist, but in such a way as to take advantage of these regulations for their own interests.

To be sure, the standard of living was improved throughout the 1970s, but at the expense of labor productivity. The oil shock in 1973–74 worsened the trade deficits in Hungary. To overcome these deficits, the government borrowed heavily from foreign banks. A great investment boom followed, but the investment was used to lower the cost of energy and raw materials. In the meantime, the severe international environment did not encourage necessary improvements in industrial structure.[73] As a result, Hungarian economic performance hopelessly lost its competitive edge in the world market within five years. A great shock during the 1970s, not merely to the Hungarians but also to all communist regimes, was that the Asian Newly Industrialized Economies (NIEs)—Hong Kong, South Korea, Taiwan, and Singapore—surpassed Hungary, the most advanced economy in the communist world, not merely in competitiveness in the world market but also in GNP.

In 1978 the economic policies of the 1970s were acknowledged as a mistake, and in 1979 the "stabilization program" and the renewed economic reform were launched. The latter tried to bring domestic prices closer to world prices, broke up enterprises, and widened the scope for private enterprises and cooperatives. These measures, which precipitously lowered the standard of living, could no longer serve as a substitute for political reform. The failure of economic reform thus inevitably led to the demand for a political reform. Political transition in Hungary began with the double processes of pluralistic tendencies, first within the Communist Party itself and then outside the party.

By 1985 basically four factions emerged within the Communist Party: the conservatives who centered around the Ferenc Munich Association (led by Janos Berec), the moderate conservatives headed by Karoly Grosz, the moderate reformers represented by Rezso Nyers, and the radical reformers led by Imre Pozsgay. The conservatives argued that socialism should be revitalized within the framework of collectivized agriculture, nationalized industry, and one-party dictatorship. The moderate conservatives accepted the need for political reform that entailed pluralism, but favored the framework of one-party dictatorship.

The moderate reformers wanted pluralism to be extended outside of the Communist Party, but they did not accept a split of the Communist Party. Finally, the radical reformers advocated a split of the Communist Party, thus expelling the conservatives and the moderate conservatives. If they could not form a majority within the party, they were prepared to walk out of the party and form a new party. Pozsgay actively sought to form a coalition of the opposition outside of the party. In competition with Pozsgay, Nyers formed the New March Front within the party, attempting to undercut Pozsgay's influence.[74] Both Nyers and Pozsgay insisted on a re-examination of the Hungarian revolt in 1956. Janos Kadar, who had mediated between the reformers and conservatives throughout the 1970s, now sided with the conservatives. At the party conference in May 1988, Kadar was forced to resign for "biological reasons." He was replaced by Grosz, who had connections with the reformers as well as the conservatives. Nyers and Pozsgay were elected Politburo members. Grosz quickly lost credibility. He mishandled the problem of Hungarian refugees from Romania, and he remained unresponsive to the demand for pluralism outside the party.[75]

This hopeless division within the Communist Party corresponded with the resurgence of the opposition in Hungary. The only opposition movement that existed outside the party in the 1970s was a human rights movement. But in the early 1980s suddenly various study groups, discussion groups and lecture series sprang up. What are known as "informals" in the Soviet Union had already emerged in the early 1980s in Hungary. One such group was the Donau Circle, which criticized the project to construct a dam in the Donau. In 1985 the first multicandidate election for the parliament was held in Hungary, although candidates were restricted to the Communist Party members. Nevertheless, this "founding election" galvanized opposition movements that had been underground. A conspicuous, full-fledged opposition came into the open to challenge the legitimacy of the ruling party.[76]

The first opposition group, the Free Democrats, issued a manifesto in September 1987 that included the following platforms: transition to a market economy except for energy and public services, equalization of various forms of property, integration of the Hungarian economy with the world market, freedom of association, freedom of the press, abolition of cultural control, strengthening of legislative power of the parliament, guarantee of local self-government, and establishment of civil rights.[77] Also in September 1987 the Democratic Forum was formed. In competition with radical reformers, regarded as Westernizers, the Democratic Forum had a distinctly nationalistic, even anti-

Semitic flavor. In a way the polarization of the Hungarian opposition movement anticipated the similar split in the Soviet opposition movement.

The first major step for extrication from Box 6 began in Hungary with "settling past accounts." By the mid-1980s the reformers within the party became convinced that the party was no longer an instrument of reform, and they began to advocate the end of the party's monopoly of power. To carry out political reform, they chose to attack the past by establishing a historical commission in 1988 to investigate the events of 1956. The commission concluded that the event was not a counterrevolution, but a genuine popular uprising. When the Communist Party Central Committee accepted this verdict in February 1989, "it signaled . . . the abandonment of the party's claim of a right to a monopoly of power."[78] Transition to a multiparty system was approved, and negotiations with the opposition movements began. Hungary was now ready to move from Box 6 to Box 7.

Nevertheless, it was Poland that moved first. Since the Polish transition serves as one of the basic prototypes of communist transitions, it is necessary to describe its pattern briefly here. The Round Table negotiations between Wojciech Jaruzelski and Solidarity began in February 1989, and both sides signed a compromise "pact" in April. Both sides expected victory by Poland's Communist Party, the Polish United Workers' Party (PUWP), but Solidarity candidates swept 160 of the 161 open seats in Sejm and 92 of the 100 Senate seats.[79] The "founding election" in Poland was turned into a plebiscite on communist rule, and the Communist Party suffered a resounding defeat. Another compromise was struck. The government was formed with a majority of Solidarity ministers and four key ministers preserved by the Communist Party with Tadeusz Mazowiecki as prime minister, while Jaruzelski was elected president by the narrowest margin. A democradura was created, but the most important characteristic of this democradura was that the opposition rather than the former ruling party controlled and dominated it. The Mazowiecki government immediately launched a drastic economic stabilization program led by Finance Minister Leszek Balcerowicz, and it prepared for transition to a market economy. Poland moved from Box 6 to Box 7 and then quickly to Box 11. Balcerowicz's "shock therapy" was a hard pill for many Polish citizens, particularly the Polish workers, to swallow, and it led to the crucial split of Solidarity. In the meantime the Polish democradura led by Solidarity fostered further democratization. The presidential election in November and December 1990 won by Lech Walesa was a genuine pluralistic election. It ushered

Poland into a polyarchy. From Box 11 Poland moved quickly to Box 12, although the economic transition within Box 12 was still at the initial stage.

The negotiations in Hungary began in June 1989 immediately after the Polish Communists' election defeat. The formation of the Mazowiecki government in Poland and the Soviet nonintervention had important repercussions on Hungarian domestic development. On the one hand, the Soviet government's willingness to let Eastern Europe develop its own course made it impossible for the Hungarian Communist Party to adhere to one-party rule. The best it could hope for was power sharing with the opposition. In fact, "the main division within the party leadership was now between those who expected change to stop at power-sharing, and those who saw the future in terms of open, competitive, multi-party politics."[80] As Judy Batt states: "the unique and extraordinary feature of the Hungarian negotiated transition from communist rule was the extent to which the process was promoted and facilitated by the deliberate action within the [Communist Party] itself, namely, its radical-reformist wing led by Imre Pozsgay."[81]

The Soviet nonintervention also emboldened the opposition. But perhaps because of the Soviet nonintervention, the opposition had the luxury of an internal split between the Democratic Forum and the Free Democrats over the election of a new president. In September the Round Table negotiations finally reached an agreement with a provision to hold a presidential election before parliamentary elections. The radicals in the Free Democrats, suspecting that this was a manipulation engineered by Pozsgay to maintain the Communist Party's ruling position, refused to sign it. The pact that would have led to the formation of a democradura was ruined by the radical reformers, who played a breakdown game by appealing directly to the populace to call for a parliamentary election first before calling a presidential election. The radicals won by a narrow margin in the referendum in November.[82] Thus, the parliamentary election was to be held first, and the position of the presidency was to be determined by the newly elected parliament. Hungary moved straight from Box 6 to Box 8, skipping Box 7.

Democratization was accompanied by disintegration of the Communist Party. The party held a special congress in October. The moderate reformists within the party wanted to transform the party into a Western type of social democratic party by changing its name from Hungarian Socialist Workers' Party to Hungarian Socialist Party. But the conservatives refused to join the new party, and they formed a new party by the old name. Not only was the party split, but also the newly constituted Hungarian Socialist Party managed to recruit only 50,000 members (out of the total of 720,000 former members of the Communist Party) by the end of the year.[83] The final blow was dealt in the October session of the National Assembly, which passed laws outlawing party organizations in workplaces and requiring the communist successor parties to account for property owned by the former Communist Party.

In contrast to Poland, where democratization was accompanied by marketization, in Hungary democratization proceeded without any marked improvement in economic reform. On the contrary, the economic situation worsened. Despite the mounting pressures from the IMF to take unpopular measures, the lame duck communist government of Miklos Nemeth was paralyzed because of its total lack of legitimacy, unable to take any decisive measures.[84]

The parliamentary election in March 1990 produced an ambiguous result: the Democratic Forum gained 42 percent of the votes cast (165 of 386 seats), while the Free Democrats captured only 24 percent (91 seats). The Democratic Forum formed a coalition government, led by Jozsef Antall. It invited the Small Farmers Party (11 percent, with 44 seats) and the Christian Democratic People's Party (5 percent, with 21 seats). The victory of the Democratic Forum meant that the Hungarian populace rejected, for the time being, westernization as advocated by the Free Democrats. It appears that the new democratic government in Hungary does not intend any quick marketization measures like those taken by Poland. It also has not taken any comprehensive economic measures to stabilize the economy plagued by inflation. Moreover, it has offered no long-term vision as to how to reconstruct the economy.[85]

Hungary demonstrated again the fundamental difficulty in communist transition. It achieved democracy; nevertheless, it still cannot find a proper way to make a transition to a market economy. Enormous foreign debts continue to be an onerous yoke for the economy. Deetatization of state property and genuine price reform that does not trigger hyperinflation are difficult tasks even for a democratic regime to implement. In Poland, the most advanced country in the marketization process, or in the former German Democratic Republic, which was merged into the capitalist Federal Republic of Germany, marketization is not smooth sailing. The Hungarian transition has clearly demonstrated that democratization in itself does not automatically lead to marketization.

China. Box 6 presented a crucial test for China as well. Nevertheless, the nature of stalemate in Box 6 was quite different in China than it was in Poland and Hungary. In China the very success of economic reform bred new problems. It was largely party officials who seized the new opportunities. This was in a way an important factor for the initial success of the Chinese transition since the conservatives entrenched in the state and party bureaucracy, who might have turned into a conservative opposition to economic reform, were bought off and integrated into the decentralization process. Nevertheless, the negative aspects of this policy emerged when the initial stage of transition was successfully carried out. Corruption (*guandao*) was elevated to a higher stage; the nomenklatura deeply infiltrated the new production and distribution networks and gained huge profits. In the meantime open economic policies invited a huge influx of Western influence, especially Western values and ideas. Students demonstrated in late 1986 and early 1987 with demands for democratization. Deng Xiaoping's reaction was swift. He could not tolerate any criticism of the leading role of the Communist Party. The reform leadership was split into moderates led by Deng and radicals led by Hu Yaobang. Hu, who advocated democratization, was dismissed as general secretary of the party.[86] Hu's defeat represented a setback, when a Chinese dictablanda could have been transformed into a democradura while the Communist Party could have maintained its leading role as the party of reform. This solution would have gained the support of a majority of the intellectuals. With Hu's defeat, the Chinese transition failed to move from Box 6 to Box 7.

Hu Yaobang's fall was a setback only and not an irreparable backlash. Zhao Ziyang, who succeeded Hu, was fundamentally a soft-liner reformer, though more moderate than Hu. In October 1987 Zhao presented his report on "the first stage of socialism." One of the most important long-term goals of the reform was to "establish a socialist regime that is highly democratic, fully equipped with legal systems, efficient, and full of vitality." In the short term the objective was to establish an efficient guiding system to carry out economic reform. More specifically, Zhao proposed to separate the party from the state, change the role of the party from an implementer of policies to an arbiter of conflicts, create a modern system of civil servants, and institutionalize consultations and dialogues among various social groups.[87] Zhao's political program aimed to postpone far-reaching pluralization-democratization until later. He believed that all that was required in political reform for the time being was to streamline the current political system without changing its foundations so that the system should implement economic reform more efficiently. In other words, he wanted to move the reform process from Box 6 to Box 10 through limited political reforms within a dictablanda, but without creating a democradura.

Moderates led by Deng strenuously resisted this modest program. They believed that marketization should be guided by a dictablanda without any political concessions. The hard-liners were opposed not only to liberalization but also to decentralization. Zhao's program was also seen as insufficient by the radical opposition.

In the meantime the economic transition ran into trouble. Growth in agriculture leveled off. The coexistence of a fixed price and a market price led to rampant corruption. Inflation soared. Inequities in income widened. As Harry Harding states,

> China's incremental strategy of reform gave local enterprises and officials greater autonomy from central planning, but did not subject them to stringent discipline from either market forces, legal constraints, or financial institutions. This enabled individuals to engage in corruption without fear of prosecution, factories to increase wages and raise prices without fear of competition or bankruptcy, and local governments to fund unprofitable investments without concern for the financial consequences. Partial reform had created an unstable economy whose achievements were rapidly being overshadowed by its liabilities.[88]

In China, as in Hungary, these problems were mainly the results of contradictions between the positive achievements of the economic reform and the persistent structural impediments that hindered further reform. Nevertheless, economic problems strengthened the hard-liners' resistance to change.

Economic problems and political frustrations merged again in 1989. This time the situation became more explosive than it was during the student demonstrations in 1986–87. The faster liberalization-democratization process in the Soviet Union fueled the frustrations of those who were dissatisfied with the unresponsiveness of the Chinese leadership to their demands for democracy. Within the leadership the moderates led by Deng Xiaoping, who favored economic transition but opposed any concessions to pluralization, allied themselves with the hard-liners led by Li Peng and Yang Shangkun. The soft-liners were defeated. They were led by Zhao Ziyang, who attempted to push the transition toward a democradura, partly in the hope of being able to widen support for a mixed market economy. The end result was the Tiananmen Square incident on June 3 and 4, 1989, when the regime brutally suppressed the popular upsurge. Although there were some indications that the military's support for the backlash was not solid, in the end the military backed the regime.

The Tiananmen incident signified a backlash in the political transition. The liberalization process was reversed: ideological conformity was reintroduced, censorship was restored, and the party reasserted its intrusive influence in all social organizations. Nevertheless, the impact of the Tiananmen incident on the Chinese reform process should not be exaggerated. Despite the backlash, the hard-liners failed to turn the political system back to the Maoist dictatorship. The moderates committed to economic reform, not hard-liners, continued to dominate the political process. A wholesale purge of the radical reformers did not take place. Nor was it possible to dislodge their influence completely without affecting the economic reform process. More importantly, the political backlash has not been accompanied by a reversal of the economic transition, although the government adopted a retrenchment policy designed to curb inflation by reducing investment, decreasing industrial production, and restricting price increases.[89] The Seventh Plenum of the Central Committee held at the end of December 1990 reaffirmed the continuation of a "reform and open" policy, but its decisions indicated a compromise between hard-liners and soft-liners. Thus, it is possible to conclude that, whatever change took place after the Tiananmen incident, China was still within Box 6.

The Tiananmen incident indicated several important lessons in the transition of the communist system. First, it proved that a backlash has tremendous costs. Although the incident did not reverse the economic transition, it made it impossible to move to the next stage—marketization. The backlash inevitably strengthened the hard-liners who opposed this economic process. The backlash is incompatible with an ideological relaxation and an expansion of the participants in the decision-making process—two prerequisites for such a transition. Second, the opposition's intransigence made the compromise position of the soft-liners untenable. This underscores the importance of the opposition's tactics to induce the soft-liners to initiate pluralization. In the game of democratic transition, it is important to avoid checkmating the king, as O'Donnell and Schmitter insist.[90]

The Soviet Union. Box 6 was also a critical test for perestroika. But the Box 6 problem in the Soviet Union was neither a political stalemate as in Poland and Hungary, nor a stalemate caused by the imbalance between economic reform and political reform as in China. The problem for Gorbachev was that as soon as perestroika crossed the boundary into a mixed command economy, its economic transition was halted by conservative resistance and so decentralization could not be completed. To regain the momentum of economic transition, Gorbachev had to dislodge the bureaucratic opposition. Glasnost was intensified. It was during this period that the target of attack shifted from Brezhnev's time of stagnation to Stalinism itself. Various social groups were encouraged to participate in the political process. Nevertheless, these tactics backfired, producing unintended consequences. Political forces unleashed by liberalization were no longer confined within the boundaries set from above, and liberalization snowballed into pluralization, and then eventually into democratization.[91]

Here we can recognize a crucial difference between the Soviet transition and the Chinese and Hungarian transitions. China and Hungary moved from Box 1 to Box 6, but Gorbachev decided to move straight from liberalization to pluralization without completing decentralization. In other words, the Soviet Union moved from Box 2 to the very left edge of Box 6, then straight up to Box 7. Gorbachev made this choice out of conviction and for strategic reasons. He did not start the pluralization process reluctantly under pressure from below. Rather, he perceived it as the goal of perestroika. To Gorbachev, pluralization—socialist pluralism—was intended to rid the Soviet Union of the Stalinist legacy, and to recapture truly democratic principles embodied in the concept of the Soviet system. By transferring the locus of power from the party to the soviets, he hoped to create a law-governed state. He also decided to proceed with pluralization before decentralization was completed for strategic reasons. The failure of his economic reform measures in 1987 that were intended to achieve decentralization convinced him of the necessity of dislodging the source of conservative opposition before he could undertake decentralization again.[92]

What Gorbachev wanted to achieve by pluralization was not exactly democratization (in other words, not a pluralistic democracy), but a democradura at best since he hoped at this point to continue the ruling role of the Communist Party. He opened the floodgate, however, by conducting a multicandidate election for the Nineteenth Party Conference in 1988 in the hope that he could turn the party into an instrument of reform. This election and the televised conference itself revealed unmistakably the hopeless division within the Communist Party. The myth of the monolith of the party was broken.[93] What happened within the party was similar to the process that proceeded within the Hungarian Communist Party.

The "founding election" for the Congress of People's Deputies in March 1989 quickly turned into a referendum for the Communist Party dictatorship. In cities such as Moscow, Leningrad, and Kiev, the party candidates suffered resounding defeats. Boris Yeltsin, Gorbachev's political opponent from the left, captured 90 percent of the votes in Moscow. Through this election a new opposition force in the parliament, the Interregional Group, was formed. More ominous was the emergence of nationalism. Alarmed by these results, Gorbachev had to postpone the local elections scheduled in the fall of 1989 to the spring of 1990. Nevertheless, anticommunist sentiment became even more pronounced in local elections; Moscow and Leningrad were captured by the radical reformers, who formed a loose coalition called Democratic Russia.[94] The pluralization process, which developed more quickly than anyone expected, resulted in the formation of a democradura. In other words, the transitional path quickly moved from Box 6 to Box 7.

It may be possible to make a general conclusion based on the Soviet experience. If the pluralization-democratization process begins without full decentralization, a destabilizing situation tends to be created for three reasons. First, the transition to a democradura, while the command economic structure remains intact, tends to generate more powerful resistance from hard-liners. Second, a democradura established by a popular election is often so divisive and contentious that it makes the decentralization process difficult. Third, pluralization-democratization without decentralization lacks a central core that supports this process. There are no emerging economic groups or classes that demand pluralization-democratization out of their economic interests.

Liberalization-pluralization in the Soviet Union unleashed powerful forces that threatened the very existence of the Soviet Union. It damaged the three fundamental adhesives that have glued the Soviet state together: the Marxist-Leninist ideology, the Communist Party, and the coercive power.[95]

Glasnost dealt a fatal blow to Marxism-Leninism as the regime's monopoly ideology. The dismantling of ideology came in three stages. First, the moment pluralism of opinion was accepted, Marxism-Leninism vacated its sacred seat as the holder of the absolute and single truth. Then began the onslaught on Marxism-Leninism itself. The sacrosanct dogmas of Marxism-Leninism have been discarded one by one. Many now argue that the ills of the Soviet state and society can be traced, not to the aberration of Marxism called Stalinism, but to Marxism itself. For all practical purposes, Marxism-Leninism is dead as an ideology that can achieve social and political cohesion in the Soviet Union. At its July plenum in 1991, the Central Committee of the Communist Party approved Gorbachev's proposal to part with Marxism-Leninism as its official ideology and espouse social democracy.

Once people are permitted to say under glasnost what they have already known—namely, that the emperor had no clothes—the next logical step is to shout "Down with the Emperor." The erosion of the authority of the Communist Party as the sole ruling party is closely associated with the collapse of the official ideology. Once people were given a chance to voice their opinions in multicandidate elections, they unceremoniously booted out party apparatchiki in major cities. In the name of a law-governed state, the locus of power was legally and institutionally to be shifted to the Congress of People's Deputies at the national level, and to the soviets at the republic and local levels. The Central Committee Plenum in February 1990 removed Article 6 of the Soviet Constitution, thus self-abrogating the Communist Party's status as the sole ruling party. The Twenty-Eighth Party Congress in July 1990 demonstrated how quickly the once powerful ruling party had become a splintered political force, unable to muster strength for reform or for counterreform. The disarray of the Communist Party was further demonstrated by the presidential election in the Russian Federation (RSFSR) on June 12, 1991. The Russian Communist Party could not select its own official candidate. Four communist candidates challenged Yeltsin, and they were defeated at the first ballot. The party further demonstrated its hopeless disintegration when the reform wing formed a "Democratic Reform Movement." Former Politburo members such as Eduard Shevardnadze and Aleksandr Yakovlev took a lead.

Three fundamental crises threatened the very foundation of the Soviet state: a crisis of power, a crisis of the federation, and a crisis of the economy. First, the Communist Party was irreparably discredited as the almighty political force to glue together diverse elements in society. This meant that the central government rid itself of the very instrument needed to implement its decisions. Suddenly the central government was floating in the ocean without ballast to stabilize it. The soviet-type of government, which resembled direct participatory democracy more than a hierarchically structured government, decentralized the locus of power. Thus, instead of creating an effective political system to replace the communist dictatorship, Gorbachev's political reform started "the war of laws." Republics' governments competed with the union government over jurisdiction, while local soviets challenged the union and republican governments. Faced with this crisis, Gorbachev concocted the presidential system. He managed to be elected president. Under the presidency, the Presidential Council was created. But this system was nothing but a severed head without the nerves connecting the body and limbs. In November 1990 Gorbachev presented a proposal for a new federal treaty with another set of major constitutional amendments with regard to the central governmental structure. The Presidential Council was abolished and replaced by the ministerial system and the Council of Federation composed of the heads of the republics. This change, approved by the Congress of People's Deputies in December, tremendously increased the presidential power in theory, but the constant reshuffling of the central government structure further eroded the power of the central authority. A democradura in the Soviet Union produced a hopeless stalemate in which neither the opposition nor the hard-liners could present an alternative to Gorbachev's leadership, while Gorbachev himself continued to hang by a thread.

The death of ideology and the erosion of the Communist Party authority removed once and for all the lid that had contained ethnic tensions within the Soviet Union. The Baltic Republics, Georgia, Armenia, and Moldova (formerly Moldavia) declared their independence. They played what Di Palma calls the "breakdown game."[96] Armenia and Azerbaijan became embroiled in an inter-republic civil war, and Georgia faced inter-ethnic civil war within its own republic. Ukraine, Belarus, and the Central Asian Republics increasingly began to take independent actions by defying the authority of the center, although they did not seek secession from the Soviet Union. Even the Russian Federation under Yeltsin competed with the federal authority in jurisdictional disputes over fundamental issues. In this unprecedented crisis of federation, Gorbachev had only two alternatives: let the breakaway republics go or force them into submission against their will. If he had chosen the former, he would have alienated the hard-liners, particularly the military and the KGB, on which he had to rely to prop up his power. If he had chosen the latter, this would have been a dangerous signal of a backlash reversing the democratization process.

Gorbachev's right-wing tendency that began in the fall of 1990 and culminated in the use of force in Vilnius and Riga in January 1991 should be understood in this context. Under the pressure from the conservative-reactionary groups such as "Soyuz," the military, the KGB, and the party apparatchiki, Gorbachev moved dangerously close to instituting direct presidential rule over the Baltic Republics. Nevertheless, this reactionary move provoked profound reaction abroad and at home. The danger of perestroika sliding down to a dictablanda, if not pure dictatorship, alarmed the reformers, both the soft-liners in power as well as the radical reformers in the opposition. Despite the radical reformers' propaganda against the referendum on the federal system on March 17, 1991, it resulted in the overwhelming support for the maintenance of the federal system except for the breakaway republics that boycotted it. Weakened though his power base might have become, Gorbachev proved to be indispensable for both reformers and hard-liners. Realignment of political groups had been undertaken. On April 23, Gorbachev and nine republics that decided to remain in the federation concluded an accord at Novo-Ogarevo to reconstitute the federal system on the new principles. This formal "pact" on May 16, 1991 (known as the "9 + 1 accord") represented an important landmark for democratization. Both Gorbachev and Yeltsin, realizing the cost of breaking away, affirmed the advantage of remaining within the democratization process.

The third crisis that threatened the foundation of the Soviet state was the economic crisis. The timid half-measures adopted in 1987 deepened the economic crisis, which by the end of 1990 had come to a head. Gorbachev's leadership politics should be blamed for the failure in economic transition. In March 1990, when Gorbachev acquired enormous presidential power, he could have used this power to implement radical economic reform. A 400-day program drafted by Grigory Yavlinsky and his associates (later the basis of the Shatalin Plan) had already been presented to Gorbachev in February 1990.[97] Instead, Gorbachev chose to test his presidential power in a futile tug of war with Lithuania. He wasted his precious time and whatever authority he managed to maintain in his new office. It was not until the summer of 1990 that Gorbachev began to pay serious attention to economic reform. Nevertheless, the Shatalin Plan, a most radical document, which mapped out the strategy for transition to a market economy in four stages within 500 days, was strongly opposed by conservatives in the military-industrial complex. Under this pressure Gorbachev rejected it in November 1990.[98] The economic deterioration has proceeded drastically since then. The most urgent task was to prevent the complete collapse of the economy.

From the end of 1990 to the spring of 1991, the new cabinet under Prime Minister Valentin Pavlov adopted a series of measures designed to achieve stabilization. It became apparent, however, that for these "anticrisis measures" to be successfully implemented, the federal government needed cooperation with the republics as well as massive aid from the West. Presumably, this led Gorbachev to seek a *modus vivendi* with Yeltsin and other leaders of the republics. The "9 + 1 pact," which demarcated federal and republican property and resources and delegated more authority to the republics, was supposed to serve as a basis for the belated decentralization-marketization process.

The political situation that existed between April and August 1991 can be characterized as a stalemate. Neither the radical reformers nor the conservative hard-liners could provide an effective alternative for extrication. Gorbachev managed to maintain power only because no political forces opposing him dared to upset this stalemate and jeopardize their own interests. The fragile stalemate seemed to be the only guarantee that the Soviet Union could accomplish democratization-marketization while maintaining a loose confederation. The Soviet Union seemed to have reached the crucial point described by O'Donnell and Schmitter and Di Palma, where the players would stay within the democratization process for fear that the cost of upsetting it would far outweigh the cost of staying in.[99]

The Soviet process, however, did not faithfully follow the theory presented by these theorists of democratic transitions. The stalemate, which was supposed to serve as a felicitous beginning of democratization, was shattered by the conservatives' abortive coup d'état against Gorbachev on August 19–21. Fearing that "the 9 + 1 accord" would annihilate their interests once and for all, the conservatives took a decisive step to oust Gorbachev and prevent the signing of the accord. Judging from the declaration issued by the Committee for the Emergency Situation, as the conspirators called themselves, their aim was not to move history's clock back to dictatorship (Box 1), but at best to restore a dictablanda (Box 6) for the moment. It was this indecisiveness of the coup that spelled its doom. The conspirators obviously counted on the old power structure (represented by the KGB, the Ministry of Internal Affairs, the military, the military-industrial complex, and the Communist Party apparatus) to rally behind the dictablanda, although they were not bold enough to part with the institutional framework created by perestroika. If those forces had responded to support the coup d'état government, the inchoate masses that rallied behind Yeltsin's call to defend democracy would have been easily crushed. Actually, the institutions that were supposed to be the bulwark of the old system had been decayed from within by perestroika. The KGB elite corps and the military units summoned to defend the Committee for the Emergency Situation and to move against democratic forces disobeyed the order. By the third day it became apparent that the coup had failed.

If the theorists on democratic transitions were right, the cost of getting out of the stalemate turned out, indeed, exorbitantly high to the conservative plotters. In fact, what followed after the coup was exactly what the plotters had been attempting to prevent. The central government, which cooperated with the Committee for the Emergency Situation, collapsed. The fragile balance that was barely maintained by the "9 + 1 accord" was completely destroyed. The precipitous disintegration of the Soviet Union began, as republic after republic declared independence. Gorbachev, whose prestige was greatly tarnished by the coup, desperately tried to salvage the union structure by forging a loose confederation. But after the Ukrainians overwhelmingly voted for independence in a referendum on December 1, Yeltsin seized this opportunity to do away with both Gorbachev and the Soviet Union by creating a Commonwealth of Independent States. On December 25, Gorbachev reluctantly accepted the inevitable. He announced the end of the Soviet

Union and resigned as president. The Soviet Union finally died after 74 years of existence.

In the meantime, the Communist Party, whose top members were either involved in the plot or at least sympathized with it, was outlawed, and its properties confiscated. The KGB, whose head was the main architect of the plot, was irreparably compromised, and the entire organization (with the exception of a few divisions) was disbanded. Likewise, the military, whose highest ranking minister was involved in the plot, lost prestige. Deprived of the Communist Party apparatus and the coercive powers, the union government had no chance of survival.

How can we interpret the development after the August coup in our diagram? The destruction of the Communist Party and the KGB may be identified as signs of further democratization. Nevertheless, the end of the Soviet Union in itself cannot necessarily be equated with democratization. In many republics the disappearance of the Communist Party paved the way for expanded democratization, but in others authoritarianism reemerged. The disappearance of the Soviet Union means that henceforward it is impossible to talk about the transition of the Soviet Union as a whole. The transition in each independent republic must be examined. This task, however, goes beyond the scope of this chapter.

As far as the economic transition was concerned, the end of the Soviet Union meant the disruption of the integrated economic unit. Henceforward, economic transitions must be traced in each independent republic. Nevertheless, due to its dominant position, the economic transition in the Russian Federation will have a decisive influence on the course of development of other republics.

Vietnam. The *doi moi* policy pushed Vietnam into Box 6. But before the Vietnamese transition proceeded further along within Box 6, two important factors intervened.

First, the East European revolutions in 1989 created an acute sense of crisis in the Vietnamese Communist Party leadership. In response to this crisis, the communist leadership in Vietnam tried desperately to uphold the communist dictatorship by emphasizing the differences between Vietnam and the East European countries. The party propagandists contended that in contrast to East European countries, where socialism was imposed by the Soviet Army, the socialist revolution and independence in Vietnam were carried out by the indigenous revolutionary party led by Ho Chi Minh. Moreover, they argued that East European countries had experienced a European type of capitalist development and a pluralistic political system in the past. Vietnam's past was predominantly agrarian, Asiatic "feudalism," and, therefore, pluralistic democracy was not appropriate.[100] The emphasis on Vietnam's uniqueness compared to Eastern Europe also led to Vietnamese communists' distancing of themselves from the Soviet Union. They began to see in perestroika in the Soviet Union the poisonous germs that would eventually doom the Communist Party dictatorship everywhere.

This acute sense of crisis led to the reversal of political reform. The new party platform adopted in December 1990 proclaimed that "the Communist Party of Vietnam is the political vanguard of the whole society, representing the interests of the working class, the laboring people and the entire nation."[101] No longer did the party allow the discussion on the separation of the state from the party. In fact, the moderate leadership headed by Nguyen Van Linh began to silence the voices within the party that advocated political reform. A group of influential war veterans known as the Club of Former Resistance Fighters in the South had been critical of the leadership in its handling of both economic and political reform. In February, 1990, Linh severely attacked the Club, and in the following month the club's chairman and vice-chairman were forced to resign.[102] In the same month a Politburo member, Tran Xuan Bach, who called for the introduction of political pluralism, was suddenly dismissed. The party severely warned that rapid political change would undermine the economic progress achieved under *doi moi*.[103]

The second event that negatively affected the transition process was the end of Soviet economic assistance and Soviet aid. During the 1980s the Soviet Union accounted for more than 60 percent of Vietnam's total trade. Until 1989 most of Vietnam's fuel and 80 percent of its fertilizers came from the Soviet Union. Since Vietnam was accorded a preferential exchange rate with CMEA, the economic association of socialist countries, this trade was in fact tantamount to direct aid from the Soviet Union. In January 1991, Vietnam and the Soviet Union signed new agreements on economic cooperation, which placed trade on a commercial basis and cut off Soviet aid to Vietnam. Supplies of fuel and fertilizer were drastically cut back. Price increases caused by shortages of oil and fertilizers contributed to inflation. Shortage of fertilizer caused a poor rice crop, which led to higher prices for rice. Unemployment was rising at an alarming speed.[104]

Despite these setbacks, the leadership continued to advocate the *doi moi* policy. The new platform adopted in December 1990 reaffirmed the continuation of economic openness, the role of the private sector, and foreign capital.[105] Nevertheless, what the platform aimed at was not full marketization, but rather "multi-sector commodity economy," where "the state's managerial function vis-à-vis the market and all economic and social activities" would be strengthened.[106] Obviously, this platform indicated a product of compromise.

The Seventh Party Congress held in June 1991 adopted this platform and reaffirmed the principle of one-party dictatorship. Linh resigned as general secretary, and his position was taken over by 74-year-old Do Muoi.[107] Do Muoi is believed to be a moderate reformer, but because of his role in disastrous economic policies in the South in the 1970s, he is disliked by radical reformers. His election thus seems to symbolize the position that Vietnam takes in its transition: marketization under dictablanda. This pattern is strikingly similar to China's.

IMPEDIMENTS IN THE TRANSITIONAL GAME

The Regime Level

To craft a successful transitional path, a number of requirements must be satisfied. The regime must be flexible and assertive enough to take the initiative for the transition with a firm commitment to the ultimate goal of democratization-marketization. It also must be strong enough to suppress the hard-liners who want to resist change. The opposition must be flexible enough to participate in the gradual, evolutionary process of transition, yet firm enough to restrain extremists within its own ranks as well as the destructive reaction of the masses. In reality, however, few regimes can satisfy all these requirements. Thus, it is necessary to discuss what impediments exist for successful transition from communism at the following three levels: regime, opposition, and society.

Once the transition process begins, the ruling Communist Party becomes divided between what O'Donnell and Schmitter call hard-liners and soft-liners. The first are those who believe that the perpetuation of the communist system is possible and desirable. They resist any attempts at liberalization and decentralization. As the transition proceeds, each group tends to split further: hard-liners into the conservatives and the reactionaries and soft-liners into the radicals and the moderates.[108] The conservatives reject liberalization "out of opportunism, indifferent to longer-term political projects, and preoccupied instead with their own survival in office and retaining their share of the spoils."[109] Conservatives do not have their own ideology, and it is possible to buy them off by securing their position and granting them better opportunities in the transitional process. Reactionaries are more difficult to manage since they are ideologically committed to the perpetuation of the communist system and "reject viscerally" the "cancers" and "disorders" of democracy and the market economy.[110]

Soft-liners are those who are aware that the rigid communist system cannot sustain economic progress. They believe that "if its eventual legitimation is to be feasible, the regime cannot wait too long" before introducing certain political and economic reform measures.[111]

The radical soft-liners advocate total dismantling of the communist system in the economy and in the political sphere. The moderates may be aware of the structural problem of the command economy, and they may support some decentralization and marketization measures to revitalize the economy. They oppose, however, any weakening of the Communist Party dictatorship. In fact, they may argue that a strong dictatorial power is essential to carry out economic reform.

Reforms in Hungary, China, the Soviet Union, and Vietnam were possible only when soft-liners assumed power. The reforms intensified the power struggle within the top leadership. Nevertheless, it was not the radicals, but the moderates, who provided the crucial impetus for reform.

There are two paradoxes at this level. The first paradox concerns ideological justification for liberalization. Since soft-liners usually present their program in the midst of a serious power struggle with hard-liners and opposition from reactionaries and conservatives alike, and since they have to maintain a coalition with some of the conservatives, they must couch their liberalization-decentralization program in the traditional ideological framework. The ideological trappings necessarily limit the scope of liberalization-decentralization. The need to justify liberalization-decentralization poses an inevitable dilemma for reforming soft-liners.[112] Nevertheless, these ideological impediments are relative to the strength of conservative-reactionary resistance.

The second paradox is that by initiating liberalization-decentralization, the top leadership breaks its cohesion. Liberalization-decentralization that is designed to legitimate the monopolistic position of the ruling party actually opens the way to making the party more democratic. This paradox can be observed in all four reforms under examination, but the degree of pluralism within the Communist Party varies. In Hungary and the Soviet Union pluralism within the party led to genuine pluralism in the political process, and eventually to the end of the monopolistic status of the Communist Party. Both in China and Vietnam, despite internal factional struggles, the Communist Party still maintains its cohesion.

The division between hard-liners and soft-liners is replicated at the lower level of the bureaucratic structure of the state and the party. On the whole, the bureaucracy, particularly the party apparatchiki, is conservative if not reactionary. Liberalization-decentralization threatens conservatives' material and ideological justification for existence. There-fore, personnel policy involving appointments and dismissals of party and state bureaucrats is an important battleground in the power strug-gle between hard-liners and soft-liners at the top level. There are basi-cally three paradoxes at this level. First, the party apparatus at the lower level is the key to the economic performance of a command econ-omy and to the implementation of political decisions made at the top. It is not possible to accomplish liberalization-decentralization and plurali-zation-marketization without dislodging the party apparatchiki or at least neutralizing them. And yet the apparatchiki are an important cog and lubricant for the machinery of a command economy. As long as the basic structure of a command economy is maintained in the first phase of economic reform, dislodging the apparatchiki may result in paralysis of the economy. *Thus, the soft-line leadership must design a strategy of liber-alization-decentralization in such a way that the apparatchiki's interests are enhanced, or at least not damaged.* Decentralization must precede plurali-zation-democratization so that the economic gains derived from decen-tralization are strong enough to offset the expected resistance of the apparatchiki at the local level. In Hungary, China, and Vietnam this process has been relatively successful. In the Soviet Union, however, Gorbachev made a cardinal mistake when he singled out the party and state apparatchiki as enemies of perestroika early on. This brings us to a second paradox. If the apparatchiki are bought off and bribed to accept the arrangements set up by the decentralization process, the public may become indignant. This may lead to political instability. Clearly this was the case in China, and potentially Vietnam faces the same danger.

The third paradox at the lower level of the party apparatus becomes apparent when political transition moves from a dictablanda to a de-mocradura. This transition is accompanied by the inevitable erosion of the party's authority and power. The party drastically loses its effective-ness as an instrument through which the central leadership can imple-ment reforms. Ultimately, the question of whether an emerging civil society can replace the old party apparatchiki is determined by the strength of the civil society in a communist regime. Furthermore, the vitality of the civil society depends, first, on whether a nation has the historical memory of civil society before the communist takeover, and second, on the degree of modernization. In Hungary new political forces, with remarkable ease and speed, took over the vacuum left by the collapse of the communist dictatorship. In the Soviet Union the paralysis of the CPSU imperiled the very existence of the state and society. The catastrophic consequences that are likely to result from the collapse of the communist dictatorship may explain the uncompromising adamancy with which the Chinese and the Vietnamese communist parties hold on to their power.

There is another issue closely connected to the leadership conflict: the position of the military and the secret police. On the one hand, the secret police is usually associated with the past abuses. In the process of liberalization-pluralization-democratization, the power of the secret police is curtailed. Thus, the secret police is likely to ally itself with hard-liners to resist change. On the other hand, in the communist system where the access to free information is severely restricted, the secret police is in a position to know the true conditions of the country as well as those of the capitalist countries. Thus, it is not surprising that some in the secret police favor a limited liberalization-decentralization process, provided that law and order are maintained. Nevertheless, when the transition game reaches the point where the foundations of social order are shaken, the secret police tend to stand decisively for the maintenance of order. In the Soviet Union, China, and Vietnam, the secret police seem to side with the conservative wing of the party. Hungary is an exception: with the collapse of the Soviet support, the secret police simply disintegrated.

The position of the military is more complicated. Unlike many authoritarian regimes, the communist system is not a military dictatorship. The military is usually under the firm control of the party. To ensure the military's subordination to the party, the military is granted a coveted status and privileges. Ideological indoctrination is thoroughly pursued in the military, and the military-political administration serves as a watchdog to prevent Bonapartism from emerging within the military. Nevertheless, the military has its own bureaucratic interests to pursue, and in the power vacuum where the authority of the party is diminished, the military often steps in to restore order. Moreover, it is impossible to insulate the military completely from political, social, and ethnic conflicts in society at large. When society goes through the growing pains of transition, the military cannot be expected to avoid these pains. It will experience the same political, social, and ethnic illness as the society—perhaps with a higher fever. This threatens the very existence of the military as an institution.

At this point hard-liners within the military are likely to seek alliance with hard-liners in the party to save their institution from disintegration. The position of the military becomes a crucial element, not only in the dynamics of power politics within the leadership, but also in the dynamics of national politics as a whole. Examined from completely the opposite side, *it thus becomes essential for soft-liners as well as the opposition not to alienate the military completely and to ensure its cooperation for moving the transition along.*

The Level of Opposition

Liberalization tends to open the window for the resurrection of a civil society. Political liberalization involving a certain degree of freedom of expression tends to catalyze the forces that are buried under the communist system. The seeming stability in the communist system is often illusory since under totalitarian repression citizens tend to escape from politics and immerse themselves in the pursuit of private goals. Passion for nonpolitical matters, however, is a disguised form of political criticism that may resurface once a space is opened up by liberalization.

Before liberalization is launched by the regime, two important movements are likely to exist within the communist system. The first is a dissident movement concerned with human rights. The second is a cultural movement that demands freedom of expression. These movements are repressed, and they usually fail to capture mass support. Nonetheless, they are important in the sense that they test the limit of the regime's tolerance.

The most dangerous moment for the communist system is when a privileged segment of society, the mainstay of the regime, realizes that the communist system no longer promotes social and economic progress. The more conscientiously engineers, scientists, economists, and other professional people want to do their job, the more painfully they become aware of the deficiencies of the system itself. The confidence and pride that they have in their professions drive them into moral revulsion with the communist system. Some experts in research institutes begin to form an opposition group within the party, often under the protection of soft-liners higher up in the party apparatus.

Liberalization initiated by soft-liners legitimates the opposition's status. But the initial liberalization process, timid as it may be, has momentum to broaden the scope of political activities, drawing in new actors and resulting in a merger with the former dissident movement and the artistic movements. Ideas and thoughts that existed only in fragments and in isolation tend to coalesce into a new intellectual current that seeks an alternative to the regime. To some extent, the soft-line leadership uses this aspect of liberalization to mobilize the support of some segments of society for intended reform measures and to damage the hard-liners' opposition. New issues are articulated, and the opposition begins to argue that the satisfaction of these demands will be contingent upon pluralization and eventually upon democratization. Thus, plurality of opinion moves toward plurality of interests, and plurality of interests moves toward plurality of political parties. The strength of the opposition that appears at first among the professional class corresponds to the maturity of modern society.

Opposition can be united as long as it is opposed to the Communist Party dictatorship. Nevertheless, the moment it succeeds in extracting concessions from the regime, it is faced with the danger of an internal split. Within the opposition itself, there emerge the radicals, who wage an uncompromising struggle against the party, and the moderates, who are flexible enough to choose cooperation with the regime for a gradual, evolutionary transition. The split within the opposition greatly affects the balance of power between the regime and the opposition and between the opposition leadership and the mass movements.

There is one fundamental difference between transition from communism and transition from noncommunist authoritarianism in terms of the composition of the opposition. In transition from communism, the business class is conspicuously absent. This absence tends to make the intellectuals the major driving force of the opposition. This intellectual dominance has an inherent weakness: it deprives the opposition movement of economic muscle. Economic transition can be seen as a process of producing a viable business class.

At the critical juncture of political transition, there comes a time when the regime and the opposition confront each other in roughly equal balance. The resulting stalemate is a crucial moment for political transition. There are two ways to end this stalemate. The first option is for both sides to agree on a pact. The Hungarian Round Table and "the 9 + 1 accord" exemplify pacts that were made to end stalemates. The second option is to use coercion to crush the opposition. The Tiananmen incident in China and the August coup in the Soviet Union are examples of this option. The experience in communist transition shows that neither option is favorable to solve the twin transition.

The Social Mobilization Level

One condition of stability for dictablanda is that "the articulation of interests, while permitted in principle, must never be allowed to take the form of a mobilization of the masses on behalf of them." Nevertheless, the momentum of liberalization-decentralization will eventually push the reform effort to pluralization-marketization, and it becomes inevitable that the masses are mobilized in the process. Decentralization accentuates economic differentiation. In a mixed command economy where the market price coexists with the official fixed price, opportunities for speculation present themselves. People's indignation is often directed toward those who make huge profits in such speculation. When economic reform moves from decentralization to marketization, it inevitably undermines social entitlements that have been taken for granted as the gains of the communist system. State subsidies are either eliminated or drastically reduced, while full employment is abandoned. Inflation becomes rampant, and unemployment increases. Enterprises losing large sums of money most go under. It is impossible to accomplish marketization without such social costs. The inevitable reduction of the standard of living of a large segment of the population increases the chance for mass mobilization.

The working class bears the brunt of this social cost. There can be two ways in which the working class reacts to the marketization process. The first is resentment at the economic sacrifices. Mass dissatisfaction finds an avenue for articulation through the spaces opened up by liberalization. Hard-liners, who oppose transition, often use this mass discontent in their attempt to arrest the reform process. Nevertheless, it is also true that the command economy has miserably failed the working class's expectations. It is therefore possible for the working class to accept economic sacrifices in exchange for participation in the political process from which they have been excluded. But the opposition united against the regime inevitably splits itself into those who favor differentiation and those who advocate social protection.

Once the soft-liners take advantage of liberalization to discredit the hard-liners, groups concerned with various issues—such as ecology, ethnic problems, and human rights—spring up and try to mobilize the masses for their purposes. The accumulated ills of the communist system are exposed clearly and discussed openly. The masses may then rise up to take political action. Ethnic problems frequently galvanize the most explosive and destructive elements in the process of transition. They may set the path of political transition at cross-purposes to the economic transition.

The popular upsurge presents a serious challenge to reform-minded soft-liners as well as to moderate opposition leaders. Suppression of the popular upsurge is inevitably accompanied by a conservative backlash in the reform process, as happened in China. This will lead to radicalization of the opposition (as in the Soviet Union after the Tbilisi incident and in Lithuania and Latvia after the Bloody Sundays) and/or demoralization of the professional class on which further economic reform depends (as in China). Making concessions to the popular upsurge will mean further erosion of the dictatorial power or the precarious demo-cradura, while such concessions on the economic transition produce uncertain outcomes, not necessarily favorable for the decentralization-marketization process.

One cardinal rule for a successful transition is to avoid a mass up-surge. In fact, this was the secret motivation behind the "9 + 1 accord." In this respect, the August coup that triggered the mass upsurge can be considered the most shortsighted folly. In Hungary throughout the political transition, the masses were conspicuously absent. This may be the result of the economic reform during the 1970s, which despite many fundamental failures accomplished one thing: transformation of the Hungarian population into a complacent middle class.

PROSPECTS

Events in Hungary, China, the former Soviet Union, and Vietnam are changing so rapidly that it is hazardous to predict what may happen next. Nevertheless, the different paths these countries have traversed may suggest certain patterns that provide a clue to future connections between political and economic transition.

In Hungary the political transition to democracy has been completed, but this has not ensured success in either the political or the economic transition. Although the Democratic Forum headed by Jozsef Antall formed a coalition government, this government lacked economic ex-perts necessary to draw up a comprehensive economic reform strategy. Tasks that confronted the democratically formed Antall government were exactly the same as those that confront all communist regimes: balancing the budget to stabilize the economy, introducing equilibrium prices, de-nationalizing state enterprises, achieving convertibility of cur-rency, creating new private firms, and liquidating unprofitable enter-prises. The challenge to the new democracy in Hungary was whether it would be able to accomplish these tasks without serious social conse-quences and without causing political instability.

The Antall government rejected from the very beginning the kind of "shock therapy" implemented in Poland. Nevertheless, the government's gradualism was tantamount to inaction. Where the government took action, it contributed to worsening the situation. Hungary ended up with the "shock" without "the therapy."[113]

The government's inability to come up with an effective economic measure created a political crisis. The general strike in October 1990 triggered by the government's decision to increase the price of gasoline contributed to the complete breakdown of the government's authority. The Minister of Interior attempted to use force, but the police refused to obey his order. In the midst of crisis, it was neither the government nor the parliament, but the National Interest Coordinating Council, which represented various interest groups in society, that intervened to solve the crisis. The popularity rating of the government plummeted to zero, but the oppositions and the National Assembly also suffered. In March-April 1991 new Round Table negotiations consisting of six parties were organized outside of the National Assembly to forge a consensus on fundamental issues for Hungary's economic and political transformation.[114]

The Hungarian transition indicates that democratization in itself does not ensure marketization, and that without marketization, democratization that has been once achieved may face the danger of sliding back to democradura.

The former Soviet Union offers an interesting contrast to the Hungarian transition. In the first place, the end of the Soviet Union makes it impossible to treat the transition of the former Soviet Union uniformly, although all the independent republics officially reaffirm the need to accomplish the twin transitions to democracy and to a market economy. But without question the most important case is the Russian Federation.

Yeltsin was elected in a democratic, multicandidate election in June 1990. It is possible to consider, therefore, that the Russian Federation accomplished democratization, although the Soviet Union as a whole was still at the stage of democradura. After the coup, when the Soviet Union disintegrated, Yeltsin's government adopted a radical economic program. In contrast to the Hungarian government, what Yeltsin adopted was precisely "shock therapy." The economic reform program drafted by Yegor Gaidar, deputy prime minister on economic reforms, started with lifting price controls on most goods on January 2, 1992. This measure was to be followed by the privatization of 70 percent of retail and public food services by the year's end, and by balancing the budget by drastically slashing defense spending, privatizing agriculture, selling land, and purchasing farmers' produce on the basis of negotiated contracts in 1992. The difference between Gaidar's plan and all previous economic reform programs was that Gaidar's was actually being implemented. As soon as the price controls were lifted on January 2, prices of most products increased sharply. Because lifting price controls occurred under the condition of state monopoly of most industries, price hikes were not accompanied by increased availability of goods. In industry, supplies were supposed to increase with greater profits, but in actuality demand was sharply reduced with higher prices. Russia's GNP, which shrank by 15 percent in 1991, is expected to be reduced further by 15 to 20 percent in 1992.[115]

Expecting criticism to rise, Yeltsin decided to take full responsibility for Gaidar's economic program by assuming the post of prime minister himself. He also postponed parliamentary elections. In an attempt to overcome a war of competing laws with local authorities, Yeltsin implemented the appointive system of local government. All these efforts indicate a tendency on the part of Yeltsin's government to create a strong government to carry out marketization. Nevertheless, it is doubtful if he has succeeded in creating an executive power strong enough to enforce its will throughout Russia. Yeltsin's government remains a miniature copy of Gorbachev's government: a severed head without limbs.

As soon as the price controls were lifted on January 2, voices of criticism and protest were raised, even from Yeltsin's supporters. Yeltsin's own vice-president, Colonel Aleksandr Rutskoi, openly criticized Yeltsin's economic program.[116] Even Ruslan Khasbulatov, chairman of the Supreme Soviet and Yeltsin's former comrade-in-arms, called for Yeltsin's resignation as prime minister. Undaunted by these criticisms, Gaidar's team announced the second stage of the reform: sale of state-owned shops, factories, and other property.[117]

Three fundamental questions may be raised about Russia's transition. First, there is a serious question as to whether Gaidar's program is, from a purely economic standpoint, a sound strategy for marketization. One of the fundamental issues for marketization is whether the price reform should precede de-nationalization of state properties or vice versa. Gaidar's program starts from the assumption that without price reform the value of state properties cannot be determined. Critics of Gaidar's program argue that without creating a market at first by de-nationalizing state properties and thus by creating competition, deregulated prices cannot be market prices. In this situation, they contend, the entire economy degenerates into a racket economy, dominated by monopolies and criminal groups. The answer to this question cannot be given at this time, although the weight of evidence seems now to favor the critics. The second question concerns the political implication of Gaidar's program. Even if the program works purely from the economic standpoint, the political reaction that inevitably arises from popular dissatisfaction may undermine it. This danger is particularly great because dissatisfaction with the economic situation can easily be combined with the resurgence of Great Russian nationalism awakened by the breakup of the empire. The failure of Gaidar's economic program may topple Yeltsin. Should this happen, the alternative government to replace Yeltsin is likely to have an authoritarian character. The third, most important question is the relationship between democratization and marketization. At least in Russia's case, democratization has not created an executive power strong enough to enforce marketization. In fact, the conflict between the president and the parliament has the potential of undermining any attempt at marketization. Moreover, Russian democratization has not created the kind of hierarchical administrative system essential for implementation of any economic program. There seems to exist, therefore, an inherent contradiction between the requirements for economic transition and the consequences of democratization.

If Hungary and Russia represent the transition through complete destruction of the communist system, China and Vietnam offer another path through preservation of the Communist Party dictablanda. In China renewed liberalization seems inevitable if China seeks further economic modernization. In fact, recent rehabilitations and promotions of the deposed radical reformers may indicate a move in this direction[118] The current Chinese leadership, still under the influence of the moderate reformer, Deng Xiaoping, will no doubt continue the course of economic modernization that aims at marketization without making any compromise on the guiding role of the Communist Party. With regard to China's transition, two fundamental questions are raised. First, what impact may the change to a new generation in leadership have on the course of transition? Certainly, the octogenarian leaders such as Deng Xiaoping, Yang Shangkun, and Chen Yun will exit from the scene within the next decade. The order in which these leaders disappear may affect the course in the short run. But in the long run, the disappearance of these leaders is likely to bring reform-minded technocratic cadres to center stage. Nevertheless, even the new leaders will be extremely careful in introducing political reforms that might undermine the leading role of the Communist Party.

This brings us to the next question: whether it is possible to achieve marketization under the condition of the Communist Party dictablanda. Although a definitive answer cannot be given on this question at this point, it seems premature to conclude that further marketization of the Chinese economy requires prior pluralization. Yet sooner or later such marketization will lead to new pressures for pluralization.

In Vietnam the two processes of the *doi moi* policy—transition to a market economy and opening—proceed under the Communist Party dictablanda. The question here is how long the present communist leadership can contain a demand for political reform that is voiced within the ruling party. Criticisms raised by the Club of Former Resistance Fighters and Tran Xuan Bach are not isolated cases. Bui Tin, the former deputy editor of *Nhan Dan,* the party daily, and a hero who presided over the surrender of Saigon in 1975, also called for political reform.[119] The situation in Vietnam is more volatile than in China, because the division between the North and the South is more sharply drawn in Vietnam than the divisions between the coastal region and the hinterland in China. Ideological regimentation from the northern leaders in Vietnam may trigger violent southern regional reaction. Moreover, Vietnam is a country of the young, and unemployment among the young is increasing at a staggering rate.[120]

This volatile situation gives the current Vietnamese leadership no alternative but to seek a policy of acceleration of the *doi moi* policy. That is why the Vietnamese leadership is desperately seeking ways to end isolation and invite foreign investment from abroad, particularly from Japan and the United States.

CONCLUSION

The transitional paths we examined in the four countries demonstrate the difficulties in making a transition from the communist system. The dynamics of leadership politics, the level of conservative-reactionary resistance, and the strength of the opposition to the regime all conspire to make it virtually impossible for the communist leadership to attain a synchronized path for political as well as economic transition. In China economic transition went ahead without the significant pluralization process. This uneven transitional path engendered a dysfunctional political situation, which led to the Tiananmen incident. In the Soviet case the political liberalization-pluralization process has gone rapidly without significant economic transition, resulting in the erosion of political authority and the eventual end of the communist rule and the Soviet state. Even in Hungary, where a democracy has been established, success in economic transition has not been ensured. Vietnam, which has belatedly initiated the transitional process, will certainly face difficulties that are plaguing transitions in China and the Soviet Union.

It is possible to extrapolate several hypotheses from the four examples of transitions I have examined. First, a transition from communism must begin with the liberalization-decentralization process, and liberalization is a prerequisite for decentralization.

Second, Box 6 represents a key moment for transition from the communist system. It is important to ponder the pattern of extrication from Box 6. Hungary as well as the Soviet Union moved vertically along political reform before moving horizontally along economic reform. China and Vietnam, at least thus far, have adamantly refused political reform. In fact, both China and Vietnam insist that the maintenance of the one-party dictatorship is a precondition for economic transition to the market economy. Three factors help explain these different patterns. First one must look at history. Did a civil society and a pluralistic political system ever exist in the past? Second, one must consider the legitimacy of the Communist Party. Although communism was an imposed regime in Eastern Europe, and to some extent even in the Soviet Union, in China and Vietnam communism was and is closely associated with national liberation and national unity. The third factor is the degree of modernization in the country.

This brings us to the third point. Beyond Box 6 there cannot be an optimal path in transition from communism. All four regimes ran into difficult problems when they chose one of many alternative paths for extrication. Nevertheless, there is no guarantee that, had they chosen other alternatives, the transitional process would have been smoother and better. Having seen the state of affairs in the Soviet Union and Hungary, the Chinese and Vietnamese leaders may be justified for their adamant refusal to yield to the pressure for pluralization-democratization.

Fourth, this point also raises a question: is it possible for the communist system to make the transition at all? China and the Soviet Union seem to present two extreme prototypes. One may be able to argue that despite the Tiananmen massacre and its aftershock, China seems to be ahead of the transition game. It has managed to accomplish the decentralization process, and the retrenchment that followed Tiananmen Square has not undone the gains of decentralization. Economically as well as politically, China remains more stable than the Soviet Union. But by choosing too hasty political reform without the benefits of economic reform, the Soviet Union ended up destroying itself. With severe instability it is impossible to play the transition game. On the other hand, one could argue that the Chinese economic transition will not be successful without political reform. Only on the ashes of the completely destroyed communist political system can a genuine market economy be resurrected, some claim. The verdict is not in yet as to which argument is correct.

NOTES

1. See Vladimir Bukovsky, "Totalitarianism in Crisis: Is There a Smooth Transition to Democracy?" in Ellen Frankel Paul, ed., *Totalitarianism at the Crossroads* (New Brunswick and London: Transaction Books, 1990), pp. 9–30.
2. Giuseppe Di Palma, *To Craft Democracies: An Essay on Democratic Transitions* (Berkeley and Los Angeles: University of California Press, 1990); Giuseppe Di Palma, "Tran-

sitions: Puzzles and Surprises from West to East," a paper presented at the Conference of Europeanists, Washington, D.C., March 23–25, 1990.

3. Ibid.
4. F. A. Hayek, *Road to Serfdom* (London: Routledge & Kegan Paul, 1944; reprinted, 1979); and Roger Scruton, "Totalitarianism and the Rule of Law," in Paul, ed., *Totalitarianism at the Crossroads*, p. 172.
5. Hayek, *Road to Serfdom*, p. 5.
6. Ibid., p. 55.
7. According to Di Palma, democratization involves the following four aspects: the quality of the finished product, the mode of decision-making leading to the selection of rules and institutions, the type of craftsmen involved, and the timing and tempo imposed in the transition. Di Palma, *To Craft Democracies*, pp. 8–9. I will discuss all four aspects in the political transition from the communist system.
8. Guillermo O'Donnell and Philippe C. Schmitter, *Transitions from Authoritarian Rule: Tentative Conclusions About Uncertain Democracies* (Baltimore and London: Johns Hopkins University Press, 1986), p. 7.
9. Ibid., pp. 7–14; Richard Lowenthal, "On 'Established' Communist Regimes," *Studies in Comparative Communism* 7 (1974): 344–45.
10. Di Palma, *To Craft Democracies*, p. 154.
11. O'Donnell and Schmitter, *Transitions from Authoritarian Rule*, pp. 7–9.
12. Di Palma, *To Craft Democracies*, p. 82.
13. O'Donnell and Schmitter, *Transitions from Authoritarian Rule*, p. 37; see also Di Palma, *To Craft Democracies*, chap. 4, for three scenarios for *garantismo*.
14. O'Donnell and Schmitter, *Transitions from Authoritarian Rule*, p. 38.
15. Di Palma, *To Craft Democracies*, p. 56.
16. Ibid., pp. 56–57.
17. Ibid., pp. 83–84.
18. O'Donnell and Schmitter, *Transitions from Authoritarian Rule*, p. 57.
19. Di Palma, *To Craft Democracies*, pp. 17–18.
20. Ibid., pp. 19–20.
21. Ibid., p. 21.
22. Ibid., p. 36.
23. Ibid., p. 30.
24. Ibid., pp. 60–61.
25. This is precisely why A. Migranian and Igor Kliamkin advocated "iron hands" for marketization. See A. Migranian, "Dolgii put' k evropeiskomu domu," *Novyi mir*, no. 7 (July 1989), pp. 166–84; A. Migranian/I. Kliamkin discussion, "Nuzhna zheleznaia ruka," *Literaturnaia gazeta*, no. 33 (16 August 1989), p. 10, and Migranian's contribution to the round table discussion in "Zapadnaia demokratiia i problemy sovremennogo obshchestvennogo razvitiia: kruglyi stol 'ME i MO,' " *Mirovaia ekonomika i mezhdunarodnye otnosheniia*, no. 1 (1989), pp. 71–84. A similar argument finds an echo in China, where there emerged a theory of "new authoritarianism" among young technocrats, most notably Chen Yizi. See Kojima Tomoyuki, "Chūgoku kyōsantō: ittō dokusai no sonzoku to henyō," Iwanami kōza, *Gendai chūgoku*, 1, Nomura Kōichi, ed., *Gendai Chūgoku no seiji sekai* (Tokyo: Iwanami shoten, 1989), p. 137.
26. To underscore this point, it is sufficient to recall how the first national competitive election was held in Mongolia.
27. But a system with an authoritarian dictatorship and a market economy is possible. The differences between authoritarian dictatorship and communist dictatorship should be more precisely defined, but this requires another essay.
28. Di Palma, *To Craft Democracies*, p. 42.
29. Morita Tsuneo, *Hangarī kaikakushi* (Tokyo: Nihon hyōronsha, 1990), pp. 46–48. According to Tsuneaki Satō, four characteristics are important for the traditional Stalinist economy: (1) public ownership of means of production, (2) dictatorship of the Communist Party over politics and economy, (3) unitary hierarchical structure,

and (4) a command-planning economy. Satō Tsuneaki, "Keizai kaikaku no hikaku-ronteki kōsatsu," Iwanami kōza, *Gendai chūgoku*, 2, Yamauchi Kazuo, ed., *Chūgoku keizai no tenkan* (Tokyo: Iwanami shoten, 1989), p. 93.

30. O'Donnell and Schmitter emphasize the importance of "settling the past accounts" in transitions from authoritarianism. See O'Donnell and Schmitter, *Transitions from Authoritarian Rule*, pp. 28–32.

31. Judy Batt, *East Central Europe from Reform to Transformation* (London: The Royal Institute of International Affairs, Pinter Publishers, 1991), pp. 4–5.

32. Morita, *Hangarī kaikakushi*, pp. 65–73.

33. Satō, "Keizai kaikaku," p. 97.

34. Morita, *Hangarī kaikakushi*, pp. 80–100.

35. Satō, "Keizai kaikaku," pp. 97–100.

36. Batt, *East Central Europe*, p. 6.

37. Ibid., p. 7.

38. Ibid., p. 5.

39. Ibid., p. 6.

40. Ibid., p. 12.

41. Nomura Kōichi, "Gendai Chūgoku seiji no tenkai to dōtai," Nomura, ed., *Gendai chūgoku*, p. 42.

42. Yamauchi Kazuo, "Chūgoku keizai kindaika e no mosaku to tenbo," Yamauchi, ed., *Chūgoku keizai*, pp. 25–26.

43. See Nicholas Lardy's chapter in this volume.

44. Ibid.

45. Ibid.

46. Ibid.

47. Harry Harding, "China in the 1990s: Prospects for Internal Change," in *Analysis*, published by National Bureau of Asian and Soviet Research, no. 1 (September 1990):6. On China's political reforms, see Harry Harding, *China's Second Revolution: Reform After Mao* (Washington, D.C.: Brookings Institution, 1987), chap. 7.

48. Mōri Kazuko, "Seiji taisei no tokuchō to sono kaikaku," Nomura, ed., *Gendai chū-goku*, pp. 56, 85–86.

49. Kojima, "Chūgoku kyōsantō," pp. 98–99.

50. Mōri, "Seiji taisei," p. 87.

51. Ed A. Hewett, *Reforming the Soviet Economy: Equality Versus Efficiency* (Washington, D.C.: Brookings Institution, 1988).

52. See Ed A. Hewett and Victor H. Winston, eds., *Milestones in Glasnost and Perestroika: The Economy* (Washington, D.C.: Brookings Institution, 1991), part 1.

53. I disagree with Marshall Goldman and Merle Goldman, who argue that Gorbachev should have started his reform with privatization of agriculture. See Marshall I. Goldman and Merle Goldman, "Soviet and Chinese Economic Reform," *Foreign Affairs* 66 (1987/88): 551–73.

54. Hewett and Winston, eds., *Milestones: The Economy*, part 2.

55. Watanabe Toshio, *Ajia shin chōryū: nishi taiheiyō no dainamizumu to shakaishugi* (Tokyo: Chūkō shinsho, 1990), pp. 143–56; Vo Nhan Tri, *Vietnam's Economic Policy since 1975* (Singapore: Institute of Southeast Asian Studies, 1990), pp. 58–121.

56. Vo Nhan Tri, *Vietnam's Economic Policy*, pp. 106–7.

57. Ibid., pp. 132–33.

58. Watanabe, *Ajia shin chōryū*, pp. 156–65; Vo Nhan Tri, *Vietnam's Economic Policy*, pp. 162–69.

59. Vo Nhan Tri, *Vietnam's Economic Policy*, pp. 93, 112.

60. Ibid., pp. 187–93.

61. Ibid., pp. 199–200.

62. Ibid., p. 199.

63. Ibid., pp. 215–16.

64. Tsuboi Yoshiharu, "Betonamu: Doi moi to kokusai kankyō," *Sekai*, no. 7, 1991, p. 114; Michael Leifer and John Phipps, *Vietnam and Doi Moi: Domestic and International*

Dimensions of Reform, RIIA Discussion Papers, 35 (London: The Royal Institute of International Affairs, 1991), pp. 3–4.

65. Watanabe, *Ajia shin chōryū*, pp. 165–67; Tsuboi, "Betonamu," p. 114.

66. Tsuboi, "Betonamu," pp. 111–15; Leifer and Phipps, *Vietnam and Doi Moi*, pp. 4–5.

67. Tsuboi, "Betonamu," pp. 108–9. Also see Gerald Segal's chapter in this volume.

68. Leifer and Phipps, *Vietnam and Doi Moi*, p. 7.

69. Vo Nhan Tri, *Vietnam's Economic Policy*, p. 125.

70. Carlyle A. Thayer, "The Regularization of Politics: Continuity and Change in the Party's Central Committee, 1951–1986," in David G. Marr and Christine P. White, eds., *Postwar Vietnam: Dilemmas in Socialist Development* (Ithaca: Southeast Asia Program, Cornell University, 1988), pp. 177–94.

71. Leifer and Phipps, *Vietnam and Doi Moi*, p. 3.

72. Morita, *Hangarī kaikakushi*, p. 105.

73. Ibid., pp. 133–34.

74. Ieda Osamu, "Hangarī seiji kaikaku no kiseki to genjō, 1," *Mirai*, no. 282 (March 1990), pp. 5–6.

75. Morita, *Hangarī kaikakushi*, pp. 142–56; Ieda Osamu, "Hangarī no kaikaku," in Minamizuka Shingo and Miyajima Naoki, eds., *Tōō kaikaku* (Tokyo: Kōdansha, 1990), pp. 38–39.

76. Ieda, "Hangarī seiji kaikaku, 2," *Mirai*, no. 283 (April 1990), pp. 6–9.

77. Ieda, "Hangarī seiji kaikaku, 4," *Mirai*, no. 286 (July 1990), pp. 28–31.

78. Ieda, "Hangarī seiji kaikaku, 3," *Mirai*, no. 284 (May 1990), pp. 28–31.

79. Batt, *East Central Europe*, pp. 31–33.

80. Ibid., p. 34.

81. Ibid.

82. Ibid., pp. 35–36.

83. Ibid., p. 36.

84. Ibid., p. 37.

85. Ieda, "Hangarī no kaikaku," pp. 45–63; Batt, *East Central Europe*, p. 37.

86. Nomura, "Gendai Chūgoku seiji," pp. 42–45.

87. Mōri, "Seiji taisei no tokuchō," pp. 88–89.

88. Harding, "China in the 1990s," pp. 5–6.

89. Ibid., pp. 7–8.

90. O'Donnell and Schmitter, *Transitions from Authoritarian Rule*, p. 69.

91. For liberalization and democratization in perestroika, see Seweryn Bialer, ed., *Politics, Society and Nationality Inside Gorbachev's Russia* (Boulder, Colo.: Westview Press, 1989); Tsuyoshi Hasegawa and Alex Pravda, eds., *Perestroika: Soviet Domestic and Foreign Policies* (London: Sage Publications, 1990); Wada Haruki, *Peresutoroika: seika to kiki* (Tokyo: Iwanami shinsho, 1990); Ed A. Hewett and Victor H. Winston, eds., *Milestones in Glasnost and Perestroika: Politics and People* (Washington, D.C.: Brookings Institution, 1991); Hewett and Winston, eds., *Milestones: The Economy;* Michael E. Urban, *More Power to the Soviets: The Democratic Revolution in the USSR* (Hants, England, 1990); and Thomas Remington's chapter in this volume.

92. See Urban, *More Power to the Soviets;* Hewett and Winston, eds., *Milestones: Politics and People*, part 3.

93. Seweryn Bialer, "The Changing Soviet Political System: The Nineteenth Party Conference and After," in Bialer, ed., *Politics, Society, and Nationality*, pp. 193–240; Ed A. Hewett with Thane Gustafson and Victor H. Winston, "The 19th Party Conference," in Hewett and Winston, eds., *Milestones: Politics and People*, pp. 112–31; Jerry F. Hough, "The Politics of the 19th Party Conference," in Hewett and Winston, eds., *Milestones: Politics and People*, pp. 132–38; Urban, *More Power to the Soviets*, pp. 15–34.

94. For the national and local elections, see Urban, *More Power to the Soviets*, pp. 89–162; Jerry F. Hough, "The Politics of Successful Economic Reform," in Hewett and Winston, eds., *Milestones: Politics and People*, pp. 246–86; Timothy J. Colton, "The Mos-

cow Election of 1990," in Hewett and Winston, *Milestones: Politics and People*, pp. 326–81.

95. Tsuyoshi Hasegawa, "Perestroika in Historical Perspective: Reevaluation," in Takayuki Ito, ed., *The World Confronts Perestroika: The Challenge to East Asia* (Sapporo: Hokkaido University Press, 1991), pp. 225–62.

96. Di Palma, *To Craft Democracies*, chap. 6. For nationality problems, see Gail W. Lapidus, "Gorbachev and the 'National Question,'" in Hewett and Winston, eds., *Milestones: Politics and People*, pp. 190–237.

97. Ed A. Hewett, "The New Soviet Plan," *Foreign Affairs* 69, no. 5 (Winter 1990/91): 151.

98. See Hewett and Winston, eds., *Milestones: The Economy*, part 4.

99. O'Donnell and Schmitter, *Transitions from Authoritarian Rule*, pp. 38–39, 71–72; Di Palma, *To Craft Democracies*, pp. 56–57.

100. Tsuboi, "Betonamu," pp. 106–7.

101. Leifer and Phipps, *Vietnam and Doi Moi*, p. 15.

102. Ibid., p. 11.

103. Ibid., p. 16; Tsuboi, "Betonamu," p. 116.

104. Leifer and Phipps, *Vietnam and Doi Moi*, pp. 8–10.

105. Ibid., p. 13.

106. Ibid., p. 15.

107. Tsuboi Yoshiharu, "Betonamu dokuji no shakaishugi wa kanōka," *On the Line*, no. 12 (December 1991): 10.

108. O'Donnell and Schmitter, *Transitions from Authoritarian Rule*, pp. 15–16.

109. Ibid., p. 16.

110. Seweryn Bialer distinguishes bureaucratic resistance from conservative opposition. Seweryn Bialer, "The Changing Soviet Political System," pp. 199–203. I use the term "conservatives" for Bialer's former group, and "reactionaries" in the latter sense.

111. O'Donnell and Schmitter, *Transitions from Authoritarian Rule*, p. 16.

112. Lowenthal, "On 'Established' Communist Party Regimes," p. 347.

113. Batt, *East Central Europe*, pp. 90–91.

114. Ibid., pp. 92–94.

115. "Recipe for Market Economy Hasn't Served up Recovery," *Los Angeles Times*, 25 January 1992.

116. "Russia's VP Slams Yeltsin's Economic Policy," *Los Angeles Times*, 9 February 1992; "Yeltsin Deputy Calls Reforms 'Economic Genocide,'" *New York Times*, 9 February 1992.

117. "Russia Outlines a Program To Sell State-Owned Shops," *New York Times*, 8 February 1992.

118. *Nihon Keizai Shimbun*, 3 June 1991.

119. Leifer and Phipps, *Vietnam and Doi Moi*, p. 16; Tsuboi, "Betonamu," p. 116.

120. Tsuboi, "Betonamu dokuji no shakaishugi," pp. 12–13.

II

REGIONAL VARIATIONS: CHINA, THE SOVIET UNION, AND ASIA

3

Reform, Revolution, and Regime Transition in the Soviet Union

Thomas F. Remington

How do regimes cross the threshold from communism to democracy? The extraordinary transformation of world politics in the late 1980s and early 1990s poses major questions about the circumstances under which some communist systems collapse and give way to successor regimes, while others persist in stubborn isolation. Why do some regimes undergo crisis only to emerge under a new dictatorship and others yield to democratic institutions? Are there any centripetal forces short of force majeur that can check the powerful urge of ethno-national communities to secede under conditions of freedom? The Soviet case—or rather, cases—may shed light on these questions. Although the region continues to change profoundly and rapidly, the botched coup d'état of August 1991 and its revolutionary aftermath served as a catalyst for events that had been waiting to happen: the dissolution of the former union and its replacement by fifteen independent nation-states groping for new forms of relationships among themselves.

In this chapter I shall discuss the relationship of reform to revolution in communist systems, with particular reference to the transformation of Soviet politics. By "reform" I mean changes in policy and authority relations that leave the two essential features of communist rule intact: the leading role of the single party and state ownership of the major means of production. "Revolution," on the other hand, is so sweeping a change in the structure of power and property that the communist regime itself surrenders. It is, therefore, equivalent to the notion of regime transition.

My argument, briefly, is as follows. Under Mikhail Gorbachev the communist leadership in the Soviet Union initiated reforms that liberalized political life. The government tolerated the expression of demands and grievances that had been generated by the long-term processes of social and economic change. These include a peculiar and explosive combination of modernization and system decay. In turn, liberalization—specifically glasnost and demokratizatsiia—led to a mobilization of popular demands for deeper change. The outcome of the challenge to the ruling elite depended on the interaction of three factors: whether leaders were willing to share power with the opposition, the organization of popular social movements, and the referent national community. Since associational life outside the state is a good deal stronger at subcentral levels than across the union as a whole, the most intense confrontation between state and society has occurred at the level of the union republics and subrepublican jurisdictions, where the outcomes have been very diverse in their regime character, but alike in their aspiration for national independence. In turn, the struggle over republican rights prompted a search for a new framework for the union. Agreement on a radically decentralizing union treaty was followed by a counterreaction (a brief and unsuccessful putsch), which was followed by the rapid dissolution of nearly all political bonds uniting the republics in a union. Agreement between Yeltsin and President Kravchuk of Ukraine in December 1991 produced a framework for a new form of association falling well short of statehood but preserving unified control of the Soviet strategic arsenal.

The extraordinary events in the communist world in the late 1980s and early 1990s can be understood, in a Hegelian spirit, as the transformation of quantity into quality. That is, the consequences of deep reform spilled out into political change that could not be contained within the existing Communist Party–state system. In China the regime had not tolerated a sufficient political liberalization to allow the forces of popular opposition to raise the "costs of repression" so high that they outweighed the "costs of tolerance," in the famous formulation advanced by Robert Dahl and developed in recent regime transition literature.[1] Elsewhere in the communist sphere, however, the weakening and division of the ruling elite, coupled with the pressure of organized popular opposition movements, resulted in revolutionary overthrows of communist power. How, then, did reform lead to revolution?

In the 1980s, several communist regimes initiated deep reform programs. Some emphasized economic reform over political reform; others coupled the two.[2] Hungary's government resumed the push for implementation of the New Economic Mechanism (NEM) first adopted in 1968, and it combined this with modest steps toward democratization in the political system.[3] In China, beginning with the December plenum in 1978, the regime actively encouraged commercial enterprise in agriculture, trade and services, and to some extent in industry. Then it fought to contain popular demands for political reform.[4] Yugoslavia adopted a new campaign for market reform in 1982. Poland's government sought popular approval for a program of radical economic reform through a national referendum in 1987, but popular mistrust for the authorities (Solidarity was not legalized until early in 1989) prevented the issue from receiving the two-thirds vote required to carry it. In 1985, following the successive deaths of three ailing leaders, an exceptionally young and energetic leader was elected general secretary of the party in the Soviet Union. Initially Gorbachev was dedicated to a broad-gaged program of "acceleration" of economic progress through fairly traditional measures (stepped up investment, more foreign trade, improved labor incentives, more reliance on "economic" levers, and technical innovation). In time he embraced more radical positions, and by 1990 he had eliminated the Communist Party's monopoly on power. By shifting the government to a presidential system, he tried to preserve a measure of central control over policy amid a worsening breakdown of the system.[5]

These reforms and their outcomes strongly influenced one another. The member states of the former communist sphere were closely connected not only through organizations such as the Warsaw Pact and Council for Mutual Economic Assistance, but also because of the traditionally powerful forces of mutual awareness and diffusion of ideological influences among them. For this reason, we cannot treat these reform initiatives as entirely independent events. Above all, the radicalization of perestroika in the Soviet Union created ultimately irresistible pressures for democratization in Eastern Europe. One reason was external: the removal of "Brezhnev-doctrine" constraints on Eastern Europe through Gorbachev's new effort at partnership with the West. The other reason was internal: the demonstration effect of democratization in the Soviet Union on populations in the region. By 1989 efforts by communist regimes to reach negotiated compromises on power-sharing with opposition forces had proved futile in every case. By the end of the decade, the wave of economic and political reform in the communist world had been overtaken by a revolution: the collapse of the communist system itself, both as a bloc of states and as a regime type. To be sure, the outcome of the changes occurring in the Soviet regime remained cloudy. China's regime clung to a repressive and orthodox position. Bulgaria was governed by a renamed version of the Communist Party and Romania by a group of ex-communists. Peripheral members of the system such as Cuba, North Korea, and Vietnam had not yet followed the example of the regimes in the core. Nonetheless, the pressure for regime transition from communist rule brought about a full collapse of the communist model throughout Europe.

This chapter will discuss the relationship of reform to regime transition in communist systems, particularly the Soviet case. By "regime transition" I mean change in a communist regime's political system such that the Communist Party no longer holds a monopoly over political functions—ideological dominance of communications and culture, elite recruitment via the nomenklatura power, and policy making. Under the structural configuration common to communist regimes, social change (change defined as modernization, as well as change associated with reverse modernization or decay) produces powerful counterpressures that block successful reform. Reform is swallowed up in bureaucratic routine, producing little if any useful effect, or it generates strong popular opposition movements mobilized against the power and privilege of the communist political elite itself. The outcome of the regime transition process is a function of the three factors discussed earlier: the willingness of a regime to grant political liberties to independent groups, the density of social pluralism, and the nature of the referent political community for social groups.

REFORM AS MANAGED CHANGE

Scholars differ over the degree to which communist institutional arrangements can adapt to demands for change arising from the domestic and international environments. Because of the complementarity of their political and economic structures, reform in communist regimes, some argue, tends to be either too feeble to achieve the desired breakthrough to a self-sustaining condition of rising productivity and living standards, or else it allows the burden of accumulated frustrations and resentments in society to turn a limited opening in the political system into a general mobilization and radicalization of society. This school of thought therefore argues that communist regimes cannot be reformed, but only destroyed. Another school asserts that long-term processes of social change—rising levels of educational attainment, urbanization, communications, and diffusion of professional qualifications—have created irresistible pressures for democratization of the political regime. Clearly, an adequate theory of transition must take into account the degree to which communist political institutions can adapt to pluralism, party competition, and the rule of law, as well as the long-term changes in social attitudes and values associated with modernization. Elsewhere I deal with the interaction of these factors in more detail.[6]

Observers such as Martin Malia (in his "Z" article) and others are correct: Communist institutions are ultimately incapable of accommodating the explosion of participatory demands that follow a liberalization of political rights.[7] The only choice is surrender to the opposition or suppression of the opposition. The important question for understanding the course and outcome of the transition process is the character of political demands that the opposition movements raise, and this depends upon the way in which social factors such as leadership, values, and interpersonal trust are distributed. These influence whether democracy or some noncommunist form of bureaucratic or military authoritarianism results from the transition process. The greater the social pluralism under the ancien regime (meaning the more the society is bound by ties of solidarity and mutual constraint), the faster is the spread of organized opposition when the crisis occurs, and the less likely is violence and disorder.

The confrontation between regime and society reinforces popular antagonism toward established political authority, and specifically toward the ruling elite. In some cases alienation is linked strongly with the assertion of ethnic-national claims; in others, with labor or regional demands. For this reason, it is necessary to know the referent political community—whether loyalty is focused upon the larger state or upon particular ethnic-national or territorial identities within the state. Always, however, the popular movement protests the concentration of power in the communist political elite, and therefore it rejects power-sharing pacts between the opposition and the regime except as temporary expedients. This phenomenon is, in part, the consequence of the distribution of power and privilege in communist society. It is also a reflection of social decay, including growing structural imbalances between occupational qualifications and the labor market, worsening corruption, and the consequences of wasteful and destructive strategies of industrialization.

My analysis of the Soviet case is congruent with Tatsumi Okabe's analysis of reform in China.[8] That is, pressure for national modernization motivated ruling elites in each state to undertake deep economic reform. In each, economic reform produced pressures for deep political reform, partly in reaction to the inequities produced by market-oriented reform in a state socialist economy. Economic liberalization releases severe inflation and nurtures a corrupt "nomenklatura capitalism" in which political elites devise ways to collect rents through their monopoly control of state property, thus converting "power into money." And in each case, the limited political opening granted for the articulation of demands quickly produced pressures that threatened the regime's ability to manage the process of change. In the Soviet Union the new political movements that were most dangerous for Gorbachev were those that took power in the union republics. In China, where political integration between nation and state is greater but social modernization less advanced, pressure for change took the form of an intelligentsia-led democracy movement in Beijing and other cities. In both systems the disjunction between economic and political reform was a consequence of the structural inability of communist regimes to carry out successful reform and simultaneously preserve communist rule. As Professor Okabe further notes, the military in China is the only organizational structure (other than the party) that can integrate the nation, and it may at some point replace the party as the ruling force in the state. Gorbachev's turn for support to the KGB, military, and economic bureaucracy in the fall of 1990 had perilous consequences, as the violence in Vilnius and Riga in January and the miners' strikes in March demonstrated. Then when he turned for support to the union republics and agreed with them on the terms of a new treaty of union that would conclusively dismantle the central governing structures of the old union, it was precisely these forces that struck back in an astonishingly clumsy effort to restore the old order. A counterreaction by the combined forces of republican nationalism and popular democratic liberalism followed.

MODERNIZATION AND POLITICAL CHANGE

Many scholars have argued that, in the long run, democratization is implicit in the logic of modernization. Usually they view change in political institutions as a function of long-term processes in the social and international environments of the political system. Political elites have little direct control over these processes and in the end must accept them. Although there may be a temporal lag before political structures catch up with qualitative social changes, and some resistance to the inevitable loss of control which they entail, regimes must bow to the impersonal forces of history. For the Soviet Union, these include urbanization, education, professionalization, and communications.

Eighty percent rural at the time of the revolution, Soviet society was 66 percent urban in 1990. Between 1950 and 1980 the urban population rose by 100 million people. This change broke down many of the attachments and norms associated with village society, and it had, on balance, two effects: individualism increased and large-scale, impersonal social associations grew. Psychologically, urbanization awakens individual and group aspirations, expectations, and identities that in the aggregate can have enormous political power.

Soviet society also experienced a striking rise in educational attainments over the seven decades of communist rule. By 1987 half of the Soviet population over ten years of age had a secondary education (the same as the proportion for the United States), and 9 percent had a higher education (nearly the U.S. rate).

Occupational structure was transformed, particularly through the rapid increase in the number of individuals employed in professional and specialist occupations. Before the war not quite 1 million specialists with higher education were employed in the economy; by 1970 there were close to 7 million, and nearly 10 million with specialized secondary education. Of these the number of engineers with higher education increased from not quite 300,000 to nearly 2.5 million. Technical personnel more than doubled their share of a fast-growing stratum, the group with specialized secondary education, increasing from 324,000 out of one and one-half million, to 4.3 million out of nearly 10 million.[9] We can add to these "industrial" categories of specialists two other very rapidly growing groups, those employed in science (whose numbers roughly quadrupled in the 1960s and 1970s to 1.3 million by 1980) and the group made up of planners, economists, and statisticians (who increased their ranks sixfold over the same period and numbered 3 million by 1980).[10]

Access to the media of communications, including print media and radio and television broadcasting, became universal. This includes state-sponsored media and many forms of communication outside state control, such as foreign radio broadcasting and the private circulation of tapes of favorite musicians as well as the unfalteringly powerful circuits of interpersonal face-to-face conversation. Television, the cinema, and videotapes conveyed visual impressions of life to a formerly isolated population, while travel to and from the Soviet Union diffused direct impressions of the contrast between life "here" and "there."

Analysts have identified the qualitative changes generated by modernization. Above all, they stress the profound change in popular expectations and in the capacity for organized collective action. Where once society could be ruled through great hierarchies of state power, the differentiation of identities brought about by social development required the state to establish a less unequal relationship with society. The revolution built a state that commanded society as if it were permanently at war, calling forth sacrifice and faith from the populace and enforcing its power with ruthless force. But the postwar decades of peace and slowly accumulating fruits of modernization subverted this model and demanded the political accommodation of new interests and loyalties. An urban, educated, and increasingly self-directed society was capable of forming autonomous social structures with distinct interests that sought outlets on the political plane. Demands for political expression and for a standard of living resembling that of the developed societies in the West created a constituency for democratic and market-oriented reform larger than many in the West imagined.[11] Moshe Lewin, Fred Starr, Blair Ruble, and other writers have noted that as vertical structures of command, control, and indoctrination weakened, forces of individualism, competitiveness, and acquisitiveness gained strength. In addition, resilient communities of independent opinion and action emerged. Simplifying slightly, we can describe interpretations in this vein as a theory of political change emphasizing the consolidation of a civil society that was brought about through modernization. Gilbert Rozman observes that "economic modernization normally brings with it a civil society."[12]

To dramatize the social-psychological effect of modernization on the Soviet population during the past seventy years, Jerry Hough compared the Russian Revolution of 1917 with the Nazi movement (and with Khomeini's revolution in Iran) in its nativist rejection of pluralist, secular, and democratic influences from the global civilization spreading from the West. He argued that the early effects of industrialization in Russia created fear and disorientation among the newly urban and semi-urbanized workers, many of whom still retained strong ties to village society and the rural culture. They responded to an extremist revolutionary movement that closed Russia off to the economic and political development of the West. Now, however, social change has reduced the insecurities associated with early industrialization. As Hough put it, "the lives of today's youth in a large Soviet city are far closer to the lives of the young in a large American city than to that of their great-grandparents in a rural Russian village."[13] These changes and the incipient consolidation of autonomous social structures created a constituency for democratic government.

But there are problems with the theory of civil society. The social changes identified are long term, slow, and incremental, whereas political change has been rapid, spasmodic, and indeterminate. The theory excludes the influence of the international environment: the enervating drain on national resources of the arms race, the increasing cost of disastrous experiments in socialism in distant lands; and the dismaying economic success of Japan, Korea, and other rising powers of the Asian-Pacific rim.

Most simply, the theory of a rising civil society fails to offer an adequate account of politics. It neglects, for example, the degree to which leadership—its methods, style, and goals—may independently determine the timing and outcome of reform. As Rozman reminds us in his survey of the factors influencing reform in socialist systems, and as George Breslauer has argued in proposing a model of "transformational leadership" under Gorbachev, reform programs require reform leaders.[14] The leadership factor, however, is only one way in which the civil society theory understates the autonomy of politics in the transition. Another is the problem of the complex, mutually dependent relationship between organized collective action outside the state, where face-to-face ties remain the dominant form of association, and the vast domain of the state's decaying but still powerful bureaucratic structures. This factor is especially critical in communist societies where national territories are constituent members of a federal state structure. The administrative segmentation of state and other official organizations along national-territorial lines makes it especially difficult for independent social movements to organize throughout the federal union. The single most potent social cleavage for mobilizing the masses is the identification of ethnic nationalities with "homeland" territories.

Beyond nationality cleavages, however, independent forms of social association are far weaker and smaller in scale than are the great hierarchically ordered agencies of the state, which cling to their monopolistic powers and privileges. The political consequences of the sea change in popular expectations and demands, the moral bankruptcy of Leninist ideology, and the shift of attention to the West as defining the reasonable living standards of a normal, civilized society were complicated by the enormous difficulty of forming independent means of action. Old class lines were largely erased, civic values forgotten, and organizational resources scarce and closely held by state bodies. In reality it was extremely difficult for any of the autonomous, self-organizing associations of society—formed around professional, national, civic, charitable, fraternal or other axes of common interest—to gain the independence and cohesiveness that would characterize a civil society.

In short, the civil society hypothesis gives too little attention to important political structures such as leadership and the continuing power of the state to deny resources to groups outside it. It must be supplemented with an account of the gulf separating rulers from ruled. Otherwise one tends to overlook the depth of popular alienation from the elite and to overestimate the ability of the Communist Party to accommodate civil society rather than to surrender to it. This, indeed, is a problem in the interpretation provided by Moshe Lewin. He predicted that the one-party system would survive because "the party is the main stabilizer of the political system." The party, he claimed, "is the only institution that can preside over the overhaul of the system without endangering the polity itself in the process."[15] No Communist Party has succeeded in democratizing itself and preserving its power at the same time. Above all, the civil society theory must be revised to take account of the power of primordial attachments of blood and soil in filling the normative vacuum in society during a time of the breakdown and transformation of communist regimes.

COMMUNICATING VESSELS

The unpredictable, errant course of political change in communist systems—liberal openings followed by floods of protest or by relapses to orthodoxy—and the trend in communist economies to exhaust their capacity for "extensive" growth illustrate the impossibility of identifying a linear correlation between modernization in the socioeconomic realm and liberalization in the political sphere. No theory of modernization can define with any degree of probability the point at which a given level of modernization makes political liberalization necessary or even likely. The reverse relationship, liberalization as facilitator of modernization, also remains complex. Clearly, political relaxation in the post-Stalin phases of the Soviet and East European economies did release new energies that spurred growth, but they could not sustain it.

As a result, most hypotheses about the relationship between variations in modernization and variations in political transition tend to be crude and unsatisfying. Neither Poland nor Hungary was the most modernized of communist states, but they were the first to institute power-sharing arrangements between communist rulers and the organized opposition. These are the two societies in communist Europe that are the most ethnically homogeneous and that have highest concentration of population in urban centers. (One-fifth of Hungary's population lives in Budapest; one-ninth of Poland's population lives in the seven largest cities.) Presumably, these factors help explain the cohesiveness of political opposition groups and the inability of the old regime to suppress them. Much as Dankwart Rustow pointed out twenty years ago, national unity, in the sense of the established identity of the relevant political community, is a crucial factor in producing a democratic outcome.[16] At any given level of modernization, the critical condition determining the likelihood that transition will result in democracy is the degree to which the opposition can raise the costs to the regime of suppressing it; these costs are higher to the extent that the opposition is well organized, normatively cohesive, and successful in rallying popular support.

Modernization in communist societies has also been overtaken by processes of decline and stagnation. The two best-documented indexes of these problems are economic growth rates, which have showed a secular tendency toward decline, and mortality and morbidity rates, which in many cases began to rise in the mid- to late-1960s after regimes' early successes in improving public health standards. Less readily measured, of course, are the hidden aspects of decay: the loss of social morale; the rise of criminality, deviance, apathy, and cynicism; the growth of corruption among party and state officials; and the widening difference in living standards between those whose political and social status entitled them to perquisites and those for whom perquisites were inaccessible. Glasnost in the Soviet Union revealed harsh and demoralizing truths about these trends. It fueled popular antagonism toward persons who were abusing the system for their own benefit.

Let us posit a simple model of the relationship between processes of change in the social and political spheres, supposing them to form two loosely coupled subsystems: polity and society. Soviet discussions sometimes use the metaphor of "communicating vessels," which is an apt image for our model. Each subsystem is relatively but not wholly self-contained; each preserves and reproduces itself through time and in interaction with the other. Problems in each accumulate and spill over to affect the performance of the other. Radical political reform, such as that undertaken by Gorbachev, is explained by the accumulation of unresolved social and political problems that undermine the regime's power and spur it to intervene in society to set matters right: to accelerate economic growth and restore public morale and confidence, to revitalize the instruments of central control over social resources. Even before Gorbachev's accession to power, the same pressures led to the futile 1979 campaign to resurrect Marxist-Leninist ideology, as well as to the 1985–86 campaign under Gorbachev to accelerate scientific-technical progress.

In the social sphere the state's inability to overcome the Stalinist pattern of administered society led to a number of compensatory trends that preserved social stability at the expense of the system's capacity for development. Often these undermined administrative controls over the production and distribution of values. For example, the tendencies of state enterprises and organizations to become autonomous, self-contained systems intensified. A few huge and often monopolistic enterprises took on the responsibility of providing their employees with food, cars, housing, education, and many other benefits unavailable through the state's distribution channels. Inevitably, the surrounding towns and regions became dependent upon these enterprises to satisfy a variety of social needs. Ministries became giant fiefdoms. By creating their own internal functional units, they took control of nominally centralized functions such as planning, research, and material supply.

The aspiration for self-sufficiency also was manifest in extrasystemic and countersystemic behavioral patterns. Corrupt syndicates developed in various regions among the established leadership. Systems for distributing hierarchically ranked hidden privileges to the elite flourished. Currents of intellectual and cultural life emerged in opposition to the state's dogmatic insistence on Marxism-Leninism. Certainly not all of the processes of social change and development were sociopathic, nor were all relations between regime and populace antagonistic. But over time, tendencies toward rationalization and mutual accommodation between society and polity were overtaken by forms of reciprocal parasitism that sapped national power and purpose. Perhaps the clearest illustration of the problem is in the economy, which proved unable to escape its "treadmill" dilemma: Simply to maintain the same level of output took ever larger increments of inputs. In effect, the Brezhnev system was robbing the future for the sake of preserving its present.

In each of the communicating vessels of society and polity, some of the effects of decay exceeded tolerable thresholds and spilled over into the other vessel, disturbing its normal functioning. Compensatory but dysfunctional patterns of behavior in the system of economic production and distribution, like the similar compensatory but dysfunctional phenomena in the normative sphere such as dissent and social anomie, eroded the political system's ability to maintain its power. The political leadership, and particularly the echelon immediately below its sclerotic senior command, could not ignore these problems indefinitely and responded with reforms. But the atrophy of central power, on which the cohesion of the economy's administration depended, doomed reform to failure as new initiatives, when they were implemented by the bureaucracies they were intended to weaken, sputtered out and died. Reform therefore reinforced the leakage of resources in channels of private and often corrupt activity. At a certain threshold, then, society and polity held each other hostage. The effort expended by the Brezhnev-Suslov team in 1979, for example, failed to make any observable dent in the deterioration of the social fabric; perhaps nothing short of a new era of totalitarian terror could have resuscitated socialist centralism. Yet the signals of breakdown, although jammed by the impoverished systems of feedback and control that the center disposed of, did reach the center; Yuri Andropov's short-lived discipline campaign suggests that some of the state's agencies were less affected by the society's decay than were others. But the recognition of crisis in a highly bureaucratized environment is subject to many competing forces. The culture of bureaucracy, as Mary Douglas and Aaron Wildavsky have shown, works systematically to induce officials to underestimate the urgency of problems.[17]

How would a Soviet leader or an outside observer be able to identify with reasonable confidence that point in the decay of the system at which negative feedback between polity and society would reach terminal crisis—the social equivalent of biological death? Any such judgment would be subjective because it depends considerably on how much hardship the populace is willing to tolerate. In 1985 some Soviet leaders evidently believed that the system—to survive—needed a more thorough political overhaul than their predecessors in office had been willing or able to carry out. Is this fanciful speculation? The Soviet leadership, after all, was only seventy years removed from a fierce revolution that tore society apart along every imaginable line of cleavage—class, political, regional, national. At what point, Soviet leaders must often have wondered, might accumulated social tension not suddenly give way to some new explosion of generalized revolutionary fury? It came as a shock, writes Anatolii Sobchak about his electoral campaign in Leningrad in 1989 when he ran for USSR deputy, to discover people's "burning discontent with literally everything—life, work, leadership, hospitals, stores with empty shelves, lies, etc. . . . And this despite the fact that the liberal Soviet intelligentsia was always used to thinking that it understood the people."[18]

Here, however, the obstacles to communication between the two vessels of polity and society constrained the leaders' ability to reverse deeply entrenched processes of social change. The leaders found that the structures protecting them from popular opposition left them helpless to carry out meaningful reform. The pressure for new policies needed to become very strong before it spilled over and affected social behavior. For example, a change of slogans or one more ideological campaign was patently inadequate to rally the populace to new banners. Yet it is difficult to imagine Gorbachev or any leader in his place beginning with anything other than a rather conventional reform program. The political system's well-established structures of political recruitment and advancement selected out truly radical leaders long before they reached the pinnacle of power. Moreover, even a reform-minded new leader was obliged to deal with the collective opinion of the senior party leadership. Gorbachev's appeals for "acceleration" of growth by placing renewed emphasis on modern technology and especially computers, his ambitious investment and growth targets adopted by the Twenty-Seventh Party Congress in 1986, his purge of the political elite, his efforts to improve consumer goods and the quality of life, his anti-alcohol campaign, and his overtures to the Western world all found their analogues in reform programs under Nikita Khrushchev and Leonid Brezhnev. And those reforms had roughly the same overall impact: a certain halo effect that produced a one-time rise in economic growth, followed by a return to the status quo.

Certainly the glasnost campaign was comparable to similar phases of greater tolerance for frank and critical expression launched under Khrushchev and, to a certain extent, under Andropov. Glasnost under Gorbachev, however, was soon joined to a campaign for "democratization," which began in January 1987. Pressure from above for fuller and freer speech permitted the voicing of grievances generated by the accumulation of social changes—both those that had increased the educated, self-aware, and articulate strata and those that had fostered new social antagonism toward the regime and its rulers and had preserved the memory of older injustices. These, of course, would ultimately reach thresholds threatening Gorbachev's control over the very process of reform.

The notion of communicating vessels is, of course, a gross simplification of reality. A vast and intricate web of relations connects all events in the social and political realms, and the division of the two into separate compartments and the idea of levels of organization of each are only analytic constructs designed to help reveal order and regularity in the way society behaves. An individual event may have an enormous impact on society, but it may be the product of incalculably long chains of chance and contingency. A war, an accident, even a work of art may have effects for years after its occurrence, but to "explain" its origins may require so complex a model of interactions as to defy the imagination.

The Chernobyl disaster in April 1986 illustrates many of the systemic features of Soviet society under the ancien regime. The failure of the nuclear reactor at the Chernobyl plant can be blamed on a host of factors: negligence concerning safety standards in industry, the siting of dangerous facilities close to densely populated regions, and the instinct to conceal unwelcome information; but more important for our purposes are the effects of Chernobyl on the political system. The accident occurred at a point when glasnost was identified as one of the desiderata of Gorbachev-era policy, but was very weakly rooted in the practice of the mass media or official bodies, and shortly before the "democratization" campaign officially encouraged a certain amount of grass-roots political mobilization. Chernobyl thus became one of the most powerful stimuli for popular environmental and national movements in the Ukraine and Belorussia. The magnitude of the disaster, which authorities long tried to minimize and distort, and the ineptitude and inadequacy of the response gave opposition leaders a rallying cry for their demands. One Belorussian writer compared the long-term effects of Chernobyl to "a time-bomb affecting the gene pool of an entire people," while another compared the destruction caused by Chernobyl to the decimation of Belorussia by the Nazis.[19] These comments were scarcely exaggerating the scope of the accident. The release of radiation at Chernobyl exposed some 17 million people to some contamination. The government's slowness in responding and refusal to provide full and accurate information fueled severe popular mistrust toward the government at a time when it began to be possible to express mistrust publicly. This event therefore illustrates the pattern characteristic of transition periods in which a limited, controlled opening from above— in this case, liberalized opportunities for the articulation of griev- ances—produces a radicalization of opinion and more alienation from the regime.

Although Chernobyl is perhaps the single most important "shock- event" of the glasnost period, many similar cases can be cited, including the rise of an antinuclear testing movement linked to national self- awareness in Kazakhstan; the political-cum-environmental protest in Bashkiria that ousted the Communist Party ruling group in early 1990; the rise of popular front movements in the Baltic republics; the envi- ronmental (including antinuclear) mass protest in Armenia in late 1987 that led to large-scale mobilization against the mistreatment of Arme- nians in Karabakh and other parts of Azerbaijan; and the democratic protests in over a dozen large cities of the Russian Republic in February and March 1990.

Labor protests also fit the pattern of local environmental grievances becoming larger and more radical programmatic movements. Before their summer 1989 strikes, coal miners in the Donets Basin had been alarmed at the buildup of toxic wastes in the groundwaters of the region. Their demands had gone unheeded by the authorities.[20] Environmental degradation in addition to anger over housing conditions, food short- ages, and appalling work conditions sparked the massive strike of July 1989. By March 1991, when a new wave of miners' strikes swept the coal mining regions of the Donbass, Kuzbass, Vorkuta, and Karaganda, labor's demands included the resignation of President Gorbachev, the dissolution of the Cabinet and Supreme Soviet, and transfer of power to the Soviet of the Federation. Therefore, it is hard to distinguish labor from environmental or ethno-national causes of opposition in commu- nist societies. A system in which economic and political powers are fused in a single political elite produces a general sense of alienation from and resentment toward power. Environmental, labor, national, and other streams of protest converge.

In analyzing the social structure of Soviet society, some observers speak of a new middle class made up of the millions of recipients of higher or specialized secondary education. This concept obscures more than it clarifies. Protest, as expressed in the rallies and strikes that have become prevalent since 1987–88, has a populist character although much of its leadership is drawn from the intelligentsia. The results of the elections of 1989 and 1990, which above all resulted in a repudiation in many localities of the most visible representatives of the old establishment, showed the broad base of support enjoyed by the democratic insurgents. The working class clearly demonstrated its willingness to support the intelligentsia in a common offensive against the entrenched political class. Indeed, polls suggested that this centuries-old gulf was at its narrowest in Russian history.

In one sense it is possible to distinguish a "new middle class" in Soviet society according to *consumption* criteria, that is, as the beneficiaries of certain social privileges and opportunities that the regime offered, such as education and a measure of consumer well-being. Middle-class *aspirations* were present in the strong desire for a Western middle-class living standard. In fact, though, the forces breaking down class boundaries were stronger than those forming them. Millions with specialized secondary and tertiary degrees have moved into intermediate, skilled-manual jobs that were once the exclusive province of the graduate of vocational and technical schools. Others have become, in effect, self-employed, or have moved into the service sphere. The social distinction that once came with a higher education or specialized secondary education has been devalued. The economy is unable to absorb the continuing flow of new graduates into the work force. Wages of engineering, technical, and lower managerial personnel lag behind the wages of skilled manual workers. And the cleavage between rulers and ruled overshadowed other lines of social differentiation as the most politically promising members of each stratum were recruited to serve as political activists on behalf of the regime.[21] Political activism, in turn, was a channel facilitating social mobility, but for those choosing to identify themselves with the regime, a certain gap inevitably began to emerge (both in social awareness and in the enjoyment of material and immaterial privileges) between those coopted into the party's penumbra and those outside it. The relative clarity and visibility of this political cleavage owe as much to the amorphousness of social structure outside it as they do to any internal cohesiveness or common consciousness of those referred to as the "nomenklatura."

The fundamental flaw in the theory of the new middle class lies in the fact that it identifies the class by its consumption of social benefits (usually higher education) rather than by its relationship to the sphere of production. The virtual absence until the last two or three years of a labor market outside the state sphere left all equally dependent upon the state and its rulers for benefits and privileges, and stratification lines described intricate hierarchies of status and prestige according to education, gender, nationality, and political affiliations. Without a working market for capital, class relations are defined by the state's monopoly on all resources for determining every individual's career chances. Proximity to the party's own officialdom created the most meaningful status cleavage: that between those with power and those without it. To be sure, this was not a clear or distinct boundary in practice since many people occupied positions entailing only elementary political clearance and conferring only minimal, and readily rationalized, privileges, and only a few were full-time political elites. But the pervasiveness and universality of the party-state's influence over the distribution of social advantages created a strong and widespread resentment of those exercising that power. Everyone had some experience with the political elite; everyone had to make certain choices about how closely tied to it he or she wished to become. Without the goodwill of the state, it was difficult to enjoy most kinds of social benefits—whether that was the *protektsiia* (connections) needed for admittance to a prestigious school, or the clearance needed to receive the coveted right to travel abroad, or the chance to acquire a car or apartment ahead of the "line," or promotion to a responsible position at work. All of these benefits rested on the relationship one established with those in charge of the political sphere. Each person had to decide, according to a personal calculus of goals and values, how much accommodation was permissible. The political cleavage thus cut across other forms of social distinction and honor; the "leading worker" routinely elected deputy to the city soviet rubbed elbows with officials from the ruling organs of party, government, trade unions, and Komsomol.

Anatolii Sobchak in his book recalls a lathe-worker from an important Leningrad enterprise who was put forward by his enterprise to be deputy in the 1989 USSR elections. The man was chairman of the council of the labor collective of his enterprise, and he enjoyed the support and respect of the authorities. Many considered him to have the best chance of all the nominated candidates to gain the necessary number of votes to be registered on the ballot. But he ruined everything with one spontaneous, ill-considered reply to a question at the electoral meeting about the Brezhnev period, when he brightened and said, "Those were the best years of my life! I worked, I lived life to the fullest!" Sobchak comments that it was evident to everyone how his life had turned out in those years—awards, a car, a place in honorary committees. But by this sincere profession he had forfeited any popular support he might have had in an open race.[22]

Those who enjoyed some measure of political trust and privilege were an extremely diverse lot, and it is unwise to impute to them the characteristics of a social class. They were divided by the same lines of social differentiation that marked society at large, including differences in the degree of power and privilege, as well as ethnic, regional, generational, gender, and occupational affiliations. Uniting them was a certain consciousness of shared responsibility, vulnerability, and privilege, as well as dependence on a single source of power to determine the cause of their lives—namely, the party's monopoly control over political power within the state. Their many differences receded before the incontrovertible fact that their social position depended on the communist system.

The concentration of power over the distribution of status and honor in the political elite in a communist system makes opposition populist rather than class centered. Labor opposition quickly joins with many other forms of antisystem protest in a generalized movement against the ruling establishment. Lacking a basis in defined class interests, the popular movement often falls back on primordial affiliations for normative cohesion. Those who see the communications revolution as exerting a transforming influence on social development must not overlook one point: new communications links exacerbate the tension between existing cultural horizons based on old expectations and values and new, often alien, perspectives imported from the world culture.[23] With the weakening of previous leadership structures during a transition period, the popular opposition movement can usually be mobilized most successfully around demands for ethnic-national rights.

POLITICAL TRANSITION IN COMMUNIST SYSTEMS

Let us recapitulate the argument. To understand the dynamics of change in a communist system, we must examine the interaction between the "communicating vessels" of society and polity in the course of the system's development through time. Modernization in communist societies is accompanied by decay in many spheres, creating severe social tensions as grievances accumulate and are focused on the political realm, where power over the distribution of material and intangible values is concentrated. Communist society, moreover, has a distinctive structure. Its principal elements are the dedifferentiation of occupational stratification and the lack of classes defined by opposing property interests, and the superimposition of the political cleavage over other social divisions. As a result, opposition movements have a populist rather than class-specific character, expressing a broad antagonism to those representing "power." Lacking more specific interests to unite it, opposition often rallies to the most general of ideological causes, ethnic nationalism.

Before the transition period, while communist hegemony is still strong enough to suppress overt opposition, manifest protest usually takes the form of anomic, spontaneous risings or of small-scale and intelligentsia-based political dissent. The strength of the communist state's repressive capacity is demonstrated by the fact that until 1989, only in one known case, that of the Gdansk accords of 1980, did a communist regime acknowledge the need to accept a negotiated settlement with an organized opposition. What, then, has happened in the Soviet Union and other communist systems to have permitted opposition movements to gain power since 1988–89?

Only by understanding the dynamic relationship between political *and* social change can we explain the dramatic transition processes in the communist world. The model proposed by O'Donnell and Schmitter for understanding transition is helpful. They postulate an authoritarian regime riven by external pressures. Elements of the ruling elite permit an airing of grievances to shore up their social base. Instead of demobilizing after their demands have been met, however, key groups in society mobilize broader followings around demands for wider and more meaningful participation in the political process. If the rulers open the political arena still more to admit new contenders for power, they lose control over the politicization of society and ultimately are forced to hand over power to the opposition through some agreement, or pact, establishing rules for the political competition. One virtue of the model of O'Donnell and Schmitter is that it operates at a level of analysis at which interaction between societal and regime actors can be specified rather than focusing on one domain to the exclusion of the other.[24]

So we must know both the underlying structure of interests in society and, perhaps even more important, how they are articulated through organized channels of influence. Can the leaders of social organizations both rally and restrain their followers, or does political initiative pass to maximalists who reject any compromise with their opponents? At the same time, we must track the efforts of the state's rulers as they seek a strategy for coping with the spillover of social discontent into the political arena.

Why did Gorbachev move beyond the conventional limits of Soviet reform policies? Historians will be searching for answers to this puzzle for generations. Was he always a radical, or did he become one in the course of his struggle to push through his reform politics over the opposition of the vast and faceless bureaucracy? It is enough for our purposes to examine what, in fact, he did, and what the consequences were. Expressing frustration with the degree to which the party was carrying out the new "April (1986) plenum" line, Gorbachev expanded his definition of perestroika during the summer and fall of 1986. He said it embraced all spheres of state and society, and referred to it as a revolution. The party plenum he planned for late 1986 had to be postponed repeatedly because of the radicalism of Gorbachev's planned assault on party conservatives. Held finally in January 1987, it introduced the concept of "democratization" as a crucial orienting slogan both in party work, where it mobilized grass-roots opposition to those party officials Gorbachev wished to remove, and as a general call to shift more political power to the soviets. Gorbachev summoned the intelligentsia to an alliance against the forces of inertia and bureaucratic power. By activating popular criticism and debate, he sought to build pressure from below for the reforms he wanted to carry out from above.

The central policy instrument his leadership produced for activating managerial initiative, the law on state enterprise, proved a bust despite the great hopes that had been attached to it. The law itself was an inconsistent patchwork of directives that strengthened the hand of enterprise directors against the bureaucracy and the hand of the bureaucracy against the enterprises. Its implementation was even more flawed. Like many earlier policy programs to improve productivity by increasing the nominal rights of enterprises, it produced dysfunctional responses—accelerating wage and price increases without commensurate improvements in output or quality. The promised package of accompanying legislation aimed at surrounding enterprises with market-oriented structures (through reforms of prices, banking, investment policy, and the like) failed to materialize until much later. The bureaucracy had succeeded in absorbing reform policy, deflecting and distorting it, and thus preventing serious damage to itself.

Through 1987–88 Gorbachev broadened his populist strategy against party and state intransigence. He encouraged newspaper editors to continue airing "healthy" criticism and expressed confidence that minor excesses now and again produced by the heat of debate posed no threat to society. The ideological positions defended by the party retreated one by one before the steady deepening and radicalization of debate, and as environmental protest in the Baltic, Transcaucasia, and elsewhere increasingly took on a nationalist color. His own political position was buttressed by the acclaim he earned in Europe and the United States, and so he intensified his battle with the party. Evidently seeking to consolidate his ideological radicalism and to effect a major purge of the Central Committee of the CPSU, he chose the expedient of the 1988 party conference as a way of accomplishing both goals. (A party conference, as the rules were generally interpreted, had the power to release members of the Central Committee and to promote members from candidate status to full status, although not to elect an entirely new Central Committee, which only a full congress of the party could do. This power, however, would have been sufficient to allow Gorbachev to rid the leadership of many of those standing in his way.) But again he had to settle for a compromise in which he obtained most but not all of his goals. Gorbachev was unable to purge the Central Committee; indeed, the Nineteenth Party Conference made no personnel changes at all. The conference nonetheless proved a watershed in several ways.

First, since it was televised, the Soviet public could witness debate of extraordinary intensity and sincerity, including open conflict between senior party leaders. The public became privy to the party's inner struggles, and the party lost much of the mystery and majesty in which it had cloaked itself. Second, the process of electing delegates to the conference produced serious tensions in local party organizations throughout the country. The conference became a forum for airing the grievances of many rank-and-file members against the manipulative power of entrenched party officials, again serving Gorbachev's populist purposes. Finally, the conference endorsed Gorbachev's program of major political reforms, including changes that would shift political power from the party to the government and would give ultimate control over the government to the electorate. Although the full consequences of these changes were not apparent and probably were not intended at the time, they supplied the institutional framework for the dismantling of communist rule in the Soviet Union.

In a characteristically forceful, indeed authoritarian, way, Gorbachev railroaded the proposed constitutional revisions through the policy process (publication, a few weeks of public "debate," speedy ratification by the outgoing Supreme Soviet in a kind of "final service") at the end of 1988. In early 1989, elections of all-union deputies were held, and in 1990, elections to republican and local soviets.

The elections provided a focus for the mobilization of political forces around the goals and grievances that the preceding two years of glasnost and protest had prepared. Where political movements had developed strong and organized form, notably in the Baltic Republics, the popular fronts won sweeping victories and in effect replaced the local branches of the CPSU as the ruling party. Elections legitimated the national demands for sovereignty, and ultimately independence, which could now be advanced by duly and democratically elected governments. Elsewhere the races vented localized populism. In many cities of the Ukraine and in the Russian Republic, the elections activated broad public movements around the simple objective of denying victory to the established bosses. In some races popular leaders, usually from the ranks of the less political, humanistic intelligentsia (Sobchak, Gavriil Popov, Stanislav Stankevich, Ion Drutse, Olzhas Suleimenov, and many, many others), became symbols of the popular movement for democracy understood in the sense of a kind of revolutionary overturning of the existing pyramid of privilege, prestige, and status. The most dramatic but perhaps rather uncharacteristic race of all was the Yeltsin race for Moscow's at-large (national-territorial) seat, which Yeltsin turned into a plebiscite against the dimly known but keenly resented pressure of the party bosses. He won with an extraordinary margin of 89 percent.

Probably the single most important long-term consequence of the two rounds of soviet elections held in 1989 and 1990 was the mobilization of ethnic-national identity in the union republics. For if we consider the other dimension of change, the rise of organizational pluralism in society, the most striking fact is the absence of organized social movements whose influence reaches across all or even most of the republics of the union. The only effective union-wide structures were the increasingly corporatist bureaucracies of the old party-state, and nearly all of these divided along republican lines in the fall of 1991. The "republicanization" of social movements is perhaps best evidenced by the strong movement to create state structures for the Russian Republic corresponding to the state structures of all the other republics and of the union: a system of organs at the republican level directing provincial-level organs of the KGB, trade union councils, Komsomol, Academy of Sciences, and hundreds of other bodies that would either duplicate the work of their all-union counterparts or, as in fact occurred, absorbed the union's own bureaucracy.

The elections were not entirely democratic. In some areas they were open, fair, and competitive. In most cases they represented a mixture of old-style and democratic politics. Most republics elected at least some opposition leaders, and a few gave a majority to national front coalitions. In the Russian Republic forces representing the new democratically oriented insurgents and those representing the power of the traditional party-state establishment were elected in almost equal proportions but with a slight edge for the pro-Yeltsin forces.[25] This enabled Yeltsin to gain the chairmanship in the spring of 1990 over the strong opposition of Gorbachev, and to keep it in the spring of 1991 when his opponents called a Congress of People's Deputies to try to remove him.

The mobilization of national popular fronts and movements in the Baltic republics, Transcaucasia, and Moldavia created powerful political forces that replaced the previous political establishments and in most other republics became significant political forces that had to be accommodated by the party leadership. The shift in the balance of political forces brought about by the new pluralization of power was spurred by the decline in the Communist Party as the ordering, unifying force in the union. The outflow of several millions of members over 1990–91 and the refusal by even more to continue to pay dues left the party in many locations in a defensive and confused condition; its power was not so much replaced by that of the newly elected soviets, which generally were unable to exercise their nominal powers effectively, as it was paralyzed in a condition of "dual power" in which old and new structures blocked each other.

In 1990 public opinion invested enormous hopes in the new soviets. A strong wave of disenchantment followed not only with the soviets, but with most institutions of power. A poll by the Center for Sociological Research of the Academy of Social Sciences (under the CPSU's Central Committee) in October and November 1990 found a substantial level of disillusionment and pessimism among the population.[26] Fifty-two percent indicated that they had lost hope in the success of perestroika. Majorities gave the Supreme Soviet of the USSR, the president of the USSR, and the government of the USSR negative ratings (57 percent, 51 percent, and 65 percent, respectively). Asked whether they would vote for the same USSR deputy again, only 25 percent said that they would be inclined to do so, and 42 percent said that they would probably vote against the incumbent. This disenchantment was not with the principle of moving to a market-oriented economy—68 percent supported the concept of private property—but with the failure of the new political structures to defend popular interests as social conditions continued to deteriorate.

Public discussion began to shift in the fall and winter of 1990 and the beginning of 1991 to the need for stronger and more effective executive power. While a few theoreticians argued for authoritarian methods to implement far-reaching economic reforms, most of the political elements of the country focused on the need for a clearer delineation of the powers of legislative and executive structures and for a shift from a collective executive to single-person executive power. Whereas in the past, state power had been centered in the Presidium of the Supreme

Soviet of the USSR and in its constituent republics, now, the argument went, it was necessary to grant the powers of chief executive to a single person, who could enforce the unity and coherence of policy across all levels of government "vertically." Most of the republics created strong executive presidencies, and in the cities there was a marked tendency to move to a "mayor/city council" form of government. This was a far cry from the new authoritarianism often discussed, especially in the context of comparisons with China, because it represented a trend toward a clearer separation of powers between executive and legislative branches.

The political crisis in the country increasingly focused on the confrontation between the union and the republics. The spring of 1991 brought renewed waves of unrest. Harsh economic stabilization measures, including a steep across-the-board increase of consumer prices—adopted by Gorbachev's new prime minister, Valentin Pavlov—exacerbated social tension. Through March and April 1991 coal miners in all the major coal-mining regions of the Soviet Union walked out, coupling their demands for improved living and working conditions with demands for Gorbachev's resignation. The strikes spread to other industries and regions as workers throughout the country demanded an immediate transfer of their enterprises to the jurisdictions of the republics rather than the federal union. Although a referendum in March 1991 held in most republics demonstrated that three-quarters of the populace still supported some form of union, the battle for sovereignty among the regions paralyzed political authority and made it impossible to negotiate a general agreement on a new form of union that would satisfy all the national republics while preserving a dominant role for the federal center. Against this background of political and economic disorder, there were reasons to fear that the contest for preeminence between President Gorbachev and his bitter rival, Boris Yeltsin, could provoke a new period of dictatorship.

At the same time, a trend toward the institutionalization of local and regional power was gaining strength. As republics and cities claimed autonomous control over their economies, they began developing new commercial relationships with each other and with the outside world. Yeltsin actively promoted the establishment of political, economic, and other ties among the union republics on a basis of the sovereign equality of the republics. The bloody seizure of the Vilnius television center in January provoked a worldwide outcry against the violent methods used to preserve central rule and, perhaps still more importantly, demonstrated to Gorbachev that his own power and program were severely threatened by the possibility of a political victory by the forces of reaction. Ultimately, Gorbachev had little choice but to bow to the new political realities in the country. On April 23, 1991, he met with the presidents of nine union republics—the three Slavic republics (Russia, Ukraine, and Belorussia) and the six Muslim republics (Kazakhstan, Uzbekistan, Kirgizia, Tadzhikistan, Turkmenistan and Azerbaijan). He agreed with them on principles that would govern the new treaty of union defining the division of powers between the center and the republics.

The agreement amounted to a surrender to the republics' demands for independence, although it also authorized the central government to enforce order in basic industries by using harsh measures. It endorsed the republics' demands for real sovereignty over their economies and opened a new phase of political development. In a looser, more confederal type of union, the Russian Republic—and Yeltsin as its president— would inevitably be the dominant force and Gorbachev's role as federal president would diminish. In effect, Gorbachev had broken the political impasse by finding a formula under which he preserved the formal existence of the union but relinquished most policy-making power to the republics. Repeated efforts by the bodies at the center to prevent radical decentralization failed; these included Pavlov's demands for extraordinary powers in June and the short-lived "state of emergency" in August 1991.

In this growing confrontation between Gorbachev's improvised and extraparliamentary demarche through the "9 + 1" process and the "four whales" of central power (the party, KGB, military, and economic bureaucracy), the USSR Supreme Soviet played a temporizing role, backing neither side. It tabled Pavlov's request in June, having determined that Pavlov was overreaching his constitutional role as the president's subordinate, and it complained of its exclusion from the Novo-Ogarevo negotiations. When the coup occurred, the chairman of the USSR Supreme Soviet, Anatolii Luk'ianov, who enjoyed enormous influence over the parliament, neither publicly supported nor condemned the coup. Upon his return, by calling the Supreme Soviet and then the Congress of People's Deputies into session, Gorbachev quickly reconfirmed the central parliament's irrelevance to the remaking of the union.

Gorbachev's search for a new basis of a federal union may now be seen as a final and futile effort to fulfill three tasks at once: preserve central authority, acknowledge republican sovereignty, and stay in power. The Novo-Ogarevo process, which effectively allowed the republican presidents collectively to set the terms of a new union treaty, pitted the weaker against the stronger republics. This strategy allowed Gorbachev to broker an agreement that protected the former from the latter while, by maintaining some sort of union, it recognized Russia's political weight. It gave Yeltsin a weak union as shelter against other republics' suspicions of possible imperialistic strivings in a newly assertive Russia, and gave Gorbachev a role as counterweight to Yeltsin. It represented the Soviet Union's "roundtable" forum, accommodating both the declining but stubborn forces of the old order and the rising but divided forces of opposition. Unlike the Central European transitions of 1989, however, government and opposition represented different levels of system organization. Change in the USSR ran at a much faster tempo in the republics than in the union: national societies were mobilized at the republic level whereas the structures operating at the union level (its army, parliament, presidency, bureaucracy, KGB, and communist party) remained hostage to conservative forces frantic at the prospect of the center's collapse.

When it was clear that they could not bend Gorbachev to their will, those forces struck on August 19; their earlier effort to win parliamentary approval for a state of emergency failed when the parliament refused to support them and Gorbachev, pressed by the parliament to declare himself, withheld his sanction. To the extent that this hodgepodge of conspirators was acting on any calculations at all, it totally misjudged the balance of political forces. No one rallied to defend Gorbachev, but the cause of national independence joined with the democratic cause to unite a powerful popular movement of resistance. The coup became the catalyst for declarations of independence by all the republics that had not already taken this final step toward rejecting the union. Russia's need for some form of loose federation to compensate for its own internal national movements and to assure its smaller neighbors of its pacific intentions could not be served by a union dominated by reactionaries from the ancien regime. If Yeltsin overreacted in the immediate aftermath of the coup, for instance, by banning the Communist Party and nationalizing its property, his actions aimed at breaking decisively with the deep inertia of those bureaucratic structures, which could not bear to relinquish power to the republics, that were all that remained of the union.

From August until December, then, the union was a government without a country; the remnants of the vast USSR state system—presidency, rump parliament, Academy of Sciences, foreign ministry, armed forces, and some other agencies—did not correspond to a territorial space that it controlled or represented. Although these organizations soldiered on despite the union's collapse, they had no way to finance their existence. By the end of November the union's budget was merged into Russia's; this political receivership acknowledged Russia's preeminence among the successor states.

Why, many have asked, at a time when West European states are gravitating toward closer financial and political union, are the republics of the former Soviet Union gripped by centrifugal forces? A simple answer (leaving aside such issues as resource endowments and the intensity of national movements) is the absence of an equilibrium in starting positions of the former Soviet republics, compared to the relative population and territorial equilibrium of the principal actors in Western Europe. At the time of the Treaty of Rome, the big three on the continent—France, Italy and West Germany—were roughly equal in size: France's population was 45 million, Italy's 49 million, and West Germany's 55 million; the territorial difference was larger, with France's area slightly over twice that of West Germany's. In contrast, Russia contained three-quarters of the territory of the entire union and half its population. Russia's territory was over six times the size of Kazakhstan's and close to thirty times that of Ukraine's. In population, Russia exceeded Ukraine by a factor of almost three, and Uzbekistan or Kazakhstan by a factor of nine. Russia's dominance made it difficult for a middle-size power such as Ukraine to accept partnership with it in a weak union. Smaller republics would be much closer to dependencies than partners of Russia. Russia's dominance, for example, meant that when Russia liberalized prices on January 2, 1992, most of its neighbors were forced to follow suit lest their economies be emptied of goods.

Therefore when Ukraine voted by a 90 percent margin for independence on December 1, Yeltsin's only hope of rescuing some new form of association that included Ukraine, which both was the only republic that could even begin to balance Russia and was long considered a brother Slavic people with deep ties to Russia, lay in creating a framework that fell short of statehood but preserved control of the former union's nuclear weapons and could coordinate economic and other policy decisions. The agreement among the leaders of the three Slavic nations—Russia, Ukraine, and Belarus—on December 8 formally dissolving the Soviet Union and establishing a new Commonwealth of Independent States then enabled eight successor states to preserve a formal relationship with one another by signing on. Only such a framework could allow organic processes of integration across republican lines to advance: if integration were forced through preservation of a union center, it would be overridden by the power of nationalist political movements in the republics.

As 1991 ended, and with it the Soviet Union, deep uncertainty surrounded the prospects for the new Commonwealth. Russia rather than the Commonwealth began to assume more of the powers and responsibilities of the former USSR in international relations, inheriting, for example, the role as the U.S. partner in sponsoring the Middle East peace negotiations and in responding to strategic arms cuts made by the United States in the new post–cold war era. It appeared likely that some members might drop out of the Commonwealth, leaving the rest to draw more tightly together. It was not impossible that some social groups that had begun to develop their own ties across republics might press for closer integration, such as miners seeking an industrywide, cross-national labor organization capable of protecting their interests in the new environment of post-communist capitalism. Ethnic diasporas would seek interstate political agreements ensuring their rights as minority communities in the successor states. Both democratic and orthodox communist movements, stronger in individual republics than across republics, were likely to maintain cross-national ties. The leaders of the Commonwealth agreed unanimously that command of the strategic forces should remain unitary and subordinate to the Commonwealth, although Ukraine took a restrictive view of what constituted "strategic" weapons. Still, the incentives for cooperation were weaker than the powerful counter-pressures for competitive, separatist policies on the part of the former republics.

CONCLUSIONS

In this chapter I have argued that it is not enough to concentrate on the political or the social domain to the neglect of the other, since what is crucial is an understanding of their interaction *as they evolve.* A state-centered account can illuminate the consequences of the fact that, in a communist regime, economic and political structures are bundled together in complementary, overlapping, and mutually reinforcing administrative structures. Reform programs typically have attempted to relax certain controls, often by giving enterprises greater autonomy vis-à-vis central planners and ministers, to stimulate productivity. In those cases when real liberties are granted to subcentral governments, opposition parties, producers, and parliaments, the Communist Party's monopoly on power breaks down. Points intermediate between a loosened, softened version of the Stalinist institutional framework and a polyarchical, market-driven society are unstable states of the system and soon yield either to a conservative consolidation or to a revolutionary rising against the regime.

The social modernization perspective, on the other hand, underlines the enormous impact of education, urbanization, professionalization, and communications in breaking down traditional structures of political control, facilitating independent and alternative forms of opinion and behavior, and unintentionally producing a shift in consciousness toward individuation and autonomy. Without this analysis we could not explain the successes of the democratic movement in the Soviet Union since 1989. It fails, however, to take sufficient note of the accumulation of antisystem resentment induced by the system, its inequalities of power and privilege, the calamitous decline in the quality of life, the vast carelessness and wastefulness with which it deploys human and material resources. Nor does this view pay sufficient attention to the group identities that fill the void left by the breakdown of a sterile doctrine of proletarian collectivism and that form the basis of new political movements. Given the amorphousness of class identities and the strength of primordial attachments, the very structure of the Soviet state, with its ethnically defined territorial jurisdictions, nurtures ethno-national counterideologies and territorial sovereignty claims. Political transition, I argued, should be analyzed as the mobilization of discontent into an opposition movement against the system. Its outcome is determined by the degree to which existing channels of social cooperation can sustain cohesive and autonomous aggregative capacities that mediate between the state and society. In the Soviet case these capacities formed first at the republican level, following the national-territorial administrative lines set up by the federal state. Once the claims by these republican national movements were largely accepted by the union center, processes in the direction of the consolidation of social interests at the union level were reinforced.

The reciprocal feedback effects between social and political change are indirect because they are affected by changing definitions of collective interest and by changing levels of freedom for the expression and resolution of grievances. A society where social interests are not well organized and autonomous—a low level of social pluralism—and simultaneously possessing a high degree of regime repressiveness is likely to witness a long buildup of popular frustration followed eventually by anomic rage. There is little reason to expect a democratic outcome in such a case. If social pluralism at the national community level is high, there can be a peaceful negotiated transfer of power to an organized opposition even if there is only a short transition period. If the national community, however, defines itself in opposition to a larger and surrounding national community, then the transfer of power at the territorial level gives way to a new struggle for independence against the center.

Because of the immensity of its territory and the ethnic-federal character of its composition, the former Soviet Union illustrates a number of these patterns simultaneously. As the theory would predict, political opposition movements were most highly developed where social pluralism was greatest—at the level of republics, cities, and regions, rather than across the entire union. Regional differences are a significant consequence of the very different levels of national solidarity and patterns of development in different areas. Democratic transition has occurred in some republics, and transition to a new authoritarianism in others. (The Baltic states, Russia, and Ukraine illustrate the first case; Georgia, Azerbaijan, and most Central Asian states, the second.) The structures of communist rule were strongest at the union level: the state bureaucracy, the Communist Party, the military, and the KGB, particularly in the behavior of their leaders at the time of the coup, demonstrated their resistance to radical renegotiation of the balance of power between the center and the republics. Their action, intended to save the union, resulted in its final demise by provoking a new mobilization of the forces of democratic opposition and national separatism. As Robert Dahl wrote, "Thus the price of polyarchy may be a breakup of the country. And the price of territorial unity may be a hegemonic regime."[27] The Soviet transition demonstrates the prescience of Dahl's observation. Any future association between Russia and its neighbors will have to recognize the equality and independence of each as national states in a post-communist world.

NOTES

1. Robert A. Dahl, *Polyarchy: Participation and Opposition* (New Haven: Yale University Press, 1971); and Giuseppe Di Palma, *To Craft Democracies: An Essay on Democratic Transitions* (Berkeley: University of California Press, 1990).
2. Peter Gey and Jiri Kosta, "Diversity and Transitions in Socialist Economic Systems: A Comparative Introduction," in Peter Gey, Jiri Kosta, and Wolfgang Quaisser, eds., *Crisis and Reform in Socialist Economies* (Boulder: Westview Press, 1987), pp. 1–10.
3. Hans-Georg Heinrich, *Hungary: Politics, Economics and Society* (London: Frances Pinter, 1986); Andreas Wass von Czege, "Hungary's 'New Economic Mechanism': Upheaval or Continuity?" in *Crisis and Reform*, pp. 121–44; and Peter A. Toma, *Socialist Authority: The Hungarian Experience* (New York: Praeger, 1988).
4. Andrew J. Nathan, *Chinese Democracy* (New York: Knopf, 1985); Dwight Heald Perkins, "Reforming China's Economic System," *Journal of Economic Literature* 26 (June 1988): 601–45; and Robert F. Dernberger, "Economic Policy and Performance," Joint Economic Committee, *China's Economy Looks Toward the Year 2000*, vol. 1: *The Four Modernizations* (Washington, D.C.: U.S. Government Printing Office, 1986), pp. 15–48.
5. Stephen White, "'Democratisation' in the USSR," *Soviet Studies* 42 (January 1990): 3–25; Stephen White, *Gorbachev in Power* (Cambridge: Cambridge University Press, 1990); Archie Brown, "Political Change in the Soviet Union," *World Policy Journal* 6 (Summer 1989): 469–501; Archie Brown, "Power and Policy in a Time of Leadership Transition, 1982–1988," in Archie Brown, ed., *Political Leadership in the Soviet Union* (Bloomington: Indiana University Press, 1989); John Gooding, "Gorbachev and Democracy," *Soviet Studies* 42 (April 1990): 195–231; Jerry F. Hough, "Gorbachev's Politics," *Foreign Affairs* 68 (Winter 1989/90): 26–41; and Anders Aslund, *Gorbachev's Struggle for Economic Reform* (Ithaca, N.Y.: Cornell University Press, 1989).

6. Thomas F. Remington, "Regime Transition in Communist Systems: The Soviet Case," *Soviet Economy* 6 (April-June 1990): 160–90.
7. Z [Martin Malia], "To the Stalin Mausoleum," *Daedalus* 119 (Winter 1990): 295–344.
8. Tatsumi Okabe, "China: The Process of Reform," Chapter 5 of this volume.
9. S. L. Seniavskii, *Izmeneniia v sotsial'noi strukture sovetskogo obshchestva, 1938–1970* (Moscow: Mysl', 1973), pp. 317, 439–45.
10. S. L. Seniavskii et al., eds., *Aktual'nye problemy istorii razvitogo sotsializma v SSSR* (Moscow: Mysl', 1984).
11. Gooding, "Gorbachev and Democracy," pp. 217–18.
12. Gilbert Rozman, "Stages in the Reform and Dismantling of Socialism in China and the Soviet Union," Chapter 1 of this volume.
13. Jerry F. Hough, *Opening up the Soviet Economy* (Washington, D.C.: Brookings Institution, 1988), pp. 19–20.
14. Rozman, "Stages in the Reform"; and George W. Breslauer, "Evaluating Gorbachev as Leader," *Soviet Economy* 5 (1989): 229–340.
15. Moshe Lewin, *The Gorbachev Phenomenon: A Historical Interpretation* (Berkeley: University of California Press, 1988), p. 133.
16. Dankwart A. Rustow, "Transitions to Democracy: Toward a Dynamic Model," *Comparative Politics* 2 (1970): 350–51.
17. Mary Douglas and Aaron Wildavsky, *Risk and Culture: An Essay on the Selection of Technical and Environmental Dangers* (Berkeley: University of California Press, 1982).
18. Anatolii Sobchak, *Khozhdenie vo vlast'* (Moscow: Novosti, 1991), p. 21.
19. See references in Thomas Remington, "A Socialist Pluralism of Opinions: Glasnost and Policy-making under Gorbachev," *The Russian Review* 48 (1989): 302.
20. Ilona Kiss, "The Coal Miners: Spearhead of the Soviet Working Class," *Beszelo*, July 28, 1990, trans. in *Uncaptive Minds* 3 (August/September 1990): 42–44.
21. Remington, "Regime Transition," pp. 171–74.
22. Sobchak, *Khozhdenie vo vlast'*, p. 17.
23. Lucian W. Pye, "Political Science and the Crisis of Authoritarianism," *American Political Science Review* 84 (1990): 3–19.
24. Guillermo O'Donnell and Philippe C. Schmitter, *Transitions from Authoritarian Rule: Tentative Conclusions About Uncertain Democracies* (Baltimore: Johns Hopkins University Press, 1986).
25. Mark Urnov, "Osvobozhdaias' ot avtoritarizma," *Polis*, no. 1 (1991): 122–35.
26. Zh. T. Toshchenko, V. E. Boikov, and G. S. Yakovlev, "Politicheskaia situatsiia nakanune s'ezda narodnykh deputatov SSSR: Noiabr' 1990 g.," *Politicheskaia sotsiologiia: Sotsial'no-politicheskaia napriazhennost', Noiabr' 90* (Moscow: Tsentr sotsiologicheskikh issledovanii Academii Obshchestvennykh Nauk pri Tsk KPSS, 1991), pp. 5–9.
27. Dahl, *Polyarchy*, p. 121.

4

The Soviet Union and China: Coping with Modernity

Shigeki Hakamada and Gilbert Rozman

Communist leaderships are torn by ambivalent attitudes toward the modernization of society. On the one hand, as followers of Marxism-Leninism, they claim to be the masters of all genuine forces of modernity: science, planning, centralization, proletarianization, and so on. Yet on the other hand, they insist that many features associated with capitalist modernization create barriers to continued development. Voluntary associations of disparate elites, individualism, and consumerism are among the wasteful or divisive elements that can be restricted without loss to economic growth in the opinion of orthodox communists. Yet the experience of their own countries increasingly demonstrates that, contrary to expectations, policies accelerating the first set of so-called positive forces did not so much remove the forces identified as negative as it exacerbated the conflict between the two types of forces. At the center of the conflict is the question of controlling citizens, as is required by the party, or of releasing their initiative, as market forces often seem to demand.

As time passes, the problems of unbalanced modernization intensify. The more a modern society evolves, the more difficult it is for the communist system to sustain modernization and to meet the rising expectations of its people. This may be the most fundamental of the dilemmas of communist-led societies. Failing to understand the interdependent structures of modernization, communist leaders drive their countries into a dead end. Then they and their successors struggle to set things back in balance. They search for new approaches to society, including to the authority relations that simultaneously sustain order and channel initiative. Once they start in this direction, forces in the society are unleashed, and it becomes very difficult to hold back the tide of change. The modern society, even in its distorted and weakly organized forms after decades of communist molding, is capable of overwhelming the communist leadership, but the conflict may be protracted and it will begin with efforts to adjust to the modern society.

This chapter identifies four levels in a modern society. First, there is the level of the microworlds, where one finds the individual at home and at leisure. Such concepts as the family revolution and the consumer revolution are often used to describe the effects of modernization on this level. Second, there is the level of knowledge acquisition from public sources, beginning with the school and extending to the mass media. Exposure to outside knowledge has intensified with the electronics revolution, the computer revolution, and the information age. Third, there is the level of the community, both at the workplace and in the local allocation of goods, services, and welfare. This is where mass society appears and where the much ballyhooed switchover from extensive to intensive production takes place. Fourth, there is the level of national integration, where parochial allegiances recede before the identity of public citizen. Direct participation in the running of society takes many forms within the general rubric of democratization, including the active leadership of urban elites who form the spearhead of a civil society. Most of our attention centers on this level; in 1989–91 the forces from above and from below struggled, with both words and deeds, to combine the participation common to a modernized society with the order necessary for a difficult transition. Communist-led societies confront the consequences of unbalanced modernization on each of these four levels.

All modernizing societies face a fundamental transition (often many transitions) between early institutions that were, for a time, conducive to development and the emerging needs of advanced modernization. Consider America's New Deal, and Japan's postwar reforms. The shift in many countries during the 1970s from energy-intensive organizations to science-intensive organizations is another prominent example. Yet the decisive transition to a higher stage of modernization under communism has proven to be particularly acute and system threatening. This is because the command economy and the mass mobilization model of Stalinist and Maoist development accentuate elements particularly ill-suited to later modernization. They delay efforts to resolve the inevitable conflict between what have been erroneously perceived as positive and negative modernizing forces. As this conflict unfolded on each of the four levels, the reform era began to offer solutions, however complicated their realization, for coping with an increasingly modern society. The prospects for success may depend as much on the society and on the balance of social interests within it as they do on the reforms themselves.

THE LEVEL OF THE MICROWORLDS

Communism in both the Soviet Union and China rode to power, in part, on the claim that the revolutionary transformation would bring normalcy to the struggle for family survival and satisfaction. The Bolsheviks promised land to hard-pressed rural families, greater equality in income and benefits to worker households, and secularization with equal rights to women and to others identified as traditionally exploited. Within the intelligentsia, and among disadvantaged groups, the goal of family normalcy had considerable appeal. The Chinese communists claimed to be the true successors to, first, the May Fourth Movement, defending the rights of youth and women before patriarchal authority, and, second, to the tradition of peasant rebellions against exploitation by landlords who had forced impoverished families to sell their daughters and, in other ways, to forgo a normal family existence. The microworlds of Russia and especially China were far from orderly in the wartorn years leading to 1917 and 1949 respectively.

By 1953 the conditions in many Soviet families had worsened appreciably, although it was not clear whom to blame. Living conditions had deteriorated ever since the onset of collectivization. Many peasants fled to the cities, which were somewhat better supplied with food and amenities even though housing was in very short supply. Women were left without husbands due to the abnormal sex ratio following World War II. Illegitimacy and illegal abortions represented two of the desperate responses to these difficult postwar times. Continued terror and the separation of millions of families in labor camps count directly as part of Joseph Stalin's legacy. Yet in the face of the danger around them, small circles often drew more tightly together. As Moshe Lewin explains, the urban microworlds of family and friendship provided some emotional satisfaction and security in difficult times.[1] They helped to sustain educational and moral values against the accumulating forces of cynicism. Once the state relaxed its grip over them, those microworlds helped to give voice to a moral crisis.

By 1985 the post-Stalin reforms had alleviated many of the severe family problems. Time away from the workplace, including vacation days, had become quite abundant. Minimal subsistence no longer required energetic efforts. Three decades of housing construction had provided separate apartments for most urban households, despite very long waiting lists for young families. Legalized abortions, freer divorces, and an increasingly even sex ratio represented steps toward a more normal family existence among a largely urban, wage-earning population. By rechanneling energy into their private lives, the Soviet people generally could cope with the bleakness of their society under Leonid Brezhnev.[2] Yet even before Mikhail Gorbachev gained office, the Soviet Union was abuzz with talk of a deepening crisis in family life.[3] Especially among the Slavic and Baltic peoples, there arose what many labeled a demographic as well as a family crisis. The prevalence of one-child families created labor and military recruitment shortages. Tired after a day at the workplace and inadequately assisted at home by their husbands, women often did not provide the nurturance essential for their children. A health care crisis exacerbated by rampant alcoholism and sharp environmental deterioration did little to alleviate the needs of families that were becoming battered, rent by divorce, or handicapped by mental and physical incapacities. A shortage of leisure options left many households with unused savings. Moreover, there were so few choices in the marketplace that people were not motivated to work hard for more earnings. Authoritative voices spread the blame widely—to emotionally immature fathers, to unfeminine or unmaternal mothers, to egotistical single children, and to informal groups that defied the constructive norms established by the party or the Komsomol. Families were failing and the day-care centers and schools were not doing their job well, explained the authorities, but they did not address the basic problems caused by the state's one-sided modernization.

What was already known to many became officially acknowledged in the age of glasnost. The state had shortchanged the Soviet family for more than a half-century. Spending on housing, consumer goods, health care, leisure, and birth control had fallen far short of basic needs. When the state in the 1950s and 1960s tried to narrow the gap between rising aspirations and depressed living conditions, severe contradictions arose: on the one hand, more leisure time and money to spend and, on the other, a severe shortage of items to purchase or to give pleasure, apart from alcohol. Glasnost opened the floodgates to honesty about the moral deterioration of Soviet society.[4] What had been filtering out in hushed revelations to only one's closest associates under Stalin and in the omnipresent, but still carefully selected, evening gatherings of friends under Brezhnev now poured forth, publicly and privately, as the older generation felt obliged to explain its past actions in an age of immorality. The mass revelations did not persuade many youths to replace their mood of escapism with a new spirit of idealism. Crime, and other signs of the alienation of Soviet youth, worsened. Meanwhile, the problem of finding goods in state outlets abruptly reached crisis proportions, driving families to spend more of their nonworking hours to this end. In such an atmosphere people grew increasingly sullen about their daily lives and more pessimistic about relief in the foreseeable future. Leadership promises in 1986–87 for priority construction of housing, quick improvements in health care, and better funded diversity in leisure had lost all credibility. The one major program to redress the deterioration of life had been Gorbachev's anti-alcoholism campaign, which by late 1988 had ended in almost complete failure. Long lines for liquor continued through 1991, adding one more complication to daily life.

By 1978 many conditions of daily life in China had also deteriorated from the levels regained in the early 1950s after order was reestablished. The major problem for the vast majority was not coping with modernity, but coping with malnutrition or a minimal existence offering few appealing alternatives. These conditions were actually not so different from those faced in prior decades of economic turbulence. In China, unlike the Soviet Union, continuities in family life remained considerable. Spared, except for short intervals or for a small percentage of people, the worst disruptions of war, labor camps, and community breakdown, Chinese families under communism held on to the core of their traditional values and way of life much more than did Soviet families.

Paradoxically, Maoist attacks against the microworlds were at the same time more direct and less effective. They initially targeted marriage reform, but some three decades later rural areas retained patriarchal, patrilineal, and patrilocal customs typical of a premodern society. Mao's policies assailed lineage authority, yet through the overlap between the rural collectives at the team and brigade levels and the village community, they often strengthened the corporate identity of localities.[5] Red Guards tried to obliterate the "four olds" in the Cultural Revolution, freeing themselves of moral scruples in their fanatic struggle against old thoughts and old customs. Even inaction was deemed hostile to the idealized world of conformity conjured up by communism. Millions of families were shell-shocked through negative class labels, continued separation of spouses, struggle sessions in which family members were pressured to denounce one targeted by authorities, and even outright torture. The emotional suffering was enormous in a society raised on family solidarity and filial piety, but most campaigns turned out to be short-lived. Meanwhile structural conditions in China, in contrast to the Soviet Union, did not often support new lifestyles. Particularly in the 1970s, when the Cultural Revolution lingered inconclusively, families recouped by combining their own resources. Youth who had been sent away trickled back from the countryside. Separated couples awaited their brief, annual get-togethers, and concerted family sacrifices managed to ease problems of survival. In China as in the Soviet Union a quarter-century before, the family provided a necessary respite from a severe world.

The reform era in China enabled families to devise new strategies to prosper and succeed. Even though educational opportunities remained scant by Soviet standards, the sudden reestablishment of proper schooling and competitive exams absorbed the energies of many advantaged urban households. The spread of the household responsibility system and the emergence of individual property household enterprises (*getihu*) gave most people new economic prospects from drawing on the labor and resources within their grasp. As in the Gorbachev era, religion made a dramatic revival in China. Since household incomes were rising, many families could spend more on newly revived or increasingly lavish life-cycle rituals.[6] Just as second economy networks and escapism had made life for many bearable under Brezhnev, Chinese *guanxi* (connections) continued to proliferate and the intensification of work in the private sector and expanded leisure outlets helped to divert individual energies.

Although the general atmosphere of reform meant a relaxation of controls from above, there was a glaring exception in China: the one-child family campaign. Like the Soviet crackdown on alcoholism, it was aimed at reducing wasteful consumption and at improving the fit between labor resources and the needs of the workplace. It too provoked discontent and evasion. Although not abandoned as was the anti-alcoholism campaign in the Soviet Union, it eventually tolerated some noncompliance. There were other parallels between these two campaigns to achieve a more disciplined society. The anti-alcoholism program was costly to the state budget, and it was so widely evaded through moonshining that it could not achieve its goals. Moreover, it came before alternative sources of refreshment and leisure activities were made available. Stringent family planning in rural China was also unpopular. It was seen as a threat to the rural household budget at a time when the responsibility system made it attractive to increase the amount of labor the household could do. The one-child rule was sometimes circumvented through connections or the payment of fines, and it came before villagers were ready to accept a single daughter as the family's only successor. Yet there was at least one huge difference between the two campaigns. Whereas the Soviet campaign failed to restore a healthy microworld environment, the Chinese campaign little affected the ongoing improvement in family vitality. The entrenched Confucian family tradition and the communist leadership's failure to transform village life gave China a better basis than the Soviet Union for recovery in the era of reforms.

It would be hasty for us to conclude that the lowest level of Chinese society is now well suited for a new era. The reassertion of traditional entrepreneurialism and of aspirations for learning, which at first seemed very impressive, have also been accompanied by widespread skepticism. Proprietors must contend not only with corruption from above but also with the "red-eye disease" of some envious communities, which do not recognize the individual's right to the extra benefits from his or her hard labor.[7] Rewards from education have become so meager that the desire to learn cannot help but be diminished.[8] As the Soviet experience under Brezhnev demonstrates, freedom from some totalitarian restraints actually can accelerate families' moral deterioration if the struggle for daily existence becomes less intense yet the open airing of problems is not permitted. One example of the drift away from stringent controls is the emergence of tens of millions of migrants, who in their search for opportunities add to instability. Gambling and crime are spreading. Efforts by the leadership to intensify the struggle against "individualism," which they see as synonymous with "bourgeois liberalism," are unlikely to solve these problems or to thwart modernization based, to an increasing degree, on the private sector.

THE LEVEL OF KNOWLEDGE ACQUISITION

When the Soviet and Chinese communists seized power, they viewed the acquisition and dissemination of knowledge as matters of national will and of centralized organization. It was up to the state more than the intellectual community to solve these problems. National planning of education and science would enable the country to catch up with more modernized states. Beginning with new agencies above and literacy campaigns below, communists would mobilize the society in order to harness science and technology. Stirred by the spirit of nationalism and by some quick gains in quantitative indicators of schooling and professional training, even many intellectuals accepted this reasoning.

Soviets continued to find merit in this upbeat viewpoint in the 1950s. Their country was training record numbers of scientists and engineers, who, in turn, were fulfilling the quantitative indicators of central plans aimed at grandiose projects and crash programs. Despite revelations about the arbitrary suppression by the "cult of personality" of entire academic disciplines as well as of leading authorities in virtually every field, few questioned the system that produced the first sputnik and the world's fastest rates of economic growth. It was taken for granted that the communist system was superior in the mastery of modern knowledge.

By the 1980s this line of self-confident reasoning had all but disappeared. The hope, pinned in the 1960s on the "cybernetics revolution," had been dashed. Recognizing that the Soviet system had repressed the social sciences and professional management training, among other areas, advocates of reform managed to air some of their views but to little avail. For the next two decades Soviet authorities claimed that, in the new era of the "scientific and technological revolution," socialism would convincingly demonstrate its superiority.[9] The authorities, however, were having to make more and more excuses for why capitalist countries, such as Japan, were the economies experiencing so much success in applying the fruits of innovation.[10] Partial measures to increase access (legal and illegal) to foreign advances or to give Soviet innovators more autonomy continued into the early Gorbachev era. But a single stark conclusion was becoming unavoidable: intellectuals and the firms and institutions that employed them found it difficult to innovate in such a rigid, top-heavy system dominated by bureaucrats.

Under perestroika, science and technology were promised a lot. The media turned their severe scrutiny on the defects of the system, appealing for freedom, autonomy, and internationalization for scientists and journalists. Yet the mammoth Academy of Sciences and other organizations were slow to change.

At least, a foundation existed in the Soviet Union in the 1980s for the utilization of modern knowledge. There were vast numbers of Soviets trained intensively in mathematics. Foreign area specialists with appropriate language skills were far more numerous in the Soviet Union than in China at the commencement of Deng Xiaoping's reforms. These intellectuals effectively seized the opportunity for glasnost, but they were almost completely helpless before the needs of economic restructuring. Whether it was because their training was obsolete and limited to narrow needs in a socialist system or for other reasons, the intellectuals of the Soviet Union were turned into critics or bystanders rather than builders of a new system.

China's harsher treatment of intellectual resources created a more severe crisis. Beginning in the second half of 1977, when the first steps were taken to recover from the Cultural Revolution, Chinese talked disparagingly of a "lost generation." Having rejected almost all modern knowledge, the Maoist clique left China with little potential to cope with contemporary science and technology. For this reason China's post-Mao economic prospects in the absence of major reform were virtually nil, while the Soviet Union's economic prospects after Stalin's death were much better for a time. Huge projects continued to be built and to function, even if rather wastefully.

After a decade of intermittent reforms, China had made some progress in recognizing and meeting the needs of the "information age." Translated books detailing the requirements of the new era were enormously popular, and reformers picked up the rallying cry of the "worldwide new industrial revolution."[11] Disciplines that had been banned or allowed only within a narrow scope now absorbed many of the earlier advances achieved by international science. Partial glasnost allowed blame to be placed on the centralized model borrowed from Stalin. Conditions for intellectuals, however, remained unfavorable. Living conditions for them were dismal, although other groups benefited from reform. Of the tens of thousands who had left China to study abroad, few chose to return to a bureaucratically rigid and materially impoverished existence. As ideological education intensified in 1989–91, so did frustrations, as they did in the Soviet Union late in Brezhnev's rule. Aspirations once aroused are not easy to suppress. Urban intellectuals proved in 1989 that, given the chance, they will insist on reform. The pressures for Chinese glasnost continue to build.

China's leaders may face the same growing impasse of scientific innovation that the Soviets faced under Brezhnev. Because of the considerable modernization of their economy in the 1980s, the Chinese now require a large and able scientific corps to sustain an increasingly complex system. The conditions are lacking for such a corps.[12] In comparison to the Soviet Union, China has the advantage of the "open door," for applied knowledge through international business partnerships. China, however, has the disadvantage of a more alienated intelligentsia and tenser relations between the Communist Party and the academic community. Only at the end of February 1992 did the leadership begin to signal, through renewed support to economic reforms and shortened prison sentences to Tiananmen activists, a more conciliatory approach.

Gorbachev started with a large intelligentsia prepared to seek modern knowledge, and he made it the backbone of his support. Deng began with only a tiny group that sought modern knowledge, and he wavered in his approach to it, caring more about the backing of bureaucrats who take an instrumental approach to knowledge in support of party rule. The advantage is on the Soviet side. Yet many in the old Soviet intelligentsia may lack the skills to shift from bureaucratic science to international, innovative science, and the cream of the younger generation in the Soviet Union may lack the drive observed in China's successful examination candidates. In the long run China's capacity to cope with modern knowledge may be greater.

The leadership groups of both Gorbachev and Deng urgently wanted high-technology electronics and information capabilities. As the Brezhnev group had attempted before, the Deng group wants to remove the static of "spiritual pollution" from this acquisition, with some allowances for China's decentralization, special economic zones, and open door. In the short run the Chinese policies are more contradictory, although emergency conditions of order and consumption left the Soviets through 1991 unable to make much progress toward their goals. China's policies are still not responding well to a modern society. Its ideology is still a mixture of Stalinist centralization and revolutionary anti-elitism, both fed, to some degree, by "feudal" thinking.

THE LEVEL OF THE COMMUNITY

Recent thinking in the Soviet Union subscribed to the notion that communist ideals of the collectivity represent a throwback to rural, premodern organization. Such ideals could control individuals, but not offer them the necessary freedom or motivation. The need arises to abandon not only these ideals, but also the organizational mechanisms used to realize them.

Under Stalin the community did not gain a strong emotional hold over the individual, although it established a fairly high degree of dependency. Informants, secret police agents, and powerful bosses paid lip service to fostering the spirit of the collective. Under Nikita Khrushchev, there was an effort to create comrades' courts in neighborhoods and workplaces, to plan neighborhood communities as microregions, and to open the party to greater populism.[13] But such idealism produced little.

Through the early 1980s the workplace remained important as a source of pensions, housing, vacation vouchers, and disparate benefits. Under Yuri Andropov there were efforts to strengthen the linkage between such benefits and a continuous, unblemished work record.[14] Economic accountability brigades were then expanded under perestroika, further connecting the individual's contribution to the group to his rewards. As the state-run economy deteriorated, the distribution system at the workplace often filled the gap. At the same time, firms became more reluctant to hire workers because of the greater threat of layoffs. There also arose a greater possibility of keeping profits generated from reduced labor costs. Curiously, the 1980s witnessed not a freeing of labor, except for some bold departees to the private sector, but a growing fear by the majority of losing the supplies and security of the socialist enterprise. The mentality of the pensioner, guaranteed only a fixed income, characterized not only the sizable retired population of the Soviet Union, but also many workers, intellectuals, managers, and bureaucrats who feared any alternative to the umbilical cord linking them to their work organization.

The Chinese situation is even further removed from a fluid labor market. In the revolutionary period and extending for a fortunate few well into the 1950s, organizations met needs largely in kind rather than in cash. This came to represent an ideal. As Andrew Walder argues, Chinese enterprises were more politicized than were Soviet ones, making workers more dependent on superiors with discretionary powers.[15] Since so much was at stake in one's relationship at the firm, many workers competed to curry favor.

Increased dependency in China resulted from many factors. Market forces were less developed there until the 1980s. Instead of a labor shortage that offered hope to those who left their firms, China faced a huge labor surplus with countless unemployed aspirants for scant new openings. Moreover, China's leaders gave the party more authority in the workplace, insisting on frequent political study sessions and requiring approval for such personal matters as marriage and divorce decisions. As conditions improved in the 1980s, workers enjoyed more options. Yet not many in the state sector were willing to forsake the security and benefits of their firms for what might be short-term financial advantages in another type of enterprise. The severe inflation of 1987–88 reinforced this way of thinking, as did the tightening of credit and controls for the private sector during the retrenchment of 1989–90.

While portions of the urban work force were more tightly in the embrace of their units (*danwei*) in China than in the Soviet Union, most Chinese, especially in rural areas, were freer from such bonds than were the Soviets. Living in private housing built by their own families, feeding themselves largely from their personal plots, and enjoying virtually no state benefits in health, education, and retirement, the Chinese were often psychologically predisposed to individual initiative. Unemployed urbanites and even many workers in collective enterprises also had little to lose by striking out on their own. Although the *danwei* exerted a more suffocating effect on modern mobility than did most Soviet enterprises, they did not reach large numbers. This opened the way for the explosion in China's private sector employment. Even so, village and neighborhood controls often remained in place in China, limiting the individual household's independence.[16] Problems of escape from nonmodern collectivities persisted in both countries.

In June 1991 the shift from state-run collectives to spontaneous cooperatives or private family and individual enterprises was still only slowly beginning in the Soviet Union. The people were deeply divided. At the time of Boris Yeltsin's election as president of Russia, 36.8 percent of the respondents in a poll explained why they voted as they did as "an endeavor to transform the republic's economy by patterning it on the developed countries of the West." About the same number (36.2 percent) backed "an endeavor to reform the republic's economy, but without allowing it to become capitalist."[17] A few months later Yeltsin's initiative to rid all state enterprises of Communist Party cells delivered a massive blow against the existing type of collectives, but people continued to be torn about how far to shift from the "social state" to the private sector. In early 1992 price reform was also given precedence over privatization, a clear contrast to the earlier Chinese approach.

THE LEVEL OF NATIONAL INTEGRATION

In 1989 a debate opened in Russia on democratization and authoritarianism. Some people asked whether it was possible in Russia to achieve democratization and commercialization—two widely accepted goals— without an authoritarian approach. If the answer is "no," then the ends must justify the means, which are the only way to enable the country to make an orderly transition. A. Migranian and I. Kliamkin were especially forceful in emphasizing the necessity of authoritarianism. In their view no dictatorial or totalitarian system has ever directly transformed itself into a democracy. Furthermore, they pointed to a deficiency in the tradition of democracy, legalism, and civil society as well as to the low level of political culture in Russia. The destructiveness of Russian history means, to them, a national inclination toward authoritarianism, a fear of anarchy, and an attitude of reliance on order and a strong leader. The logical conclusion is that for democratization and reform to be successful a strong hand will be necessary.[18]

In contrast, others pointed to the danger of authoritarianism and to its reactionary character, even suggesting that it would produce anarchy rather than order. They observed a universal tendency for democratization, to which Russia and Eastern Europe are no exception. It followed that the democratization of Eastern Europe could positively influence the Russian case. Also with the advance of the educational and cultural level of the masses and the spread of the new information age, the forces of democracy would continue to grow. Through glasnost the criticism of Stalinism and the ideals of democracy would penetrate more deeply, changing the national consciousness. The democratic faction added that what was occurring in Soviet society was a diversification of interests, the development of pluralism, and the advancement of the people so that they could no longer be managed according to old command methods. With the spread of the democratic movement from below, accompanied by self-interest associations, strikes, and environmental movements, fear of authority was declining. For these reasons the Soviet people could build a democratic society without an authoritarian approach.[19]

At roughly the same time a similar debate raged in China in intellectual circles and to some degree in the press. By 1986 it had started to build. After a short hiatus following the firing of Hu Yaobang, the debate intensified from the middle of 1987 into early 1989. On the one side were those who insisted that China's special circumstances—a largely peasant society, the absence of a democratic tradition, the danger of regional fragmentation, and so on—required the continued dominant role of the Communist Party. On the other side were the reform thinkers who argued that the process of reform would be incomplete without counteracting the above conditions and accelerating a political and ideological shift toward democracy.[20] Both sides took into account the aged leadership's reluctance to share power. The former suggested that the slow transition of a neo-authoritarian tutelage might offer an acceptable compromise with gradual results, and the latter insisted that to keep the entire reform process from stagnating a big infusion of the popular will was required.

Recent Soviet steps toward parliamentary democracy were cited in China as evidence that this was the common and only reliable way to reform socialism.[21] In both countries roughly the same theoretical views were being aired, largely removed from the political process.

THE NEW DEBATE ON AUTHORITARIANISM

Before the spring of 1990, the debate in the Soviet Union was abstract and idealistic. Radical reformers did not yet occupy the seats of power, and there did not seem to be any realistic prospect for this outcome. In the summer of 1989, voices arose, publicly calling for the elimination of article 6 in the constitution. This article guaranteed the Party's monopoly. People did not expect, however, that the breakup of this monopoly would be easy. Accordingly, in the process of reform the presence or absence of authoritarianism was discussed as a hypothetical or theoretical question. Yet by 1990 the question had shifted from the realm of the abstract to the actual politics of the reform factions, which now held power in some areas. What brought this about in the spring of 1990 was the birth of radical reform leadership in the parliaments of Moscow, Leningrad, and the Russian Republic. The February 1990 enlarged plenum of the Central Committee ended the Party's monopoly, and the spring elections to local and regional soviets brought radical reformers actual power. For the first time the question of power became more than a matter of criticism of the system or of the party. It was a practical problem in need of urgent resolution. Although the position of Migranian and Kliamkin lost ground in the spring of 1990 as democratization under the slogan "all power to the soviets" seemed to be realized, this optimism would not last long.

Within a half year of gaining power, the radical reformers such as Gavriil Popov, the chairman of the Moscow Soviet, and Anatolii Sobchak, the chairman of the Leningrad Soviet, had begun to recommend strong administrative power. Intense criticism of the soviets was spreading. Already in August 1990 a conflict between Sobchak and the Leningrad Soviet had surfaced. The theoretical leaders of the reformers who held the seats of power now criticized the utopianism of the democratic group and started to advocate a more authoritarian approach. This exerted a deep influence on the reform intellectuals and resulted in a split within radical reform circles. The nation faced the acute question of how to integrate a new social order.

Popov preferred a strong executive power and criticized parliamentary power. By September of 1990 he was presenting the view that executive power must be strengthened in order to be able to issue orders to people and to create an iron arm capable of arresting criminals.

The political system of soviets, especially where the democratic group had won, had now been proven inefficient, just as the socialist economy had been earlier. Under the power of the Communist Party, the soviets had once seemed rather effective because behind the ornamental soviets had existed real executive power. The soviets of the reform group were also ornamental, but there was no executive power behind them. If one removes the hand operating the marionette, it becomes powerless. Citizens obtained political freedom, but even if freedom has the power to destroy, it does not have the power to create, added Popov. The frenzied activity of citizens is especially dangerous, he warned. The democratic market economy cannot be born naturally out of the administrative socialist system, in his opinion. He believed it was necessary to plant it from outside. Popov insisted that the postwar "Japanese miracle" became possible only because of the compulsory power of the occupation army.

As chairman of the Moscow City Soviet, Popov introduced the concept of "desovietization" to limit, on a large scale, the rights of the soviet. In this way he would limit the functions of the soviet to legislative ones. For him, strong executive authority had become a priority. He advocated that the president, governors, mayors, and other executive heads throughout the country should be directly elected by the citizens.

They should be given a strong position independent of the soviets.[22] In June 1991 such elections began. Yeltsin, Popov, and Sobchak were among the first directly elected to high posts.

Sobchak, Popov's counterpart in Leningrad, intensely criticized the city soviet that had elected him. He said that most of the current representatives accidentally became deputies and that they represented only themselves. He even accused them of being neo-Bolsheviks, only able to destroy but with no ability to build. Parliament, he charged, debates on and on but cannot resolve anything. To establish parliaments at the level of the city, the district, the town, and even the city ward is nonsense, he declared. Instead he urged strong executive power appointed from above. Wide authority should be granted to the mayor, he believed. In the Leningrad Soviet there was a negative reaction to Sobchak, who was criticized for being too authoritarian and self-assured.[23] The standoff continued in late 1990. Only when both Sobchak and the Leningrad Soviet were faced with a rightist drift in the Kremlin in 1991 did they find new grounds for cooperation. After Sobchak's direct election and a majority vote of the city electorate in favor of changing the city's name, they followed the abortive August coup by renaming the city St. Petersburg.

Even the reformer Stanislav Stankevich, deputy chairman of the Moscow Soviet, offered the harsh criticism that the bloated soviet is nothing more than a democratic ornament and that it has "driven us into a dead end." He urged that all power should be given to the chairman of the soviet.[24] Stankevich declared his hope that a strong state or party power could stabilize economic conditions. He also unofficially volunteered the opinion that conditions for commercialization were favorable in the Kazakhstan Republic, where party and state authority had not been destroyed. The dilemma and psychology of the reformers in power are embodied in this strange admission. Yet by no means was Stankevich endorsing a reassertion of conservative authority by the party; his goal was firm leadership for reform.

Strong criticisms of district soviets came from chairmen at that lower level. The reformer I. Zaslavskii, chairman of the Moscow Oktiabrskii district soviet, said that the slogan "all power to the soviets" may be democratic, but once it is realized the soviets themselves are proven to be useless. He criticized the fact that the functions of the soviets, which are now independent from party power, are paralyzed and that when deputies only engage fervently in debate this signifies *iazychestvo* (a loaded word meaning paganism, but also reflecting the basic word for language or language for the sake of language) or *zabaltyvanie* (babbling), both constituting a "new form of sabotage" and representing, in religious terms, the most terrible "sins." Zaslavskii added that democracy is "power chasing after the people's will" and that this power should not necessarily be limited to the parliament. He urged that the functions of the soviets should be limited to budget approval and a check on the budget.[25]

These statements of the reform leaders who had assumed power presented a fierce offensive against the illusions of the idealistic democratic group. In a lot of ways, they expressed views held also by the conservative group. Perhaps they helped to build support for emergency powers granted to Gorbachev in late 1990, but when those powers were used more to preserve the union than to accelerate economic reform, the reformers reasserted their respect for basic freedoms. When the moment of decision was reached in August 1991, the reformers lined up behind Yeltsin, rejecting a takeover by the old forces of communist order.

Also in China a new factor gained force in 1988 and early 1989 at the expense of reform group cohesion. Many blamed the galloping inflation on the loss of control by state authorities. They insisted that reformers, in a rush to create a complete market economy, had brought the country close to economic chaos. This encouraged many to write that neo-authoritarianism was needed to guide a cautious transition toward a mixed economy. As in the Soviet Union, the weakness of democratic traditions contributed to this impatience. Moreover, the most visible technocrats in office often became scapegoats for the behind-the-scenes stalemates within the inner core of party leaders. In any case reforms that seemed to be grinding to a halt heightened frustration and raised the demand for firm leadership.

Prior to June 1989 Chinese reformers used their writing about early Soviet steps toward parliamentarism as an opportunity to elucidate their domestic concerns. They praised Gorbachev's political reforms, while conservatives were tightening censorship in order to limit the spillover into China.[26] Preferences for domestic solutions led to arguing through analogy. Gorbachev was variously likened to a hero and a traitor. After June the official verdict increasingly exposed him as a traitor to communism.

THE BACKGROUND OF NEO-AUTHORITARIANISM: THE CRISIS OF TRUST

The most serious problem for the implementation of reform policy is the lack of popular trust in the government, parliament, and leaders. In general, the reason why military command methods, administrative methods, or a bureaucratic system to control people is necessary is because mutual trust between the authorities and the people is missing. In the Soviet Union an administrative system through a huge bureaucratic structure dominated for a long time because there did not exist relations of trust between the authorities and the people. As Iuryi Orlov states, "All Soviet government documents and laws presupposed that the people were potential violators of the law and, if control were lost, would become thieves, would refuse their obligations, and would be lazy. For example, the law on parasitism starts from the idea that man from his nature does not desire to work."[27]

In a crisis leaders cannot implement difficult reforms without the trust of the people, or else they must rely on force. Whether or not they can dare to implement reform policies such as price reform or the introduction of a market economy that will temporarily infringe on the interests of the people through price increases depends on the extent of trust in the leadership, government, and the parliament. The new leadership of Eastern Europe could carry out reforms because of this popular trust. In contrast, in the Soviet Union in 1990 popular trust in the government quickly declined. Trust in President Gorbachev slipped to the level of 30 percent and later to close to 10 percent, with statistics varying depending on the way the question was posed. Prime Minister Nikolai Ryzhkov's level of trust fell from 24 percent in December 1989 to 14 percent in October 1990, as calls for his resignation intensified until, following a heart attack, he left office early in 1991.[28] The ardent hopes of the people and the trust placed in the new Congress of People's Deputies and the Supreme Soviet fell quickly by the second half of 1990 (see Table 4-1). At first considerable hope was also placed in the soviets of the Russian Republic, Moscow, and Leningrad, but soon they were criticized as settings for "chattering" by the delegates and as completely useless venues for real policies. The nation experienced a great disappointment in the administration of reform leaders and in parliament. In March 1990, 30 percent still believed in the possibility of the soviet system as a system of power, but in July the figure had dropped to 11 percent.[29] The newly established Congress of People's Deputies and Supreme Soviet played a huge role at first in transforming the political consciousness of the Soviet people and destroying the prestige of the Communist Party; however, by the end of 1990 the opinion had spread that the existing soviets had already taken that mission as far as it would go.[30]

What was elicited by this crisis of confidence was economic and social disorder. Even when a new political system was introduced by reform leaders who climbed onto the stage, a political mechanism in order to overcome the crisis was not created. One author even compared the

Table 4-1
ATTITUDES OF MOSCOW AND LENINGRAD CITIZENS
TOWARD THE SOVIETS IN 1990

Attitudes of Moscow Citizens in November		
	Toward the Supreme Soviet	*Toward the Moscow Soviet*
Completely satisfied	9%	16%
Largely satisfied	9%	20%
Quite dissatisfied	16%	15%
Dissatisfied	55%	36%

Attitudes of Moscow Citizens toward the Russian Republic Supreme Soviet		
	In August	*In November*
Completely satisfied	28%	15%
Largely satisfied	31%	16%
Quite dissatisfied	15%	22%
Dissatisfied	18%	36%

Attitudes of Leningrad Citizens toward the Leningrad Soviet		
	In July	*In September*
Trusting	63%	49%
Neutral	29%	27%
Distrusting	8%	24%

Do Deputies of the Leningrad Soviet Meet Your Expectations?	
Yes	30%
No	70%

situation to a body that has been invaded by AIDS.[31] As a result of this loss of immunity, the real situation of the economy and the society does not improve at all. On the contrary, it worsens from the reforms. At the same time as the prestige of the Communist Party is lost and the command administrative system is paralyzed, the economy sinks into ruin. The partial introduction of a market economy assisted the second economy and speculation in bringing about rising shortages and inflation. On the social side, discipline and order were increasingly disturbed and crimes were rising. Most of the economic reform laws, decrees, and presidential orders, which had been enacted and issued one after another, brought only meaningless idling without demonstrating real effects. Since the center lacked the prestige, power, or structure for carrying these out, the republics adopted their own laws and made their own decisions based on their own interests. More and more clashes with the center followed. At the level of localities, laws were overlooked and anarchy was born. Especially in Moscow and Leningrad, where the reform group held the mayoral posts, disorder grew severe.

In a way the situation in China was similar. Zhao Ziyang and his reform group were blamed for worsening economic conditions in 1988. Outrage against corrupt officials led to demands for a stronger state police. Confidence in the reform process continued to dip. At least one year earlier than the Soviet morass in the summer of 1990, China reached an impasse of reforms. It could go neither forward nor backward. Each country was marking time, while discontent simmered.

Of course, there were sharp differences between the two countries. China's populace never experienced the psychological uplift of electoral campaign promises followed by victories of anti-establishment figures followed by hard-hitting speeches and parliamentary deliberations. There never was a mood of euphoria. When disappointments arose in China, the blame was quickly spread in many directions. The prestige of the party was low. Yet without any electoral diversity and without glasnost, it is likely that the psychological reaction against the party in China among most social groups, especially the peasantry and the workers, was less unabashedly negative. In any case few reform intellectuals were ready to concede that central power should be strengthened. As seen in the huge spring demonstrations of 1989, the urban populace had no trouble placing the blame on the party old-liners and on conservative resistance. After the June 4 reassertion of conservative power, the situation became even clearer. The responsibility of reformers for some inadequacies in economic policies paled before the guilt of the conservatives in stifling the popular will. Of course, the beneficiaries of Chinese reform were far more numerous than were those of Soviet reform. The greater number reduced the need for scapegoats. As microlevel conditions deteriorated sharply in the Soviet Union, the central institutions bore the brunt of the attack; the vitality at the microlevel in China—an achievement of the 1980s that was not ended by the crackdown at the center—made escape from central concerns a viable outlook.

Some of the national surveys of the political views of youth (aged up to 25 and 26 to 35) focused on attitudes toward reform, often showing that most respondents favored reform of the political system, but cautious reform. About one-fifth in each age group urged an immediate comprehensive reform and another one-sixth went further by favoring China's absorption of a broad range of thought in order to create an environment for reforming the political system. But, at the other extreme, one-fifth of respondents insisted that reform is of no use or temporarily it is best not to act. The most common response was intermediate between immediate comprehensive reform and temporary delay. Of the group aged 26–35 31.4 percent and of the younger group 24.5 percent preferred, through careful experimentation, to move forward in adjustments and reforms. This was the mainstream response. Likewise, 55 percent chose the cautious answer that China now already has some democracy and needs to advance a step in perfecting it, a far larger number than the one-fifth who chose the response that China most lacks democratic freedoms necessary for the Four Modernizations. Balancing the respondents impatient for democracy were nearly as many on the opposite side who chose one of three answers: 1) China does not need new democratic freedoms—first economic freedoms should proceed and then we can consider them; 2) China already has advanced socialist democracy; and 3) the Four Modernizations demand the united will of the whole people—to incite democratic freedoms now is not to be careful.[32]

We can contrast this hesitancy among Chinese youth with the boldness of the residents of Vilnius (50 percent Lithuanians, 20 percent Russians, 20 percent Poles, and 10 percent others) in April 1990. When asked, "With the secession of Lithuania from the USSR, will the non-Lithuanian population live better or worse than it does today?" Sixty percent said "better" while 21 percent said "worse." Only Russians were doubtful, a third answering "better" and 43 percent "worse." In retrospect, we can see that the Lithuanian and Russian respondents, unlike the Chinese, were overly confident about the short-term gains. When asked, "Will the USSR leadership use force if the Supreme Soviet of Lithuania does not renounce its decisions?" 73 percent of those polled said "no." Both Lithuanians and Russians were close to this level.[33] This expectation proved correct when Lithuania gained its independence in 1991.

Fragmentation and Regional Egoism

The nationalist movements grew sharper and sharper and almost all of the republics declared their independence or sovereignty, and republics, nationalities, and localities all stressed their independent interests in preserving their respective resources. In this way a conflict of interests occurred between the center and the localities. Within the localities the region, the city, and the district all insisted on their respective autonomous interests. For example, the chairman of the Zhitomir city soviet, V. Mel'nituk, suggested that with the region above and the districts below grasping various powers, the city was really in a powerless condition.[34] In this way, along with the crisis of the breakup of the Soviet Union as a unified state there occurred a kind of territorial egoism. Economically, too, unification was lost and a breakdown was in progress. When Gorbachev tried to respond through emergency strengthening of presidential authority and reliance on the military as the sole unifying organization, this gave rise to the resistance and despair of the republics and of the reform groups that opposed centralization. In August 1991

Gorbachev was to regret his earlier trust in the conservatives at the helm of the military, the KGB, the Interior Ministry, and even the Prime Ministership. Some months later, territorial power disputes and economic fragmentation seemed only to worsen under the Commonwealth of Independent States.

The Crisis of Ideology and Morality

The ideals of communist ideology lost their prestige. By late 1990 support for socialism had sunk to 10 to 20 percent. Communist ideology was repeatedly subjected to public attack. Furthermore, in the Soviet Union honor, duty, morality, patriotism, and virtually all values had long been linked to socialist ideology. Thus, the collapse of the ideology led to a moral collapse.[35] In China, where morality for most people was largely centered in the family and the community, the moral collapse in the letdown of the 1970s and again in the uneven reforms of the 1980s did not reach such proportions.

In June 1990, with the founding Congress of the Russian Communist Party, the coherence of the conservative group was strengthening at the very time that there was a fragmentation of the reform group and a decline of their power. The interregional group of radical reformers that coalesced with a membership of about 500 deputies in the summer of 1989 was reduced to under 230 by the end of 1990. In contrast, the conservative group *"Soyuz"* which formed in 1990, gained a membership of more than 560 deputies.[36] From the beginning of September 1990 to the beginning of October, the conservative group systematically attacked the democratic groups in *Pravda, Sovetskaia Rossiia,* and *Rabochiaia tribuna.* They exaggerated the economic and social crisis and the fear of hunger. Distrusting voices openly called for the resignation of the Gorbachev leadership. There occurred direct or indirect sabotage by the apparatchiki. Retaining administrative power, they did not give enough information to parliament, even in this era of glasnost.[37]

With the paralysis of party power and the breakup of the union, the army began to acquire special political meaning as the only unified organization with power. The possibility of political acts by the army suddenly increased. Already inside the army, information was transmitted about political actions it was taking. To stop the breakup of the union, President Gorbachev in January 1991 depended more on the army. The army played a special role at the time in suppressing the independence of the Baltic and other republics. Nonetheless in August a divided army failed to give the coup the backing its leaders expected.

Yeltsin soon took charge of a shake-up in the military leadership and an effort to reduce the military's stranglehold over the economy.

In the deepening economic and social disorder, the role of the KGB was being strengthened. The Supreme Soviet on November 23, 1990, entrusted rights to control economic sabotage to the KGB. The Moscow Soviet and other city soviets gave it full authority for unmasking economic crime.[38] It is ironical that the aid of the KGB was seen as necessary to introduce a market economy. The KGB, however, after its role in the August coup was exposed, was drastically reorganized and stripped of many of its functions.

The main reason for the mounting disorder in 1990–91 was perceived to be a lack of centralized power. It was impossible to improve the situation only through democratic means. Therefore, the theory of democratic centralism, which earlier had been rejected, again gained support.[39] Among others, Roy Medvedev intensified his criticism of the reform group that rejected centralism.[40]

Pessimism and apathy reigned in the Soviet Union in the second half of 1990 and early 1991. People lost hope in the future of reform and in the future of the Soviet Union. Tatiana Zaslavskaia wrote in December 1990 that the democratic group had been in too much of a hurry to grasp power. Men such as Popov and Sobchak seemed to have nothing to offer except their knowledge. They would have been cleverer to remain in the opposition, she asserted, adding that as the democratic power bloc collapses, the possibility of a temporary victory of the right cannot be excluded.[41]

When asked in December 1990 when the Soviet Union would get out of its crisis, respondents were not at all hopeful. Only 1 percent said in the next year, 8 percent said within two to three years, and 15 percent said within five to six years. In contrast, 16 percent answered by the year 2000, 32 percent said it would take longer, and 12 percent said that it would be impossible no matter how much time passed. Another poll asked Soviet citizens to name persons, past and present, who have a lot of meaning for them. The results were as follows: 58 percent chose Christ, 48 percent Sakharov, 36 percent Lenin, 26 percent Gorbachev, and as many as 9 percent Stalin.[42]

The Desire for Strong Leadership and Order

Disorder greatly influenced popular consciousness concerning authoritarianism, a powerful leadership, and central economic control. In May 1990 Sobchak said soviet power must be the only power,[43] but afterward he proclaimed "all power to the mayor," which, in fact, meant rejecting the soviets. In the ensuing conflict with the city soviet, 67 percent of city residents supported Sobchak, and only 7 percent backed the soviet deputies.[44]

It is said that there is nothing more terrible than to live in Russia in conditions of a power vacuum.[45] As disorder was deepening, the attitude of the nation toward the army was changing. After the April 1989 Tbilisi incident, when the army killed many civilians, the army was strongly criticized by the parliament, the government, and the people, and among the people it lost a lot of prestige, leading to the term the "Tbilisi syndrome." In various republics draft evasion became widespread. But with the intensification of nationality conflicts, unease grew about the prospects of civil war, and the army was the organization that gained the most trust of the nation. A poll of May 1990 showed that 61.8 percent of the people had complete trust in the army, 47.9 percent had complete trust in the church, and 29.5 percent had complete trust in the party.[46] In 1991 the army was to lose much of this trust.

The possibility arose of introducing in many places an antimarket mechanism through a rationing system of all foodstuffs. Concerning this extreme control measure, a survey of Moscow citizens found 53.3 percent in favor and 32 percent opposed.[47] Trust in the spontaneous force of the market was not high, nor were people reassured when Yeltsin raised prices drastically in January 1992 but the desired effect— sudden reappearance of abundant supplies on store shelves—failed to happen.

The essential differences between views of authoritarianism before and after the summer of 1990 were the following. In the Soviet Union the result of the daring attempt at political democratization created a new attitude toward authoritarianism. After they had experienced the early process of democratization, reformers stressed the necessity of combining democratization from below with some types of authoritarian methods from above. Approaches to neo-authoritarianism vary, depending on where the stress is put. A. Yakovlev said, "Strong elements of both democracy and authoritarianism will have to be combined." While placing the stress on democracy, he said, "the seat of authoritarianism is possible, inevitable, somewhere even useful, but under the control of the democratic system as a whole. Not democracy 'built into' authoritarian structures—but authoritarian subsystems 'built into' democracy and controlled by it."[48] Stanislav Stankevich also advocated a combination of authoritarianism from above and the democratic movement from below. He suggested that the Soviet savior be a joining of Gorbachev and Yeltsin, who symbolize both sides. As he reported privately, he took very seriously the split between them in mid-October 1990.

A TURNING TOWARD NEO-AUTHORITARIANISM

In China after 1978 there seemed to be many turning points as the leadership backtracked on reforms. Yet each time the momentum of reform built up again. Only the June 4, 1989, military crackdown on the demonstrations in Tiananmen Square represented a true break with the reform forces. This set the reform process back by years.

In the Soviet Union between 1985 and mid-1991 there were several times when Gorbachev appeared to step back from reform or when the forces arrayed against reform took advantage of Gorbachev's weakness. The ouster of Yeltsin from the Politburo, the ideological offensive associated with the letter of Nina Andreeva, and the unleashing of troops on Tbilisi demonstrators are among the clearest examples. Although these were less serious setbacks than the ouster of Hu Yaobang as party secretary, the Chinese Communist Party's concerted campaign against spiritual pollution, and the crackdown and imprisonment of the leaders of the Democracy Wall movement, they reveal a similar pattern of inconsistency.

If the challenge of Beijing intellectuals to Deng Xiaoping's notion of reform repeatedly proved to be the litmus test for China's march forward, the test in the Soviet Union came from the challenge of ethnic nationalists aroused by democratic forces. For example, A. Migranian argued for strengthening the center and its coercive power in the face of dangers of division and instability. In the early fall of 1990 Migranian was openly critical of the democratic forces. He charged that the democratic group is the victim of eighteenth-century rationalism, which assumes that society can be built according to a plan. Their utopianism is revealed in belief that power can be built from bottom to top or through a contract. The result of a utopian approach is not the victory of the democrats, but the dismantling of society and chaos. Democracy means more than freedom of choice, popular sovereignty, and political pluralism. It also means a breakdown leading to a strict system of submission to the state. Only the structure of force chosen by the people guarantees such submission in the face of imminent collapse. The army is the last guarantee of state stability and unity; the breakup of the army would lead to civil war. For Migranian the military becomes an instrument for reform. What obstructs commercialization or democratization, he warns, is a power vacuum at the center.[49]

Other voices sang a similar tune. T. Koriagina said that the collapse of power produced chaos. She criticized the idea that wide privatization will bring stability, and she stressed the importance of political power.[50] A. Kiba also favored a strong hand in reform; only authoritarian power can reform the system in a crisis. From the point of view of Russia's distinctiveness, he criticized the idealistic position that stresses democracy. His theory is that a nation that does not know the taste of democracy will not hunger for democracy. Only in a mature, well-fed society does democracy become the highest value, and for that developed human beings are a precondition.[51]

The argument that in the Soviet Union there are few or no conditions for the rapid emergence of democratization is related to the argument that points to large differences between Eastern Europe and the Soviet Union. There are at least five reasons why greater disorder appeared in the Soviet Union, according to Soviet theorists. First, power was dismantled without any container to hold it. Second, in the Soviet case, where earlier all the natural social, economic, and moral relations had been destroyed, order was maintained by artificial administrative means; therefore, when these were paralyzed, great disorder followed.[52] Third, the democratic group was unable to prepare for holding power, and although Sakharov and others gained moral support, they had no practical ability, political sense, or administrative ability.[53] Fourth, the breakdown of the administrative system was too rushed. Its possibilities should have been further used. Fifth, through glasnost only rejection and criticism went forward, and these alone do not yet constitute real politics.[54]

Yakovlev, who mentioned the necessity of a kind of authoritarianism, referred to the need to consider the destructiveness of a nation's history and culture. In economics, too, Popov and others for a time advocated the introduction of a rationing system—that is, an "administrative-command market." L. Piiasheva, and other democrats opposed to authoritarianism, criticized the economic program of Popov as much more conservative than the program of Ryzhkov and Leonid Abalkin.[55] Privately, Emelianov severely criticized the positions of Popov, Sobchak, Stankevich and others as reactionary and helping the conservatives.

On March 24, 1989, the newspaper *Guangming ribao* summarized a conference on neo-authoritarianism. At this time discussions about the topic were raging in what were identified as Chinese "middle-aged intellectual" circles. The paper observed that excited discussions had been initiated in Beijing by a November conference on modernization theory. One of the more recent discussions focusing on neo-authoritarianism in current political thought was summarized in the article. Among the issues raised was the notion of enlightened despotism as a means for overcoming China's crisis and advancing economic reform and political freedom. One participant was quoted as objecting to this idea because it is impossible to truly combine "enlightenment" and "despotism." History shows that the despot never can avoid regressing. Given the complexity of the contemporary social system and the tendency for the entire world to converge from many directions, conditions are now even more in evidence for "enlightened despotism" to fail, this source added.[56] The intellectual context for the crackdown on China's fledgling openness of debate and democratic participation was shaped by this debate, as was the context for Gorbachev's crackdown in January 1991 shaped by the Soviet debates outlined earlier. Loss of trust in democratic means led many who espoused reform goals to gravitate to more authoritarian approaches, however much they qualified their ideas with concerns about reverting to the past totalitarian system.

In the heady days of the Beijing spring, the democratic forces rallied in such numbers that the normal civilian control forces, mostly in party organs at the workplace, were overwhelmed. Only the military could be counted on, even if it meant bringing recruits in from the country who were uninformed about the causes of resistance in the capital. For the cause of national stability, as defined by a small circle of leaders and largely accepted by the military, security, and party apparatus, the troops killed peaceful civilian demonstrators.

On January 13, 1991, in the Baltic cities, beginning with Vilnius, a military crackdown also ensued. Here was the most decisive turning point away from reform in the Gorbachev era. One man at the top had tried to prevent this shift with remarkable personal courage in resisting his associates in the leadership, but he failed. Like Zhao Ziyang eighteen months earlier, Eduard Shevardnadze had been the second figure responsible for the major arena of reforms (for Moscow foreign policy and for Beijing economic policy). Like Zhao, he had a strong personal interest in a second arena (for Shevardnadze, a Georgian, nationality affairs and for Zhao, a close associate of economists, the democratic role of the intellectuals). The defeat for Shevardnadze personally and for Soviet reformers collectively was not as decisive or as devastating as was the defeat for Zhao, but Vilnius symbolized a shift of course that, as in China, would slow and alter the direction of reform. The military had become a central actor in the relationship between the state and the civil society.

In mid-1991 the prospects for authoritarianism in the Soviet Union were viewed in contrasting ways. With Yeltsin's resounding June 12 election as Russian president in a six-man field came the reaction that it is too late to think about an authoritarian version of modernizing the economy under the aegis of the Communist Party, following Asian models. We have hurried past that fork in the road. Yet it was rumored that forces in the party, military, and KGB were gathering to suppress the newly won democratic freedoms. These would not be champions of economic liberalization. The neo-authoritarian model seemed to have few prospects in an increasingly polarized society.

The demonstrations of April–June 1989 and the coup of August 1991 were both acts of desperation. Zhao Ziyang, like Hu Yaobang before him, lost the fight to sustain China's general course of reforms and to put democratization on the agenda. Likewise, the communist and security hierarchies in the Soviet Union were forced to watch as their opportunity to take charge disappeared and the date approached for the signing of a union treaty. Desperation spread among groups losing power at the top in each country. In this atmosphere Chinese leaders were concerned that Gorbachev's summit visit in mid-May 1989 would arouse demands for following the path of glasnost and democratization that he symbolized. Soviet reformers in the summer of 1991 were also alarmed about ominous preparations by their opponents. Days before the coup Aleksandr Yakovlev turned in his membership card in the Communist Party and followed Shevardnadze's warning of December 1990 with his own warning of the danger of a new dictatorship.

JUNE 1989 AND AUGUST 1991

Despite the flirtation with neo-authoritarian ideas in China's disquieting inflationary days of 1988 and early 1989 and again in the midst of the Soviet Union's economic deterioration of 1990, many in the population did not abandon their faith in reform and democracy, especially when confronted with the threat of a reversion to hard-line Communist Party control. In an atmosphere of polarization, the citizens of Beijing flocked to the streets in support of democracy. Leading them were the students. In the ensuing emergency, the compromise formulas for guided democratization were quickly set aside. Finally, after Deng Xiaoping and the older generation of party leaders resorted to force, they unleashed a barrage of communist dogma very different from the growing call for a mixture of centralized authority and advancing democracy. They couched their appeal in terms of a struggle between the forces of order and those of anarchy, the forces of national dignity and those of subservience to the imperialists, the forces of stability needed for economic growth and those of risking the well-being of the country. China's leadership opted for polarization, not compromise.

The Soviet leaders who briefly seized power under the flimsy excuse that Gorbachev was ill found that the popular sentiments in support of a strong leader at the center were not redounding to their benefit. Even if many citizens objected to Gorbachev remaining at the helm, they were cool to a revival of the old power hierarchy. More than in China, the legitimacy of the Communist Party in the Soviet Union had been drastically undermined during the course of several years of incessant revelations and protracted struggle. Moreover the interval from December 1990 to August 1991 had further discredited the conservative center while reinforcing the legitimacy of the reformers. This resulted from the mounting failures of the Communist Party and of the security establishment and the resounding electoral successes of Boris Yeltsin.

With Gorbachev's acquiescence, the hard-liners had resorted to military force in the Baltic republics, had confiscated large denomination bank notes to deny "speculators" their "unearned income," and had tightened censorship on television to quiet the tide of anticommunist opposition. These actions heightened tensions. When Gorbachev in April finally opted for a compromise solution with the forces of national separatism and followed that with preparations for a new opening to the world capitalist economies, it became clearer that the best way to avoid anarchy was to accept the reality of separate republics that would establish their own central authority. Yeltsin's June 12 victory produced the reaction that it is too late to turn to an authoritarian version of modernizing the economy under the aegis of the Communist Party. Glasnost and democracy in just a few years had spelled the doom of communism.

In China after Prime Minister Li Peng's participation in the United Nations Security Council session of January 31, 1992, on a new world order, there were suggestions that, two and one-half years after Tiananmen, normalcy had been reestablished. Official spokesmen even suggested that in 1949 communism had saved China and now it was China's turn to save communism. To most observers, however, this possibility seemed scarcely conceivable. Even the strategy of a gradual neo-authoritarian reform led by the Communist Party seemed far-fetched under leaders as unpopular as Li Peng. Instead, it could be expected that rising regional elites, closely tied to business interests, would play a major role in the next stage of transition. Once Chinese glasnost and democratization resumed, the survival of communism would be put to its last major test. Since much of the communist system was already being dismantled, the Communist Party itself could not be expected to retain its power for long even though uncertainty over its future leadership complicated efforts to predict the timing and process of transition.

NOTES

1. Moshe Lewin, *The Gorbachev Phenomenon* (Berkeley: University of California Press, 1988), pp. 63-71 and 110.
2. James R. Millar, "The Little Deal: Brezhnev's Contribution to Acquisitive Socialism," in Terry Thompson and Richard Sheldon, eds., *Soviet Society and Culture* (Boulder: Westview Press, 1988), pp. 3–19.

3. "Concern for Family," *Moskovskaia pravda*, September 5, 1984, p. 1, trans. in *The Current Digest of the Soviet Press*, 36, no. 37 (October 10, 1984): 21.
4. Andrei Melville and Gail W. Lapidus, *The Glasnost Papers: Voices on Reform from Moscow* (Boulder: Westview Press, 1987).
5. William Parish and Martin King Whyte, *Village and Family in Contemporary China* (Chicago: University of Chicago Press, 1978), pp. 315–16.
6. Helen F. Siu, "Recycling Rituals: Politics and Popular Culture in Contemporary Rural China," in Perry Link et al., eds., *Unofficial China: Popular Culture and Thought in the People's Republic* (Boulder: Westview Press, 1989), pp. 121–37.
7. Thomas B. Gold, "Guerrilla Interviewing Among the Getihu," in Link et al., eds., *Unofficial China*, p. 190.
8. Lynn T. White III, "Thought Workers in Deng's Time," in Merle Goldman, ed., *China's Intellectuals and the State: In Search of a New Relationship*, Harvard Contemporary China Series 3, (Cambridge, Mass.: Harvard University Press, 1987), pp. 259–61.
9. *Nauchno-tekhnicheskaia revoliutsiia i chelovek* (Moscow: Nauka, 1977).
10. *Nauchno-tekhnicheskii progress v Iaponii* (Moscow: Nauka, 1984).
11. Feng Lanrui, Sun Kaifei, and Liu Shiding, "The Worldwide New Industrial Revolution and China's Socialist Modernization," *Selected Writings on Studies of Marxism*, no. 3 (Beijing: Institute of Marxism-Leninism-Mao Zedong Thought, Chinese Academy of Social Sciences, 1984).
12. Richard P. Suttmeier, "Science, Technology, and China's Political Future: A Framework for Analysis," in Denis Fred Simon and Merle Goldman, eds., *Science and Technology in Post-Mao China*, Harvard Contemporary China Series 5 (Cambridge, Mass.: Harvard University Press, 1989), p. 396.
13. Jerome M. Gillison, *The Soviet Image of Utopia* (Baltimore: Johns Hopkins University Press, 1975), pp. 66–67 and 155–59.
14. N. Karpunin, "We Discuss the Draft Law on Labor Collectives: Where Authority Must be Exercised," *Pravda*, April 26, 1983, trans. in *The Current Digest of the Soviet Press*, 35, no. 18 (June 1, 1983): 10.
15. Andrew G. Walder, *Communist Neo-Traditionalism: Work and Authority in Chinese Industry* (Berkeley: University of California Press, 1986).
16. Jean C. Oi, *State and Peasant in Contemporary China: The Political Economy of Village Government* (Berkeley: University of California Press, 1989).
17. V. Kuvaldin, "Turning Point: For the Country There Is No Going Back," *Izvestiia*, July 3, 1991, p. 3, trans. in *The Current Digest of the Soviet Press*, 43, no. 27 (August 7, 1991): 8.
18. Li Honglin, "Socialism and Opening to the Outside World," *Selected Writings on Studies of Marxism*, no. 4 (Beijing: Institute of Marxism-Leninism-Mao Zedong Thought, Chinese Academy of Social Sciences, 1984).
19. I. Kliamkin, A. Migranian, and G. Tselims, "Nuzhna 'zheleznaia ruka'?" *Literaturnaia gazeta*, August 16, 1989; I. Kliamkin, A. Migranian, and E. Ambartsumov, "Oboidemsia bez 'zheleznoi ruki,' " *Literaturnaia gazeta*, December 27, 1989, p. 10; and R. Sakwa, "The New Authoritarianism," *Detente*, no. 16, 1989, pp. 18–25.
20. Su Shaozhi, "Understanding Democratic Reform in China" (unpublished manuscript, Bradley Institute for Democracy and Public Values, Marquette University, 1990), p. 3.
21. Wu Yaohui, "Sulian dongou guojia zhengzhi tizhi gaige de lishi kaocha," *Shehui kexue*, no. 8, 1987, pp. 11–16
22. G. Popov, "Kak vyiti iz krizisa" *Moskovskie novosti*, No. 42, 1990, p. 7; G. Popov, "Perspektivy i realii," *Ogonek*, No. 51, pp. 5–8, No. 52, pp. 6–8; G. Popov, " 'Obratsovyi gorod' stal simvolom krizisa perestroiki," *Kuranty*, no. 9, 1990, p. 5.
23. "Raivlast," *Komsomolskaia pravda*, September 20, 1990, p. 2.
24. S. Stankevich, "Dnevnik Mossoveta—gde vykhod iz tupika."
25. I. Zaslavskii, "Razmyshleniia o 'iazychestve,' *Moskovskii komsomolets*, October 16, 1990.
26. O. S. Artem'eva, "Kitaiskaia pressa o sotsial'no-politicheskom aspekte perestroiki v SSSR," *Problemy Dal'nego Vostoka*, no. 1, 1988, pp. 66–78.

27. Iu. Orlov, "Gosudarstvo-Partiia-Narod," *Argumenti i fakty*, no. 24, 1990, p. 5.
28. T. Zaslavskaia "Eto kakoe-to nervnoe istoshchenie" *Komsomolskaia pravda*, October 30, 1990, p. 2.
29. L. Shevtsova, "Krizis vlast," *Izvestiia*, September 17, 1990, p. 3.
30. Iu. Ryzhov, "Astenicheskii sindrom," *Moskovskie novosti*, no. 44, 1990, p. 7.
31. A. Telen, "Ot krizisa vlasti k vlasti krizisov," *Moskovskie novosti*, No. 44, 1990, p. 7.
32. Wen Ji, *Zhongguo zhengzhi wenhua: minzhu zhengzhi nanchande shehui shinli insu* (Kunming: Yunnan renmin chubanshe), Chap. 2 and 3.
33. "Vilnius Residents Polled," *Moscow News*, no. 16, 1990, p. 11.
34. "Khoziaeva bez khoziaistva," *Izvestiia*, September 17, 1990, p. 2.
35. T. Zaslavskaia, "Eto kakoe-to nervnoe istoshchenie," *Komsomolskaia pravda*, October 30, 1990, p. 2.
36. "Soren kaikakuha ni motomerareru mono," *Asahi shimbun*, January 10, 1991, p. 5.
37. Iu. Ryzhov, "Astenicheskii sindrom," *Moskovskie novosti*, no. 44, 1990, p. 7.
38. "KGB protiv ekonomicheskogo sabotazha," *Moskovskie novosti*, no. 49, p. 1.
39. L. Onikov, "Gde istoki krizisa," *Pravda*, December 4, 1990, p. 3.
40. R. Medvedev, "Vzaimosviaz ideologii, politiki i obshchestvennykh nauk," *Kommunist*, no. 16, 1990, p. 4.
41. T. Zaslavskaia, "Sitiuatsiia chrezvychaino slozhnaia," *Izvestiia*, December 17, 1990, p. 2.
42. "Sotsial'nyi barometr," *Moskovskie novosti*, no. 49, 1990, p. 9.
43. "Anatolii Sobchak—predsedatel' Lensoveta," *Argumenti i fakty*, no. 23, 1990, p. 6.
44. "Kredit doveriia ne ischerpan, no . . .," *Leningradskaia pravda*, October 3, 1990, p. 1.
45. A. Tsipko and I. Milshtein, "Ostorozhno! Bolshevizm," *Ogonek*, no. 47, 1990, p. 11.
46. "Vsesoiuznii tsentr po izucheniiu obshchestvennogo mneniia soobshchaet," *Ogonek*, no. 25, 1990, p. 1.
47. "Da zdravstvuiut kartochki?," *Moskovskii komsomolets*, November 25, 1990.
48. A. Yakovlev, "Traps For Democracy," *Moscow News*, no. 42, 1990, p. 5.
49. A. Migranian, "Soiuz nerushimyi?" *Izvestiia*, September 20, 1990, p. 3.
50. T. Koriagina, "Chestnaia vlast' i demokraty," *Moskovskii komsomolets*, November 11, 1990, p. 2.
51. A. Kiba, "Opasatsia li avtoritarnoi vlasti," *Izvestiia*, December 10, 1990, p. 3.
52. L. Shevtsova, "Krizis vlast," *Izvestiia*, September 17, 1990, p. 3.
53. A. Tsipko, "Ostorozhno! Bolshevizm," *Ogonek*, No. 47, 1990, p. 11.
54. S. Zalygin, "Kuda idut Russkie?. . .," *Komsomolskaia pravda*, October 3, 1990, p. 2.
55. L. Piiasheva, "Zigzagi sotsial'noi ekvilibristiki," *Literaturnaia gazeta*, March 28, 1990, p. 14.
56. " 'Xinchuanweizhuyi' taolunhui congshu," *Guangming ribao*, March 24, 1989, p. 3.

5

China: The Process of Reform

Tatsumi Okabe

To find out what kind of path China will follow in implementing its reform policies, this chapter extrapolates past trends. It takes into account China's special background and makes comparisons with the reforms in Eastern Europe and the Soviet Union. The goal is to identify some of the factors that shaped China's experience in the 1980s and to anticipate what will happen as the 1990s unfold.

CHARACTERISTICS OF CHINA'S REFORM

Nationalistic impulses behind China's reform and the open door policy have served the modernization of that nation. The Soviet Union is similar to China in this regard, but most of the Eastern European countries seem to be motivated by less nationalistic reasons (democracy, better standards of living, and so on). To understand the case of Chinese nationalism, it is necessary to recall the modern history of the country, especially since the mid-nineteenth century. Before that time China was "the Center of the World," both in its images and in reality, although its decline had already started much earlier.[1] After the Opium War China was incorporated into the existing international society.

The international society of the nation-state system originated in Western Europe and still dominates the world at the end of the twentieth century.[2] Although one of the principles of the system is the equality of sovereign nations, China until the middle of the twentieth century was a subordinate member of the system because of its weakness. One of the objectives of Chinese revolutions in modern times was to make China a truly independent member of the system by overcoming its weakness. Nationalistic fever, which was the product of the nation-state system, became the major motivating force of the revolutions including the communist one. In developed countries communists tried to overthrow regimes through "class struggle," while in China the same activities were mainly advanced under the banner of "national struggle."

In 1949 the Chinese communist revolution proved victorious, and China became a truly independent state within the nation-state system for the first time. The leadership, however, realized that without strengthening the country through modernization this independence would be fragile. Modernization of the nation, therefore, has been an objective of utmost importance since then.[3] The history of the People's Republic of China (PRC) has constituted a process of trial and error for socialist modernization. The infamous "detour" of the Great Leap Forward and the Cultural Revolution were among the remarkable errors.

A new period of modernization started at the end of 1978 with reform and the open door policy as the major means. The first aim of the reform and the open door policy has been to strengthen the country rather than to improve the life of the people. Both, of course, are related. The stability of the country has been threatened by the social mobilization accompanying modernization. Therefore, the latter aim has become more and more important.

China's reform policies have had a dual role: first, to remove the Stalinist command economy and the dictatorship of the proletariat; second, to eliminate remnants of China's tradition disadvantageous for its modernization. China introduced the Stalinist system from the "motherland of socialism," but most of the Eastern European countries had it forced upon them.

As is well known now, the Stalinist centralized planned economy and the political system that went hand in hand with it worked better in very poor or wartime situations. Even many of the capitalist countries during and just after the war suffered from a lack of needed products and had to adopt some measures of a controlled economy. The system, however, does not at all suit richer and more complicated economies. It proved impossible to plan everything people need beforehand, and the system produced queues and stockpiles. Planning failed to adjust supply and demand, which markets, not necessarily entirely free any more, can do by an invisible hand.

Another weak point of the system was the lack of incentive for technological innovation. In a planned economy the primary task of a manager is to fulfill the quantitative "norms." Therefore, before the norms are given, it is necessary for the manager to bargain with his or her superior not to be assigned too large a norm lest it should not be fulfilled. Such bargaining skills rather than managerial skills are more important in this system. In this situation and in the absence of competition, technological innovation must proceed very slowly. One notable exception was in the field of military technology. Noneconomic competition with the United States and espionage kept the Soviet Union's military technology fairly up-to-date.

Politically, the centralized system had an inherent weak point of relying on the decisions of one man behind a thick veil of secrecy. Sometimes the system, without heeding noisy public opinion, made remarkable achievements. Most of the time, however, the unchecked "fallible man" made many fatal mistakes, such as those of Mao in the Great Leap Forward and the Cultural Revolution. With the continuing diversification and pluralization of the society, the dictatorial system failed to respond to the demands of the people or to adjust to their contradictory interests. The assumption proved false that the party, or the giant at the top, can know all the demands of the monolithic "people" or "proletariat" and can represent them.

Realizing these difficulties, European socialist countries tried reform as early as the 1960s. China then advanced in quite a different direction. The Cultural Revolution was admired by many Western people (including the Japanese) who thought the end of Western civilization was coming and who wanted a new civilization to replace it.[4] But for most of the Chinese people, the Cultural Revolution was a nightmare.[5] By this China delayed the start of the reform compared to its European counterparts by more than 20 years, and made almost all the Chinese leaders who suffered during the Cultural Revolution reformers to some degree.

The second task of the reform for China, the elimination of the disadvantageous remnants of the pre-modern society, also was not present in most of the European socialist countries. China never experienced a full-fledged capitalist period that could have eliminated the traditional behavior patterns that are disadvantageous to modernization. Karl Marx and many other thinkers have noted the destructive effects of capitalism on feudal or other traditional institutions and cultures that are counterproductive in developing not only capitalism, but also democracy and other features of modernity.[6] Modernity is a prerequisite of becoming a major or independent member of the nation-state system. China has needed modernity, just as Japan did after the Meiji Restoration. The disadvantages of traditional behavior mentioned here are identified only with regard to modernization or raising the international rank of the country. It is a known fact that many Chinese intellectuals have criticized the feudal elements in China since the May Fourth Movement in 1919, and in the 1980s they repeated a similar criticism of them.

China's models for becoming modern were first the European countries and the United States, then Japan, and finally the Soviet Union. The Soviet Union, however, failed to serve as a clear-cut model for

Chinese leaders from the late 1950s through the 1970s (the Sino-Soviet conflict) and again in the early 1990s (when the Soviet Central Committee first renounced the leadership of the party, then the Yeltsin leadership insisted on eliminating the party itself, which the Chinese consider the core of any socialist system). The Soviets also accepted political pluralism, which the Chinese leadership views as bourgeois liberalization. The Chinese leaders are still searching for a Chinese way of socialist modernization.

The disadvantageous remnants of China's past that impede modernization are as follows: bureaucratism, centralization of power, paternalism, the personality cult, rule by man and not by law, a rigidly hierarchical system, noninstitutionalization of decision-making practices, despotism, special privileges for rulers, nepotism, egalitarianism in distribution of income at the expense of material incentives, conservatism, anticommercialism, and closed thinking about the country and the world.[7]

In most modernized countries these disadvantageous features were wiped away or modified through competition in the markets for profits and survival. China, however, has never experienced a competitive market under the capitalist system, and it has had no chance to wipe these remnants away. In addition, China has never been unified by an integrated national market.

The overseas Chinese in Southeast Asia or the Hong Kong Chinese after the war were different from the mainlanders from the start. Most of them came from lower classes unfamiliar with the traditional culture of elite Chinese. After they rose on the social ladder, the environments they found were quite different from those of the mainland. Nevertheless, they retained Chinese popular culture. They have, however, adapted well to capitalist developments in the resident countries after the war and changed rapidly. Chinese in the mainland did not, because of the lack of capitalism.

After the Tiananmen incident those who stressed the disadvantages of the Chinese tradition were severely criticized. There are three reasons for this. First, the seemingly total denial of the "Great Chinese Tradition," as in the famous television documentary "He-shang," can lead to westernization or bourgeois liberalization. Chinese leaders want a "Chinese way," whatever that means.

Second, it is necessary for current leaders to defend China's very early transition to socialism in the early 1950s. According to Mao's original idea of New Democracy, the new democratic period would continue for decades until the society became mature enough to suit the needs of socialist development. Suddenly Mao, against his own plan, started to move quickly to socialism. The theory of the "primitive stage of social-ism," introduced in 1987, was an attempt to make up for the stage that was prematurely jumped in the 1950s.[8] To save the legitimacy of the party, leaders do not welcome discussions on "feudal remnants" to be wiped away during the aborted period of New Democracy. Vietnam, a similar socialist country in Asia, says it is now in a transitional period to socialism. In other words, in the early 1990s it had not yet reached the level of socialism.[9] This is very similar to the original idea of Mao's New Democracy.

Third, the Chinese leadership has to resort to "patriotism" (*aiguo-zhuyi*) to unify the country now that belief in socialism is rapidly declin-ing. Any denial of the Chinese tradition would be counterproductive, the leaders felt. After all, the tradition must have good points for mod-ernization. It is telling, however, that the leaders have not been able to show many persuasive examples of remnants from tradition that are advantageous to China's modernization.[10] The glorious Chinese tradi-tion is poorly suited to Western-oriented modernization and nation-building.

To eliminate the disadvantageous features for modernization, China must have a capitalist system or some kind of market economy to replace "capitalism." Yet the traditionalism remaining in China is well suited to the despotism of the imported Stalinist system. The two were well fused during the building of socialism in China. Bureaucratism and nepotism are two of the factors Chinese tradition and the Stalinist system have in common. Rule by a "man of virtue" and networks of connections (*guanxi*) rather than rule by law are other similarities.

Socialist bureaucracy, which is characterized by sharply differentiated vertical command lines, is well suited to the decentralized situation in China. There are very few horizontal relations or communications. In this sense the warlord economy (*zhuhou jingji*), which divides the country by provincial or even prefectural boundaries, has dual ancestors in the closed systems of the Stalin era and of traditional China.[11] The country is unified as a state, not by an integrated market but by monopolistic national organizations, the party and the military.[12] This is another reason why one authoritative person must decide almost everything related to state policies or, at best, must reign as a symbolic unifier. This explains why the renunciation of party leadership and elimination of the party by the Soviet Union was so shocking to the Chinese leaders.

It is the party and the military that unify China. Therefore, it has been strictly prohibited to organize spontaneous associations even of some innocent kind. This was required by the goal of keeping China a unified state and hindering disintegration. A very different but related example was the Cultural Revolution. At that time the party was paralyzed, and the military took over the role of integrator. The party resumed its supremacy over the military only after Deng Xiaoping was rehabilitated. The situation has not changed since then. With the development of reform and the release of popular energy, the necessity for an integrator increases. China's insistence on party leadership and nationalism is the product of this situation.[13] Vietnam, though on a smaller scale, is in a similar situation.

An alternative to the "party as unifier" may be a federation. This alternative, however, is unacceptable for the Chinese leaders because of their tenacious belief in a unified state (in "unity is strength") and the traditional idea of "treasuring unification" (*dayitong*). Yan Jiaqi, one of the refugees after the Tiananmen crackdown, is a known advocate of the federation formula for China. Naturally, China's leaders would not listen to a refugee's opinion. It is ironical to recall that Mao Zedong advocated a federation for China before he came to power.[14]

Driven by their nationalistic objective of making China more modernized, Chinese leaders will not step down from the "reform race." Whether reform and the open door policy will succeed in modernizing China is unknown, but the leaders will never go back to the closed planned economy.

China and its European counterparts can be compared in terms of the following variables: capitalist development before the revolution; recent development, whether capitalist or socialist; rigidity of the Stalinist system before reform;[15] national unification before and after the revolution; size of the country in land and population; proportion of educated class in the population; degree of covert or overt "participant culture"; degree of real or potential political participation. If these variables are compared, we can know both differences and similarities among different socialist countries that are reforming themselves.

THE BEGINNING OF THE REFORM

China started its reform from the economic aspect. At the beginning China's economic reform had no clear-cut images or models. Early European socialist reforms pointed in a vague direction, but they were not models. Later, with the development of reform, the Hungarian experience became a pseudo-model, although obvious differences between the two countries made it impossible for Hungary to become a genuine model.

At any rate China's reform started from the rural areas somewhat spontaneously. The most prominent leaders were Zhao Ziyang in Sichuan and Wan Li in Anhui. The reform broke the collective farms (the People's Communes) up into family units. The peasants divided the land and created a new system of family contracts, although this was inhibited in the famous document that is said to have started the reform and the open door policy at the Third Plenum of the Eleventh Party Congress.[16] Zhao and Wan encouraged the unauthorized system to make it a standard model of the rural reform. The "People's Commune," once said to be the "spontaneous" creation of peasants, collapsed entirely by 1985.

Reform in the rural areas was a remarkable success at the beginning. During the days of the People's Commune, productivity on the family plots was much higher than on the collective farms. Success in the reform became possible mainly because the repressed energy of the peasants for development was released. Ideologically, most of the Chinese leaders and scholars still believe in the superiority of the collective style of farming.[17] This amply shows the spontaneity of the rural reforms and suggests the difficulties that occurred later. In a word, there was no well-thought-out blueprint.

The situation in cities was much the same. Although Hungarian models had been studied well by October 1984, when the famous party decision on economic reform was adopted,[18] details of the reform model were not known yet. Zhao Ziyang was later reported to have equated China's reform to crossing a river by searching for stones with one's feet to find shallow places.

The party decided that a "socialist commodity economy" should be realized. "Commodity economy" means a market economy with very little planning, although this was not clear at the outset. It became widely stated that reform means expansion of the market economy and reduction of the areas where planning operates. "Socialist," as far as substantive policies were concerned, was a mere rhetorical adjective, although using the word in the 1984 decision was and is very important for ideological and political reasons. Enterprises were expected to become "relatively independent economic entities" with sole responsibility for their profits and losses. The leadership tried to eliminate the "softness" of the "budgetary restraint" that had been the source of underdevelopment under the paternalistic economic system.[19]

If China had ever had a genuine and unified market economy, the proclamation of reform in the cities in 1984 might have produced independent enterprises. Industrial capitalism, however, did not develop in China. Entrepreneurship in large factories did not, either. As a result, release of oppressed energy, as in rural areas, was not poured into industrialism but into the traditional style of commerce that uses price

differences among areas. Because of the underdeveloped and nonuni-
fied markets, people traveled a long way to sell their products at prices
much higher than in their neighborhood. This behavior pattern is very
similar to that of entrepot traders in Singapore in the pre-industrial
days. Historically speaking, pre-modern commercialism of this kind
has not developed into industrialism or produced a genuine market
economy.

Despite the limitations, the released energy brought a booming economy to China. Many people thought the reform and the open door
policy were successful, broadly speaking. Trade expanded rapidly.
China's share of world trade reached about the same level as that for
Taiwan, whose population is less than one fiftieth that of mainland
China. Once cautious about foreign investments and loans for ideological reasons and because of its experience with foreign countries, China
started to accept them on a large scale. In this way China is gradually
being incorporated into the international economy.

The remnants of Chinese tradition are also reflected in foreign interactions. Most of the investments in China from Hong Kong or from
Chinese overseas went into tertiary industries because it is easier to
enter or leave them; tertiary industries could ensure a shorter turnover
for invested money. The shortsightedness of pre-modern commercial
capitalism and lessons from the period of political turmoil made investing in tertiary industries with short turnover natural when investing
in China. Overseas Chinese investors are in a better position to understand China's ways, including systems, practices, and economic mentality. Similar behavior patterns by Chinese bureaucrats are easy to understand, too. Therefore, long-sighted investments that would really
contribute to China's modernization met with difficulties: red tape, the
Chinese people's suspicion of foreigners, and their unfortunate desire
to buy things as cheaply as possible. In Japan there is a saying that
"buying cheap things ends up in losing money." This is what the Chinese
are doing, but so far Japanese businessmen have not been able to persuade proud Chinese on this point.[20]

After Gorbachev came to power and started perestroika, many said
that on economic reform China preceded the Soviet Union, while on
political reform the Soviet Union went ahead. This is true to some extent.
China's planned economy was a loose centralized system, but the "authentic" Stalinist system in the Soviet Union was rigid and centralized.
In a rigid system every material for production and consumption should
be controlled by the state. In China, even in areas where planning was
best implemented, there was a "three eights system": Materials allocated
to enterprises were 80 percent of the plan, ordered materials were 80

percent of the allocation, and acquired materials were 80 percent of the order.[21] Thus, even before the reform, centralized planning in China covered only half of the Chinese industrial economy. Indeed, China was politically even more rigid than was the Soviet Union, not to mention those Eastern European countries that have experienced a Western type of democracy.

The centralized planned economy disintegrated more easily in China than it did in the Soviet Union and in some Eastern European countries, but building a reformed society was not easier in China. Easy disintegration often means confusion, and it even leads to difficulty in reintegrating the society along new lines. Some may argue that the loose-rigid comparison between China and the Soviet Union is not justified because the latter disintegrated drastically. That argument, however, confuses the looseness of state economic control with the political disintegration of the last empire on earth. The Soviet disintegration is a problem of national or ethnic self-determination and too chaotic a change in its political system. On the other hand, the Soviet economy has difficulty dismantling the yoke of the old, rigid system, while the Chinese economy enjoys the looseness of its pre-reform centralization.

Political reform in China was proposed in the early 1980s. From the start this reform was very different from what was to occur in European countries that have had some experience with Western democracy. The main motivating force was the deep self-reflection caused by the Cultural Revolution. The Chinese leadership, however, never envisioned dispensing with the monopoly of party leadership. When Deng first raised the problem, the targets were decentralization of power, reduction of excessive posts, separation of party and government, and the "succession problem." To achieve these targets, Deng advocated some sort of supervision of high-up members of the party and government by general members of the party and by the masses. He also wanted rejuvenated, better educated, and more specialized cadres. Deng tried to dispense with the remnants of both Stalinism-Maoism and feudalism.[22]

The scheme did not aim at a Western style of democracy, but even so it was never fully implemented. It was not a regime transition, but a within-system change (*tizhi gaige*). Deng's proposals, however, offered some buds for Western ways of thinking. Despotism, authoritarianism, and feudal tradition in China have one thing in common: "men of virtue" know everything. Western democracy, however, presupposes the fallibility of men. "Power corrupts, and absolute power corrupts absolutely," in Lord Acton's famous phrase. The central features of democracy—whether they be participation, free elections, or the right of protest—are all related to checking this fallibility. It was natural that, just after the Cultural Revolution, any plan for political reform included schemes for checks. Since there was and is no national organization other than the party itself powerful enough to master the corruption of power, any political reform or democracy was never intended to liquidate the monopoly of power by the party. The situation caused a dilemma between the party monopoly and efforts to strengthen and institutionalize checks by independent entities. The dilemma was amply shown in subsequent events in China. One of the first examples was Liao Gailun's plan in the fall of 1980 that advocated a plan very similar to "checks and balances" along with wide participation.[23] The plan was never made official perhaps because of this radical element. This shows the difficulty of transition from despotic regimes to authoritarian or democratic regimes.

Political reform is a prerequisite for economic reform for the following reasons. First, to make enterprises relatively independent entities, administrative constraints of the command economy have to be restructured. Second, to make the market economy work, communications and information must offer open access to a wide range of markets; knowledge about matters previously monopolized by the party and the government must be shared. Third, the pluralized interests of the society will emerge, and they cannot be represented by a single-party leadership. These problems suggest the need for a democratic system, but there are other reasons to deny the necessity of the system. First, there is difficulty in reconciling the dilemma between democracy and the monopoly by the party. Second, if there is enough freedom to produce a market economy, a full-fledged democracy is not always necessary. One example is Hong Kong. Third, democracy is a luxury for many developing states. Many of the Asian societies that have shown rapid economic development were not and are not democratic. Under authoritarian rule, economic development has been possible. The problem here is whether the feudal-Stalinist regime can move into developmental authoritarianism.

In foreign policy there was a big change in China in 1982. Although reform and the open door policy started at the end of 1978, there was a time lag before the foreign policy change occurred. That can be ascribed to the mere momentum of the old policy and to the time needed for learning. One of the big emotional reasons was that the foreign policy change had to involve a drastic change of policy toward the Soviet Union. Before the early half of 1982, China's foreign policy was based on the "main enemy thesis." In other words, the main enemy was the source of all evils. This policy was well suited to a time of war or imminent conflict, but in a peaceful time of reform, when economic development became most important, a more multidimensional issue-by-issue policy was needed. The general trend remained the same even after Tiananmen.[24]

THE REFORM IMPASSE

Reform without a clear blueprint brought about many problems. Many articles that criticized Zhao Ziyang after Tiananmen contended that the economy had started to overheat in late 1984. That seems to mean that the party decision on economic reform adopted in the fall of 1984 was the source of all the evils. It is true that the overheating was, in part, the result of reforms or of loosening the economy without a clear blueprint. Building a market economy is no easy thing. In the fall of 1988, an austerity policy had to be adopted to mitigate the existing confusion. Zhao had no option but to agree. For more than one year until after the seventh plenum of the party in late 1990 the 1984 decision was seldom cited in articles and speeches. Finally, to support the legitimacy of the regime, the Chinese leadership had to admit that the ten years of reform were a great success.

Difficulties occurred here and there. Agriculture, which had started the reform through household spontaneity, first met with problems. At the outset, due to the release of untapped energy and the revival of the pre-modern style of commerce, rural areas flourished. In 1985, however, development reached a ceiling. Then, in 1990, agriculture began to revive through massive governmental help.

The causes of the problems in agriculture are many. First is the limitation to small-scale agriculture. Land per person in China is much less than in most countries (about 0.08 hectares).[25] Even if Chinese agriculture had developed for some years, the small-scale economy soon would have suffered from declining inputs. Irrigation, for example, was retarded. The short length of the contract period for land made peasants adopt a plundering approach to agriculture. Many not familiar with the market economy failed to adapt to the fluctuations of the precarious markets. Government policies of controlled buying and selling changed often, sometimes remedying the situation of peasants, sometimes worsening it. The income of peasants, once envied by city dwellers, fluctuated. Generally speaking, it is not envied anymore. The "ten thousand yuan households" are few in number, and most of them earned money by nonagricultural work, including pre-modern commercial activities that took advantage of price differentials. These households, once models, became targets of attack as "bourgeois." Local cadres increased various assessments imposed on them. Even many less privileged peasants were assessed heavily, depriving them of their rural prosperity. It was no wonder, therefore, that the eighth plenum of the party at the end of 1991 entirely concentrated on agricultural problems to improve the plight of peasants.

Another problem is the population in the rural areas. This will become one of the biggest troubles in China in the near future. With modernization, it is natural for many people to move from rural areas to cities (social mobilization). Especially in China, income gaps between coastal areas and the hinterlands are great. There are push factors in rural areas such as the rise of productivity or the overpopulation. In cities there are pull factors such as expanded needs for labor and higher income. In China for a long time this movement was artificially controlled. The major means for that are the strict registration and rationing systems.[26] It has been very difficult to change registration from rural areas to cities. After the reform started, though the system existed as before, its implementation became more difficult because of the general loosening in society. As a result, China began to suffer from a population explosion in its cities. The leadership tried to continue a policy of control by adopting measures for absorbing the rural overpopulation, not in agriculture but in township industries across small towns in rural areas. The policy of population control was about to change in a more liberal direction easing the restrictions on movement on the eve of the Tiananmen incident. The former population policy, however, was continued after the tighter austerity program started in 1988. Many who had lived for a long time in cities, both legally and illegally, were sent back to rural areas to become a potential unemployed population. Still, it is reported that there are about 60 to 80 million "floating" (*liudong*) persons in China.[27]

A related problem is the partial failure, mainly in rural areas, of the "one-child" policy. There are three consequences of this partial failure. First, the proportion of males and females in the population was distorted by the traditional male chauvinist practice of killing female babies.[28] Second, since children are a source of income in a loose, money-oriented society, peasants wanted big families and ignored the one-child policy. School attendance also decreased. Third, people tend to go to cities where they have unregistered babies (called black children).[29] As a result, the population control is not reaching its targets. The population that was supposed to grow slowly to 1.2 billion in 2000 already has reached more than 1.13 billion according to the tentative results of the national census of July 1, 1990.[30] The expanded population will exac-

erbate many social problems such as food shortages, lack of social infrastructure, environmental hazards, and even the mass exodus from rural
areas. It also will decrease the growth in per capita GNP.[31]

Remedies by the leadership are threefold. One is to encourage labor-
intensive township industries. They are not very effective except in
some well-situated areas. Second, the government has tried to increase
labor input on farms even by resorting to old-fashioned "voluntary
labor." Third, the government has tried to build a dual management
system in which collective commercial and service industries encircle
the family contract system to make the collective economy as useful as
possible, although the recollectivization of farms is impossible for fear
of peasant protest. It seems that these measures, at least in the short
term, are working to support the rural economy and to reduce peasant
discontent to a tolerable level. This seems to contribute to the relative
stability of the country.

Aside from rural difficulties, the loss of macroscopic control of the
economy is one of the biggest problems in China. Decentralization to
the level of local governments and party branches, which was seen as
one of the remedies to the overcentralized planned economy, produced
30 (provincial), or 2,000 (district), or even more (township and village)
centralized systems on a smaller scale. Without political reforms suitable
for a commodity economy (at least the separation of party and administration and the separation of party and enterprises), decentralization
will not work as intended. The loss of macrocontrol and the shift to a
"warlord economy" are the results. Besides, enterprises that were supposed to have gained independence from centralized control are still
under the rule of the local governments. The contract system prevails
now among most of the governmental enterprises. Conditions of contracts must be settled through bargaining with the same level of government administration. Therefore, the market mechanism is still not
workable. Enterprises are independent only in name. Most enterprises
still enjoy soft budgetary restraints. Deficits are still supported by the
state in most of the big and medium-sized national enterprises. Their
productivity is quite low. In addition, Chinese enterprises are self-sufficient units, responsible for almost all aspects of life including education
and medical care. This makes enterprises (*danwei*) not only economic
entities, but small worlds for every urban Chinese who belongs. These
enterprises are very different from their counterparts in market economies.

All of these factors, together with the pre-modern style of commerce
among different markets within the country and the "double-track price
system" caused by halfhearted marketization, gave power-holders an

advantage in earning money. This led to the infamous "bureaucratic broker" (*guandao*), who became one of the targets of the student movement in 1989. For good reason, it is said that "power can be changed into money." It goes without saying that connections (*guanxi*) are very important.

In this situation political reform, or at least administrative reform, is necessary. Simply put, the administrative system established during the age of the command economy cannot be efficient in the age of the commodity economy. Allocating, commanding, and bargaining are very different from market-building. Besides, there has appeared no system for achieving compromise among the diverse interests produced by the reform policy. No political channel to articulate interests exists. This often results in quarrels and fights between peasants and cadres, or, in more sophisticated ways, in bargaining and corruption using connections. A political movement was never born because of the *lack* of organizers, a role assumed by intellectuals in many other countries. The need for political reform was originally mentioned by Deng Xiaoping in 1980. The task Deng proposed, however, was shelved until 1986, and when it was introduced it brought about the resignation of General Secretary Hu Yaobang. Political reform has not progressed because of its relation with the party leadership. Political reform, even as a limited form of administrative reform, unavoidably affects party leadership and the omnipotence of the party. To limit the power of the Communist Party for the purpose of checks and balances necessarily encroaches on the party monopoly. But the party, backed by the military, is the only integrating force in a society not integrated by a unified market. According to the orthodox understanding, the party is the only representative of the people in China. Therefore, questioning the party leadership is the biggest taboo.

In 1986 the lingering political system associated with the command economy was already seen as an obstacle to promoting the commodity economy. To be more exact, under the "two track price system" caused by "melting" the loose centralized system before a more market-oriented economy is near completion, there is room for "changing power into money." In order to overcome corruption, price reform and the reform of the political system were necessary, but they are very difficult because of the limits of popular patience with inflation and bureaucratic resistance to what is called a "revolution" of interests and power. The resistance from bureaucrats, the main target of this "revolution," was severe. The more orthodox group of leaders, many of whom had grudgingly agreed to earlier, limited reforms, was behind them. There was a saying that "if there is a policy at the top, we have a countermeasure to it."[32]

Still, with the development of political reform the party started losing its controlling power to the masses. Orthodox and ideological leaders at the top, most of whom had been honored as the heroes of the revolution and had been satisfied with the golden age of the 1950s when they enjoyed the fruits of their revolution, sensed a crisis coming for the party leadership. They then ousted Hu Yaobang as general secretary of the party.

After the Thirteenth Congress of the party in 1987, Zhao Ziyang, who had succeeded Hu Yaobang, reasserted the need for political reform. Zhao was prudent enough to limit the political reform to the minimal level that would smoothly promote economic reform. After the beginning of price reform, which caused some economic confusion and social unrest, an austerity policy was introduced. This was regarded by some reform intellectuals as stagnation of the reform policy in general.[33] In order to break this "conservative" atmosphere, they started advocating radical political reforms. Above all, they rallied the students. That was the general background of the student movement in 1989 and the Tiananmen incident, which again led to the fall of the general secretary of the party.

Two other factors also hindered political reform. First, the communications network in China was thin. This can be attributed to the remaining traditional structure of the society and to the decentralization as a result of economic reform, which prevents the new initiatives in the capital or big cities from spreading to the whole of the nation. Second, the number of intellectuals, the group most susceptible to political reform, is very small. The accumulated members of university graduates from 1949 to 1990 represented only 0.65 percent of the population in 1990.[34] The real percentage may be lower because some of the university graduates were already dead, and many others are now out of the country. Most people in China (a little less than 80 percent) live in rural areas and still have a kind of "subject culture," even though they have ample political problems to be solved. Although they are changing rapidly and are much interested in the output of the political system, they have no institutionalized means to express their demands except through quarrels and violence against the cadres. These actions are closer to "peasant rebellions" of the past than to a new type of political participation. Very few urbanites pay attention to the plight of the rural areas, which have been underprivileged by the government and the party since 1949. Few Chinese democrats, either in Tiananmen in 1989 or in foreign countries before and after that incident, even mention the need for organizing the peasants as the communists have been doing since the 1920s.[35] This is why the party is still "stable" in its grasp on power.

The student or democratic movement is the movement of an absolute minority. The students scarcely tried to organize the peasants to democratize the apparatus. They tried, as a first step, to build an "elite" democracy by intellectuals. Chinese society, however, is still dominated by a rural mentality within the party, although the peasants themselves have been victims of fluctuating economic policy since 1949. The famous saying that the cities are surrounded by the villages still applies. Unlike China, European socialist countries are city oriented and more integrated as nations.

Even if a similar movement occurs in Chinese cities, its influence will be small unless rural people as well as city dwellers are organized to wage a protracted conflict.

The "neo-authoritarianism," advocated by supporters of Zhao Ziyang just before the Tiananmen incident, was an attempt to find a compromise between political reform and the Chinese constraints.[36] There were two reasons for this argument. First, there was a strong desire to emulate the "Asian Four Tigers"—mostly authoritarian regimes that developed rapidly during the 1970s and 1980s—since democracy did not seem realistic for China. The second, more urgent need was to rebuild the party authority in China. Because of the political reform that tried to separate the party from the administration and from everyday management of the enterprises, the party was losing authority. The authority crisis or power vacuum in China was a very dangerous situation as seen from the party. An answer to that was the neo-authoritarianism, which collapsed after the Tiananmen incident.

AFTER TIANANMEN

The economic tightening that started in 1988 continued and a political tightening began after Tiananmen. Economic performance in 1990 was not encouraging. Depression was accelerated by too rigid a policy. Industrial growth in the first half of 1990 was only 2.2 percent.[37] Township industries and private enterprises, which had contributed to the economic boom during the pre-Tiananmen days, were chastened for their waste of raw materials, their inefficiency, and their tax evasion. Increased supervision was necessary, but the main problem was the strong ideological prejudice against privatized or independent enterprises. During the Zhao years, these enterprises were models of profit-making management, unlike the big and medium-sized national factories notorious for their low efficiency. In post-Tiananmen days, however, the latter were said to be the backbone of the national economy.

As a result of the new policy, bankruptcy and unemployment accelerated. A "return to home" policy directed toward the peasants who labored in construction accompanied the tightening policy. Potential unemployment in the rural areas became very serious. Under the circumstances, therefore, the "floating population," most of whom are illegal, increased. A market slump was another big problem caused by too tight a hand on the reins.[38]

Faced with this crisis, the leadership had to loosen its control of finance and construction. As far as economic policy is concerned, the pre-Tiananmen policy was restored almost as it was. Township industries, once a target of attack, are again praised as good absorbers of the surplus labor. Economic performance in 1991 returned to the pre-crisis level because of this policy change, forced on the leaders by objective conditions. Even before the economic crisis became serious, the leaders emphasized that the reform and the open door policy would not be changed, including "the coastal areas development strategy," understood to be Zhao's project.[39] Aside from the economic crisis, the structural changes in China after the reform made it impossible to return to a stricter planned economy. The Communiqué of the Seventh Plenum at the end of 1990 showed this clearly.

As for the corruption under the two-track system, there are only two ways out. First is rapid implementation of reform, including political change, so that "power cannot be changed into money." Second is emphasis on the integrity of the cadres. The former is difficult to implement in a short period of time. The latter has been adopted, therefore, as the only means to cope with the corruption. It will help, but a system of checks among independent actors also is needed. Such a system, however, would be viewed as "bourgeois liberalization" in the post-Tiananmen ideological atmosphere in China.

Political changes after the Tiananmen incident were much bigger than economic ones. Relatively liberal policies toward research, speeches, and press freedom disappeared. Bold arguments about privatization and adoption of Western democratic practices were strictly prohibited, and the previous arguments by those in 1989 who took refuge in Western countries were attacked as treacherous to the state.[40] Accusations targeted bourgeois liberalization; instead nationalism (*aiguozhuyi*), socialism, and collectivism were propagated extensively by the party. The choice of nationalism as the most important value to be pursued shows that socialism is losing its attractiveness, especially among youth. It is also a reflection of a domestic crisis since nationalism against international threats is always the best means to shift the blame for the domestic crisis to the outside world. At the same time, however, the emphasis on nationalism cannot but impede reforms. As the Fourth Plenum of the Thirteenth Congress declared, "Reform and open door are the way to a strong country."[41]

One of the most important objectives of modern China is to raise its international rank. Stalinist socialism has been discredited as the way to create a "strong country." China cannot go back to it. But the indoctrination of "nationalism" has not been very effective. Nationalism (or *aiguozhuyi*, which can be literally translated as "love-state-ism") is not strong at the grassroots level. Chinese nationalism has mainly been the concern of intellectuals and cadres, those politically committed to some causes. At the same time, it cannot become a rallying point for mass opposition. Among the Han Chinese, love of people of Chinese origin, no matter where (ethnonationalism), is strong, but it lacks political implication most of the time. In this sense, nationalism cannot be the core of the political opposition, with the exception of minority nationalism.

According to the official announcements, international economic transactions such as trade and investment were not adversely affected by the Tiananmen incident despite sanctions by the West. In the political sphere, however, change was great. The Chinese leadership attacked the United States as implementing a strategy of *heping yanbian*. This term is literally translated as "peaceful evolution." Although it sounds innocent, it is not. The term was widely used during the late 1950s and 1960s in condemning American policy toward Yugoslavia. The United States was accused of conspiring to make Yugoslavia a capitalist country by peaceful means.[42] The term was also used in a famous article ostensibly criticizing Yugoslavia, but widely seen as a volley in the deepening Sino-Soviet dispute.[43] A more suitable translation of this term may be "subversive activities using peaceful means," or "indirect aggression." It reflects U.S. intervention in the domestic problems of China. President Bush made a speech in Texas in May 1989 entitled "Beyond Containment." According to the most detailed Chinese articles, Bush was trying to subvert all the socialist countries by peaceful means.[44] Bourgeois liberalization, which led to the Tiananmen incident, is a case in point as is the American intention of integrating the Soviet Union into the international community.[45] The drastic changes in Eastern Europe were similarly interpreted by the Chinese. The term *heping yanbian* has a sharp ideological connotation, and it reflects a cold war mentality.

Important sources of *heping yanbian* include not only Western influences, but also influences from Eastern Europe, the Soviet Union, Taiwan, and Hong Kong. The influence of overseas Chinese is small. They are becoming more and more disillusioned with China; their interests in China are primarily economic now. The Tiananmen incident was a final blow in changing the emotional relations between China and the overseas Chinese.[46]

Heping yanbian largely is intended for domestic consumption, but as long as that kind of criticism continues, the international environment will not be improved. The peak of the attack occurred in late 1989. The frequency of the term in Chinese documents notably declined in 1990, although it is included in most of the major policy statements by leaders and in important party and state documents as of the beginning of 1992.[47]

This declining mention of *heping yanbian* shows that China's leaders are trying to improve relations with the West, the source of needed finance and high technology. Two gestures were the lifting of martial law and the release of Fang Lizhi, who had found asylum in the American Embassy in Beijing in order to evade arrest by the Chinese authorities after the Tiananmen incident. In the United Nations China tried to cooperate during the Cambodian conflict and the Gulf War.

Such steps, except for China's moderate stance in the United Nations, were not very effective in improving relations with the United States and Western Europe. After consulting with its allies, Japan "unfroze" the yen loan, which it had promised in 1988 and had been slated to start in 1990. Japan did that because asking more of the proud Chinese would be hard and because it feared that economic deterioration would cause domestic confusion dangerous for neighboring countries. Chinese leaders, in their official statements, have carefully exempted Japan from the attacks against *heping yanbian*. The unfreezing of the yen loan may be only marginally effective in improving China's economy, but with their firsthand experiences, the Japanese reason that the country is much more underdeveloped and fragile than many people assume.

At the same time, China improved its relations with the Soviet Union a great deal with the intention of constraining the United States and substituting for the lack of technological cooperation caused by the sanctions. After the aborted coup in August 1991 in the Soviet Union, however, and the elimination of the union and the actions against the Soviet Communist Party, this strategy proved ineffective. China's strengthened ties with the Third World countries may be more important, at least symbolically. These actions were not very effective in improving China's political and economic situation.

Based on the trends analyzed above, one can say that because Deng Xiaoping plays a cohesive role in the party and the military, so long as he stays, the Chinese leadership will continue to be relatively stable. In order to continue the relative stability, a new cohesive figure will be necessary. China will stick to the goals of sovereign independence and socialism. It will continue economic reform under the name of socialism, without proceeding deeply into political reform. It may start some administrative reform, but it will fear any threat to the party leadership. China's leaders may be able to delay an eruption of political problems for a while, thanks to the "subject culture" enduring among most of its people. Besides, the party leadership is indispensable in maintaining the unity in the country.

Thus, the gap between economic and political reforms will continue for some time to come. In the long run, however, economic reform, if it becomes successful, will inevitably produce a market economy, and the plural interests in the market will conflict with each other. The situation will require some adjustments of these conflicting interests and will make political reform inevitable. The reform policy of utilizing the commodity economy will substitute for the "capitalist stage" that was supposed to be needed for modernization. At that time China may follow the pattern of Eastern Europe in 1989. Stagnation of economic reform and development, however, may delay this turning point. The lingering "subject culture" will be the biggest delaying factor in the political sphere, if no one manages to organize a large number of people to channel diverse political demands into the political system. China's elitist intellectuals may not be able to do that. The peasant-minded party leaders are more experienced in accommodating themselves to the peasants, but they will not be willing to activate peasant participation into politics except through their favored formula, "the mass line."

Unless modest reform occurs—that is, unless surplus labor is absorbed, enterprises become more independent, and efficiency or productivity increases to give China modest international competitive power—social and political confusion will follow. At that time the only integrative power will be the military. After the reform started, an attempt was made to professionalize the military and to build state armed forces rather than party armed forces. Nevertheless the military is still led by the party. In fact, indoctrination of the armed forces in Marxism, Leninism, and Mao Zedong thought has been strengthened. The biggest task of the armed forces is now to maintain domestic security.[48] If the military is divided at the time of national confusion, the picture will be tragic.

On the other hand, if modest reform with gradual development succeeds, a Chinese version of "corporatist" mediation in solving problems by pro-party but more independent interest groups may arise as party control deteriorates.[49] This may be the best possible course. It will take time and will be accompanied by confusion, but as long as the major aim of China's modernization is an established status in the international community, reform and the open door policy are a necessity. Perhaps, after trial and error, party control will gradually diminish to allow spontaneous organizations to appear.

NOTES

1. Huang Renyu, *Wanli 15 nian* (Taibei: Zhonghua shuju, 1982). For the first version of this book published in English, see Ray Huang, *1587: A Year of No Significance* (New Haven: Yale University Press, 1981).
2. Hedley Bull and Adam Watson, eds., *The Expansion of International History* (Oxford: Clarendon Press, 1984).
3. See the *Renmin ribao* editorial of January 1, 1988, which said that China must stand on its own feet in the forest of the world nations. The Communiqué of the Fourth Plenum in 1989 said that reform and the open door policy are means to build a strong country. The term "modernization" in this chapter refers to the rationalization of national capabilities to cope with stronger nations. Modernization is not necessarily Westernization, and it is not always good for the people.
4. The object of admiration is now replaced by so-called neo-Confucianism.
5. "Guanyu jianguo yilai dang de regan lishi wenti de jueyi" in 1981 was one of the moderate versions of the official criticism of Mao at that time. Many other works by those who personally experienced the Cultural Revolution have been published. One of the best is by Chen Kaige (a famous movie director living in New York), *Watashi no kōeihei jidai* (Tokyo: Kōdansha, 1990).
6. The term "feudal," as it is usually defined, is not applicable to traditional China, but the CCP has used the term since the 1920s.
7. Deng Xiaoping, "Dang he guojia lingdaozhidu de gaige" (August 18, 1980), in *Deng Xiaoping wenxuan (1975–1982)* (Beijing: Renmin chupanshe, 1983), pp. 280–302; Su Shaozhi, "Zhongguo tesede shehuizhuyi mian mian guan," *Renmin ribao* (overseas edition), July 3, 1985; "Zhengzhi tizhi gaige he fan fengjian zhuyi yingxiang," *Renmin ribao*, August 15, 1986; Tian Jujian, "Yao shenru pouxi fengjian zhuyi canyu," *Renmin ribao*, September 12, 1986. Also see Tatsumi Okabe, *Chūgoku kindaika no seijikei-zaigaku* (Tokyo: PHP Institute, 1989).
8. "Socialist construction" began sooner in China than originally planned. See Tatsumi Okabe, "Chūgoku no hatten dankai moderu to 'kindaika' seisaku," in *Gendai Chūgoku to sekai* (Tokyo: Keiō Tsūshinsha, 1982), pp. 179-215; Yan Lin, "Cong xinminzhuzhuyi dao shehuizhuyi de zhuanbian," in *Zhongguo shehuikexue*, no. 2, 1990, pp. 3-26; and Lu Zhenxiang, "Dui jianguo chuqi cong xinminzhuzhuyi guodu dao shehuizhuyi jige wenti de kaocha," in *Zhonggong dangshi yanjiu*, no. 2, 1990, pp. 58-64.
9. Communist Party of Vietnam, *Draft Platform for the Building of Socialism in the Transition Period* (undated but known to be drafted in 1990). The draft was revised before and during the Seventh Party Congress in June 1991, but the general tone did not change. My information about the Seventh Congress is based on oral communication with Professor Masahiko Ebashi, who has close contacts with the Vietnamese.
10. Gu Mu, "Jicheng chuantong jinhua jianshe shiying shidai yaoqiu de xin wenhua," *Renmin ribao* (overseas edition), October 19, 1989; and "Chuantong zhengzhi zhidu yu dangqian de zhengzhi tizhi gaige," *Renmin ribao*, July 15, 1988.
11. The term "zhuhou jingji" (warlord economy) was first used in Hong Kong to criticize the state of decentralization in China. It now appears in the articles published in mainland China. See, for example, Du Haiyan and Xin Wen, "Hongguan gaige zaici xianru shoufang xunhuan de genyuan," *Jingji zongheng*, no. 2, 1990, cited from *Xinhua wenzhai*, no. 5, 1990, pp. 49-51.

12. The relation between political integration and markets is discussed in Charles E. Lindbrom, *Politics and Markets* (New York: Basic Books, 1977), esp. pp. 12-13.
13. When the Chinese use the word "nationalism," it often means negative interethnic problems. When referring to their love for the whole nation, they prefer the term "aiguozhuyi" (love-state-ism), which may be translated as "nationalism."
14. Mao Zedong, "Lun lianhe zhengfu," *Mao Zedong ji* (Tokyo: Hokubosha, 1971), p. 220. This part is deleted from the Chinese official version of *Mao Zedong xuanji*.
15. Katsuji Nakagane, "Chūgoku—shakaishugi keizai seido no kōzō to tenkai," in Masayuki Iwata, ed., *Keizai taisei ron IV Gendai shakaishugi* (Tokyo: Tōyō keizai shinpōsha, 1979), pp. 297–309.
16. "Zhonggong zhongyang guanyu jiakuai nongye fazhan regan wenti de jueding (draft)." About a year later, when the draft was formally adopted, there was only a slight revision to admit exceptional cases. The former document is classified, but the latter is declassified. For the latter, see Shen Chong and Xiang Xiyang, eds., *Shinianlai: lilun, zhengce, shijian* (Zhangjiakou: Qiushi chupanshe, 1988), vol. 2, pp. 11–31.
17. Words like "scale of the economy" and "cooperatives" were revived in Chinese official documents after the Thirteenth Congress report by Zhao Ziyang.
18. "Zhonggong zhongyang guanyu jingji tizhi gaige de jueding," October 1984.
19. Janos Kornai, *Fusoku no keizaigaku* (Selected writings of Janos Kornai, ed. and trans. by Tsuneo Morita (Tokyo: Iwanami shoten, 1984), pp. 27-30.
20. As for the difficulties of foreign ventures in China, see Jim Mann, *Beijing Jeep* (New York: Simon & Schuster, 1989).
21. Liu Guoguang, "Guanyu guomin jingji zonghe pingheng de yixie wenti," *Jingji yanjiu*, no. 3, 1979, p. 36.
22. *Deng Xiaoping wenxuan*, pp. 287-98.
23. Liao Gailong, "Rekishiteki keiken to wareware no susumubeki michi" (October 25, 1980). This is a Japanese translation of a classified document in *Chūgoku sōran, 82 nen* (Tokyo: Kazankai, 1982), pp. 716-90.
24. Tatsumi Okabe, "Kaikaku to Chūgoku no gaikō shisō," in Tatsumi Okabe and Kazuko Mōri, eds., *Kaikaku kaihō jidai no Chūgoku, Gendai Chūgoku ron II* (Tokyo: Nihon kokusai mondai kenkyūjo, 1991), pp. 39-68.
25. Calculated from *Zhongguo tongji nianjian 1991 nian*.
26. Tomoyuki Uchida, "Koseki kanri, haikyū seido kara mita Chūgoku shakai," in Kazuko Mōri, ed., *Mōtakuto jidai no Chūgoku, Gendai Chūgoku ron I* (Tokyo, Nihon kokusai mondai kenkyūjo, 1990), pp. 258–90.
27. *Renmin ribao* (overseas edition), February 14, 1990.
28. *Renmin ribao* (domestic edition), March 5, 1989.
29. Ibid., August 11, 1989.
30. Ibid., October 31, 1990. *Asahi shimbun*, September 15, 1990, reported that the actual number is 1.4 billion.
31. The target figure of per capita GNP ($800) in the year 2000 is seldom mentioned. One reason is the yuan depreciation. See Yu Quanwei and Li Xiaonan, "Xi renjun guomin shengchang zongzhi 300 meiyuan," *Renmin ribao*, January 22, 1990.
32. Pinlunyuan, *Renmin ribao*, "Shouqi duice zhixing zhengce," February 5, 1985; and Wang Limin, "Luelun dui 'xia you duice' de duice,' " *Renmin ribao*, December 8, 1988. Here is the authority crisis of the party.
33. For example, Yan Jiaqi and Wen Yuankai, "Guanyu shiju de duihua," in *Jingjixue zhoubao*, December 4 and 11, 1988 (quoted from *Xinhua wenzhai*, no. 2, 1989, pp. 7–11).
34. Calculated from *Zhongguo tongji nianjian 1991 nian*.
35. Chen Yizi, *Zhongguo: Shinian gaige yu bajiu minyun* (Taibei: Lianjing chuban gongsi, 1990), p. 167.
36. For articles on the new authoritarianism, see Liu Jun and Li Lin, eds., *Xin quanweizhuyi, dui gaike lilun gangling de lunzheng* (Beijing: Jingji xueyuan chupanshe, 1989).
37. *Renmin ribao*, July 21, 1990.

38. Niu Renliang, Song Guanmao, and Ding Baoshan, "1988 nian yilai jinsuo de zongti xiaoying fenxi," in *Jingji yanjiu*, no. 5, 1990, pp. 13–22.
39. Press conference by Jiang Zemin and others in *Renmin ribao*, September 27, 1989.
40. On Yan Jiaqi, see *Renmin ribao*, August 3, 1989, September 21, 1989, February 19, 1990. On Su Shaozhi, see April 25, 1990; on Chen Yizi, April 21, 1990; on Wan Runnan, August 17, 1989.
41. See *Renmin ribao*, June 24, 1989. Also see the title of the editorial of the paper on that day.
42. One of the first articles to use the term was Wang Jiaxiang, "Boxi xiandai xiuzheng-zhuyi fandong guojia lun," in *Hongqi*, no. 2, 1958, quoted from *Xinhua banyue kan*, no. 13, 1958, p. 139.
43. *Renmin ribao* and *Hongqi* Editorial Staff, "Nansulafu shi shehuizhuyi guojia ma?" September 26, 1963. This is the third article of the "nine criticisms" against the Soviet Union. See the book that was later compiled, *Guanyu guoji gongchanzhuyi yundong zongluxian de lunzhan* (Beijing: Renmin chupanshe, 1965), pp. 188–89.
44. The most detailed argument is Pan Tongwen, "Zhaoyue ezhi zhanlue chuxi," *Guojiwenti yanjiu*, no. 1, 1990, pp. 30–35.
45. Speech by President George Bush, "Beyond Containment," May 12, 1989, Texas A & M University.
46. Right after the Tiananmen incident, there was a run on the Bank of China in Singapore.
47. For example, see Li Peng's Political Report to the People's Congress, *Renmin ribao*, April 6, 1990, and Jiang Zemin's speech on intellectuals in *Renmin ribao*, May 4, 1990. There are many restricted (*neibu*) publications on this subject. See, for example, Li Zhencheng, ed., *Wu xiaoyan de zhanzheng—"heping yanbian" yu duice* (Tianjin: Tianjin shehui kexue chupanshe, 1991).
48. Deng Xiaoping's speech at the Enlarged Central Military Conference was reported in *Renmin ribao*, November 13, 1989. As is well known, the chairman of the Central Military Conferences of both the state and party, which are one and the same, is the party general secretary, Jiang Zemin.
49. Tatsumi Okabe, "Kokusai kankei no naka no Chūgoku minshuka undō," in *Minshuka undō to Chūgoku shakaishugi* (Tokyo: Iwanami shoten, 1990), p. 133, refers to this possibility. Kazuko Mōri developed the idea in her "Chūgoku no seiji kaikaku no henyō—Tō Shōhei jidai no imi," in Okabe and Mōri, eds., *Kaikaku kaihō jidai no Chūgoku*, pp. 26–32.

6

China: Sustaining Development

Nicholas R. Lardy

In 1989 and 1990 Western analysts raised increasing doubts about the long-term efficiency of China's approach to economic reform. This reassessment stemmed from two developments in 1989. The first was internal to China—the tragedy of Tiananmen followed by policies that appeared to many to constitute a retreat from economic reform and a recentralization of decision making. The second was the dramatic events of 1989 in Eastern Europe, where several communist regimes virtually evaporated overnight and where in one case, Poland, a revolutionary program replacing central planning with a market economy was adopted shortly thereafter. These doubts were reinforced by the collapse of the Communist Party in the Soviet Union. China increasingly was seen as anachronistic, isolated from the trends sweeping through the communist world.

In short, China's decade-long economic reform program appeared badly tarnished. Some, particularly those who believed that political reform was a prerequisite for sustained economic reform, doubted the long-term viability of the latter. Others compared its somewhat laborious pace either with Poland's big-bang approach or with various proposals for an accelerated transformation of the Soviet economic system. The presumption that the key features of the centralized economic system could be successfully thrown off within a year or two reduced the attractiveness of China's gradualistic approach to economic reform for other former socialist states.

By the end of 1991 the optimism concerning the transformation of the former socialist states of Eastern Europe had been replaced with a more sober assessment. The vision of a rapid and relatively painless transition from central planning to market economies was tempered by rising inflation, falling output, increasing unemployment, and a range of other problems unanticipated by the advocates of the big-bang approach to reform. The situation in the former Soviet Union was in some ways even more bleak. The long-term deterioration of the economy continued. The unified Soviet state had been replaced by a loose coalition of the independent republics. However, agreement among the republics on trade, monetary and currency systems, and other critical economic policies was conspicuously lacking.

In China, by contrast, economic performance by 1991 had somewhat improved. The regime was able to contain the hyperinflation that had threatened in the late 1980s. It lowered the rate of price increases to the low single digits without sending the economy into a sharp recession. Growth in 1989–91, although lower than in the 1980s, averaged 5 percent annually. Reforms in many areas (such as foreign trade and exchange control, domestic banking and finance) and the increasing use of markets continued in the late 1980s and early 1990s.

This chapter attempts to provide some perspective on the transition from central planning toward more market-oriented economies by addressing both the short-term issue of whether 1989 marked the high watermark of economic reform in China and the broader issue of whether the reform experiences of other socialist states have discredited China's more incremental, ad hoc approach to economic reform. Is a program of sweeping, comprehensive reform the most effective strategy for sustaining economic development? What are the conditions under which gradualistic reforms may be a viable or even a preferred alternative?

ECONOMIC REFORM SINCE 1989: A RETREAT?

The consensus view during much of the 1980s was that China's reform was outpacing that of the Soviet Union and the Eastern European countries. After June of 1989 there was a widespread Western perception of Chinese retrogression. Three areas frequently have been mentioned: a more stringent monetary policy, a squeeze on rural enterprises and other nonstate firms, and a recentralization of foreign trade. Some of these policy changes, however, predate June 1989. They stem largely from decisions reached in September 1988 at the Third Plenum of the Chinese Communist Party. More significantly, these changes represent midcourse corrections to consolidate reform rather than an abandonment of basic reform policy.

The chief objectives of the adjustment program announced by the party in September 1988 were to reduce excess demand and inflationary pressure and to correct certain excesses that had emerged in the mid-1980s. This is particularly evident in the restrictive monetary policy that emerged after the fall of 1988. The goal was not to roll back economic reform.

The credit offered to state enterprises, which grew only moderately more rapidly than did the economy in the early 1980s, grew excessively after the mid-1980s. These expanded credits were used to add to industrial capacity and to raise the wage bill. The growth of the money supply was soon out of control. Currency in circulation expanded by almost 50 percent in 1988 alone.[1] A major reason for this sharp increase was that local branches of the specialized state banks, such as the Industrial and Commercial Bank, were beholden almost entirely to local governmental authority. These governments urged banks to extend more credit to stimulate local economic growth, in the process usurping the authority of the newly established central bank, the People's Bank of China.

In the second half of 1988 China was heading for a major economic crisis. Excess demand from an inappropriately high rate of investment and huge increases in money in circulation quickly became apparent. Panic buying in the summer and fall of 1988 stripped many commodities from store inventories, and prices began to rise rapidly. The official cost of living index in December 1988 was 28 percent higher than it had been in December 1987.[2] Without the austerity program initiated in the fourth quarter of 1988, China would soon have been consumed by hyperinflation.

As a result of monetary tightening and other financial reforms, currency in circulation rose only 9.8 percent in 1989 and 12.8 percent in 1990, compared with 46.8 percent in 1988.[3] Although the annual rate of inflation in 1989 was still high by China's standards, it fell during 1989, and in the closing months of the year retail prices fell in absolute terms. In 1990 retail price inflation was held to 2 percent.

In the absence of a policy of monetary restraint, the prospects for economic reform in China would have become quite bleak. Reform in a highly inflationary environment, particularly the adjustment of relative prices, is problematic at best. Equally important, the erosion of the real incomes of large segments of the population, an inevitable result of high inflation, would undermine popular support for further economic reforms.

A second area of retreat from reform trends was a supposed squeeze on nonstate firms, particularly the rural firms classified as township and village enterprises. Rural enterprises grew more rapidly than did state-owned industry throughout the 1980s. Some Chinese writers argued that these firms competed unfairly with state-owned firms for raw materials and intermediate goods and that they should be subject to more state regulation. In the late 1980s these firms appeared to be under increasing pressures from the state. Their access to state credit was curtailed, and some of the firms went bankrupt as a result. This was widely viewed as a crackdown against the more liberal economic environment of the 1980s and part of the central government's policy of favoring state-run firms. According to one account at that time, "China's austerity plans are wreaking havoc on the most visible beneficiaries of reform: rural enterprises."[4]

External perceptions of the threat to rural industries were, however, exaggerated, and the aims of the central authorities were misinterpreted. The number of township and village enterprises did shrink slightly both in 1989 and 1990. There were 18.882 million rural enterprises at the end of 1988, and only 18.504 million by the end of 1990.[5] But this small reduction may not have been the result of adversarial state policies. Rural enterprises, like state-owned enterprises, were strained by a reduction in the credit available after the late fall of 1988. Perhaps the specialized state banks, in their allocation of credit, did sometimes favor state firms over township and village enterprises. Several additional factors, however, must be taken into account. First, rural firms are less dependent on the state banking system than are state-owned firms. They are able to draw on informal credit markets that are largely unimpeded by state regulation. Second, rural enterprises are exempt from paying most taxes for an initial period of three years. These tax regulations provide a stimulus for rural firms to go "out of business" periodically and to shortly thereafter reappear under a different name. As a result, data on the number of these firms do not necessarily provide a very good barometer of the economic health of the sector they form.

A far more accurate reflection of the economic viability of this sector is its rate of growth relative to that of state-owned firms. Township and village enterprises outperformed the state-owned sector by a wide margin in 1989 and 1990. During these two years, the value of output of township and village enterprises in the industrial sector grew twice as fast as that of state-owned firms.[6]

Indeed, in manufacturing the whole nonstate sector, including collective and private firms of all types as well as joint ventures, expanded its share of total manufactured goods output throughout the 1980s. These firms accounted for under a fifth of industrial output in 1978, when reform was just getting under way. Their share reached a third by 1985, and it stood at 43.2 percent in 1988. In 1989 these entrepreneurial firms produced 44 percent of all manufacturing output, and their share rose further to just over 45 percent in 1990. In short, there is very little evidence that state policy in the closing years of the 1980s constituted a significant crackdown on the nonstate sector.

From the perspective of the early 1990s, China's strategy of transforming the ownership of its industrial sector compares quite favorably with the strategies of the Soviet Union under Gorbachev and the former socialist states in Eastern Europe. In Poland state-owned firms produced 95 percent of all industrial output in the late 1980s. Although Poland's big-bang reform called for the rapid privatization of state firms, this process proved to be painfully slow and fraught with difficulties that were not anticipated by Polish reformers or most of their Western advisors. In the first year of Poland's big-bang reform, the state divested itself of only five large enterprises.[7] Although many small firms were privatized and many new small private firms were established in 1990, 90 percent of manufactured goods output was still produced in state-owned enterprises. In the Soviet Union in 1990 more than 80 percent of all firms, producing a significantly higher share of output, were still state run. Despite the creation by late 1990 of more than two hundred thousand small cooperatives, "the industrial sector consists almost entirely of huge state-owned firms."[8]

Foreign trade is a third area where the Chinese state supposedly pulled back from reform. Critics charged that the center reduced the authority of locally run foreign trade companies and expanded the powers of the central trade corporations directly controlled by the Ministry of Foreign Economic Relations and Trade. Curtailing the monopoly power of the handful of foreign trade corporations was one of the most significant decentralization measures of the 1980s. Thus a recentralization of control of trade authority would have constituted a major retrogression in the reform process.

The authorization of new foreign trade corporations in the 1980s undercut the monopoly powers traditionally exercised by the Ministry of Foreign Economic Relations and Trade. In 1979 the ministry directly controlled all foreign trade. By the mid-1980s more than eight hundred independent foreign trade corporations had authority to make international transactions in specified product ranges. By the late 1980s the number had soared to more than five thousand. Some of those corporations were controlled by national production ministries, others by provincial governments, and a few by large enterprises with extensive foreign trade.

Competition among foreign trade corporations (national and local) made it possible for manufacturing firms to bargain to get better domestic prices for the goods they produced for export. Under the old system, producers were required to deliver goods to the national foreign trade corporations at officially established ex-factory prices. Producers had no incentive to produce for the international market since the prices they received for such sales were the same as for domestic market sales. The rapid expansion of trading companies spurred the growth of Chinese exports in the 1980s, but it also began to create problems for China's trading partners. Under the traditional pre-reform system, China enjoyed an outstanding international reputation for meeting the terms of its international trade contracts. In the mid-1980s this reputation began to erode, largely because the decentralization of foreign trade "meant the appearance in foreign trade circles of inexperienced newcomers who have sometimes signed contracts which they could not perform."[9]

In response to these problems, the Chinese State Council and the Central Committee of the Chinese Communist Party in 1989 approved a program to consolidate and reorganize the foreign trade corporations. Although the formal approval of this campaign postdates the Tiananmen disaster, its antecedents can be traced to a campaign in 1985 to delineate the business scope of new foreign trade corporations. The cutback in the number of foreign trade corporations appears to leave substantial room for competition among these firms. It did not restore the monopoly position of a handful of centrally controlled, national corporations in foreign trade. By the spring of 1990, the state had examined roughly 70 percent of all foreign trade corporations to determine whether they complied with all regulations, and only eight hundred corporations had been closed down or forced to merge with another corporation.[10] If that survival rate of firms continues to the end of the campaign, China will still have 3,850 foreign trade corporations.

In short, the campaign seems designed to eliminate the firms that failed to live up to the terms of their signed contracts. It was those weaker firms that tarnished China's image with foreign traders in the second half of the 1980s. Although there has been some recentralization of control of foreign trade, there is little evidence that the campaign has expanded dramatically the powers of the remaining national-level foreign trade corporations under the jurisdiction of the Ministry of Foreign Economic Relations and Trade. Julia Leung's argument that the reorganization "will return China to the system of the early 1980s, when a few specialized state-owned trading companies handled the nation's trade" seems to be an exaggeration.[11]

In the three policy areas I have discussed, China did not make a wholesale retreat from reform. The introduction of a more stringent monetary policy dates from decisions in the fall of 1988, and it was not an unreasonable initial response to rapidly rising inflation. The nonstate sector grew more rapidly than did the state sector in 1990, as it had during the previous decade. There is little evidence that the state sought to squeeze this dynamic area of the economy. And although the state has shuttered a few hundred foreign trade corporations, thousands more remain. There is little evidence that the state seeks to restore the pre-reform system in which all trade was controlled by a handful of centrally run foreign trade companies.

REFORM STRATEGY

In recent years a growing number of Western economists have offered detailed advice to the Soviets and to the reforming former socialist states in Eastern Europe. Their recommendations have several common features. First, Western economists generally propose comprehensive reform, arguing that partial reforms lead to internal contradictions that can discredit the reform process. The republics of the former Soviet Union and Eastern European countries should simultaneously free prices, slash budget deficits, curb expansive bank credit, eliminate subsidies to money-losing state enterprises, curtail subsidies of urban housing and certain consumer goods, open their economies to foreign competition, and move rapidly toward convertibility of their currencies. Most plans also incorporate provisions for rapid privatization of state enterprises, particularly in manufacturing. Some internal reform packages, such as those advanced by Stanislav Shatalin in the Gorbachev era in the Soviet Union and by Boris Yeltsin's economic advisers, were similarly comprehensive.

Second, Western economists argue that all of these radical changes should be instituted rapidly—within a matter of months (as in the Polish case) or at least on a relatively short, preannounced schedule (five hundred days in the case of the Shatalin plan). They emphasize proceeding rapidly to reduce the prospects for backsliding, which may occur if reform opponents have time to mobilize support among those who become unemployed or who suffer declines in their real income during the transition from a centrally planned economy to a market economy. Better, they say, to suffer a steeper but briefer downturn on the path to the market.

China's incremental, ad hoc approach to reform lacks the drama of Poland's big-bang approach and the theoretical elegance of comprehensive reform plans discussed in the Soviet Union in the Gorbachev years and actually instituted in Russia under Yeltsin. Nonetheless, the first decade of Chinese reform must be judged a success by at least two important criteria.

First, economic output in China, unlike that in the Soviet Union and the countries of Eastern Europe, did not shrink as reform was getting under way. Quite the opposite. In the 1980s Chinese economic growth accelerated significantly to an annual average rate of over 10 percent or about 9 percent on a per capita basis.[12] By comparison, gross domestic product in Poland fell by more than 10 percent in 1990, paced by a drop of almost one-fourth in manufactured goods output.[13] In the Soviet economy a deceleration of the growth of output since at least the 1970s led to economic stagnation during the reformist era of Mikhail Gorbachev.[14] In 1990 gross national product dropped 2 percent. This negative trend accelerated in 1991 when gross national product fell by more than 10 percent.

Second, although the Chinese Communist Party never endorsed the creation of a market economy, resource allocation in the Chinese economy by the end of the 1980s was probably more market driven than in either the Soviet Union or the states of Eastern Europe. A few examples show just how dramatic this transformation has been.

The first is the external sector where the Chinese have moved quite far toward allowing supply and demand on an open market to determine the value of their currency. This process began by making the fixed exchange rate more realistic. The Bank of China devalued the yuan repeatedly throughout the 1980s. The official exchange rate at the end of 1990 stood at 5.2 yuan to the dollar compared with 1.5 yuan to the dollar at the beginning of the 1980s. The state also began to use the market to allocate scarce foreign exchange as early as 1980–81. At that time it allowed the Bank of China and its local branches to facilitate foreign exchange transactions among state units at prices diverging from both the official exchange rate and the internal settlement rate used by the Bank of China to settle merchandise trade transactions in the period 1981 to 1984. More formal foreign exchange markets were established in major urban centers and in several special economic zones in the mid-1980s to allow joint venture firms to buy and sell foreign exchange among themselves. In 1987–88 the state opened these markets up to domestic firms including nonstate firms, and the state authorities abandoned their most blatant efforts to control prices of these transactions

The volume of foreign exchange transactions expanded from $4 billion in 1987 to $6.3 billion in 1988.[15] In 1989, when some argue reform was in full retreat, the volume of transactions rose almost 40 percent to reach $8.6 billion.[16] The upward trend has continued. In 1990 transaction volume rose 54 percent to $13.164 billion.[17] In the first half of

1991, turnover on the foreign exchange market reached $8.75 billion, a 50 percent increase over the same period in 1990.

As a result of the growing use of the market to allocate foreign exchange for a large and growing share of Chinese trade transactions, importers are paying the opportunity cost of earning foreign exchange rather than continuing to be subsidized by the still somewhat overvalued official exchange rate. In 1988, when the official exchange rate was 3.7 yuan per U.S. dollar, the average swap market price of foreign exchange was 6 yuan, a premium of almost two-thirds over the official rate. Moreover, in 1988 the black market rate for foreign exchange was about one-fourth higher than the swap rate. The swap market rate may be a reasonable measure of the true value of foreign exchange. Thus the subsidy to imports financed with foreign exchange provided by the Bank of China at the official exchange rate as part of the import plan was 2.3 yuan per dollar. Based on the volume of imports financed at the official exchange rate (that is, excluding imports financed by enterprises using their own foreign exchange or foreign exchange purchased on the swap market), the subsidy to imports in 1988 was more than 80 billion yuan, or an astonishing 7 percent of national income.[18]

After late 1990 this massive subsidy to imports financed at the official rate was reduced significantly. The swap market rate in late 1990 was 5.4 yuan per dollar, a premium of only a few percentage points over the new official exchange rate.[19] The swap rate rose slightly in the first half of 1991 to a premium of about 10 percent.[20] It appeared as if the official exchange rate was much less overvalued than it had been at any time in recent years. Thus, the subsidy to officially financed imports fell dramatically.

Moreover, revisions of the foreign trade contract system introduced in 1991 suggest that the volume of transactions on the swap market for foreign exchange will continue to expand, as occurred in the late 1980s. The share of foreign exchange earnings retained by firms producing export goods, local foreign trade companies, and local governments was to expand to 50 percent from about 40 percent in 1988. And compensation for three-fifths of the remaining foreign exchange remitted to the central government was to be at the swap market rate rather than at the official rate. Thus, exporters could convert up to 80 percent of their earnings to domestic currency at the swap market rate. That means the penalty to exporting, which existed in the early 1980s as a consequence of the highly overvalued official exchange rate, has all but vanished. And, at a minimum, half of all imports were to be financed at the swap market rate, eliminating all subsidies for these transactions.

In little more than a decade, what the World Bank once described as an "airlock system" separating the Chinese domestic economy from the world economy has largely broken down.

Contrast this situation with that in the Soviet Union. The official exchange rate for trade transactions in the late 1980s was .625 rubles per dollar. Unlike in China, this rate in the Soviet Union played no role in the allocation of resources.[21] The exchange rate on the black market in 1989 varied between 10 and 15 rubles per dollar, an astonishing premium of up to 2,400 percent over the official rate. Most significantly, foreign exchange was allocated by the state rather than through a market-like process in which importers had to pay something approaching the opportunity cost of foreign exchange. An auction for foreign exchange, run by the Vnesheknom Bank, was initiated in 1989. But the volume of foreign exchange that was sold for rubles was tiny, only $13.7 million in the first month's auction.[22] In the first eleven months of 1990, transactions totaled only $150 million, only .3 percent of estimated 1990 convertible currency imports and about 1 percent of the volume on the Chinese foreign exchange market.[23] Moreover, the auction rate was initially 15.2 rubles per dollar—comparable to the black market rate. By the summer of 1990, the value of the ruble on the auction market had fallen to 23 rubles per dollar.[24] The devaluation of the currency to 1.8 rubles to the dollar for trade transactions in the fall of 1990 still left the ruble grossly overvalued. The botched currency reform of January 1991, in which ruble bank notes in large denominations were made worthless, increased the demand for foreign exchange even further. In February-March the price of foreign exchange rose to 35 rubles on the limited auction market. The gap between the official and the market rate rose further in the second half of 1991 as centripetal political forces raised fundamental questions regarding the future of the monetary system and confidence in the ruble eroded further. A plan announced at the end of 1991 to stabilize the value of the ruble collapsed, and by early 1992 the market value of the ruble plummeted. More than 200 rubles were required to purchase one dollar on the market.

At the beginning of the 1990s, the Chinese appear to be significantly closer than the Russians to achieving internal convertibility of their domestic currency for trade transactions. This is somewhat paradoxical since virtually every reform plan put forward in the Soviet Union in the Gorbachev years and in Russia under Yeltsin embraced convertibility as a goal. By contrast, Chinese officials rarely state publicly that convertibility is a goal of reform. Although the Chinese have never announced a timetable for achieving internal convertibility, they have made much more progress than did the Soviet Union or has Russia toward achieving that end. At least in this area, incremental, ad hoc reform appears to have been more successful than the relatively dramatic proposals periodically advanced in the Soviet Union in the Gorbachev era and in Russia under Yeltsin.

A second little-noticed area of economic reform in China is domestic financial markets. In this realm Chinese reforms are well ahead of those in the Soviet Union. For example, Chinese financial institutions during the past decade began to offer a broad range of financial assets at more competitive interest rates, and the state began to use interest rate adjustments as a policy tool. Chinese banks since the late 1970s have offered long-term savings deposits, effectively certificates of deposit, that pay higher interest rates than do conventional savings accounts. Beginning in late 1988, banks, for the first time, offered so-called value preserving deposits. The interest rate is linked to the underlying rate of inflation, as measured by a price index, during the time the deposit is held. Thus, prior to reform the banks relied largely on relatively cheap sources of funds—savings deposits on which they paid an interest rate of only 3.24 percent. By the end of the first decade of reform, banks were paying substantially more for their funds. Interest rates on savings deposits had risen to around 10 percent for short-term deposits and over 13 percent on longer term certificates. And value preserving deposits were offered at potentially even higher rates. Since the mid-1980s, China's banks have also begun to lend one another short-term funds at market-determined interest rates. Turnover on this interbank market reached 520 billion yuan in 1988.[25]

The state even began to adjust interest rates on consumer deposits with a view to influencing aggregate demand. As already noted, value preserving deposits were introduced in the inflationary environment of 1988 in an attempt to encourage individuals to hold financial assets rather than convert them into goods. This conversion had been contributing to excess demand and inflationary pressure in consumer goods markets. After the austerity program took hold in 1989, individuals began to form deflationary expectations, and consumer demand collapsed. This contributed to a very marked slowdown in domestic economic growth in 1989 and 1990. The interest rate on value preserving deposits naturally declined in line with lower inflation. But in April 1990 the state, in an effort to increase consumer spending, reduced the interest rate paid on fixed deposits by a uniform 1.26 percent. The People's Bank lowered deposit rates by an additional percentage point in the spring of 1991.

Beyond the somewhat broadened range of financial assets offered by banks, the government issued more than a 100 billion yuan in government and treasury bonds to finance a significant portion of the fiscal deficit in the 1980s. The state initially required individuals and enterprises to purchase these bonds. Thus, interest rates were not market determined. However, this, too, gradually began to change.

The first significant step was the development of a secondary market for government bonds. Traditionally, bonds were held to maturity with a fixed rate of interest paid when the bonds matured. The development of a secondary market for bonds (a market in which bond prices reflect supply and demand) provided the first market-determined interest rate in China. Informal secondary markets in government bonds, which have existed since 1984 in several cities, had expanded to more than sixty cities by 1988. The state authorized the formal opening of the Shanghai Securities Exchange in the fall of 1990. Government bonds initially were the primary instrument traded in Shanghai and most other securities markets.

A secondary market can have far-reaching significance for two reasons. First, it places enormous pressure on the state to adjust the yield on its future new bond issues in order to be competitive with yields of existing issues traded on the secondary market. A formal secondary market in government securities gives the public readily available information on market interest rates. For example, if yields on government bonds in the secondary market were 9 percent, the Ministry of Finance would be compelled to offer a comparable rate of return on new issues of a similar maturity length.

In short, the government faced pressure to move from a system of compulsory assignment of new bond issues to a system of voluntary purchases. This market pressure was evident in the fall of 1989. As the government found it increasingly difficult to "place" a growing volume of government bonds, the Ministry of Finance, in order to ease these difficulties and compete more effectively with banks for funds, introduced a value preserving bond that promised to pay a 1 percent premium over comparable length certificates of deposit issued by banks.[26] In 1991 the Ministry of Finance fundamentally changed the method of distribution of state bonds by moving to sell up to 60 percent of its bonds on a voluntary basis. This broad, voluntary distribution of bonds required the creation of an underwriting syndicate of about seventy domestic financial institutions to sell the bonds to the public.

Second, an active secondary market for government debt is a prerequisite for open market operations by China's central bank, the People's Bank of China, as an instrument of monetary policy. To date, the bank has been handicapped in its execution of monetary policy by the absence of this instrument, by far the most important instrument of monetary policy in many market economies.

Financial market developments in China and in the Soviet Union are markedly different. Until November 1990, consumers in the Soviet Union were offered only traditional savings accounts bearing nominal rates of interest of 2 to 4 percent. These rates had not been adjusted in years. Indexing of savings deposits, to prevent inflation from eroding their purchasing power, has been discussed in the Soviet Union, but unlike in China it has not been carried out.[27] The state finances its burgeoning fiscal deficit by the highly inflationary means of government borrowing from the banking system, rather than by selling bonds to the public. Beginning efforts to create a central banking system in which the money supply is controlled indirectly through open market operations and discount rate policy (rather than through quantitative ceilings on lending) are evident. In principle, state banks in the Soviet Union have been allowed to lend to and borrow from each other since 1988, but there is no evidence that an interbank market in short-term funds actually has developed as it has in China.[28] Unlike the Chinese, the Soviets do not use interest rate policy as an instrument of aggregate demand management.

China's lead in the development of varied financial markets and in the use of interest rates to attract consumers' savings deposits appears to give it a far-reaching advantage over the Soviet Union in economic reform. Many Western analysts and Soviet reformers are worried about the huge quantities of rubles held by the population as either currency or savings deposits. These rubles, presumably held because of a shortage of consumer goods on the domestic market, are frequently referred to as "forced savings." Since these funds are relatively liquid and could be used to bid up prices for scarce goods if prices were freed, forced savings are perceived as a permanent threat to price stability. Thus, it is argued that the regime must somehow absorb the ruble overhang before introducing greater reliance on markets.

Two methods of absorbing the ruble overhang have been discussed most often. The first is the sale of state assets (privatization). However, in the absence of well-established markets, the sale of machinery and other assets owned by state enterprises could be manipulated and could result in huge transfers of wealth to a few well-placed individuals. Thus, unless markets are well established, the ruble overhang cannot be addressed by the sale of state assets. But the overhang itself is an obstacle to allowing the markets to develop that are a prerequisite for the efficient and equitable dispersal of state assets. The most commonly proposed solution, to simply distribute shares to the work force and allow a secondary market in the shares for enterprises to develop later, would not reduce the ruble overhang, although it might successfully be used to privatize a large share of state assets.

A second proposal is either to borrow internationally or to sell a portion of the state's gold holdings and use the proceeds to import large quantities of high-quality consumer goods from the West. These then could be resold at high ruble prices. Although this might absorb a portion of the ruble overhang, it would not increase the capacity of the state to export to earn foreign exchange either to repay the initial foreign borrowings or to restore the initial level of state foreign exchange and gold reserves.

Superficially, it appears that China suffers from a similar problem. Individual savings soared in China during the first decade of reform— from 31 billion yuan in 1978 to 604 billion yuan at the end of 1990.[29] Individual savings accounts in 1990 were the equivalent of 35 percent of China's gross national product, roughly the same proportion as in the Soviet Union.

However, the favorable interest rates on long-term deposits in China have resulted in a significant reduction in the liquidity of these savings. By the third quarter of 1989, more than 80 percent of all individual savings deposits were in certificates of deposit ranging from six months to eight years in maturity. Only 18 percent were in demand deposits that could be withdrawn without notice.[30] In short, although market forces have been introduced in the determination of interest rates in China, Chinese citizens have voluntarily shifted a significant portion of their financial assets into long-term deposits that cannot be immediately spent. In the Soviet Union financial reform has not yet begun. Soviet savers predominantly hold sight deposits that pay a low nominal fixed rate of interest and may be withdrawn on demand. This threatens price stability.

Moreover, the extremely rapid growth of the Chinese economy over the past decade has placed it in a fundamentally different position than the republics of the former Soviet Union. The Chinese economy in the late 1980s and early 1990s suffered from a surplus, not a shortage, of many consumer goods, even consumer durables. Indeed, the regime in 1990–91 tried to stimulate consumer demand by reducing the interest rates paid on savings deposits. As inventories of durables piled up, the regime was forced to curtail production of cameras, bicycles, household refrigerators, washing machines, and even color televisions. Chinese citizens were sitting on mountains of savings not because there was nothing to buy but largely because they expected prices to fall. And

Chinese reformers were not preoccupied with the threat of *renminbi* overhang.

Finally, a broader measure of markets in China is the growing share of output produced outside the state-owned sector. Needless to say this is an imperfect measure. Various levels of the state impinge on the activities of the nonstate sector. Nonstate firms do not operate totally in the market. But many state-owned firms do purchase a significant share of their inputs and sell a significant share of their outputs on the market.

By the end of the 1980s, the nonstate sector accounted for as much as 65 percent of China's national income. Almost half of all industrial goods were produced in what might be loosely called the entrepreneurial sector—township and village enterprises, collective firms (what would be called cooperatives in the Soviet Union), private firms, and joint ventures. In farming, which accounted for a third of national income, as much as 95 percent of output was produced by family farms. Their access to land is ensured through a system of long-term contracts that provide many of the characteristics of private property. The right to use land can be transferred to others on a short- or long-term basis, and the contracts also can be transferred to one's heirs.

It is more difficult to judge the contribution of the nonstate sector to the three remaining components of national income—construction, transportation and communication, and commerce. In construction, which accounted for 6 percent of national income, the share of state employment fell during the 1980s from more than half to under a third. The difference was made up by rapidly rising employment in collective construction firms and rural construction teams. This shift largely reflects the housing boom in rural areas, all of which is private.

In transportation and communication the state still dominates, despite significant long-distance private hauling of agricultural products. The state owns and operates the rail system, which accounts for almost all long-distance transport, as well as all modern telecommunications facilities. Although this sector is strategically important, it accounted for less than 5 percent of national income in 1989.

In the commercial sector the role of the state has shrunk. Less than 40 percent of retail sales, for example, were via the state retail system in the late 1980s, down significantly from their 55 percent share of 1978. The once dominant role of state-owned commercial establishments in wholesale trade also eroded dramatically in the 1980s.

This approach understates the role of the market since a large share of the output of state-owned firms, too, is distributed via the market. The varieties of materials and equipment distributed by the state fell throughout the 1980s. By 1990 only seventy-two varieties of materials and equipment were under state distribution, two hundred less than in 1988.[31] And even for these commodities, the state's distributive role is partial. More than 50 percent of steel products and coal, 75 percent of timber, and 90 percent of cement produced in China are distributed via the market.

CONCLUSION

This brief summary of China's reform strategy in only three areas—foreign exchange, domestic financial markets, and product markets—is hardly the basis on which to generalize. But it does suggest that incremental economic reform can lead to fundamental changes in an economic system. This does not mean that the Chinese path of reforms in the 1980s was optimal or that it will succeed. At the beginning of the 1990s, the Chinese economy was still burdened with a large state-owned sector kept afloat by substantial fiscal subsidies. The slower pace of growth of the agricultural sector, after unprecedented growth in the first half of the 1980s, also posed fundamental challenges for the leadership.

Despite these and many other difficulties, China's reforms were far more successful than those of Mr. Gorbachev. Even with the collapse of the Communist Party, it seems unlikely that the "shock therapy" reforms announced and at least partially implemented by Mr. Yeltsin in the Russian Republic will lead to economic results comparable to those achieved in China. At least in the short run Russia's economic difficulties have deepened. The decline in output has accelerated, the magnitude of the fiscal deficit has burgeoned, price inflation has accelerated, confidence in the currency has collapsed, the prospects for foreign direct investment have become quite bleak, and access to international commercial credits effectively has ended. Moreover, the republics have yet to agree on the basic principles and institutional arrangements that will govern their economic interactions.

Incremental reform may have been politically feasible. But won't the lag in China's political reform ultimately short-circuit its economic reform? Over the long run a competitive, market-oriented economy must be paired with a pluralistic political system. In the short run, however, this linkage can be quite loose, as the experience of countries in East Asia reminds us. Not one of the six Asian economies that grew fastest in the past twenty-five years—China, Indonesia, South Korea, Taiwan, Singapore, and Hong Kong—could be characterized as democratic. None experienced a transfer of power to another political party.[32] In East Asia pressures for far-reaching political reform, such as those observed in the second half of the 1980s in Taiwan and South Korea, emerged only after decades of sustained economic growth created per capita incomes several times those of present-day China.[33] If the East Asia pattern continues to hold in China, the Chinese Communist Party may be able to postpone sweeping political reform for another decade or more.

Incremental economic reform has had some success in China for several reasons. First, it has been politically feasible. China's Communist Party in the late 1970s would never have approved a comprehensive reform package, however appealing it might have been in economic terms. It took all of Deng Xiaoping's considerable political resources to persuade the party to approve cautious reforms largely limited to the rural sector.

A second reason for the success of China's incremental reforms was their initial focus on the agricultural sector, where prospects for short-term gains in output and productivity appeared brightest. The incremental approach gave reformers the wherewithal to build a coalition for broader, more far-reaching reforms. Agriculture from 1978 through the mid-1980s grew far more rapidly than it had at any other period of comparable length since the Chinese Communist Party came to power in 1949. Agriculture's contribution to the growth of gross national product surpassed that of industry for the first time ever, providing the state with a huge increase in the most important wage good.

Thus, in the first half of the 1980s, the state was able to introduce wage reforms and bonus systems in manufacturing in an effort to raise productivity without the development of significant inflationary pressure. In short, the acceleration of the growth of agriculture made the transition toward a more market-oriented economy much smoother.

Rejecting an incremental approach, the Soviet Union under Gorbachev attempted to map out a comprehensive reform program in advance. Ensuing conflicts of interest among bureaucratic, regional, and social interest groups left the Soviet economy in a state of collapse. The conflict among these contending interests was exacerbated by the declining rate of economic growth in the Soviet Union during the 1980s. Output then shrank in absolute terms at the close of the decade. The prospects for Mr. Yeltsin's reforms in Russia also seem bleak.

A third reason incremental reform in China has had some success is that its unanticipated consequences have pushed Chinese leaders to adopt policies that otherwise they almost certainly would have rejected. Consider, for example, what happened in 1979. Enterprises were allowed to retain a portion of the foreign exchange earned from the sale of commodities on international markets. This was adopted initially to provide greater incentives for exporting. But by the mid- to late 1980s, it had led to the need to open a foreign exchange market. Some enterprises were so successful in exporting that they generated more foreign exchange than they either could or were allowed to spend. Thus, they demanded the right to sell it to others. Initially, these transactions were relatively informal, but as the volume of them grew, the need developed for a more formal market. By 1988 so-called foreign exchange adjustment centers had been opened in dozens of cities to facilitate these transactions.

Similarly, beginning in the early 1980s, the state let enterprises retain a large share of their depreciation funds and a growing share of their earnings or profits, rather than remitting them largely if not entirely to the state treasury. As a consequence, state revenues grew relatively slowly. State fiscal revenue as a share of gross national product fell from 31 percent in 1978, a level well above that of most developing countries, to 23 percent by 1990. Spending exceeded revenues, and budget deficits became a matter of increasing concern. As a result, the state has been under enormous pressure to reduce subsidies to the few branches of manufacturing where significant losses are incurred because of state pricing policy. Although the steel industry, the railroads, and other major users of coal and oil have lobbied against price increases for energy, the state has gradually raised prices for these commodities in order to contain a growing financial crisis. For example, because the average wellhead price of crude oil, 103 yuan per ton, was unchanged for seventeen years (1971 to 1988), while production costs rose 90 percent between 1975 and 1985, in the late 1980s one major field after another fell into the red. Opponents of higher prices held a 1988 increase to only 10 yuan per ton or about 10 percent. But beginning in 1989, the state acted much more decisively. It raised the average wellhead price per ton of crude to 137 yuan in 1989, to 167–171 yuan per ton in 1990, and to 205 yuan per ton beginning January 1, 1991.[34]

From the perspective of the early 1990s the continued rule of the world's most populous country by a communist regime seems anachronistic. While the Chinese Communist Party has largely preserved its monopoly of political power, it has presided over or at least tolerated the development of an increasingly marketized economy. The economic results of its reforms to date are arguably more favorable than those achieved in the former socialist states of Eastern Europe and likely will compare favorably with economic performance of the republics of the former Soviet Union. Ultimately the very success of China's economic reform will generate growing pressure for far-reaching political change. Only after this process has been under way for some time, and after the long-term results of reforms elsewhere in the former socialist world are known, will scholars be able to make more definitive comparisons of the alternative strategies for combining sustained economic development with political reform.

NOTES

1. State Statistical Bureau, *Chinese Statistical Abstract 1989* (in Chinese) (Beijing: Statistical Publishing House, 1989, p. 74.
2. *China Statistics Monthly* (Chicago, Ill.: China Statistics Archives, March 1989), p. 57.
3. State Statistical Bureau, *Chinese Statistical Abstract 1990* (in Chinese) (Beijing: Statistical Publishing House, 1990), p. 35; and *Chinese Statistical Abstract 1991* (in Chinese) (Beijing: Statistical Publishing House, 1991), p. 35.
4. Adi Ignatius, "China's Economic Reform Program Enters Hibernation: Political Crackdown Clouds Free-Market Policy's Future," *Wall Street Journal*, September 26, 1989, p. A18.
5. *Chinese Statistical Abstract 1990*, p. 65; and *Chinese Statistical Abstract 1991*, p. 65.
6. *Chinese Statistical Abstract 1990*, p. 68; and *Chinese Statistical Abstract 1991*, p. 68.
7. Keith Crane, "Poland's Economic Performance in 1990: Taking Stock of the 'Big Bang' " (Paper presented to the United States-Polish Economic Roundtable, Jackson School of International Studies, Seattle, Washington, June 7–9, 1991), p. 13.
8. International Monetary Fund, World Bank, Organization for Economic Cooperation and Development, and the European Bank for Reconstruction and Development, *The Economy of the USSR* (Washington, D.C.: World Bank, 1990), p. 26.
9. Stanley Lubman, "Investment and Export Contracts in the People's Republic of China: Perspectives on Evolving Patterns," *Brigham Young University Law Review* 3 (1988): 557.
10. "Pay Close Attention to the Work of Rectifying Various Kinds of Foreign Trade Corporations," *Guoji shangbao*, March 20, 1990, p. 1.
11. Julia Leung, "Beijing Is Reasserting Centralized Control: New Guidelines Mark Undoing of Economic Reforms," *Wall Street Journal*, November 28, 1989, p. A10.
12. World Bank, *World Development Report 1990* (New York: Oxford University Press, 1990), pp. 180, 228.
13. Crane, "Poland's Economic Performance," p. 2.
14. International Monetary Fund, World Bank, Organization for Economic Cooperation and Development, and the European Bank for Reconstruction and Development, *A Study of the Soviet Economy*, 3 vols. (Paris: OECD, 1991), I: 11, 23.
15. "Initial Steps in the Establishment of China's Foreign Exchange Market," *Jinrong ribao*, February 15, 1989, p. 1.
16. Zhang Guanghua and Wang Xiangwei, "Swap Centers Will Be Updated," *China Daily*, May 6, 1990, p. 1.
17. Han Guojian, "Foreign Exchange Market Opens Wider," *Beijing Review*, June 3–9, 1991, p. 38.
18. Nicholas R. Lardy, *Foreign Trade and Economic Reform in China, 1978–1990* (Cambridge: Cambridge University Press, 1992), pp. 121, 167.
19. "Shanghai Exchange Sees Record Cash Deals," *China Daily*, November 21, 1990, p. 2.
20. Han, "Foreign Exchange Market," p. 38.
21. *A Study of the Soviet Economy*, I: 363.
22. "Ruble Shrinks Again," *Wall Street Journal*, November 13, 1989.
23. *A Study of the Soviet Economy*, I: 369.
24. Philip Hanson, "New Exchange Rate to Govern Ruble for Trade and Investment," *Report on the USSR*, vol. 2, no. 46 (November 16, 1990), p. 4.
25. Zhao Xiaodi, "Market Mechanism Proves Successful," *China Daily*, December 8, 1990, p. 4.

26. World Bank, *China, Financial Sector Review: Financial Policies and Institutional Development* (Washington, D.C.: World Bank, 1990), p. 108.

27. *A Study of the Soviet Economy,* I: 372.

28. Ibid., III: 365.

29. *Chinese Statistical Abstract 1991,* p. 35.

30. *China: Between Plan and Market* (Washington, D.C.: World Bank, 1990), p. 145.

31. Li Hong, "Materials Ministry to Take on Market Role," *China Daily,* December 4, 1990, p. 1.

32. "Freedom and Prosperity: Yes They Do March Together, But Sometimes Out of Step," *The Economist,* June 29, 1991, p. 15.

33. Nicholas R. Lardy, "Is China Different? The Fate of Its Economic Reform," in Daniel Chirot, ed., *The Crisis of Leninism and the Decline of the Left* (Seattle: University of Washington Press, 1991), p. 147.

34. Lardy, *Foreign Trade,* p. 91; and State Commodity Price Bureau News Center, "A Special Column on Price News," *Jiage lilun yu shijian,* no. 4, 1991, p. 64.

7

Socialism in East Asia: Vietnam, Mongolia, and North Korea

Akihiko Tanaka

When communist regimes in Eastern Europe changed drastically and even the Soviet Union abandoned the leading role of the Communist Party, questions were raised about the fate of communist states in Asia. Are they following the pattern of their counterparts in Eastern Europe? How are they different from other communist (or former communist) states? What are their economic prospects? This chapter is an attempt to answer these questions concerning three relatively small socialist countries in Asia—Vietnam, Mongolia, and North Korea. First, I present a brief history of economic and political reforms (or lack thereof) in the three states. Then I compare structural characteristics of the three countries—commonalities and differences that may account for behavioral variations in the reform process. Based on this comparative analysis, the chapter concludes with a look to the future.

VIETNAM

At the Fourth Congress of the Vietnamese Communist Party in December 1976, the first party congress after the unification of the country in 1975, the second five-year plan (1976–80) was adopted. This ambitious plan turned out to be an utter failure. Its intent was to double most production by 1980 through rapid collectivization, both in the North and the South, and further nationalization in all areas. But industrial production grew only 0.6 percent annually, agricultural production decreased from 13.49 million tons in 1976 to 12.26 million tons in 1978, and in 1979 Vietnam had to import 2.1 million tons of agricultural products.[1] According to To Huu, then vice-premier and a Politburo member, "the national income per capita decreased 20 percent in 1975 and continued to decrease 2 to 3 percent annually in the following years."[2]

To cope with this crisis, the Sixth Plenum of the Fourth Party Congress in September 1979 adopted a series of reforms later to be lumped together as the "new economic policy." Major reforms included: (1) a five-year (1981–85) freeze on the quota to be turned over to the state by agricultural cooperatives; (2) a 500 percent price increase for agricultural products purchased by the government; (3) a new "production responsibility system"; (4) a policy to allow national enterprises to retain some of their production as well as to increase management initiative and fiscal independence; and (5) changes in the wage system (the introduction of incentives and bonuses, for example). The beginning of the new economic policy coincided with the inception of the third five-year plan (1981–85) and led to growth in both agriculture and industry. Despite adverse climatic conditions, agricultural production grew annually at an average of 4.9 percent compared with 1.9 percent in the second five-year plan period. Food imports also decreased substantially; in 1983 Vietnam imported only 60,000 tons of food. Industrial production grew 11.8 percent on the average.[3]

The new economic policy, however, also created serious problems including inflation and corruption. Consumer prices increased 90 percent in 1981, 80 percent in 1982. Higher agricultural prices paid by the government gave incentives to farmers to increase production under the new production responsibility system, but they tremendously increased the government's budget deficit. The government now bought agricultural products at more than 500 percent of the previous prices while rationing them to the consumer at very low prices; the difference between the price that the government paid and the price that it received from the consumer was, in fact, the government's subsidy to the consumer. For example, the government bought rice at 40 dong per kilogram, but the rationed price of rice remained at 0.4 dong for forty years (1946–86).[4] The deficits, previously covered by massive assistance from the Soviet Union and other socialist countries, were managed by an increase in the money supply, thus causing more inflation. Subsidies to consumers and producers comprised 67 percent of the government budget deficit in 1984; the money supply increased from 2.4 billion dong in 1980 to 21.9 billion dong in 1984.[5]

To remedy these conditions, the Eighth Plenum of the Fifth Party Congress in June 1985 decided to make overall reforms in prices, wages, and currency: first, the rationing of basic products was abolished in the summer; second, wages were raised so that workers could afford the unrationed basic products; third, a currency reform was undertaken in

September 1985 to redesignate currency units (ten old dong were now exchanged for one new dong) and to devaluate the exchange rate of the dong vis-à-vis U.S. dollars. One U.S. dollar was now exchanged for 15 new dong (150 old dong), as opposed to the previous exchange rate of one dollar for 12 old dong.

Despite the state's intentions, this price-wage-currency reform brought about disastrous confusion in the economy. Instead of controlling the already bad inflation, the reforms accelerated it. In 1986 the annual inflation rate was as high as 700 percent. Budget deficits climbed to 2.2 times more than those in 1984. Partial retreats from the price-wage-currency reforms were observed in early 1986.

The rampant inflation and the confusion of the economy did not stop the reform efforts, however. At the Sixth Party Congress held in December 1986, three senior leaders of the Vietnamese Communist Party— Truong Ching, Pham Van Dong, and Le Duc Tho—resigned from the Politburo and the Central Committee. A new leadership centered around pragmatists replaced them. One of the new leaders, Nguyen Van Linh, had long experience in the South before the unification. The catchword introduced at the Sixth Party Congress was *doi moi* (renewal). The Party Congress adopted a policy to utilize "nonsocialist economic sectors" to revitalize the national economy. It also decided to adopt the "three major economic programs" and the goal of "four decreases." The "three major economic programs" were to give top priority to investment in agricultural and food production, production of consumer goods, and production of export goods. The "four decreases" were meant to decrease the budget deficits, the money supply, inflation, and the hardship of life. However, real reforms were not, in fact, implemented until 1989. The Sixth Plenum in March 1989 represented the turning point; radical reforms were finally introduced. Almost complete fiscal independence was given to national enterprises; price regulations were abandoned with only a few exceptions; foreign exchange rates were completely floated; and the private sector was allowed to do business in the distribution of goods as well as in financial markets. Farmers' rights under the "responsibility system" were expanded to the extent that private ownership of land was revived.

These radical reforms have born fruit. The average monthly inflation rate in 1989 was 2.8 percent as compared with 19.4 percent in 1986, 12.7 percent in 1987, and 12.4 percent in 1988.[6] Before floating the dong in November 1988, Vietnam had a tremendous gap between the official rate and the black market rate. By the middle of 1989, however, the exchange rate had been stabilized at 4,000 to 4,200 dong per U.S. dollar.[7] Industrial production, which declined until 1987, also began to pick up. In 1989 the GNP grew at 3.5 percent and industrial production by 3 percent. Agricultural production exceeded the goal of 20 million tons. For the first time since its unification, Vietnam was able to export 1.3 million tons of rice, becoming the third largest exporter of rice in the world.

At the same time, the Vietnamese economy faced serious challenges. For years it had depended on aid from the Soviet Union and on earnings from labor sent to Eastern Europe, the Soviet Union, and the Middle East. The aid from the Soviet Union was virtually terminated by the end of 1990. In early 1991 Vietnam concluded a new economic cooperation agreement with the Soviet Union based on the "market mechanism" (that is, to be settled by hard currency).[8] In the spring of 1989, it was reported that 220,000 Vietnamese were working abroad. There were 80,000 Vietnamese in the Soviet Union, 60,000 in East Germany, 37,000 in Czechoslovakia, and 16,000 in Iraq. But by the middle of 1991, most of them had returned home.[9] Prices began to rise in 1990; one estimate says that the retail price inflation in 1990 was 85 percent.[10]

Despite these hardships and the continuing budget deficits, the Seventh Party Congress in June 1991 confirmed *doi moi* and set the goal of doubling Vietnam's GDP by the year 2000. Private business, especially in the South, began to thrive. The number of foreign visitors increased from 10,000 in 1986 to 100,000 in 1990.[11] As the political resolution of the Cambodian conflict was finally made in late October 1991, foreign interest in investment in Vietnam increased. Considering the domestic and international difficulties facing Vietnam, the overall performance of its economic reforms can be graded fair to good when compared with that of communist or former communist countries.

Unlike economic reforms, political reforms have not proceeded very far. While Mikhail Gorbachev's glasnost proceeded in the Soviet Union and dramatic changes toward democratization took place in Eastern Europe, Vietnam retrenched its political system. The Sixth Plenum of 1989, which initiated a really remarkable economic liberalization, declared that no fundamental political reforms were necessary; it also emphasized the primacy of the Communist Party in socialist development. The Tiananmen Square incident in China in June 4, 1989, and the defeat of the Polish Communist Party in the June election of parliament shocked Vietnam's communist leaders. The Seventh Plenum, hurriedly convened in late August, charged that U.S. imperialism was waging "an unprecedented offensive against socialist countries." Regulations on the media were strengthened in 1989; by mid-July eight journals had been banned.[12]

The overall attitude of the Vietnamese leaders toward political reforms is quite similar to that of the Chinese communist leaders. Nguyen Van Linh, who stepped down as party general secretary at the Seventh Party Congress in June 1991, said in his departure speech that though economic pluralism of a "multisector economy" should be pursued, political pluralism should be ruled out.

MONGOLIA

Substantive reform efforts (*öörchilölt shinechlel*) came late in Mongolia, the second oldest socialist country in the world, and they were mainly inspired by Gorbachev's perestroika in the Soviet Union. Long overdue, these reforms were not simply a matter of keeping up with the socialist Joneses. They were badly needed. Despite the introduction of cooperative farms, mostly completed in 1960, livestock farming, the most important branch of production in Mongolia, has not exceeded the level once achieved in 1940. Although industrial production has grown more rapidly than has agriculture, its growth rate has gradually declined from about 10 percent in the 1970s to 7.9 percent for the 1981–85 period.[13] Nevertheless, it was the changes in Moscow that in fact gave critical impetus to the reform process in Ulan Bator.

Yu Tsedenbal, general secretary of the Central Committee of the Mongolian People's Revolutionary Party (MPRP) for some forty years, was replaced in August 1984 by J. Batmönh. The Fifth Plenum of the Nineteenth Party Congress in December 1988 criticized Tsedenbal in these words: "As more and more power began concentrating in his hands, the more strongly were manifested such negative aspects as departure from adherence to principles on issues of Party and state leadership and cadres, diminution of the significance of collective leadership, wilfulness and deafness to others' opinions, and discrepancy between words and actions."[14]

Actual reforms, however, had not been really started by Batmönh until the Third Plenum of the Nineteenth Party Congress in June 1987, when *öörchilölt shinechlel* was used for the first time. The general trend of reforms was very similar to the Soviet perestroika. Prime Minister Dumaagiyn Sodnom emphasized in his report revitalization of the economy, efficient investment, adoption of new technologies, and independent management of state enterprises, but he did not argue for introducing the market mechanism.[15] Large-scale reorganization of the bureaucracy was conducted in the 1986–88 period; eighteen ministries and committees were abolished, and nine new organizations were created. This reorganization seemed to be conducted to make the Mongolian system compatible with the reorganization efforts in the Soviet Union. The State Enterprise Law, approved by the Great People's Hural in November 1988, was virtually a copy of a similar law introduced in the Soviet Union. No wonder its implementation to "promote the decision-making powers of industrial enterprises" did not proceed very far. The economic reforms in Mongolia closely followed the Soviet pattern. They appeared to be efforts to adapt to the changes in the northern neighbor.

Political reforms in Mongolia also reflected political reforms in the Soviet Union. In December 1988 Batmönh advocated more democratization of the MPRP and *il tod* (glasnost), greater openness of the party, socialist pluralism, and a reevaluation of Mongolia's traditional culture. In particular, Genghis Khan was reevaluated. A postage stamp to commemorate the eight hundredth anniversary of Genghis Khan's coronation was issued in April 1989, and it was decided to call a new hotel under construction in Ulan Bator the Genghis Khan.

At the Seventh Plenum early in December 1989, Batmönh insisted that reforms did not imply retreat from socialism, and he affirmed the MPRP as the vanguard of society. What he said, however, was more an expression of puzzlement over the dramatic changes in Eastern Europe than determined resistance to democratization.

On December 10 the Democratic League, the first noncommunist political party, was organized, and on almost every Sunday thereafter a substantial number of demonstrators appeared to appeal for more democratization. On January 18, 1990, the MPRP accepted the legitimacy of the Democratic League by saying "it is not surprising that a movement is organized by the free will of workers at this period of democratization and such movement is guaranteed by the Constitution."[16] On January 25 Deputy Prime Minister Dashiin Byambasuren revealed that the MPRP was considering revisions of the constitution and the party charter including the adoption of a multiple party system. The Mongol Democratic Party, based on the Democratic League, was inaugurated on February 18, and Batmönh sent a message to the ceremony. On March 4 the four noncommunist groups led by the Democratic League organized a large scale demonstration of more than twenty thousand participants. The protestors demanded that a provisional People's Great Hural be convened to write a new constitution, that an extraordinary MPRP party Congress be convened within the month of March, that the current leadership resign, that the party and the administration be separated, and that members of the Central Committee of the party be reelected. The protestors started a hunger strike, which increased pressure on the party leadership. The MPRP accepted most demands of the opposition on March 9, and its Eighth Plenum decided to renew the party leadership, to introduce a multiparty system, and to revise the constitution. All the Politburo members submitted their resignation and Batmönh was replaced by Punsalmaagiyn Ochirbat as general secretary of the party. On March 21 the People's Great Hural decided that the leadership role of the MPRP should be deleted from the Constitution and that P. Ochirbat should assume the role of the head of state.

Based on the revision of the constitution and the electoral law, the first free elections were held on July 29, 1990. Under the new constitution, the Great People's Hural, the supreme organ of the state composed of 430 representatives, has the power to appoint the president and to revise the constitution, but it convenes only once a year. The Small People's Hural, composed of fifty-three representatives, is a standing legislative body that can appoint the cabinet and conduct normal legislative activities. The Great People's Hural election is based on a single-constituency system. The Small People's Hural election is based on a proportional representation system. Mainly because of this difference in electoral systems, the MPRP in the July election won as many as 357 seats (83 percent) in the Great People's Hural, while it won only 31 seats (62 percent) in the Small People's Hural.[17]

Despite the overwhelming victory of the MPRP in the election of the Great Hural, the first Great Hural, held in early September, decided to create a coalition government. P. Ochirbat was elected president with the support of 372 votes; some members in the opposition parties voted for him. But the important position of vice president, who *ex officio* assumes the chairmanship of the Small Hural, went to R. Gonchigdorj, the head of the third opposition party, the Social Democratic Party. He received 279 supporting votes. D. Byambasuren of the MPRP was elected prime minister, and D. Ganbold of the National Progressive Party and Ch. Purevdorj of the Democratic Party became deputy prime ministers.[18]

In 1991 political reforms continued. The political party law was revised in January to ban organizational activities of any political party in the governmental bureaucracy as well as state enterprises. Further revision of the constitution was under deliberation in the Small Hural. Unification of the Great and the Small Hurals and direct election of the president was being considered.[19]

In contrast to political reforms, economic reforms in Mongolia have barely started. The deterioration of the Soviet economy has severely hurt the Mongolian economy. In 1990 Moscow notified Ulan Bator that it would decrease oil exports to Mongolia by half and require payment in foreign hard currencies. In December 1990 a ban was placed on taking consumer goods out of the country. In January 1991 wages, prices, and interest on bank deposits were doubled, and ten major goods were rationed.[20]

Not until late November 1990 did Prime Minister Byambasuren disclose a systematic program to transform the Mongolian economy into a market economy in three years. Some of the measures included private ownership of property, redistribution of two-thirds of the state properties among the entire population, privatization of state enterprises, and liberalization of prices based on reforms in foreign trade and financial institutions. Redistribution of the national properties would be achieved by giving each citizen a bond worth 10,000 tugrik ($1,825). With this money citizens could obtain stocks of state enterprises when they were privatized.[21]

In 1991 several concrete steps were taken. In May a new bank law was written. In June the tugrik was devalued; one U.S. dollar became 40 tugrik as opposed to an earlier rate of 7 tugrik. The government "Committee on Privatization" disclosed in June that stocks of privatized enterprises could be purchased by foreigners and foreign firms without any conditions. It was announced that the first national bonds would be issued in September and that a security exchange would be opened in the autumn. But industrial production as well as foreign trade had declined in 1990, and there was no guarantee that the reform measures would alleviate hardship.

NORTH KOREA

North Korea's economy in the 1980s was, it seems, no less gloomy than the economy of any other socialist country in the world. How bad the economy of North Korea was, however, is not at all clear because, even by the standards of other socialist countries, economic statistics are few in number and dubious in quality. State revenues—virtually the only state-level statistic that has been published every year—grew by more than 10 percent annually during the 1970s, but the average growth rate in the late 1980s was only about 5 percent.[22] Statistics on gross industrial production and grain production have not been published since 1983 and 1985, respectively.

North Korea has been affected not only by its bad economic performance but also by reforms in other socialist countries. These internal and external factors, however, have not brought about the economic and political reforms observed in other socialist countries. Rather, the result has been more political retrenchment as well as a bizarre campaign for investment in counterproductive monuments.

The most easily observable domestic developments in North Korea's politics during the 1980s were the efforts to legitimize a future transfer of power from Kim Il Sung to his son Kim Jong Il. At the Sixth Congress of the Korean Workers' Party in October 1980, Kim Jong Il was elected a member of the Politburo as well as its Standing Committee, a member of the Party Secretariat, and a member of the party Military Committee. The only other person who ever held positions in all three critical party organs—the Standing Committee of the Politburo, the Secretariat, and the Military Committee—was his father. Though Kim Jong Il had not even served as a Central Committee member until then, he had become by the mid-1970s the sole authoritative interpreter of Kim Il Sungism based on Juche Thought. Following his father's initiative, he developed on the cadre level the "movement of small groups for the three great revolutions"—a thought revolution, a technology revolution, and a cultural revolution. On the mass level Kim Jong Il started the "grab the red flag movement for the three great revolutions." Its purpose was to increase production as well as to spread and consolidate Juche Thought in the minds of all citizens in North Korea. He also started a "movement to learn from hidden heros." Kim Jong Il found "hidden heroes" who showed their strong loyalty to Kim Il Sung by working hard and sacrificing themselves.

Since the 1980 elections, Kim Jong Il has formally acted as the sole legitimate successor of Kim Il Sung and, just like his father, he has been deified. In the 1980s he averaged about seven on-the-spot guidance tours through the country each year. In June 1983, at the invitation of Hu Yaobang, then general secretary of the Chinese Communist Party, he visited China. In the same year he hosted the Chinese delegation headed by Peng Zhen to Pyongyang. In the following years, he attended meetings between Kim Il Sung and foreign dignitaries. In July 1989 Kim Jong Il attended the opening ceremony of the World Festival of Youth and Students. The bizarre personality cult of Kim Jong Il grew and grew. His birth year was changed from 1941 to 1942 so that the year 1982 would become the ninetieth anniversary of the birth of Kim Il Sung's mother, the seventieth anniversary of the birth of Kim Il Sung, and the fortieth birthday of Kim Jong Il. Kim Jong Il's birthplace was changed to the foot of the revolutionary mountain of "Paektu." In 1989 this mountain was designated "Jong Il Peak" and the cultivation of a "Kim Jong Il flower" was reported.[23] Supposedly, Kim Jong Il can expand space (Kim Il Sung could shrink space), can transform the ocean into land, and can make the blind see.[24]

The necessity of economic reforms was acknowledged in the 1980s. In January 1984 the Supreme People's Congress declared that North Korea should develop economic and technical exchanges with capitalist countries that would respect its independence. In September 1984 the first joint venture law was issued. The following year a policy to activate tourism was started. In 1987 Kim Il Sung told Japanese visitors that "our third economic plan needs technological as well as financial assistance from Japanese business."[25] Kim Jong Il reportedly said, "Building an independent national economy on the principle of self-reliance does not mean building an economy in isolation. An independent economy is opposed to foreign economic domination and subjugation, but it does not rule out international economic cooperation."[26]

The North Korean government also conducted a large-scale reorganization of the Administration Council. In 1985 the twenty-two ministries, thirteen committees, and one agency were reorganized into nineteen ministries, thirteen committees, and one agency. Two new ministries were the Electronic and Automation Ministry and the Joint-Venture Industry Ministry.[27] These changes in orientation and organization have not been accompanied by significant reforms. Some twenty joint ventures (many with Korean residents in Japan) are now in operation, but they are small in size and scope. The number of foreign tourists has fallen far short of the goal of one hundred thousand per year. The 1987 figure was only 15,000.

In its domestic economic policy North Korea does not seem to be making any constructive reforms; it continues to target an expansion in the scale of production without proposing means to improve labor productivity.[28] It continues to rely on mobilization methods to fulfill the artificially created targets. A "two hundred day battle" was waged in early 1988 and then a "new two hundred day battle" followed. If these mobilization efforts had been targeted at productive investments, they might have boosted production. But the exploitation of workers was not for productive investment; workers were used to build such wasteful things as the Juche Thought Tower, the Arch of Triumph (bigger than the Arc de Triomphe in Paris), a hotel in Pyongyang more than one hundred stories high, and huge athletic facilities for the World Festival of Youth and Students, to name a few examples.

The dramatic collapse of communist dominos in Eastern Europe certainly affected North Korea, but in a peculiar manner. In his 1990 New Year message, Kim Il Sung recalled 1989 as a time when "antisocialism maneuvers by imperialists were of unprecedented intensity."[29] Hungary normalized relations with South Korea in February 1989; in October 1990 Moscow and Seoul normalized relations. Perhaps because of such manifest international isolation, Pyongyang finally began to show some flexibility in foreign policy. When a senior Japanese politician, Shin Kanemaru, visited in 1990, North Korea agreed to release two Japanese fishermen held hostage for more than six years, and it dramatically announced its desire to normalize relations with Japan.[30] In May 1991 Pyongyang returned the remains of an American who had been missing in action. In still another diplomatic turnaround, North Korea joined the United Nations simultaneously with South Korea in September 1991. In December 1991, Pyongyang reached a historic reconciliation agreement with Seoul. This series of flexible diplomatic steps may be interpreted as efforts to attract badly needed foreign capital. Furthermore, Pyongyang declared in the same month that a "free economic and trade area" be established around Najin in the northeast of the country. But it remains to be seen whether this will lead to real economic reforms. There is still little other evidence that North Korea has started serious domestic economic reforms, let alone political reforms.

SIMILARITIES

One common feature of Vietnam, Mongolia, and North Korea—and, for that matter, of all the communist regimes in the world—is a stagnant economy. Vietnam recognized its bad economic conditions as early as 1980, five years after the unification of the country. Tsedenbal's reign in Mongolia was described as "years of stagnation." North Korea has been unable to achieve its economic targets, and in some years (1985 and 1986, for example) it did not even write an economic plan. Central planned economies simply do not work.

A second characteristic of the three countries is their dependence on the Soviet Union. Vietnam conducts about two-thirds of its trade with the Soviet Union; for the 1976–80 period, the Soviet Union extended $1.45 billion in economic assistance (mostly in the form of grants) to Vietnam. For the 1981–85 period, Soviet aid to Vietnam was about $6 billion, and for the 1986–90 period it was about $12 billion (believed to be mostly soft loans).[31] Mongolia has depended on the Soviet Union for 90 percent of the economic assistance it receives from abroad, and its trade with Moscow constitutes 85 percent of its entire trade.[32] North Korea's trade with the Soviet Union is a substantial share of its entire trade (more than 50 percent in the late 1980s).[33] Though details are unknown, it seems apparent that North Korea has received various forms of assistance from the Soviet Union.

The third obvious similarity is adjacency to China. Traditionally and culturally, the three countries have long been affected by Chinese civilization. Since the establishment of the People's Republic of China in 1949, their relations with Beijing have been very important. The fact that China started its economic reforms as early as the end of the 1970s should certainly have been taken into consideration in the regimes in the three countries.[34]

DIFFERENCES

Despite these three commonalities—stagnant economy, dependence on the Soviet Union, and adjacency to China—developments in the 1980s significantly differed in Vietnam, Mongolia, and North Korea. Mongolia followed the Soviet pattern of reform. Vietnam started its economic reforms earlier than did the Soviet Union, but it has not accepted the Soviet or Eastern European type of political reform. Vietnam's pattern may be rather close to China's, albeit exaggerated in some respects. Both have been very active in economic reforms, especially in agriculture, while very reluctant in political reforms. North Korea, despite hints at some sort of open door, has not initiated any significant reforms, economic or political. Kim Il Sung's North Korea appears, in many ways, very similar to Nicolae Ceausescu's Romania.[35] Several factors explain such behavioral differences.

First, the levels of communist centralization in the three countries are different. Nationalization and collectivization of industry and agriculture had been forcibly achieved in North Korea by the end of the 1950s; many peasants were moved from their agricultural communities to artificially created collective farms.[36] Significant private sectors have not existed in North Korea since the end of the 1950s. Although Mongolia became a communist country as early as 1921, collectivization of agriculture was not completed until the late 1950s when two hundred thousand small farm households joined in more than seven hundred cooperative farms.[37] But Mongolia, like North Korea, has maintained a basically nationwide collective production system. Vietnam's case is more complex. Although the North had collectivized agriculture by 1975, socialism came to the capitalist South only after it was forcefully unified. Even in the North, collectivization did not seem to reach the "perfection" of North Korea.[38] In the South, collectivization was started in 1976–80 but because of the utter failure of the economy, it was abandoned when the economic reforms started.

Second, the levels of penetration of the Communist Party into society differ among the three countries. North Korea has an abnormally high percentage of Communist Party members in the population. The Korean Workers' Party had about 2 million members in 1980. That year North Korea's population was 18 million, so one out of nine people was a member of the Communist Party.[39] The Mongolian People's Revolutionary Party had 91,100 members and candidate members in 1988 (about 4.5 percent of the population).[40] The Vietnamese Communist Party at the time of the Fourth Party Congress had 1.53 million members (about 3 percent of the total population).[41] The percentage of Communist Party members in the society is clearly a misleading indicator of the loyalty of the population to the party. It is a relatively useful indicator, however, of the penetration of the Communist Party into society. It suggests how effectively the party can control people's lives under normal circumstances.

Third, the leadership of the three countries has differed. Kim Il Sung is the founding father of North Korea. During the 1950s and 1960s he successfully purged potential challengers to his position. He lives on as the demigod of the nation. In Vietnam Ho Chi Minh is long gone, and the current leaders belong to the second and third generations of the revolution. Khorloogiin Choibalsan, Mongolia's Stalin, died in 1952, and his successor Tsedenbal was replaced in 1984. In North Korea alone, the charisma of the leader can still play a significant role.

Fourth, the exposure to and experience with a market economy is different. South Vietnam, though rather chaotic and corrupt, was a market economy, and Vietnamese leaders from the South, such as Nguyen Van Linh, have some sense of what a market economy is all about. But Mongolia was a feudal and nomadic society before it became a socialist country. It is quite understandable that Mongols have a hard time implementing laws to deregulate and encourage private initiative. Entrepreneurship is an alien concept. Despite its years as a colony of Japan, North Korea lacks experience as well as human resources that could be useful in market competition.

Finally, the living standards in the three countries are different. Given the dubious nature of available monetary values for living standards especially of centrally planned economies, it is difficult to make a sound comparison. But if the estimates have some value, Vietnam's per capita GNP is by far the lowest among the three countries. North Korea's per capita GNP was an estimated $1,114 in 1988; Mongolia's, $1,054; and Vietnam's, $100 to $150.[42]

Given these differences, it makes sense that Vietnam was most active in economic reforms. People's living standards were low; the economy was stagnant; collectivization had not proceeded very far; party control was weak; charismatic leaders eager to stop reforms did not exist; and human resources more adaptable to a market economy were available. A contrasting picture can be drawn for North Korea. Although the economy was stagnant, living standards were not terrible; collectivization was almost complete; the party almost completely permeated the society; and the leader still maintained high charisma in his grip on state power. Even if the country had wanted to liberalize, it lacked the experience or knowledge of a market economy. Mongolia is probably positioned in between the other two. Because conditions for reforms were not as ripe as in Vietnam, Mongolia did not initiate its own reforms. Yet because it was not as tightly controlled as North Korea, and because of overwhelming dependence on Moscow, once the Soviet Union started its reforms, it followed the Soviet patterns.

PROSPECTS FOR REFORM

Are these three countries likely to follow the Soviet Union and Eastern Europe in terms of political liberalization? The communist regimes in Asia, unlike those in Eastern Europe, were established to gain independence from foreign subjugation. These indigenous forces were nationalist first and communist second. Even in Mongolia, communist rule was not imposed by the Soviet Union. Mongolia's overwhelming dependence on the Soviet Union was motivated in many ways by nationalistic aspirations for independence from Chinese rule. Ho Chi Minh was clearly a symbol of Vietnam's nationalist aspiration for independence. Although Kim Il Sung's regime was largely created by the Soviet occupation forces immediately after the defeat of Japan, he was perceived by many Korean nationalists, not as a Soviet puppet, but as a symbol of anti-Japanese nationalist movements. In fact, he has grown to be an independent figure not controlled by Moscow.[43]

Nationalist sentiment was very strong also because these three countries were homogeneous, more homogeneous than many Eastern European countries. North Korea and Mongolia have few if any ethnic minorities. Although Vietnam is heterogeneous compared with these two countries, 90 percent of its population is Vietnamese, and few strong divisive movements exist. The Communist Parties in these countries could still depict themselves as the sole champions of the nationalist sentiment.

Thus, the demise of the Communist Party in many East European countries had little direct impact on the Communist Party in the three countries. It is true that an almost knee-jerk tendency toward political liberalization occurred in Mongolia in 1989–90. But the MPRP has not disintegrated; on the contrary, it won the free elections in July 1990. In Vietnam, although the situation is in flux, the Communist Party still remains in power with no visible alternative forces; if it can depart from the current rigid and doctrinaire position, it can still have a chance to manage the initial transition to capitalism. The North Korean government, although shocked by the fall of Ceausescu, can continue its policy of retrenchment. As long as Kim Il Sung is alive and as long as he continues to keep tight control over the information flow in his society, his regime probably will be able to survive.

But clearly there are differences in the prospects of these three countries. One difference among the three countries that could make a difference for their future is the degree of political institutionalization. In this respect, despite its current effective repressive control of the population, the Korean Workers' Party seems weakest. The fact that it has not experienced any leadership transition makes the survival of the party as a viable organization extremely doubtful. Kim Il Sung painstakingly has tried to prepare a smooth leadership transition to his son for many years. But the preparation does not really increase the level of political institutionalization. To the extent that the preparation has been made at the initiative and power of the Great Leader, it does not strengthen the viability of the party or the regime. Once the leader is gone, the survivability of the party and the regime will face a real test. Compared with North Korea, Mongolia and Vietnam have experience with leadership transition. All their transitions were made peacefully. The MPRP won the first election under the new leadership of Ochirbat, and this increased its viability as a national institution. In Vietnam the party's nomination of Nguyen Van Linh, a southerner once demoted in the early 1980s, strengthened the institutional life of the party.

The critical tasks facing the three countries differ. Foreign aid from the West and Japan is sorely needed in Vietnam as is change within its Communist Party. Vietnam has introduced one of the most radical economic reforms of any communist country. It has survived three-digit inflation without anything like China's Tiananmen Square massacre. This indicates the Vietnamese government's strength as a political institution. To accomplish more economic development, however, it needs to allow more openness and freedom, the inevitable consequence of successful economic reforms.

The critical challenge of Mongolia is a challenge of economic development. Introduction of capitalism is a formidable task for a country that has long depended on Soviet aid. Uncertainties abound. Will enough financial assistance come from abroad? Is the population ready for the hustle and bustle of capitalistic competition? And can the government create economic management mechanisms to cope with the peculiar problems of capitalism?

North Korean problems are simple and intractable. They are simple because they depend on when and how the leadership transition occurs. It is hard to conceive of substantive changes in North Korea's political economy as long as Kim Il Sung survives. The current system with its tight controls, indoctrination, and repression has been able to manage internal stagnation as well as external pressures during his lifetime. Real reforms will be possible only when Kim Il Sung dies or is incapacitated.

North Korea's problems are also intractable. No one can predict what will happen once the senior Kim passes the scene. Can Kim Jong Il assume his father's leadership position? Will other leaders emerge? Can the Korean Workers' Party survive? How bad will the North Korean economy become by that time? Is the unification of the Korean peninsula more likely? No ready and easy answers exist, but it seems clear that among the three Asian socialist countries North Korea is the most resistant to reforms and its future could be the most volatile.

NOTES

1. Kimura Tetsusaburo, "Indoshina shakaishugi no genjitsu," in Kikuchi Masanori, ed., *Shakaishugi to gendai sekai*, vol. 2 (Tokyo: Yamakawa, 1989), pp. 335-36.
2. Mio Tadashi, "Betonamu no keizai kaikaku: moderu naki jikken to shikosakugo," in Mio Tadashi, ed., *Indoshina o meguru kokusai kankei: taiketsu to taiwa* (Tokyo: Nihon kokusai mondai kenkyujo, 1988) pp. 42–43.
3. Ibid., pp. 45–49.
4. Ibid., p. 57; Takeuchi Ikuo, "Yutakasa e no kutō: seiji to keizai," in Sakurai Yumio, ed., *Motto shiritai Betonamu* (Tokyo: Kobundo, 1989), p. 162.
5. Ibid., pp. 159–61.
6. Mio Tadashi, "Sonbō kakeru Betonamu no kaikaku rosen," *Kaigai Jijō* 38 (March 1990): 106.
7. Ibid.
8. *Asahi shimbun*, February 2, 1991.
9. *Asahi shimbun*, February 1, 1991; June 22, 1991.
10. The Economist Intelligence Unit, *Indochina: Vietnam, Laos, Cambodia, Country Report*, No. 2 (1991).
11. *Asahi shimbun*, September 26, 1991.
12. Murano Tsutomu, "1989 nen no Betonamu," *Ajia dōkō nenpo 1990* (Tokyo: Institute of Developing Economies, 1990), p. 236.
13. Koibuchi Shinichi, "Mongoru: keizai kaikaku no hōkō," *Ajia Kenkyū* 35 (March 1989): 27–28.
14. The Academy of Sciences, Mongolian People's Republic, *Information Mongolia* (Oxford: Pergamon Press, 1990), p. 158.
15. Hanada Marohito, "Mongoru," *Chūgoku soran 1990* (Tokyo: Kazankai, 1990), p. 592.
16. Koibuchi Shinichi, "Mongoru: ayumidashita minshuka e no michi," *Kaigai Jijō* 38 (April 1990): 72.

17. The election was held on July 29th. In twenty-eight districts where the results were undetermined a reelection was conducted on August 26th. *Asahi shimbun*, August 1, 1991; August 30, 1991 (evening edition).
18. Koibuchi Shinichi, "1990 nen no Mongoru," in *Ajia dōkō nenpo 1991* (Tokyo: Institute of Developing Economies, 1991).
19. *Asahi shimbun*, January 31, 1991; June 26, 1991.
20. *Asahi shimbun*, December 16, 1990; January 25, 1991.
21. *Asahi shimbun*, November 18, 1990.
22. Komaki Teruo, "Chōsen minshushugi jinmin kyōwakoku: keizai," *Chūgoku soran 1990* (Tokyo: Kazankai, 1990), p. 562.
23. Kong Dan Oh, "North Korea in 1989: Touched by Winds of Change?" *Asian Survey* 30 (January 1990): 77.
24. Yee Myonyong, "Kin Nichisei fushi shinkakuka no keika to sono seikaku," *Kaigai Jijō* 38 (May 1990): 63.
25. Heiwa anzen hoshō kenkyūjo, *Chōsen hantō no shorai to Nihon no anzenhoshō*, vol. 3 (Tokyo: Research Institute for Peace and Security, 1988), p. 84.
26. *Far Eastern Economic Review*, November 5, 1987, p. 24.
27. The real motivation behind the continuous reorganization is not at all clear. In Mongolia's case, the reorganization was to make the system more compatible with the Soviet Union under perestroika, but this does not seem to be the case in North Korea because the basic bureaucratic organization in North Korea was much closer to the Chinese system since 1972. The increase in the number of ministries may have been made to increase the number of high-ranking posts that Mr. Kim could distribute to his loyalists.
28. According to my private communications with some foreign visitors to North Korea, the unit of collectivization was broken down to much smaller groups of households sometime in the 1980s. The quota was assigned the group, and the group could dispose of the excess products. Some private plots were allowed to each household, and some free markets began to exist. But the scale of the decentralization and liberalization of the economy is still extremely limited. As travelers to both Pyongyang and Beijing know, the availability of various products differs in the two cities.
29. Quoted in Izumi Hajime, "Chōsen minshushugi jinmin kyōwakoku: gaikō, gunji," *Chūgoku soran 1990* (Tokyo: Kazankai, 1990), p. 559.
30. Negotiations between the two countries have not proceeded smoothly. One obstacle is North Korea's reluctance to accept unconditional inspection by the International Atomic Energy Agency (IAEA) of its nuclear facilities.
31. Vo Nhan Tri, "1975–87 nen no Soren to Betonamu no keizai kyōryoku," in Mio Tadashi, ed., *Indoshina o meguru kokusai kankei: taiketsu to taiwa* (Tokyo: Nihon kokusai mondai kenkyūjo, 1988), p. 178–79. These figures are based on the official exchange rate between ruble and dollar. The real value could be greatly overestimated.
32. Koibuchi, "Mongoru: keizai kaikaku," p. 33.
33. Komaki, "Chōsen minshushugi," p. 565.
34. The direct impact of Chinese economic reforms on the three countries was not so significant, however. Vietnam seemed to go through reforms of its own anyway; Mongolia was not affected very much. In North Korea the joint venture law and the limited responsibility system may have been introduced to emulate Chinese practices, but their significance was very limited in any case.
35. Striking are the degree of personal cult as well as almost dynastic tendencies in both countries. Tight political control as well as resistance to any meaningful economic reforms are also common to them. There are clear differences between North Korea and Romania, however. Kim Il Sung has more revolutionary credentials than has Ceausescu. North Korea has virtually no ethnic minorities. Romania has a far smaller military (179,500 personnel) than has North Korea, which has the third largest army in the world with more than a million military personnel. Political culture is vastly different between the two countries. North Korea has never been exposed to democratic institutions. For these comparisons, I owe John Phipps very much.

36. Tamaki Motoi, "Kyūchi ni tatsu Kitachōsen keizai kensetsu," *Kaigai Jijō* 38 (May 1990): 5.
37. *Information Mongolia*, p. 128.
38. The percentage of farm households organized into cooperatives reached 86 percent in 1960 and 96 percent in 1975, but the percentage of higher cooperatives was less than 50 percent until 1964. During the Vietnam War, the share of free markets increased from 9.2 percent in 1960 to 19.7 percent in 1975. See Kurihara Hirohide, "Betonamu no shakaishugi," in Sakurai Yumio, ed., *Motto shiritai Betonamu*, pp. 189–93.
39. Rajio Puresu, *Kita Chōsen no Genkyō 1990* (Tokyo: Rajio puresu, 1990), pp. 10, 112. Tamaki Motoi says that the membership in 1980 was 3 million; if his figure is correct, the percentage of the Communist Party members in the population was 16.7 percent. See Tamaki Motoi, "Kitachōsen no kaihō seisaku, sono tenbō to seiji kōzō," in Okonogi Masao, ed., Kiro ni tatsu Kitachōsen (Tokyo: Nihon kokusai mondai kenkyūjo, 1988), p. 42.
40. *Information Mongolia*, p. 153.
41. Kimura, "Indoshina shakaishugi," p. 323. Furthermore, the membership distribution between the North and the South was extremely skewed; the South had 273,000 members (about 18 percent), whereas its population constituted 47.5 percent of the entire nation.
42. Far Eastern Economic Review, *Asia 1990 Yearbook* (Hong Kong: Review Publishing Company, Ltd., 1990), pp. 6–7.
43. Kim Il Sung changed his name several times. Kim Il Sung was the name of a legendary general in the 1920s who was believed to have heroically fought against the Japanese. Several generals called themselves Kim Il Sung during the resistance movements in the 1930s. In 1945 Kim Songju was introduced by the Soviet forces as the great "General Kim Il Sung" to the Korean public and he started his career of becoming a demigod in North Korea then. Yee Myonyong, "Kin Nichisei fushi shin-kakuka no keika to sono seikaku," *Kaigai Jijō* 38 (May 1990): 53–54. For a detailed biography of Kim, see Dae-Sook Suh, *Kim Il Sung: The North Korean Leader* (New York: Columbia University Press, 1988).

III

REGIONAL VARIATIONS: EASTERN EUROPE

8

East-Central Europe: From Reform to Transformation

Judy Batt

In this chapter I will use the word "transformation" to describe the systemic change in Poland, Hungary, Czechoslovakia, and the German Democratic Republic. Clearly, what has gone on in East-Central Europe is more than "reform," a word that has long been applied to too many different—and equally unsuccessful—attempts to make the economic system of "real socialism" work within the limits set by the Communist Party's monopoly of political power. The events of 1989 or the subsequent programs of the new postcommunist governments also cannot properly be described as "revolutionary."[1] Radical, far-reaching change in the political, economic, and social order is now on the agenda, but the situation in East-Central Europe has not displayed the elemental, uncontrolled, and above all violent qualities characteristic of the classical revolutions.[2] In 1989 the ruling elites lost the will and the ability to defend their positions by force. The exhausted and sceptical populations had no stomach for violence, suspecting it would only provoke direct Soviet intervention. The opposition elites identified revolutionary violence as the "original sin" of the totalitarian power they sought to dismantle.

The word "transformation" is intended to capture the distinctive accent on legal continuity, self-restraint, and deliberate compromise that has marked the process of change in East-Central Europe. Transformation involves three phases: the breakdown of the communist regime; the transfer of power; and the reconstruction of politics. In the countries covered in this chapter, two paths to systemic crisis and breakdown are identified: the path of intransigent resistance to reform in Czechoslovakia and the German Democratic Republic and the path of failed reform in Hungary and Poland. The regimes that totally rejected reform faced total collapse; the regimes that embarked on reform with the aim of shoring up communist power suffered, in the end, the same fate. Half-way reform turned out to be even worse than no reform at all, while radical reform—that is, reform that would bring about the intended economic results—could not be achieved without sweeping away communist power.

Although they led to the same end—the breakdown of the communist regimes—the different paths had significant implications for the subsequent phases of transformation. The transfer of power from failed reformist regimes in Hungary and Poland was effected through a protracted and relatively orderly negotiation between ruling and opposition elite groups. In Czechoslovakia and the GDR, the intransigent ruling elite was unprepared for negotiation, and it effectively collapsed in the face of spontaneous mass mobilization of the population. These different patterns have created different opportunities and obstacles in the latest phase of transformation, the reconstruction of politics. This phase involves not simply the replacement of one political regime by another but a reconstruction of the sphere of politics per se. First in this reconstruction is the separation of politics from economics. The system of central planning based on state ownership is dismantled and replaced with a market economy based on private property. The second step in the reconstruction is the establishment of an authentic state, one that is not a creature of Soviet domination but is accepted as the legitimate institutional expression of the national will.

THE BREAKDOWN OF THE COMMUNIST REGIMES

Failed Reform: Poland and Hungary

Economic reform was the central plank of the political strategy of the Polish and Hungarian communist regimes. It was an attempt to stabilize power after traumatic political crises had exposed the coercive basis of the party's power and its role as the instrument of national subordination to the Soviet Union. Economic reform was intended to inject new life into the communist ideology and to revive the legitimacy of the political system by demonstrating the party's efficacy as the agent of economic and social modernization that would lead to a level of personal consumption and social welfare comparable, if not superior, to those of the West. Party leaders promised that economic reform would offer new career opportunities and high material rewards for the ambitious, well qualified, and hard working.

In fact, economic reform was adopted as a form of substitute politics: purposes that are properly those of politics were thrust onto the economy. The expression, competition, and reconciliation of interests and the enjoyment of individual freedom were all to be realized in the economic sphere, while the sphere of politics remained monopolized by the party as before. The replacement of command planning by the "regulated market" was expected to transform the basis of party rule from coercion to consent. Economic efficiency would translate into moral legitimacy.

The structure of power that evolved as a result of the reformist strategy in Hungary and Poland in the 1970s can be described as a form of "state corporatism" or "consultative authoritarianism" in which the eventual crisis and breakdown were already prefigured.[3] Partial decentralization of control over the economy diffused power to regional party apparatuses, sectoral ministries, and large industrial conglomerates, all of which were heavily represented on the Central Committee. The party leadership and government policy making became highly responsive to these bureaucratic interests, even dependent on them. At first sight, this could be taken as evidence of political development, in the sense of evolution toward a more pluralistic and rational politics based on interests.[4] In fact, it was a highly imperfect form of political decentralization that transmitted social interests in a selective, distorted way and that seriously weakened the ability of the central authorities to construct and implement coherent policies and, in particular, to maintain overall macroeconomic control.[5] In Hungary this was indicated by the compromises and modifications to the New Economic Mechanism between 1972 and 1975, which amounted to a major reversal of the reform; in Poland Edward Gierek was unable to impose the necessary economic adjustment policies in the second half of the 1970s and therefore he could not prevent the slide into crisis in 1980.

Market-type reform was undermined by the organizational system in which powerful conservative interests were entrenched. The branch ministries, superfluous once traditional directive planning was abolished, were left in place. Organizational reforms not only failed to break up the economically (and often technologically) unjustified large industrial enterprises, but even promoted mergers and concentration. These firms enjoyed monopoly positions on the domestic market, and they also were not exposed to the rigors of competition from imports. They could evade or manipulate central price and wage regulations and secure privileged access to investment resources and budgetary subsidies.[6] In both countries wage payments ran ahead of output and productivity growth. In Poland, this was a result of the regime's deliberately expansionist incomes policy and its powerlessness in the face of mass pressure from the working class.[7] In Hungary the official trade unions built themselves up as an effective lobby. Self-appointed defenders of the workers' interests, they derived their political clout from acting in concert with the lobby of large enterprises and from playing on the party leadership's fears of Polish-style social unrest.[8]

Sustaining this pattern of political economy entailed a sharp rise in external indebtedness, but the improvements in export performance on which the strategy depended did not materialize. The Western recession could be blamed for this, but the underlying reasons were in the poor quality of goods and low technological level of production. Thus, after a decade of modernizing and reformist rhetoric, Hungary and Poland began the 1980s with massive, unmanageable hard currency debts, inefficient and outdated production structures, budget deficits, and intense inflationary pressures.

At this time the political system in both countries began to break down. This was obvious in Poland in 1980–81 with the emergence of Solidarity, the collapse of the Polish United Workers' Party (PUWP), and the imposition of martial law. But in Hungary the turn of the decade saw the beginning of gradual and rather more subtle change as the power of the Hungarian Socialist Workers' Party (HSWP) eroded. Both regimes' commitment to economic reform was renewed at the start of the 1980s, but the relationship between economic reform and political power was changed. Economic reform in the early 1980s was to be introduced in conditions of profound economic difficulty in Hungary and open crisis in Poland. Now, in contrast to the previous attempts, therefore, it had to be accompanied by harsh economic policies—leading in Hungary to stagnation in the standard of living and in Poland to swinging price rises and a sharp fall in real wages. In such an economic environment, economic reform could no longer substitute for political reform. In fact, economic reform became conditional upon political reform. But in Eastern Europe in the 1980s, political reform was impossible.

The turning point came in Hungary at a series of plenary sessions of the HSWP Central Committee in October 1977. The following year it was acknowledged that the economic policies of the 1970s had been mistaken and, in particular, that the reversal of the economic reform had contributed in large part to the looming threat of national insolvency.[9] In the summer of 1979 a stabilization program was introduced. Austerity measures cut investment in order to improve the convertible-currency trade balance while protecting social consumption. The economic reform was relaunched with the introduction of price reform to bring domestic prices closer to world prices. New measures introduced in the early 1980s not only returned to the original principles of the

1968 reform, but in many respects extended and went beyond them. The industrial branch ministries were merged into a single Ministry of Industry in 1980; many of the large enterprises were broken up into smaller, more viable and competitive units; new small and medium-sized firms were promoted, and new legislation increased the scope for private enterprises and cooperatives. In 1984–85 worker self-management and elected enterprise councils were introduced. The right to make managerial decisions and to select the top managerial personnel was transferred from the branch ministries to enterprises. Some liberalization in the foreign trade system took place. The Ministry of Foreign Trade was merged with the Ministry of Internal Trade, and foreign trade rights were granted to state enterprises. New legislation on joint ventures with Western firms was introduced.

In Poland the introduction of martial law under Gen. Wojciech Jaruzelski was accompanied (in contrast to post–1968 Czechoslovakia) by the clear reaffirmation of commitment to the economic reforms prepared in 1980–81. In fact, Jaruzelski and his advisers looked to Kadarist Hungary as a model of social pacification through economic reform.[10] In 1982 the "3-S" program of self-direction, self-financing, and self-management was introduced.[11] Obligatory central plan targets were abolished except for a few strategic industries (for example, coal mining, the key source of hard currency exports). Foreign trade rights were extended to more enterprises, and new legislation was passed permitting the founding of small foreign firms and later joint ventures with foreign capital.

Because of the profound economic disequilibrium early in Jaruzelski's rule, the reforms could be only partially implemented: enterprise autonomy, for example, was crucially vitiated by centralized control over access to most key inputs. Economic recovery in the mid-1980s was weak, and a familiar pattern of political economy quite soon reestablished itself: monopolistic producers and industrial lobbies reasserted themselves, and levels of consumption were allowed to run ahead of economic performance, thus eroding the benefits won in the drastic austerity measures of 1982. Convertible currency trade had begun to show a surplus, but not enough to allow reduction in the huge accumulated debt. Indeed, to maintain even modest growth, further borrowing seemed inevitable. By 1987 it was recognized that the main objectives of the 1982 reform had not been achieved, and a renewed, more radical proposal for a second stage of reform was unveiled.

In Hungary a similar pattern could be discerned: "Despite these reform measures, one senses a reluctance to pursue reform as vigorously as in the past as well as a suspicion that reforms increasingly appear to deal with issues peripheral to Hungary's fundamental economic problems and are more style than substance."[12] The government, overoptimistic after weathering an acute liquidity crisis in 1981–82 and seeing signs of economic recovery in 1983–84, attempted to accelerate the growth rate in 1985, but the underlying weakness of the economy was rapidly revealed in the doubling of the country's convertible currency debt between 1985 and 1987 from (gross) $8.8 billion to $17.7 billion.[13] The stage seemed set for a repeat performance of the Polish crisis of 1980–81.

Political disintegration in Poland and Hungary was both cause and consequence of these economic developments. This was apparent at every level of the power structure. Leadership immobilism and drift set in in the face of the intractable politico-economic conundrum[14]: within the framework of the traditional political stucture, the reformist leaderships remained prisoners of conservative bureaucratic interests embedded in the party-state hierarchy over which they presided. Economic reform required political reform in order to mobilize new sources of social support, but political reform was blocked by seemingly immovable external and internal obstacles.

Jaruzelski's program of socialist renewal tried to bridge the yawning gulf between the regime and society by developing a "coalitional method" of rule, according to which pliable, moderate partners for a controlled social dialogue might be co-opted, and responsibility for policy making thus shared.[15] But this strategy was continually opposed by the more orthodox hard-line element in the political leadership. Moreover, these hard-liners periodically engaged in provocative incidents (such as the murder of the priest Jerzy Popieluszko) that undermined whatever shreds of popular credibility Jaruzelski's efforts might have gathered. The opposition to Jaruzelski's attempts at controlled pluralization had solid foundations. On the one hand, the hard-liners had good reasons to doubt whether such an approach could work without political concessions that would undermine the basic logic of a regime founded on martial law; indeed, the manifold new channels for organized participation set up by Jaruzelski remained obstinately lifeless. On the other hand, these misgivings were shared by the Soviet leadership, which provided crucial backing and encouragement to the hard-line elements in Poland. Jaruzelski's persistence in what looked like a self-destructive course could be explained by the countervailing pressures from Western creditors insisting on some evidence of progress toward political stabilization. In a freely conducted referendum in No-

vember 1987, Polish society rejected the second phase of economic reform. Jaruzelski was left flailing hopelessly in the web of mutually irrec-
oncilable international and domestic pressures.

The Kadarist regime, to which the Polish refomers had looked for
inspiration as a model of political integration through economic reform,
also went adrift under the impact of economic failure. The pivot of the
regime had been Janos Kadar's personal role as a "centrist" mediator
between the conservative ideologues and bureaucratic lobbies on the
one hand and technocratic and reformist economic experts on the other.
Conflict had thus been contained within the power structure, while
intellectuals were incorporated with some success. But the party's acknowledgment of its mistaken path in the 1970s brought this political
structure into question, and Kadar personally was discredited. When
reformist economists began to advocate a "reform of the reform" in the
early 1980s, Kadar lashed out against them.[16] In so doing, Kadar placed
himself firmly in the conservative wing of the party, thus forfeiting his
mediating role in the leadership and his popular credibility as guarantor
of the reformist course, while alienating the economic experts. Particularly after the HSWP Congress in 1985, these experts defected to the
extraparty opposition and began circulating highly critical materials
through the medium of *samizdat*.

At the same time, Kadar's advanced age brought the question of the
party leadership onto the agenda. The Kadar era had reached its "biological limits," as Karoly Grosz, a leading contender in the succession
struggle, put it. Kadar began to display the typical characteristics of an
authoritarian leader. He refused to step aside, and his tactic of dealing
with his challengers by shifting them away from the center of power in
the party backfired. The powerful Budapest party secretary, Karoly
Grosz, was appointed prime minister in 1987. Instead of languishing in
the mire of the crisis-ridden economy, Grosz energetically used his position as a vantage point from which to appeal outside the party for new
sources of social support. He talked with hitherto excluded experts and
technocratic groups, and he drew up a promising program for tackling
the economic problems. When he presented this program to parliament
in September 1987, his crisp and decisive style made a favorable impression at home and abroad. By contrast, Kadar increasingly appeared
tired, old, and confused.[17] Grosz's emergent rival in the reformist wing
of the party, Imre Pozsgay, was using his position as chairman of the
Patriotic People's Front, to which he had been "exiled" by Kadar in
1982, to stimulate further public debate on the state of the nation. Thus,
the party itself appeared to be the main obstacle to change. This was

confirmed when Grosz succeeded Kadar. Grosz reverted to his more natural authoritarian style as the new head of the party and attempted to consolidate his power against Pozsgay by stalling the reform debate.

In both countries the party's "leading role" underwent irreversible decay in the 1980s under the combined impact of economic reform and economic crisis. The beginnings of the rot can be traced back to the 1970s, when cadre policies had downplayed ideological criteria in order to attract a younger generation of well-trained technocrats:

> To most of them the party career was like a job for which they expected to be properly rewarded. Accordingly, the ideology of the party became a kind of window dressing. . . . As a result, the party came closer to resembling society, but at the same time one of its integrating forces was weakened: the sense of a common political mission.[18]

In Hungary this "sense of common political mission" had, in the 1970s, been very much bound up with economic reform. Many able and independent-minded people had been induced to join the party and pursue "establishment" careers by the not unreasonable calculation that the cause of reform could be most effectively furthered from within the apparatus. These people were disappointed and felt morally compromised by the failure of the reform. In the 1980s they provided a substantial constituency in favor of radical change within the party. By the mid-1980s many of them had come to share Imre Pozsgay's conviction that the party's monopoly of power was neither workable nor desirable. Ready to make a decisive break with the past, these people reassessed the entire Kadar era going all the way back to its roots in the 1956 revolution. A historical commission, set up at the end of 1988, concluded that the events of 1956 had not constituted a "counterrevolution," the prevailing myth of the Kadar regime, but a genuine "popular uprising." The HSWP Central Committee accepted this finding in February 1989. This signaled not only the final defeat of the conservative-Kadarist faction in the leadership, but also the abandonment of the party's claim of a right to a monopoly of power. The same plenum approved the transition to a multiparty system, opening the way for negotiations with the opposition movements that had sprung up.

In Gierek's Poland the new brand of apparatchiks had been blamed for the spread of corruption; the purges carried out under Jaruzelski reasserted discipline and central control over cadres. They also weeded out genuine party reformists who had compromised themselves politically in 1980–81. Thus, the party proved to be of little use to Jaruzelski in his attempts to bridge the gulf between regime and society. During martial law, the party was thrust to one side, or at least shared power with the military and security apparatus. But when martial law was lifted, it remained irretrievably compromised by association with coercive rule, and it failed to regain its "leading role." Membership fell from just over 3 million at the end of 1980 to 2 million in 1985. Recruitment remained a constant problem, and the share of workers and young people declined dramatically.[19] It was not just a question of moral repugnance. The incentives to join the party were greatly diminished because the party was no longer the key channel for access to power or material reward. Jaruzelski's coalitional strategy sought to revive or create a wide variety of institutions: Patriotic Council for National Rebirth (PRON), the other political parties, the official trade unions, enterprise self-management. "At the local level, the party organization was only one among several groups, and was generally not the most active or influential."[20]. At the central level, Jaruzelski preferred to give high visibility to the Sejm, and he set up his own Social Consultative Council as an adjunct to the Council of State.[21]

In both countries the nomenklatura system underwent a process of dilution and, as a result, the central element of the power structure, party control over the economy, weakened. The introduction of enterprise self-management significantly weakened the direct control of the party apparatus over the recruitment and promotion of managerial personnel. Where economic reforms took hold, incomes began to depend more on economic performance and less on political connections and access to centrally controlled processes of redistribution of resources. Moreover, as production in the state sector stagnated, new resources increasingly eluded direct party control. The small but dynamic private sector, new cooperative enterprises, foreign-owned firms, and joint ventures were the major sources of what growth took place in the economy.[22] Demands for the formal abandonment of the nomenklatura system were made openly in the late 1980s, and its impending demise was signaled in Poland in June 1988, when the PUWP Central Committee approved proposals for a radical restriction of its extent,[23] and in Hungary in early 1989, when the new prime minister, Miklos Nemeth, presented to the parliament a new government team that had not received the prior approval of the HSWP Politburo.

The final component of the impasse at which Poland and Hungary had arrived by the late 1980s was stalemate in the strategy of social control. Both regimes tried to hide their essentially coercive nature by efforts to manufacture social consent through what has been called "covert legitimation" and "demobilization" of society.[24] Opposition was controlled not only by outright repression but also by co-optation or marginalization of its most articulate representatives. The economic crisis and increasing incoherence of the political structure undermined the regimes' ability either to repress or co-opt opposition, but they were "successful" in preventing the upsurge of mass social unrest. The price of this success, however, was an alienated society that had become ungovernable. The root of the problem in Poland was, of course, the suppression of Solidarity, which Jaruzelski had been quite unable to replace with PRON, or the official unions, or any other channel of communication. "This is the secret of the Polish situation," Adam Michnik commented in 1987. "For six years Jaruzelski has been paralysed by his insistence that Solidarity does not exist."[25] Solidarity, however, suffered badly under martial law, and once martial law was lifted it failed to win support from an angry young generation for whom Solidarity was "a symbol of cowardice and conformity."[26]

In Hungary the population began to show signs of "reform fatigue," as described by the intellectuals of the Democratic Opposition in a proposal for a new social contract produced in June 1987:

> The public at large is showing increasing dissatisfaction, but nothing more. They are not thinking about alternatives; they raise no demands. . . . There are many obstacles to people starting to make demands. First, pessimism; the feeling that economic decline is unstoppable. Then, the discrediting of reforms; since 1979, everything has been "reformed" but nothing has changed, except the fall in living standards. And the perception of an immovable power elite: it does not matter what "we" think, "they" will do what they like anyway.[27]

Notwithstanding the growth and maturation of organized opposition movements from the mid-1980s onwards, the society remained largely "demobilized" and atomized. It diverted its frustrated energies in the "internal emigration" of family life, religion, participation in the "second economy," or escapism of various sorts, including alcoholism. But these forms of adaptation began to act as a constraint on the regime itself. It was unable not only to generate positive support for any of the projects for reform or renewal but also to control the status quo. For example, alcoholism and exhaustion from moonlighting in the second economy were a drain on labor productivity in the state sector. Public health deteriorated markedly in the 1980s. This was attributed not just to drastic underfunding of the health service but also to a sociopsychological crisis closely connected with economic and political decay.[28] The second economy certainly filled in gaps where the first economy had manifestly failed, but it also was parasitic. It relied heavily on pilfering and corruption for its access to supplies and on the endemic "economy of shortage" for levels of profit that had a high rental component.[29] The two economic sectors became more interdependent, thus creating new vested interests against reform. The second society was unable to evolve naturally into a civil society to challenge the official society of state and party. Rather, "the two societies' paradigms have collapsed into each other and reciprocally obstructed each other's normal functions, leading to a further worsening of our current crisis."[30]

Resistance to Reform: Czechoslovakia and the GDR

In many respects the breakdown of communist rule in Czechoslovakia and the German Democratic Republic is easier to explain than the breakdown in Poland and Hungary. The regimes in Czechoslovakia and the GDR centered their strategy for maintaining power not on risky domestic reforms but on firm alliance with the Soviet leadership. Instead of attempting to win popular consent, they built up a formidable coercive apparatus, justified according to the tenets of traditional Marxist-Leninist ideology and ultimately dependent on Soviet backing. When the Soviet Union began to depart from these ideological principles and finally abdicated its role of ultimate guarantor of the regimes of Eastern Europe, communist rule in Czechoslovakia and the GDR simply collapsed.

From a comparative perspective, what is interesting about these regimes is not so much why they collapsed, but why they were able to resist reform for so long. The answer is not simply that Soviet penetration was more intensive than in Poland and Hungary: From the Soviet geostrategic perspective, control of the GDR was of paramount importance, but this depended as much on control of Poland as on the maintenance of ideological conformity and an efficiently coercive regime in the GDR. Hungary was less important from the purely geostrategic perspective than any of the other three "northern tier" states; but it is not immediately obvious that this gave it much more latitude to experiment with ideologically unorthodox methods of rule than was available to Czechoslovakia. The Kadar regime proved able to convince the Soviet leadership that its reformist course was necessary to stabilize communist power after the trauma of Soviet armed intervention in 1956; a "Kadarist" course may not have been precluded in Czechoslovakia after 1968, but it was not taken by the Husak regime. In other words, East European regimes had a choice of political strategies, and their choices were conditioned as much by the preferences of the particular local party leaderships and by domestic conditions as by specific Soviet directives. The choice of antireformism in Czechoslovakia and the GDR thus suggests certain domestic factors, which continued to exert their influence on events once Soviet support was withdrawn.

The origin of the divergence of paths in East-Central Europe can be traced to the immediate post-Stalin period. The crises of 1956 were a watershed for communist rule in Hungary and Poland. Both the HSWP and PUWP leaderships had been shocked by the events of that year to such an extent that they recognized reform could not be kept off the political agenda. Of course, Czechoslovakia and East Germany had experienced mass popular revolts in Pilsen and East Berlin in 1953, but the crucial difference was the timing. The restoration of order in 1953 was effected according to the Stalinist principles still dominant in the Soviet Union, rather than the more flexible approach characteristic of Nikita Khrushchev's leadership. The 1953 crises strengthened the faction of neo-Stalinist authoritarians in the Communist Party of Czechoslovakia and the Socialist Unity Party of East Germany, whereas the 1956 crises significantly and permanently reduced their influence in the PUWP and HSWP. In all four cases the crises of the 1950s were a major formative experience of the generation still in power in the 1980s.

From the 1950s to the 1980s, groups inclined toward reform, when they emerged within the communist parties of Czechoslovakia and the GDR, were always embattled and on the defensive. Over time the strength of the hard-line opposition to reform was only enhanced by the crisis-ridden progress of reform both at home and elsewhere in the bloc. Thus, reforms were perceived not as a response to crisis but as its cause. The experience of 1968 was the ultimate confirmation of this for the Communist Party of Czechoslovakia (CPCS) and the Socialist Unity Party (SUP); shortly afterwards, both parties saw a resurgence of traditional hard-liners and the establishment of new leaderships tied to the reaffirmation of neo-Stalinist ideological principles that definitively excluded even modest experiments with reform.

In Czechoslovakia in 1969 and 1970, some of the new party leaders, including Husak, had expected to be able to follow a Kadarist course. They maintained in public a commitment to the economic reform, albeit "cleared of revisionist deposits," as Gustav Husak put it.[31] An important conference of economic specialists as late as April 1971 heard CPCS Central Committee Secretary Miloslav Hruskovic affirm that outright rejection of economic reform "would be equal to a step backward in the political, as well as theoretical sense, and would hurt the interests and needs of the Party and the economy."[32] But economic reform in the wake of political coercion was no more possible in Czechoslovakia in the 1970s than it was in Poland in the 1980s. In contrast to Poland, however, political conditions in Czechoslovakia favored the consolidation of neo-Stalinism. A sizable cohort of convinced neo-Stalinists, not only in the leadership but throughout the apparatus, had been shaken but not dislodged in the nine short months of reformist rule. The party purges of 1971–72 accentuated the weight of hard-liners by comprehensively eliminating the reform communist faction.[33] Economic recentralization began initially as an ad hoc emergency response to the profound economic disequilibrium that had been allowed to develop unchecked in 1968–69 as a result of the Dubcek leadership's preoccupation with the political crisis; but the momentum of economic recentralization built up as the political purges cut a swathe through the most competent, qualified, and reform-minded managerial cadres.[34] Finally, in 1972 the word "reform" was officially outlawed from the public vocabulary and the Academy of Sciences issued a comprehensive ideological repudiation of reform economics.[35]

Thereafter, even the most modest proposals for improvement of the economic system were suspected of "creeping counter-revolution," even more insidious than the open variant exhibited in 1956. The creeping counter-revolution protested loyalty to socialism and pretended to want it to work better.[36] Even pragmatic technocrats were put on the defensive. Prime Minister Lubomir Strougal, who advocated economic reform in January 1987, was removed from the Politburo the following year. The ghost of 1968 thus spooked reform in Czechoslovakia, just as the ghost of Solidarity haunted Jaruzelski.

The change of leadership of the SUP in May 1971 was related to the question of economic reform. Soviet dissatisfaction with Walter Ulbricht's intransigent opposition to the new *Ostpolitik* was the immediate reason for his removal, but dissatisfaction had been growing within the SUP over Ulbricht's ideological innovations, not the least of which was his "New Economic System" of 1963, upgraded in 1967–68 to the "Economic System of Socialism." The 1967–68 innovation, less radical in concept than the Czechoslovak and Hungarian economic reform models of the 1960s, was nonetheless discredited in the eyes of ideological hard-liners by the events of 1968. They found unacceptable its implicit claim to be a distinctive and superior model to that of the Soviet economy. Moreover, as a half-way model of reform, it created a certain amount of economic dislocation and did not live up to expectations of radical improvement in economic performance.[37] The danger of such heterodox tinkerings with the fundaments of the economic, political, and ideological order was heightened, from the perspective of East German neo-Stalinists, by the changing international context. The problem the Honecker regime now faced was how to sustain the credibility of a separate East German state in the era of *Ostpolitik* and rapprochement with the Federal Republic. The answer was *Abgrenzung*. A new "law" of historical development was pronounced by the leading ideologue of the new regime, Albert Norden. He declared that as socialism progresses, "there takes place between the systems an objective process of ever-clearer political, ideological and economic delimitation."[38] Economic reform, the introduction of market elements into the socialist planned economy, blurred the distinctions between capitalism and socialism; it smacked unacceptably of "convergence," a fashionable "bourgeois" social science theory of the late 1960s and early 1970s. Thus, economic reform was perceived as a threat to the very *raison d'être* of the German Democratic Republic: Otto Rheinhold, director of the SUP's Academy for Social Sciences, posed the question with unexceptionable clarity in 1989: "What kind of right to exist would a capitalist GDR have alongside a capitalist Federal Republic?"[39]

Resistance to reform was the pivotal principle of these regimes. Their durability and strength present a mirror image of their reformist counterparts' weakness. They had the advantage of clear and uncompromisingly consistent ideological principles, upheld by a disciplined nomenklatura and an extensive internal security system, whose efficiency no doubt owed much to a long tradition of bureaucratic administration. Competent and qualified East German citizens were induced to stay at home, rather than try their luck in West Germany, by the promise of high rewards: rapid promotion and access to the hidden privileges of special distribution networks.[40]

Loyalty to the leadership in the Czechoslovak apparat was guaranteed by the political purges, to which many owed their careers. The introduction of reform for these people meant not merely the likelihood of losing a comfortable, well-rewarded position, but also the psychologically and morally distressing possibility that the former occupants of those positions would reappear in person, demand their jobs back, and even seek some retribution for twenty wasted years.

A centralized, closed economy proved to have certain political advantages. In comparison to the reformist regimes, success was no greater in long-term growth rates, efficiency, or technological dynamism,[41] but this could be concealed by manipulating the statistics and avoiding the prying eyes of Western creditors and the International Monetary Fund, to which Poland and Hungary acceded in the early 1980s. What could be avoided by this course was more significant—loss of control over basic macroeconomic development and exposure to the fluctuations and shocks transmitted from the world economy. To be sure, the GDR ran up large debts in the 1970s, but its "special relationship" with the Federal Republic eased the acute payment tensions of the early 1980s.[42] More restrained in its borrowing, Czechoslovakia was (in the short term) successful in imposing a centralized adjustment policy. It accumulated instead an "internal indebtedness," effectively borrowing against its future by neglecting infrastructural and environmental investment.[43] Information on these issues, however, was closely controlled, and public discussion stifled.

Above all, centralization had the advantage of putting at the disposal of the regime the vast bulk of economic resources that could be redistributed according to political criteria in order to guarantee full employment, subsidize prices, satisfy populistic concepts of social justice in income distribution, and sustain the welfare state. Personal consumption and the provision of social welfare may have stagnated throughout the 1980s, but at least the regimes could point to the unhappy lot of the workers in Poland and Hungary—and Thatcherite Britain—to head off criticism of their own record. Those for whom the proper standard of comparison was West Germany emigrated or avoided expressing their doubts in public. These regimes supplemented outright coercion with the same tactics of "demobilization" of the population employed by the Hungarian and Polish regimes. The effects on social morale were similarly devastating.[44] But the regimes in Czechoslovakia and the GDR, unlike those in Hungary and Poland, did not require a more active role for society in the realization of their politico-economic strategies. Therefore, they were less affected by the negative consequences of demobilization tactics.

In short, Czechoslovakia and the GDR were virtually immune to the emergence of reformism from within: they had settled into a pattern of "self-stabilizing oligarchy."[45] Generational change in the leadership, on the horizon in both countries in the 1980s, did not seem likely to be used as an opportunity for a change of course. Husak was replaced at the head of the CPCS in December 1987 by Milos Jakes, the man who had conducted the devastating purges of party reformists in the early 1970s. The leading representatives of the rising generation were Egon Krenz in the SUP and Miroslav Stepan in the CPCS. Krenz praised the resolute stand of the Chinese leadership in Tiananmen Square. He discovered the need for reform only when the GDR was irretrievably set on the course of transformation. Krenz distinguished himself as the prime mover of the brutal police repression of Prague students on November 17, 1989, which brought down the whole regime. Serious internal problems could readily be identified, but the complete breakdown of the regime supposed an unprecedented challenge from outside—from mass revolt, which because of the effectiveness of coercion and social demobilization was likely only with a radical change in people's perceptions of the possible. This depended on the withdrawal of Soviet backing of the regime, which seemed hardly conceivable right up to the late summer of 1989.

THE TRANSFER OF POWER

Negotiated Transition: Poland and Hungary

By the end of 1987, the unavoidable necessity of a new "social compromise" or "anticrisis pact" had become obvious to the regimes and the opposition elites in Poland and Hungary. For the Communist Party, compromise entailed recognition of the right to exist of groups it had perceived as enemies and had sought to repress; reluctance to admit the complete failure of its monopolistic rule was compounded by genuine fear of retribution by aggrieved opponents. The spectre of a "white terror" from the regime's opponents was raised by the resistant factions in the ruling parties. Even those who could claim some credit for advancing the cause of political reconciliation were insecure and not immune to the sense of guilt at complicity with the old regime. Taking the initiative in securing a way out of the impasse was partly motivated by the desire to redeem, as far as possible, their own situation. Competing concepts of the purposes of negotiation with the opposition were therefore present on the regime side. "Defensive liberalization" was an attempt to control negotiation from above. By freezing the political balance of forces and blocking the emergence of new political organizations, it hoped to ensure the continued position of the Communist Party. "Power sharing," however, was based on compromise with the new political movements. This concept would still guarantee the Communist Party a place in the coalition, but the opposition would accept joint responsibility for managing the economic crisis.[46]

For the opposition, the advocacy of dialogue with the regime involved the abandonment of the high moral ground that had sustained morale during the dismal period of repression and marginalization. Behind the rethinking was the painful recognition of their isolation and possible rejection by their societies. Solidarity may have continued to enjoy respect underground, but it was no longer able to rely on a massive response to its calls for election boycotts or token strikes. The "democratic opposition" in Hungary had always been a small group of intellectuals, regarded as a narrow elite and confined to the capital.

The idea of a negotiated pact also raised moral questions for would-be democrats. Pacts "move the polity toward democracy by undemocratic means."[47] What right had a few disorganized intellectuals to negotiate on behalf of society? The answer was that it was not a right but a national duty to avert revolution. As usual, Adam Michnik provides the most lucid rationale for this position:

> Solidarity does not exist just for itself, it exists for Poland. Our union had no right to turn down any chance that presented itself simply in order to keep its hands clean or to please certain radicals. . . . Nobody has a right to turn down a chance because of their grievances, disaffection or prejudice—a chance, of course, born largely thanks to widespread resistance and to widespread support for Solidarity, but also, let's face it, thanks to the very courageous political reorientation of those around General Jaruzelski. . . . That reorientation deserves respect.[48]

The strategy of compromise was also perceived as risky for the opposition: Compromise could mean that the old regime would not be fully dislodged from power, and thus that political change might not go far enough to win social support. Not only would the basic problem remain, but the opposition would be tarnished and further isolate itself from society. This was the fear of the radical opposition to negotiation in Poland, which rejected the strategy and fiercely attacked Walesa and his advisors.[49] In Hungary the propensity to accept a leading role for party reformists—in particular, Imre Pozsgay—divided the self-styled "centrist" Democratic Forum from the other major opposition group, the radical-liberal Alliance of Free Democrats.

The outcome of the negotiations in the spring and summer of 1989 was more satisfactory from the point of view of the transition to democracy in Hungary than in Poland. Poland paid the price of being the first: It was not so much that the Hungarians were able to learn by the experience of the Poles but that the all-important but absent partner in the negotiations, the Soviet leadership, changed its position after observing the outcome of the agreement in Poland.[50]

At the Polish Round Table, which finally convened in February–March 1989, the two sides, regime and opposition, shared the basic assumption that the Soviet Union would not permit the PUWP to relinquish ultimate control. The opposition negotiating team's central objective was therefore limited to the relegalization of Solidarity as an independent social movement, thus restoring the *status quo ante* of 1980–81 and securing freedom of the media. The Polish regime sought Solidarity's cooperation in elections to produce a Sejm and a new coalition government with the participation of noncommunist representatives, but it was able to insist on retaining ultimate PUWP control. The compromise agreement signed in April reconciled the competing aims by relegalizing Solidarity in exchange for partially free elections. The opposition refused to be inveigled into a predetermined distribution of seats, which went beyond what could be accepted by a democratic movement, but agreed to an election where only 35 percent of Sejm seats were fought on the basis of free competition, leaving 60 percent of seats for the PUWP and its allies, the United Peasant Party and the Democratic Party. The remaining 5 percent of seats were reserved for the official Catholic organizations. But to win any of the seats would require an absolute majority. A significant concession by the regime, facilitating the final agreement, was the establishment of a new upper house, the one-hundred-member Senate, to be elected on the basis of free competition, but enjoying lesser powers than the Sejm. The Sejm and Senate together were to elect by absolute majority the president of the Republic. The regime was satisfied with this arrangement. Although the PUWP's dominant position was no longer set in concrete, the regime expected the elections to produce the basis for sufficient PUWP control. The opposition assented because the PUWP's dominant position was no longer set in concrete, and it had secured agreement that the following elections would be wholly free. Both sides expected a rather extended transition, with room for further negotiation and compromise over the next four years.

Both sides were taken aback and unprepared for the results of this deal. In the first round of the elections, Solidarity candidates won by outright majority 160 of the 161 freely contested Sejm seats and 92 of the 100 Senate seats.The PUWP was utterly humiliated: Only five of the establishment candidates won outright majorities in their 295 reserved Sejm seats. Worse still, the "national list" of leading establishment candidates standing unopposed for thirty-five Sejm seats was decimated by negative voting: More than 50 percent of the electorate had not only failed to vote for them, but had used the opportunity to cross out all their names. The PUWP and its allies thus faced a second round of balloting in considerable disarray. When the final results were obtained, the Senate was entirely composed of Solidarity candidates with one exception, an independent; in the Sejm the PUWP had 173 seats (38 percent), the United Peasant Party 76 seats (17 percent), the Democractic Party 27 seats (6 percent), the Catholic organizations 23 seats (5 percent), and Solidarity 161 seats (35 percent).[51] The regime had "won" the largest share of the Sejm seats, but it had suffered a terminal defeat.

Having renounced the right to preserve its position by force, it had failed to gain electoral legitimacy.

The astounding and quite unexpected success of Solidarity's candidates immediately called into question the basic assumptions of the Round Table agreement. The formation of a PUWP-dominated government on the basis of these results could not be justified in the eyes of the population. It appeared that the opposition had underestimated its strength, and radical voices were once again raised urging abandonment of the strategy of negotiated transition in favor of immediate transition to a wholly noncommunist government. Instead, an ad hoc renegotiation of the agreement (in close consultation with the Soviet Union) took place around the formation of the new government headed by a Solidarity prime minister, Tadeusz Mazowiecki. The majority of posts (twelve) would go to Solidarity representatives; the establishment parties would share the remaining nine. In order to satisfy what were then taken to be the minimal demands of the Soviet Union, the PUWP was allocated the ministries of Interior and Defense, as well as Foreign Economic Relations and Transport and Communications. A final element of the renegotiated deal was the election of General Jaruzelski, by the narrowest of margins, to the presidency. Most of the Solidarity group of deputies opposed his candidacy, but his election was secured by the abstention or invalid votes of a minority of them. On this basis, a government was formed with sufficient parliamentary backing and popular democratic legitimacy to embark on a drastic economic stabilization program and to prepare a radical economic reform. But the imperfections inherent in the compromised form of democratic legitimation, and the emergent divisions within Solidarity itself, gave grounds for doubt about the stability of the political settlement and its capacity to survive the originally envisaged four-year term. The political system itself remained in transition.

Negotiations began in Hungary in June 1989, six days after the PUWP's electoral debacle, and they continued during negotiations for the formation of the Solidarity government. The Soviet government's responses to the Polish events undermined the possibility of the HSWP pursuing "defensive liberalization," and it became clear that power sharing was the best that the HSWP could hope for. A new four-man HSWP leadership was established that checked the conservative influence of the first secretary, Grosz, by appointing Rezso Nyers party chairman, supported by the Prime Minister Nemeth and Imre Pozsgay, who led the regime's team in the negotiations. The opposition, which comprised a Round Table of nine major groups including the Democratic Forum and the Free Democrats, entered the negotiations with the clear-cut expectation that wholly free elections were a realizable objective, which was soon confirmed.

The major point of contention turned out to be the proposal for a new, directly elected presidency. At stake in this issue was the future place of the HSWP in the state, and it divided radicals and centrists. The key candidate for the presidency was Imre Pozsgay, the party reformer who had enjoyed high visibility for at least eighteen months during the open power struggle in the HSWP. He had been associated with the formation of the Democratic Forum from its beginnings in September 1987.[52] The Democratic Forum was deeply distrusted as populist and covertly antisemitic by the Free Democrats, urban-based intellectuals, many of Jewish origins, and vulnerable to stigmatization as an "alien elite." Pozsgay's promotion of the Democratic Forum appeared to them to be motivated by a Machiavellian design to preserve a major place for himself and for the HSWP in a coalition with the Forum. Rumors circulated about a secret deal whereby the Democratic Forum would be guaranteed the prime ministerial post in exchange for Pozsgay's accession to the presidency. The elections might be free, but the HSWP would salvage its position by skillful backstairs manipulations.

The centrist line prevailed at the negotiations, and the agreement reached in September included the provision for direct election of the president before parliamentary elections. The radical groupings of the Opposition Round Table did not veto the agreement, but they refused to sign it. Instead, they mounted a campaign in favor of a referendum on the presidency. The referendum, held in November in place of the planned presidential election, resulted in a slender victory for the radicals. General elections would be held first, and the constitutional position of the presidency would be decided by a democratically elected parliament. The date for the general elections was set for the end of March. In the interim a protracted election campaign was held in free conditions. Although this period was highly undesirable from an economic point of view, leaving the Nemeth government suspended without either coercive power or democratic legitimacy to introduce urgent measures to stave off complete economic collapse, it had a rather positive effect on political development. The choices facing voters in March were clarified by the pluralization of the political forces. On the one hand, the crisis within the HSWP came to a head with its split in October into a would-be "West European-style" Socialist Party and a traditionalist communist HSWP. The membership of both was reduced to a shadow of the former HSWP. This, in turn, afforded the opposition parties the luxury of focusing their polemics as much on each other as on the communists. The divisions that Solidarity concealed were brought into the open. Thus, a relatively developed party system, already beginning to resemble West European models, was in place by the time of the March 1990 elections.

The only major problem seemed to be that the election would not produce an overall majority of seats for either of the two main parties, the Democratic Forum or the Free Democrats. This would reopen the question of communist participation in the government or an unstable coalition between the two major parties, whose mutual animosity intensified in the course of the campaign. These fears were confounded by the results: a center right government coalition of the Democratic Forum, which won 164 parliamentary seats (42.5 percent), the Independent Smallholders' Party with 44 seats (11.4 percent), and the Christian Democrats with 21 seats (5.4 percent), facing an articulate and well-represented opposition from the Free Democrats and their close allies, the Young Democrats. The Socialist Party won 33 seats, but the HSWP was annihilated, failing to clear the 4 percent barrier built in to the proportional electoral system.[53]

Regime Collapse: Czechoslovakia and the GDR

In neither Czechoslovakia nor the GDR were conditions present for a negotiated transfer of power. This was reaffirmed by the regimes' responses to events beyond their borders: Overt approval for the Chinese authorities' suppression of the protesting students in Tiananmen Square in June revealed to their domestic audience their own preparedness to use force to maintain the status quo. Unprecedented warnings to Gorbachev about the dangers of the course he was pursuing, and unrestrained criticism of developments in Poland and Hungary, signaled determination to continue along the old course, and no attempts were made to conceal the gearing up of the domestic repressive apparatus. In the wake of demonstrations in Prague in January, leading opposition activists were tried and imprisoned. Their appeals for negotiation were spurned. Indeed, they looked hopelessly naive in the face of the regimes' intransigence.

Neither negotiation nor open revolt was possible, but the East German regime could not prevent its population from voting with its feet: Hungary opened its border to Austria in the spring of 1989, and then East Germans began to attempt to get to the West via Hungary. In September the Hungarian government renounced its treaty with the German Democratic Republic according to which it was obliged to refuse exit from its territory to the West of East German citizens unless they had an East German exit permit. Over the following weeks thousands of East Germans abandoned their homes and possessions to leave for West Germany. Nevertheless, the GDR regime pressed on with preparations for the increasingly farcical celebration on October 5 of the nation's fortieth anniversary. It not only refused to recognize a new grouping of would-be negotiators in the oppositional New Forum, but disregarded the urgings for a new approach from its own Liberal Democratic "coalition" partner. As a result, mass demonstrations broke out in Leipzig and other provincial capitals with gathering momentum over the weeks. Gorbachev's arrival for the celebrations finally prompted the SUP leadership to act, but characteristically it was action on its own terms—a minimalist variant of the "defensive liberalization" strategy. A two-day session of the Central Committee on October 10–11 declared the party "open to discussion" on reform, but ruled out "bourgeois democracy." Erich Honecker met with the coalition party leaders, but he ignored the New Forum, which was still branded a subversive organization and denied legal registration. Mass pressure continued to build, as the flow of emigrants surged into a flood. Demonstrations increased weekly in number and spread throughout the country. When Honecker was finally forced to step down on October 18, his successor, Egon Krenz, showed little more understanding of the depth of the crisis. A new law on emigration designed to regain popular confidence was rejected by the crowds as hopelessly inadequate. The only remaining device to win credibility was opening the Berlin Wall, which took place on November 9.

The party itself began to disintegrate: Krenz had failed to win any popular credibility, and regional officials began openly to pursue their own courses of negotiation with the New Forum. With the party in crisis, the structures of power rapidly disintegrated, and the institutions of the state and government were left to pick up whatever means were left to prevent total collapse. The weekly mass demonstrations continued unabated, but their demands became progressively more radical: from demands for democracy and the right to free travel to the demand for reunification with West Germany. At this point, however, the extraordinary international position of this evaporating state came into play. Astonished at the pace of events, the West was absolutely uncertain as to the limits of the Soviet Union's toleration and very much aware that an inappropriate response could further destabilize Gorbachev's position in Moscow. This caution counseled support for a new government formed by Prime Minister Modrow, an SUP member, but a man who had won some credibility by his role in Dresden. The new government was formed from representatives of the SUP and former official "block" parties. The New Forum at first was suspicious and unwilling to participate in it, but was able to influence it from outside by means of its role on the Round Table, set up to coordinate the transition to democracy. "Negotiations" in these conditions fundamentally differed from those in Poland and Hungary because they came after communist power had collapsed and their aim was to regain control of a society mobilized for revolution.

Free elections were perceived by all sides as urgently necessary in order to stabilize the situation and establish a more legitimate basis for the government. In an atmosphere of continuing emergency, with the resumption of high levels of emigration to West Germany, the date for elections had to be advanced to 18 March. It became increasingly clear that democratization and reunification were inseparable. The role of the Federal Republic, and in particular of the West German political parties, became the decisive force shaping political development. The New Forum, which had played a commendable part in the autumn events, was marginalized this time—not by the communist regime's repression but by the steamroller of West German parties that stepped in to adopt other partners among the East German parties. The Federal Republic's financial resources, campaigning expertise, and, above all, governing party's ability to offer the East Germans the quickest, most sure route out of the morass of uncertainty determined the outcome of the elections. The conservative "Alliance for Germany," a coalition comprising the CDU, one of the former "block" parties (now adopted as "sister party" by the West German CDU), and two new right wing parties, carried off 192 of the 400 *Volkskammer* seats. The major opposition group in parliament turned out to be the Social Democrats, with eighty-eight seats. The re-formed and re-named Communist Party, the Party of Democratic Socialism, won 16.4 percent of the popular vote and sixty-six seats. The stance of the parties on reunification turned out to be the decisive factor in their electoral support.[54]

The opening of the Berlin Wall made the survival of the communist regime in Czechoslovakia patently untenable. In fact, a section of the CPCS apparatus was not impervious to the evidence before it and sought to avert the impending disaster facing the regime: It intended to use the student demonstration on 17 November as the occasion for a "palace coup" against the hard-line party leadership. By abstaining from immediately arresting leading opposition activists, it hoped to set the stage for controlled negotiations.[55] But this group completely failed to grasp the limits of the regime's ability to control events from above: The bankruptcy of a strategy of defensive liberalization was exposed by the unexpected, spontaneous force of the popular reaction. Czechs and Slovaks followed the example of their East German neighbors. They took to the streets in numbers that were simply beyond the capacity of the coercive apparatus to contain and channel to its own ends. After a week of mass demonstrations, the CPCS Central Committee met in crisis session and removed the most discredited leaders. It retained, however, the familiar, highly conservative complexion of the regime.

Prime Minister Adamec, apparently acting independently of the party leadership, opened negotiations with the Civic Forum, which had sprung up on the initiative of veteran Charter 77 activists. Adamec won sufficient confidence to be entrusted with the formation of a new government, but his proposed new team, comprising only five noncommunists, revealed the extent to which even the more flexible personalities in the ruling elite were captive to the assumptions of defensive liberalization. When negotiations began in Czechoslovakia, the two sides were not interdependent, as had been the case in Poland and Hungary. The opposition—previously small, weak, and disorganized—was buttressed by the mass support of the people. The party had been weakened to the point of dependence on the opposition leaders to avert its complete obliteration. Adamec was forced to resign, and a new government was sworn in on 10 December under Marian Calfa (a CPCS member of the outgoing government). The majority of ministers in the new government were not communists.[56] Most of the communist ministers, including the prime minister, renounced their party membership.

Free of the acute international complications that played a key role in East Germany, events in Czechoslovakia unfolded with extraordinary speed toward their logical destination. If Poland was paying the price of being first, Czechoslovakia was enjoying the advantage of being last. By the end of the year, it had achieved more radical change in the political leadership than had any of its East-Central European neighbors. Cowed in defeat, the CPCS was anxious to salvage some vestiges of credit by contributing to the orderly and legal transfer of power. It offered to recall a majority of its deputies from the Federal Assembly, and replacements were duly coopted on the basis of arrangements agreed to by the Civic Forum and the other parties and movements represented in a round table. President Husak agreed to swear in the new government, and then he resigned. The new parliament removed from the Constitution the clause on the "leading role of the Communist Party," and it elected Vaclav Havel, the leader of the Czechoslovak opposition for nearly two decades and founder of the Civic Forum, as president of the Republic on 29 December 1989.

The new president and government made free elections their first priority. Held on 8 June 1990, the elections produced a clear majority for the Civic Forum and its sister movement in Slovakia, Public Against Violence, in both houses of the Federal Assembly and in the national governments of each republic.[57] Marian Calfa, by now accepted as a member of Public Against Violence, was confirmed for a second term as prime minister. He headed a wholly noncommunist government comprising a coalition of Civic Forum–Public Against Violence with the Christian Democratic Movement of Slovakia. The new and fully democratic Federal Assembly reelected Havel as president in June 1990.

THE RECONSTRUCTION OF POLITICS

The distinctive feature of the transfer of power in East-Central Europe in 1989 was the determination of the opposition elites to avoid violence and to act wherever possible according to the legal framework and the Constitution. The new regimes self-consciously eschewed revolutionary legitimation, but they did not thereby acquire full democratic legitimacy. In Poland, of course, the June 1989 elections had been only partially free, but the political crises in the other countries also could not be resolved simply by holding free elections and changing the government. The legitimacy of the state itself had become an open question.

This was most apparent in East Germany, where the logical culmination of developments moved inexorably toward the disappearance of a separate German Democratic Republic by reunification with, or absorption by, the Federal Republic. In Czechoslovakia, too, the crisis of identity of the federal state structure, long suppressed under decades of totalitarian rule, rapidly reemerged.[58] Slovak nationalism has brought onto the postcommunist political agenda an issue that can be resolved only by a radical redistribution of powers from the federal government to national governments. Secessionist aspirations have been expressed not only by the extremist Slovak National Party, but also by the increasingly successful Christian Democratic Movement, a coalition partner in the federal government and the Slovak National Council (republican government). The problem of redefining an acceptable and workable federal framework dominates debate over the meaning of "democratization" and the introduction of economic reform, and it may act as a brake on both.

A nationalist challenge to the legitimacy of the state as presently constituted is also present in Hungary: The existence of substantial Hungarian minorities in neighboring Romania and Slovakia exerts a significant pressure on domestic politics. The claim by the new prime minister, Jozsef Antall, to represent the interests of "16 million Hungarians" (only 10 million of whom inhabit the territory of the Hungarian Republic) is a tacit acknowledgment of popular concern on this issue, but it did little to enhance Hungary's standing with its neighbors. Revisionist aspirations, however, are confined to a minority, and Antall has steered his party, the Democratic Forum, away from its nationalist-populist origins toward a political approach modeled on West European Christian Democracy. The current dependence of Hungary's economy on the West serves to underpin this orientation, as does the increasing cultural openness of the country and the rapid development of educational links and exchanges with Western Europe. In these circumstances, nationalist sentiment, if used by the new regime with sensitivity and moderation, may offer an opportunity to integrate and stabilize the new state. The same possibility is open in Poland. In both cases, however, continuing economic crisis and the accompanying severe social dislocations hardly provide conditions conducive to a liberal-democratic evolution of East and Central European nationalism, and the danger of a reversion to the interwar patterns of xenophobia and inward-looking parochialism cannot yet be ruled out.

A significant issue in the debate about state legitimacy has been the constitutional distribution of authority between parliaments and presidents. For Hungary, this issue, the source of much controversy in 1989, was put to rest in 1990 after the election. Having secured the post of prime minister on the basis of its electoral victory, the Democratic Forum lost interest in the establishment of a powerful, directly elected presidency and became more concerned with the consolidation of a single center of authority in a government resting on a parliamentary majority. The Hungarian parliament subsequently elected Arpad Goncz, a leading member of the Free Democrats, as president.

In Poland the presidency rapidly became a central issue with Lech Walesa's challenge to the legitimacy of the political order that had come about as a result of the Round Table agreement. This issue had three aspects. First, the continued incumbency of General Jaruzelski in the presidential office was an unnecessary and unacceptable token of compromise and continuity with the communist past. Second, the individual with undoubtedly the greatest personal legitimacy as national leader, Lech Walesa, had chosen not to take formal political office, presumably expecting to be able to influence the government without forfeiting his popularity and prestige as head of Solidarity. This did not work out. Walesa began to feel powerless and excluded as the Mazowiecki government began its work.[59] Moreover, Walesa's personal authority was an asset that the government could not do without. The radical economic program of Finance Minister Balcerowicz prompted strikes and farmers' protests in the summer of 1990.[60] Walesa stepped forward to play a vital mediating role between the new government and the strikers. Soon it became clear that he had to be incorporated in the formal power structure. Walesa attacked "his" Solidarity government for its alleged failures to promote political development and its "elitist" lack of responsiveness to the people. This fostered a split in Solidarity that brought into the open not only the original division in the opposition about the legitimacy of compromise in the negotiated transfer of power, but also deeper divisions in general political orientation between nationalistic, Catholic and populist spokesmen and secular, Westernizing liberal intellectuals such as Michnik.[61] The need for a clearer pluralization was recognized by all sides. The main dispute was whether the time was ripe for such development, at the height of economic transformation. But Walesa's actions forced the pace: The original scenario for the transition collapsed, and a free, direct election of a new president was brought forward to the autumn of 1990.

The presidential election accelerated the process of pluralization, but exacerbated tensions between the Solidarity factions backing the candidates Walesa and Mazowiecki. The unpreparedness of Polish society for this latest phase in the political transition may be judged from the outcome of the presidential election. The first round humiliated Mazowiecki, who won only 18 percent of the votes, but it did not produce the outright victory Walesa had confidently expected. He won just under 40 percent of the votes. Instead, an unknown and, to say the least, dubious character, Stanislaw Tyminski, captured over 23 percent of the votes. In the second round the two warring Solidarity factions were forced to pool their resources in order to head off Tyminski's challenge. Although they were successful, and Walesa became president, political stabilization and the establishment of legitimate state authority have not been much advanced, and some would say they have even been set back. The resolution of such fundamental constitutional issues as the power of the president and the Sejm was not possible until after the Sejm itself had undergone a further general election according to fully democratic rules. This election took place in October 1991. In the meantime the Polish public is becoming more disaffected from political institutions.

Democratic legitimation resting on popular participation remains fragile throughout the region. In both Poland and Hungary the first general elections met with less than wholehearted enthusiasm. Voter turnouts (62.1 percent and 63.2 percent, respectively, on the first ballots) were satisfactory by international standards, but dropped sharply for the second ballots in each country. The Polish local government elections in May 1990 saw turnout fall below 50 percent. Turnout in the presidential election was over 60 percent in the first round, but fell back to 53 percent in the second. Turnout in the general election of October

1991 fell to 43 percent. In Czechoslovakia and the GDR, by contrast, the general elections of 1990 saw massive turnouts of 96 percent and 93.2 percent, respectively. This may well be the legacy of the greater role of mass mobilization in securing the change of regimes in the latter two countries, as compared with Poland and Hungary, where negotiations between elites were in part motivated by fear of the consequences of mass mobilization. In Hungary and Poland, therefore, the mechanism by which power was transferred seems to a significant extent to have perpetuated the demobilization of society and the mentality of "without us but for us," and it may prove a brake on the development of state legitimation.[62]

Symptomatic of this have been the problems in establishing political parties. In Hungary, where the process of pluralization was allowed to unfold relatively unhindered after late 1987, the crystallization of coherent alternative groupings into parties has advanced the most. But the parties still have a rather artificial air: Their mass memberships are limited, and the basic dividing lines are drawn from competing quasi-tribal loyalties within the Hungarian intelligentsia (the Democratic Forum and Free Democrats). Otherwise, they are based on so-called historic parties (such as the Independent Smallholders), revived from the interwar period. A promising, vigorous newcomer on the Hungarian political scene is "Fidesz," the Alliance of Young Democrats. The Czech Civic Forum and the Slovak Public Against Violence, within a few months of their resounding electoral success, began to show some of the same difficulties experienced by the Polish Citizens' Committees of Solidarity. All three movements originated as grand coalitions, uniting society against communism. It was inevitable that after the fall of communism, significant divisions would appear within them. These divisions, in the case of Public Against Violence, led to a crisis within the PAV-dominated Slovak government in the spring of 1991. As a result, the PAV prime minister, Vladimir Meciar, was dismissed by the Slovak National Council and replaced by a Christian Democrat prime minister. The Christian Democratic Movement now dominates the governing coalition in Slovakia. PAV has split, with Meciar forming a new "Movement for a Democratic Slovakia." Meciar's movement has now become the major opposition party, enjoying substantial popular support on the basis of its eclectic (and opportunist) program combining national populism and paternalistic socialism. The rump of PAV, comprising the secular liberal intelligentsia leadership faction favoring radical and rapid economic transformation, still has minority representation in government, but its popular support has fallen dramatically to around 4 percent. Civic Forum, which began to fall apart in the late autumn of 1990, has split into two competing parties: the Civic Democratic Party led by the federal minister of finance, Vaclav Klaus, which strongly supports the radical economic transformation program he has promoted so energetically, and the Civic Movement, which represents the more gentle "human face" of transformation as a centrist, less formally structured movement with progressive-liberal orientation, rather close to President Havel's own political preferences. But in Czechoslovakia, as in Poland and Hungary, the number of people willing to engage actively in building parties remains small.

There remains among the new publics of East-Central Europe a certain aversion to parties. The word "party" is associated with the authoritarian hierarchical structure of the Communist Party. But power itself tends to be seen as inherently a bad thing, and politics as a morally dubious activity. President Havel has referred to the need to "rehabilitate politics." Bargaining, compromise, and material interests must be recognized as legitimate components of politics; at present, however, in East-Central Europe moralistic and emotional appeals are the dominant motive force—hence the recurrent success of ethnically based appeals, as compared with more policy-based and interest-based demands.

The problem of party formation and political development has much to do with the weakness of the articulation of material interests. The new regimes' problems of political legitimation lie in the diffuse and vague nature of the popular aspiration for change. When it comes to the implementation of specific measures of economic transformation, the governments discover that they lack a clear and coherent constituency of active social supporters. In the meanwhile, the breakdown of the hierarchical, bureaucratic organization of the economy, as a result of economic dislocation and the beginnings of economic transformation, is shattering the social structure and creating great volatility and unpredictability in the structure of interests. What we see is a "quicksand society," Moshe Lewin's description of Soviet Russia in the 1920s.[63] Interests are confused, incoherent, and changing. It is no wonder that interest-based parties have yet to arrive on the scene, that the language of politics harks back to the distant past, that energy is wasted on disputes with little relevance to the pressing problems of today. But despite this, remarkable development has taken place. Governments have managed to pass vast amounts of legislation of fundamental significance, and social order has not broken down. The current atmosphere of crisis and uncertainty is inevitable, and many questions remain unresolved about the future. In my view, however, the major question has been resolved: there can be no turning back to the way things were.

NOTES

1. Ralf Dahrendorf, *Reflections on the Revolution in Europe* (London: Chatto Counterblasts Special; 1990).
2. J. Dunn, *Modern Revolutions* (Cambridge: Cambridge University Press, 1972); and Chalmers Johnson, *Revolutionary Change*, 2d ed. (London: Longman 1983). For Johnson, violence is the defining characteristic of revolution.
3. For definitions see P. Schmitter, "Still the Century of Corporatism?" in P. Schmitter and G. Lehmbruch, eds., *Trends Towards Corporatist Intermediation* (Beverly Hills: Sage Publications, 1979), pp. 1–52. See V. Bunce, "The Political Economy of the Brezhnev Era: The Rise and Fall of Corporatism," *British Journal of Political Science* 13 (April 1983); and H. G. Skilling, "Group Conflict and Political Changes," in C. Johnson, ed., *Change in Communist Systems* (Stanford, Calif.: Stanford University Press, 1970), pp. 215–34.
4. For the optimistic view of Hungarian political evolution, see W. T. Robinson, *The Pattern of Reform in Hungary* (New York: Praeger, 1973).
5. See J. Batt, *Economic Reform and Political Change in Eastern Europe* (London: Macmillan, 1988).
6. G. Blazyca, "The Degeneration of Central Planning in Poland," in J. Woodall, ed., *Policy and Politics in Contemporary Poland* (London: Francis Pinter, 1982), pp. 99–128; and K. Poznanski, "Economic Adjustment and Political Forces: Poland Since 1970," in E. Comisso and L. Tyson, eds., *Power, Purpose and Collective Choice: Economic Strategy in Socialist States* (Ithaca: Cornell University Press, 1986); and J. Batt, "The Political Limits to Economic Reform in Hungary, 1968–78," Chap. 7 in *Economic Reform*.
7. Poznanski, "Economic Adjustment."
8. Batt, *Economic Reform*.
9. See I. Berend, *A Magyar Gazdasagi Reform Utja* (Budapest: Kozgazdasagi es Jogi Konyvkiado, 1988), pp. 370 ff.
10. See Z. Gitelman, "Is Hungary the Future of Poland?" *East European Politics and Societies* 1 (Winter 1987).
11. See Economic Commission for Europe, *Economic Survey of Europe in 1989–90* (New York: United Nations, 1990), Chap. 5.2: 237–43.
12. J. Brada, "Is Hungary the Future of Poland, or Is Poland the Future of Hungary?" *East European Politics and Societies* 2 (Fall 1988): 468.
13. E. Kerpel and D. Young, *Hungary to 1993: Risks and Rewards of Reform*, Special Report 1153 (London: Economist Intelligence Unit, November 1988), p. 106.
14. For a discussion of "leadership drift" and its applicability to different communist regimes, see a special issue of *Studies in Comparative Communism* 22 (Spring 1989).
15. See G. Kolankiewicz, "Poland and the Politics of Permissible Pluralism," *East European Politics and Societies* 2 (Winter 1988).
16. R. Tokes, "Hungarian Reform Imperatives," *Problems of Communism* 33 (September–October 1984): 1–23.
17. See G. Schopflin, R. Tokes and I. Volgyes, "Leadership Change and Crisis in Hungary," *Problems of Communism* 27 (September–October 1988).
18. Poznanski, "Economic Adjustment," p. 287.
19. P. Lewis, "The Long Good-Bye: Party Rule and Political Change in Poland Since Martial Law," *Journal of Communist Studies* 6 (March 1990): 32–33.
20. P. Lewis, *Political Authority and Party Secretaries in Poland* (Cambridge: Cambridge University Press, 1989), p. 299.
21. Kolankiewicz, "Permissible Pluralism."
22. M. Csanadi, "Beyond the Image: The Case of Hungary," *Social Research* 57 (Summer 1990): 321–46.
23. Lewis, "The Long Good-Bye," p. 36.
24. On the first term see M. Markus, "Overt and Covert Modes of Legitimation in East European Societies," in T. Rigby and F. Feher, eds., *Political Legitimation in Communist*

States (London: Macmillan, 1982) pp. 82–93. The term "demobilization" is elaborated fully in E. Hankiss, "Demobilization, Self-Mobilization and Quasi-Mobilization in Hungary, 1948–1987," *East European Politics and Societies* 3 (Winter 1989).

25. Michnik, "Towards a New Democratic Compromise," p. 26.

26. See the account by Solidarity's historian, Jerzy Holzer, "Seven Years After August," *East European Reporter* 3 (1987): 4.

27. "A New Social Contract: Conditions for a Political Renewal," trans. in *East European Reporter* 3 (1987): 55.

28. This aspect of the crisis is emphasized by Schopflin, Tokes, and Volgyes, "Leadership Change." See also G. Kolankiewicz and P. Lewis, *Poland: Politics, Economics and Society* (London: Francis Pinter, 1988), chap. 2, 19–65. The sociologist Elemer Hankiss spoke of the "escape into illness," a passive and self-destructive response on the part of society to the regime's strategy of social control by demobilization. See Hankiss, "Demobilization."

29. J. Batt, "The Second Economy in Hungary: Private Economic Activity and the Legitimation of a Communist Regime" (Paper presented to the Annual Conference of BISA, Birmingham University, December 1983).

30. Elemer Hankiss, "First Society, Second Society," *East European Reporter* 3 (Winter 1989): 63.

31. Husak to the XIV Congress of the CPCS. See XIV.sjezd KSC (Prague: Svoboda, 1971), p. 153.

32. M. Hruskovic, "Towards the Further Development of Economic Science," *Czechoslovak Economic Papers*, no. 13, 1972, p. 17.

33. See V. Kusin, *From Dubcek to Charter 77* (Edinburgh: Q Press, 1978), pp. 69–89.

34. J. Batt, "Czechoslovakia Under Gorbachev" (Paper presented to the conference by Radio Free Europe on Gorbachev's Eastern Europe, Munich, June 1988). Official statistics show the effect of the purges on enterprise management. The number of enterprise managers and administrative workers with the requisite education and qualifications for their posts declined by 1972, particularly in the Czech Lands. *Statisticka Rocenka CSSR* (Prague: SNTL, various years).

35. See "Analyze vyvoje ekonomicke teorie v Ceskoslovensku v sedesatych letech," special issue of *Politicka Ekonomie*, no. 9, 1972: 799–838.

36. See the CPCS Central Committee document "Lessons of the Crisis Development in the Party and Society After the XIII Congress" (Prague: Svoboda, 1970).

37. See M. Melzer "The GDR: Economic Policy Caught Between Pressure for Efficiency and Lack of Ideas," in A. Nove et al., eds., *The East European Economies in the 1970s* (London: Butterworths, 1982).

38. Quoted in A. James McAdams, *East Germany and Detente* (Cambridge: Cambridge University Press, 1985), pp. 107–8.

39. Quoted by B. Donovan, "Reform and the Existence of the GDR," *Radio Free Europe Background Report* 158, August 25, 1989. See also O. Rheinhold, "Das Programm unserer Partei hat sich in Leben bewahrt," *Neues Deutschland* 3–4. December 1988, p. 5.

40. D. Granick notes the exceptional degree to which the East German regime offered opportunities to young, well-trained technocrats. D. Granick, *Enterprise Guidance in Eastern Europe* (Princeton N.J.: Princeton University Press, 1975). A similar picture is presented by T. Baylis, *The Technical Intelligentsia and the East German Elite* (Berkeley: University of California Press, 1974).

41. See K. Dyba, "Adjustment to International Disturbances: Czechoslovakia and Hungary," *Acta Oeconomica* 34, no. 3–4 (1985): 317–37.

42. J. Garland, "FRG-GDR Economic Relations," in U.S. Congress Joint Economic Committee, *East European Economies: Slow Growth in the 1980s*, vol. 3 (Washington D.C.: U.S. Government Printing Office, 1985).

43. K. Dyba, "Dve Desetileti Dvou Ekonomik" (a comparison of Hungary and Czechoslovakia), *Hospodarske Noviny*, no. 29, 1988, pp. 10–11.

44. See, for example, the essay by the Czechoslovak Chartist, Petr Pithart, "Social and Economic Developments in Czechoslovakia in the 1980s," pts. I and II, *East European Reporter* 4 (Winter 1989/90 and Spring/Summer 1990).

45. The concept was elaborated by T. H. Rigby with respect to the Brezhnev regime in the early 1970s. T. H. Rigby, "Soviet Leadership: Towards a Self-Stabilizing Oligarchy?" *Soviet Studies* 22 (October 1970).

46. These concepts are derived from L. Bruszt, "1989: The Negotiated Revolution in Hungary," *Social Research* 57 (Summer 1990): 365–87.

47. G. O'Donnell and P. Schmitter, "Negotiating (and Renegotiating) Pacts," in O'Donnell and Schmitter (eds.), *Transitions from Authoritarian Rule*, pt. IV, *Tentative Conclusions About Democracies* (Baltimore: Johns Hopkins University Press, 1986), p. 38.

48. "The First Steps Towards Democracy: An Interview with Adam Michnik," *East European Reporter* 3 (Spring/Summer 1989): 37.

49. On this approach see M. Siedlecki, "Time for Positive Action," *East European Reporter* 3 (Spring/Summer 1989): 35.

50. See V. Kusin, "Mikhail Gorbachev's Evolving Attitude to Eastern Europe," *RFE Background Report*, no. 128 (20 July 1989); M. Shafir, "Soviet Reactions to Polish Developments: Widened Limits of Tolerated Change," *RFE Background Report*, no. 179 (20 September 1989); and R. Asmus, "Evolution of Soviet–East European Relations Under Mikhail Gorbachev," *RFE Background Report*, no. 153 (22 August 1989).

51. For a more detailed account of the Polish elections, see P. Lewis, "Non-Competitive Elections and Regime Change: Poland 1989," *Parliamentary Affairs* 43 (January 1990): 90–107.

52. On political development in Hungary in general since 1987, see J. Batt, "Political Reform in Hungary," *Parliamentary Affairs* 43, no. 4 (October 1990): 464–81.

53. On the electoral system and the results in detail, see J. Batt, "The Hungarian General Election," *Representation* 29 (Summer 1990): 7–11.

54. On the GDR elections in detail, see A. Hyde-Price, "The Volkskammer Elections in the GDR, 18 March 1990," *Representation* (Summer 1990).

55. See the report of the commission of inquiry set up by the Federal Parliament to investigate the events of November 17th, reproduced in translation in *BBC Summary of World Broadcasts: Eastern Europe*, no. 0763 B/3–4.

56. See P. Martin, "The New Czechoslovak 'Government of National Understanding' " and "Biographies of Members of the Federal Government," *RFE Report on Eastern Europe* 1, no. 2 (12 January 1990): 3–5 and 6–8.

57. See J. Batt, "After Czechoslovakia's Velvet Poll," *The World Today* 46 (August–September 1990): 141–43.

58. On the term "crisis of identity," see L. Binder et al., *Crises and Sequences in Political Development* (Princeton, N.J.: Princeton University Press, 1971).

59. See A. Sabbat-Swidlicka, "The Walesa Factor," *REF Report on Eastern Europe* 1, no. 17 (27 April 1990): 14–17.

60. See L. Vinton, "The Polish Rail Strike: A Lesson for All Sides," *RFE Report on Eastern Europe*, 1, no. 24 (15 June 1990): 36–40; and R. Stefanowski, "Is the Government's Period of Grace Coming to an End?" *REF Report on Eastern Europe* 1, no. 22 (1 June 1990): 37–39.

61. See the undisguisedly partisan account of the division by A. Michnik, "The Two Faces of Europe," *New York Review of Books* (19 July 1990), p. 7.

62. On Hungary see L. Bruzst, " 'Without Us But for Us': Political Orientations in Hungary in the Period of Late Paternalism," *Social Research* 55 (Spring/Summer 1988); and M. Marody, "Perceptions of Politics in Polish Society," *Social Research* 57 (Summer 1990): 257–74.

63. See M. Lewin, *The Making of the Soviet System* (London: Methuen, 1985).

9

Eastern Europe: Achieving Legitimacy

Takayuki Ito

SOME CONCEPTUAL PROBLEMS

Nineteen eighty-nine witnessed dramatic political changes throughout socialist countries, particularly in Eastern Europe. These changes had a systemic character, that is, the principles that had governed political rule in these countries for four decades or longer underwent a fundamental change. One of those principles is legitimacy. The legitimacy of the old regime was seriously challenged and shaken to its foundations. In Eastern Europe a new regime with new legitimacy emerged, while in the Soviet Union a search got under way for such legitimacy. Only in China did the leadership refuse to make this effort.

What kind of legitimacy did the old regime enjoy? Why did that legitimacy break down so easily? What is the legitimacy of the new regime? Those are the questions that this chapter attempts to address. Attention is focused on Eastern Europe, where the most serious change occurred. The implications of these questions, however, are not limited to Eastern Europe since all the socialist countries are at present caught up in a legitimacy crisis of more or less the same nature.

In this section I examine four conceptual problems. The first is the concept of legitimate rule (*legitime Herrschaft*). Political rule cannot be maintained solely by naked force or coercion. It requires some positive acceptance or consent by the ruled. The acceptance or consent by the ruled is to be provided by belief in the legitimacy of the political rule. Therefore, rulers try to kindle and cultivate belief in the legitimacy of their rule among the ruled. This is the understanding of legitimacy by German sociologist Max Weber. Weber gives three types of legitimate rule: charismatic, traditional, and legal.[1] Japanese political scientist Masao Maruyama gives five: traditional rule, rule by natural law, rule by authorization from God or Heaven, rule by the elite, and rule based on authorization from the people.[2]

This is classification by the type of belief and does not imply normative evaluation of a political order. Furthermore, the classification does not mean that a political system enjoys a substantial legitimacy. In other words, they are value-free concepts. Those who live under socialism and are critical of the system often contend that the value-free concepts cannot be applied to their system. They argue that the communist regime is devoid of any legitimacy since it knows no democratic procedures and relies mainly on coercion. This is perhaps just one of many cases in which a Western concept, originally value free, becomes value charged when transplanted to Soviet or East European soil. For instance, the concept of "political culture" is value charged in the Soviet Union and Eastern Europe.

The Soviets and East Europeans may be partly right in the case of "legitimate rule" because the concept is contradictory. Legitimacy emerges when the ruled voluntarily subordinate themselves. No political rule is possible, however, unless the authorities have coercive means to exact the obedience of the ruled. The original German word for rule, *Herrschaft,* makes this clear beyond any doubt since it explicitly means use of force or coercion. A more adequate English translation for it would be "domination" or "rulership." Thus, the concept of legitimate rule has double roots: voluntary subordination and coercion, two factors that seem to contradict each other. If we understand legitimate rule in a value-free sense, however, there is nothing contradictory about it. There is even a mutually reinforcing relationship between voluntary subordination and coercion: If the ruled are willing to subordinate themselves, they should show all the more readiness to accept coercion. No political system including the communist one should be excluded from scholarly analysis, and the concept of legitimate rule should not be used to denounce a certain regime.

The types of legitimate rule applicable to socialist countries are all ideal types. They are theoretical constructions that do not exist in reality but are helpful to understand reality. The types of legitimate rule that actually exist are mixed types. If none of the types or mixed types apply to the political system under investigation, we should construct a new type that is more suitable. In a first attempt to apply Weber's three types of legitimate rule to socialist countries, it immediately turns out that none of them exists there in pure form.

According to Weber, the charismatic type of legitimacy is most likely to emerge in a revolutionary situation. This is true of most of the communist regimes that were established as a result of an authentic revolution. There appeared a charismatic leader, and the Communist Party played the role of a collective charisma. Suffice it to mention Russia's Lenin, China's Mao Zedong, Vietnam's Ho Chi Minh, and North Korea's Kim Il Sung. In Joseph Stalin's case a military charisma was added to the revolutionary charisma; he was the Soviet Union's indisputable leader during the victorious Great Fatherland War. We may talk of a charismatic rule with regard to these countries. The charismatic rule is difficult to maintain, however, when the leaders with charismatic appeal pass away. The Communist Party of the Soviet Union always stresses that it is Lenin's party, suggesting that it inherits Lenin's charisma. But such an association did not work as the case of Soviet prisoners of war in German camps during the Second World War shows: Almost all of them glorified Lenin, but criticized the Soviet state and party. Weber suggested a concept of "inherited charisma," for instance, for Japan's emperor system. If Kim Il Sung succeeds in establishing a kind of dynasty, the concept may be applied to North Korea as well. But the chance of success seems to be rather bleak. In China the collective charisma of the Communist Party lives on in the minds of some of the people, particularly peasants, but after the Tiananmen massacre in June 1989 not in the minds of the urban population and intellectuals. The spell of charisma was broken in the Soviet Union by the death of Stalin and in Vietnam by the death of Ho Chi Minh.

In Eastern Europe and Mongolia, where an imported revolution rather than an authentic revolution took place, no charismatic leaders appeared. In the early 1950s there were attempts to create a small Stalin for each East European country: Beleslaw Bierut for Poland, Walter Ulbricht for the German Democratic Republic, Klement Gottwald for Czechoslovakia, Matyas Rakosi for Hungary, Gheorghe Gheorghiu-Dej for Romania, and Vulko Chervenkov (later Todor Zhivkov) for Bulgaria. None of these small Stalins, however, was able to develop charismatic qualities. The same may be said about Mongolia's Khorlogijn Choibalsan and Yumdzhagun Tsedenbal. Only Yugoslavia and Albania, where a more or less authentic revolution took place, produced truly charismatic leaders: Josip Broz Tito and Enver Hoxha. Once they passed away, their charisma could hardly help the system to survive.

No communist regime can refer to immemorial traditions of legitimacy because it could not come to power without effectively destroying those very traditions. Of course, any political system with some length of existence can refer to a tradition, but legitimation through that tradition will be out of the question if the tradition can go back only within the memory of one or two generations (as in the communist regimes in

China and Eastern Europe). During its history of more than seventy years, the Soviet Union may have established some tradition, but that tradition, if any, is very weak since Stalin's "revolution from above" destroyed the early postrevolutionary tradition.

In the wake of transformation in 1989–90, some respectable political parties in Eastern Europe, such as Small Holders in Hungary and National Liberals in Romania, put forward the resurrection of the monarchy as a political platform. From a Western perspective it sounds like a joke. It is no joke. It is a serious problem. There is no other tradition for the new regimes in these countries to rely on as a source of legitimacy than the monarchy. In Poland Lech Walesa, immediately after being elected president, held a pompous ceremony to take over state insignia from the government-in-exile in London. The government-in-exile, nothing but a club of old timers, had long been effectively defunct. From the point of view of legitimacy, however, Walesa's actions were not insignificant. President Walesa acted as if he had taken over, not from the communists (now regarded as illegitimate in every sense of the word), but from the government-in-exile, which enjoyed traditional legitimacy. Even in the Soviet Union voices lament the deceased Romanovs and the decimated Russian aristocracy. In any event these episodes reveal that the communist regime did not and could not enjoy traditional legitimacy.

The communist regime cannot be regarded as a legal rule, but not because it is undemocratic. Weber's concept of legal rule is very specific: Formal, impersonal procedures, once accepted, have preference over circumstances, including the very goals the political system pursues. Surely when creating his ideal type of legal legitimacy, Weber had in mind the modern bureaucracy. Legitimacy is not necessarily related to democracy. In Weber's sense, legal legitimacy existed in Wilhelmine Germany—far from a democracy in our sense. The communist regime is not a legal rule because it is not based on formal procedures. The communist regime is a bureaucracy, but not a modern bureaucracy as defined by Weber, states British sociologist Maria Hirszowicz.[3] It freely bends formal procedures if they hinder goal attainment. Australian political scientist T. H. Rigby distinguishes between task-achieving bureaucracies and rule applying bureaucracies. Industrial or army bureaucracies in the West and communist bureaucracies belong to the former type, while state bureaucracies in the West belong to the latter. He deduces from this that in communist countries authority is legitimized in goal-rational terms, while in Western countries it is done in terms of formal-legal rationality.[4]

In short, communist regimes cannot be neatly classified as one of the three Weberian types of legitimate rule: charismatic, traditional, or legal. It is not easy to think of a mixed type, either. We must contrive something new. Consider the relationship between legitimacy and stability. Legitimacy is regarded as conducive to political stability. Indeed, many political scientists think that the most important function of legitimacy is to bring about and maintain political stability. The question is whether the reverse is true. Is there legitimacy where there is political stability? Properly speaking, this should be the case. In a value-free sense any political rule enjoys some kind of legitimacy, to say nothing of a political rule that boasts of a long life. We must say, however, that legitimacy is neither a necessary nor a sufficient condition of political stability.

There is a wide range of attitudes between positive acceptance of authority and active defiance of it. Polish political scientists make a fine distinction between legitimation and compliance (*przyzwolenie*). "Legitimation" means that citizens obey the authorities because of a certain psychological relationship and not because of fear and naked force. "Compliance" means that the ruled agree with the rulers' authority over them; this agreement is not tinged with a positive, accepting relationship with the authorities. Stanislaw Gebethner argues that this differentiation is important for understanding the social and political crises in Poland in 1956, 1970, and 1980–81.[5] If the mass compliance with authority is given, it is possible to maintain political rule without legitimacy and without resorting to force, which would otherwise be necessary.

Legitimacy is one of many pillars, and not necessarily the most successful one, that support political stability under communism. To understand how the communist system is reproduced, we must pay due attention to other sources of stability. We may call them *ersatz*-legitimacy or quasi-legitimacy.

Lastly, consider the distinction between legitimacy and popular support. Rigby criticizes "the frequently encountered view of political legitimacy which more or less equates it with positive popular acceptance or support."[6] Legitimacy relates to the constitutional structure of the system; popular support relates to popularity of individual politicians or political parties. Even if individual politicians or political parties representing the system are unpopular at a given moment, the political system as a whole may remain legitimate in the eyes of the public. For instance, the popularity of President Richard Nixon was almost nil during the Watergate hearings, but the legitimacy of the American constitutional system remained unshaken.

This is conventional wisdom in Western political science, but it applies only to the ongoing state of a parliamentary democracy. In a crisis the legitimacy of the system is questioned, and the popularity of individual

politicians or political parties representing the system is bound to decline. It is conceivable only theoretically that when the legitimacy of the
system is questioned in a fundamental way, politicians or political parties
representing it can maintain popularity. Toward the end of the Weimar
Republic in Germany, the Nazis and the communists, two political forces
hostile to parliamentary democracy, won together the majority in elections, condemning to political insignificance all the parties committed
to parliamentary democracy. Thus, in a crisis popular support is one
indicator of the extent to which the political system enjoys legitimacy.

We can approach opinion polls in the same way. In a normal situation
popularity scales of politicians or parties based on opinion polls cannot
be treated as indicators of the system's legitimacy. In a critical situation,
however, they can be a correct index of legitimacy. Unfortunately, neither free elections nor opinion polls are conducted on a regular basis in
communist countries. This makes it extremely difficult for researchers
to measure in quantitative terms the extent to which the communist
regime enjoys legitimacy.

THE OLD REGIME: HOW LEGITIMATE?

From a scholarly point of view, it should be possible to tell what type of
legitimacy a regime *enjoys*. It also should be possible to tell what type of
legitimacy the regime *does not enjoy*. We ask another question, however:
Is the regime legitimate at all? If so, in what sense and to what extent?
This question will not be easy to answer because legitimacy is basically
a question of belief system, which does not always lend itself to a yes or
no reply.

Thus, the question of how far a regime enjoys legitimacy comes close
to the question of how far the ruled believe the rulers' justification for
their rule. This is difficult to establish when the ruled do not have
representatives to articulate their interests. It is naive to think that the
ruled always know what they want and are able to articulate it. In many
political systems including the communist one, however, the ruled are
not allowed to have representatives. If they were, what would their
representatives say? They are most likely to question the rulers' justification for their rule because it is the simplest way for them to prove to
their mandate-givers that their position, as opposed to the rulers' position, is right; therefore, they are more entitled to power than are those
in power. An American political scientist specializing in Chinese affairs
makes an interesting statement that "if pushed hard enough, no government can stand up to the standards of political and moral theory
imposed by the theorist."[7] Indeed, in any country popular commitment
to constitutional principles is rather difficult to assess. Take, for in-

stance, the postwar regime in Japan. It will never be possible to tell exactly how far it enjoys legitimacy.

Despite the difficulties, it is still worthwhile to try to identify the extent of legitimacy of the communist regime, especially because many people supposed that the regime, particularly in Eastern Europe, was *not legitimate*. There were a few sources of information about it (for instance, information that emigrants brought to the West, the number of emigrants or would-be emigrants, activities of antigovernment organizations, and so on). None of these sources, however, was reliable enough for a variety of reasons. Information about elections and opinion polls, if it had been available, would have been more reliable, although it might have been misleading as well.

The results of normal parliamentary elections in communist countries seldom are helpful as indices of legitimacy, although they are intended to serve that very purpose. Voters are given little choice among candidates or platforms. They have virtually one choice: to go vote or not. Therefore, the turnout rate, not the share of votes cast for a particular party, is important. The higher the turnout rate, the greater the popular support for the regime, suppose the rulers. It is a special kind of plebiscite. But because the election takes place under strong pressure from the authorities, it has little meaning in practice. It discloses only the rulers' psychological need for legitimacy.

The last local elections in the GDR before the great transformation were held in May 1989. As usual, the Election Commission announced that the turnout rate was high (98.78 percent), and that the unity list of the government bloc received a whopping majority of all votes cast (98.89 percent)! Nobody took the election seriously. What was new was that a church-related citizens' group contested the figures and accused the Election Commission of violating the election ordinance and falsifying election results. This was a harbinger of the civic revolts a half year later that brought down the communist regime.

Free elections were finally introduced in 1989–90 in Eastern Europe and the Soviet Union. They were the first free elections since 1946 in Czechoslovakia, since the 1920s in many other East European countries, and since 1917 in the Soviet Union. They should not be confused with one of the parliamentary elections in a Western democracy.

Although East European and Soviet elections have much in common in their timing and character, they have crucial differences. In Eastern Europe people did not go to the polls to make a choice among individual politicians or political parties. Most of the voters wanted to pass judgment on one issue only: Should the communists remain in power? In other words, it was a plebiscite on communism, not a normal election. What mattered was a constitutional question, but not a political platform of this or that politician or party. The new parliament constituted on the basis of elections was a kind of constituent assembly. It would abrogate the old communist constitution and adopt a new one.

The same cannot be said of Soviet elections to the Congress of People's Deputies in 1989. These elections were indeed free, but only in a qualified sense. One-third of the seats were assigned arbitrarily to socalled social organizations, including the Communist Party. In many districts no competitive elections were held. The number of candidates who were allowed to run was limited to the number of seats, so no choice was left for voters. In districts where there were more candidates than seats, elections still took place under the one-party system. Again, the choice was limited: Voters could choose among candidates of the same party, not between communists and noncommunists. Had the elections taken place in late 1990 (that is, after abrogation of the party's leading role) the results might have been completely different. The elections might have been a plebiscite on communism as in Eastern Europe.

Therefore, through 1990, only East European elections may be used as a source of information on the extent of the regime's legitimacy. As I observed earlier, free elections in Eastern Europe became a plebiscite in a reversed way. The election results varied from country to country, but generally they were a crushing defeat for communists. Polish communists, together with satellite parties, could obtain only about 17 percent in the first ballot of national elections in June 1989.[8] In local elections a year later, they scored even worse. Social-Democrats, a successor organization of the Polish United Workers' Party (Communist Party), and the communist-oriented trade union combined, received only 0.92 percent. East German communists, now calling themselves Democratic Socialists, obtained 16.3 percent of the votes in the March 1990 elections. Hungarian communists, now Socialists, did not fare better. They won only 10.9 percent of the votes in the first ballot of elections later in the same month. Czechoslovak comrades recorded 13.6 percent in June 1990.

The exceptions were Bulgaria and Romania. Bulgarian communists, now Socialists, scored a remarkable 47.15 percent of the votes in proportional election districts and 58.5 percent of the seats in single-seat districts in June 1990. In Romania no successor organization of the Communist Party was established, but the National Salvation Front appeared to be a successor at least to the party's anti-Ceausescu wing. It captured 85.1 percent of the votes in the presidential election and 66.4 percent of the seats in the Lower House elections in June 1990. In spite of such a phenomenal election success, the communists could not achieve political stability either in Bulgaria or in Romania. In Bulgaria a power vacuum emerged after the June elections and continued for almost half a year when the communists decided to give up the presidency and the premiership to the opposition forces. In Romania political disturbances persist.

In the countries where communists made great efforts to reform the system—namely, in Poland and Hungary—they fared badly, while in those countries where they undertook almost nothing—Bulgaria, East Germany, and Czechoslovakia—they fared rather well. In Poland the communist government made desperate efforts to stabilize the system and introduced a whole series of noncoercive mechanisms for that purpose. All the efforts, however, were to no avail. The Polish communists fared the worst of all in the elections.

To sum up, the free elections in 1989–90 in Eastern Europe were a verdict on communism. It turned out that people did not believe the communists' justification for their rule, contrary to the long-time official propaganda. But this was the vox populi in a critical moment, and we should be cautious not to generalize it over the entire postwar period. The communist regime in Eastern Europe enjoyed a varying degree of legitimacy. Communists referred also to a varying principle of legitimacy. We also should be cautious in applying the East European experience to other communist countries.

After elections, the next most reliable source of information on the regime's legitimacy is opinion polls carried out by independent organs or groups of scholars. Indeed, in a number of Soviet bloc countries, opinion polls on leading personalities or institutions of party and government were introduced in the early 1960s. The results were seldom published, with the notable exceptions of Czechoslovakia in 1968 and Poland since the beginning of the 1960s.[9] Opinion polls after the Western pattern were systematically conducted in Poland by researchers at universities, and the results were published. After the martial law, the government established an independent opinion poll institute (CBOS), which conducted large-scale opinion polls on every possible issue and freely published the results. How legitimate was the old regime in Poland against the background of these opinion polls?

Polish sociologists Andrzej Rychard and Jacek Szymanderski analyzed a questionnaire in the summer of 1984 and adopted a unique typology of legitimation. Respondents indicated the following seven types of legitimation in Poland: full legitimation (14.3 percent), legitimation without compliance (5.0 percent), compliance without legitimation (8.3 percent), ideological legitimation (8.4 percent), non-ideological legitimation (1.1 percent), compliance without political and ideological legitimation (4.3

Table 9-1
TRUST IN POLISH INSTITUTIONS

Institution	Trust/ Not trust	1984	1985
State organs[a]	Trust	26.2%	36.2%
PZPR	Trust	37.0%	42.1%
Army	Trust	65.4%	70.8%
Catholic Church	Trust	82.4%	85.6%
	Not trust	7.7%	5.9%
Underground Solidarity	Trust	12.7%	10.8%
	Not trust	57.5%	52.4%

a. Sejm (Parliament), State Council, Council of Ministers (government), Justice Courts, Public Prosecutor's Office, and National Councils (local diets). Stanislaw Gebethner, "Legitymizacja systemu politycznego," pp. 110–11.

percent), and full delegitimation (13.2 percent). The remaining 45.4 percent did not indicate which of the seven types of legitimation they accepted. Probably they are people characterized by passivity or retreat from reality.[10]

Of those questioned, 23.8 percent consider the contemporary political system in Poland legitimate, 58 percent grant weaker or stronger compliance to it, and about 15 percent regard the system as illegitimate. Stanislaw Gebethner comments: "This may be large or small depending on the point of view. It is enough for the system to survive, but, with such a great portion of the public that grants only passive compliance, it is decidedly insufficient for the political system to actively influence its environment."[11]

For a political system to be legitimized, institutions of the system, as well as persons holding office in the structures of power, must enjoy a high degree of trust among the population. Results from opinion polls on the trust that those institutions and persons enjoy may be a useful index of how strong the legitimizing force of the given system is. According to Szymanderski, in 1984, 21.8 percent of the sample population trusted the three institutions that are supposed to represent the authorities: PZPR (Communist Party), the Public Prosecutor's Office, and the police. In 1985 the percentage increased to 28.1 percent.[12] Gebethner gives somewhat different figures (see Table 9-1).[13]

The Catholic Church and the Army enjoy relatively high prestige among the population. Trust granted to the underground Solidarity is surprisingly low, lower than that granted to the PZPR. On this point, Gebethner tells us that the people who trust Solidarity are more or less the people who disapprove of the legitimacy of the political system. For Gebethner, however, the essence of the problem is the lack of general consensus in Polish society, which weakens the legitimacy of the institutions constituting the political system and makes the level of compliance with them very shaky.[14] The deep cleavage that runs through Polish society is vividly described in the famous reportage by T. Toranska entitled *They*. People call party functionaries simply "they" and see an insurmountable wall dividing "them" from "us." The cleavage is also confirmed statistically. To the question whether the "We and They" division exists in Poland, 38.2 percent answer yes, 29.3 percent no, and 31.8 percent do not have an opinion.[15]

The picture of the regime's legitimacy that appears from these figures is different from the one that appears from the election results in 1989–90. The election results in 1989–90 indicated that the Communist Party, the mainstay of the regime, enjoyed little support, or at least not enough support to stabilize the system, but the opinion polls in 1984 revealed that the regime rested on a foundation, albeit a shaky one. The opposition, a political force that would bear the responsibility of government in five years, was clearly devoid of legitimacy at that time. Which picture is closer to reality?

In sociological surveys in Poland in the 1980s, the following two questions were often asked: (1) Do you wish that the world will develop to that form of socialism that exists in Poland? (2) Do you wish that the world will develop to some form of socialism? Almost 40 percent more people responded positively to the second question. The support for "actually existing socialism" was rather weak, but "theoretical socialism" found considerable acceptance. Fifty percent of respondents accepted the view that under capitalism there is more injustice and exploitation than under socialism (27 percent disapproved it). Forty-six percent accepted the view that socialism is more progressive than capitalism (25 percent disapproved it). Seventy percent accepted the view that socialism assures people of work and of security for tomorrow better than does capitalism.[16]

Of course, this cannot be taken as an index of popular commitment to constitutional principles, so long as questions of cardinal importance for the communist regime, such as the party's leading role, are not addressed. But the discrepancy between theoretical socialism and actually existing socialism may be compared to that between commitment to constitutional principles and support for concrete politicians or political parties in the West. In my view the political system in Poland before the great change in 1989 was not totally deprived of legitimacy.

Poland's case cannot be generalized for other East European countries, not to speak of other communist countries. However, it should be taken into account that the years these polls were conducted in Poland were a time when the regime's legitimacy was at an all-time low. The memory of freedom in the Solidarity years and of repressions under the martial law was still fresh, and the underground Solidarity was active. In the recent past no communist country had experienced such a terrible shake-up of the system as had Poland. Thus, presumably the extent of the regime's legitimacy in the rest of Eastern Europe and other communist countries may have been higher or at least not lower than in Poland.

FROM TELEOLOGY TO FUNCTIONALISM

What kind of legitimacy did the old regime enjoy? In order to answer we must investigate how the communists tried to justify their rule. They were Marxists of a dogmatic school, and as such they were not free to adopt any legitimating formula or legitimacy claim. The Marxist ideology imposed a narrow limit on their freedom. Within the ideological confines, however, their legitimating formula underwent a subtle change with the passage of time. We can identify at least three legitimating formulas: the revolutionary-millennial formula, the rapid industrialization formula, and the economic effectiveness formula.

The revolutionary-millennial formula is directly derived from the ideology. The Communist Party and its leaders supposedly knew what the people wanted and how to achieve it better than did the people themselves. They were allegedly the only ones that were far-sighted enough to know what is historically inevitable and, thanks to this knowledge, able to avoid a wrong path called capitalism and to realize a paradise on earth called communist society. With dedication to a utopia, they engineered a revolution for the people and in the name of history. Obviously, the communists could not refer for legitimacy to religious principles, immemorial traditions, or formal procedures as could their predecessors. Instead they referred to goals in the distant future, goals they allegedly would lead the people toward. Hence, the communists had a teleological argument for legitimacy. The newness and suggestive power of their goals and ideas were their main claim to rule. They wanted to rule on credit, since their goals were not yet achieved, but they already had a need to justify their right to political power.[17]

How many people believed this teleological argument for legitimacy—that is, the revolutionary-millennial formula? The answer depends largely on the circumstances of revolution. In countries where the communists had an indigenous base and were strong enough to take power without foreign assistance (Russia, Yugoslavia, and China), the people embraced the communist gospel more or less enthusiastically. The idea of a communist utopia was sufficiently captivating that Mao Zedong could mobilize millions of people in the late 1960s and early 1970s when he set in motion the so-called Cultural Revolution. Utopianism haunted the de-Stalinizer Nikita Khrushchev. Even Mikhail Gorbachev resorted to utopian paroles like *uskorenie* (acceleration) and *sovershenstvovanie* (perfecting) for a while after he took power. In Czechoslovakia and Bulgaria, where popular support for communists was considerable, although not enough for them to take power alone, the revolutionary-millennial ideology also found a strong following among certain segments of society.

In Poland, Hungary, Romania, and the part of Germany that later became the GDR—countries where the communists had little backing—the situation was different. Few people had ears for whatever the communists, henchmen of a foreign power, preached. There is a general assumption, however, that at least in the first postwar years these countries showed a certain popular enthusiasm for the communist revolution. Polish sociologist Jacek Tarkowski questions this and suggests that the myth of popular support for the communist revolution may have come about because many intellectuals, people of "wide public visibility," enthusiastically embraced the communist ideology and actively supported the new system. In addition to intellectuals, many workers and poor peasants who had advanced socially thanks to the revolution supported the new regime. Tarkowski admits that "the new regime and the new elite, in the first years of their functioning, enjoyed an authentic, though not very massive, support and powerful legitimacy."[18]

The second legitimating formula is the formula of rapid industrialization. Rapid industrialization after the revolution was not envisaged by Marx. Rather, it was considered a prerequisite for the revolution. Since the revolution took place, contrary to the prediction, in the economically backward Russia, and not in a highly industrialized country, industrialization became the foremost task of the revolutionary regime. No revolutionary goals could be achieved without industrial progress. In the Soviet Union the First Five-Year Plan started in the late 1920s and was followed by successive five-year plans. With industrialization, wholesale collectivization of agriculture was started and brought to completion. The time of industrialization in the Soviet Union was full of sharp contrasts: great achievements in industrialization and in certain aspects of cultural and social life, on the one hand, and mass political repressions and economic hardships, on the other. In Eastern Europe an ambitious industrialization program was launched in 1948–49. This coincided with the advent of the cold war and the establishment of a total communist dictatorship. A first attempt at collectivization of agriculture started at the same time. In China the same process began with some time lag.

In the Soviet Union the apparent success of industrialization, rather than the revolutionary-millennial gospel, captured the imagination of many intellectuals of developing nations. They came to believe that industrialization is the main objective of a socialist revolution. Industrialization and only industrialization makes it possible for their countries to catch up with the West. There was an outburst of mass enthusiasm for the industrialization program in Eastern Europe, China, and North Korea. Tarkowski states, "The heroic and romantic vision of industrialization to be realized under the guidance of the Communist Party legitimized the system and the ruling elite in the eyes of a part of society, first of all among those who migrated from the countryside to urban areas, and among a part of the youth." The most important change was a subtle shift from an abstract revolutionary-millennial vision to a concrete program of economic and social progress. "The most mass effective formula of legitimation was more or less concrete promises of material benefits—liberation from hunger and poverty—and promises of satisfaction of basic needs, still kept on a modest level. At that time nobody dreamt of consumerism."[19]

The third legitimating formula is the formula of economic effectiveness. Communist society is supposed to be a society in which all people work according to their ability and obtain according to their needs. Needs, however, have no natural limits. The vision of an ideal communist society inevitably leads to a consumption society. When the ascetic and heroic phase of the communist revolution is over, the regime can no longer rely on the public's readiness to sacrifice today for benefits tomorrow. The leadership starts to promise a constant and tangible improvement of the living standard. The teleological formula for legitimacy gives way to a functional one. Its basis is effectiveness in achieving goals that were ideological promises stemming from the official doctrine. The shift from teleological to functional argumentation is related to erosion of ideological beliefs not only among the masses, but also among the rulers and the groups subordinated to them.[20]

In the Soviet Union this shift coincided with the death of Stalin in 1953. Georgii M. Malenkov was the first Soviet premier that pleaded for an investment policy to give preference, not to the "productive sector" (the heavy industries), but to the "nonproductive sector" (the light industries). Khrushchev severely criticized this policy although later he appropriated it. The Twenty-Second Party Congress in 1961 solemnly declared that the Soviet Union would catch up with and even surpass the United States in per capita GNP by 1980 and that the main task of the economic plan was the realization of this objective. The "consumption first" policy was not consistently pursued under Brezhnev, but the regime remained committed to raising the nation's consumption life.

In a number of East European countries, the policy of sacrificing the present for a glorious future had to be abandoned in the mid-1950s. Worker-consumers started to air their discontent with economic hardship, and the belief system of communist intellectuals was put to a severe test under the shock of de-Stalinization. The Communist parties promised to improve consumption to stabilize the system, which became then a permanent component of their legitimating formula. In China it was only after the Cultural Revolution and Deng Xiaoping's rise to power that economic effectiveness became the main legitimating formula.

Normally the three legitimating formulas appear in successive order: When all the possibilities of the first formula are exhausted, the second one appears, and then the third one follows, but there will be no fourth one. The sequence and timing of succession depends on the country. One formula may last long in some countries, but endure only for a short time or be skipped over entirely, in others. One formula may persist while another appears so that two or even three formulas can coexist at the same time. The legitimating formula may be modified in accordance with the country's specific conditions. For instance, the pattern in Yugoslavia is not typical: The revolutionary-millennial formula in varying disguises persisted for a long time. In Albania, Romania, and North Korea the industrialization phase lasted very long without ever coming to the third phase. It is doubtful whether transition from teleology to functionalism has ever taken place in these countries.

Concerning the last formula, economic effectiveness, political scientists and sociologists debate whether it is a legitimating formula or a substitute for legitimacy. Seymour M. Lipset explains the relationship between effectiveness and legitimacy as follows: "While effectiveness is primarily instrumental, legitimacy is evaluative. Groups regard a political system as legitimate or illegitimate according to the way in which its values fit with theirs."[21] He relates effectiveness to stability rather than to legitimacy. In contrast to this, Thomas Baylis in his book on East German technical intelligentsia elevated the "performance-based legitimacy" to an independent category that is distinct from "rational-legal legitimacy."[22]

Most Polish scholars and foreign specialists on Poland are critical of the notion of performance-based legitimacy. They regard economic performance just as a substitute for legitimacy. In Poland after the March incident of 1968 the revolutionary-millennial formula of legitimacy (including its revisionist variant) finally exhausted its attractiveness even among the power elite. Among the power elite a firm conviction struck root that legitimacy is simply a dependent variable of economic effectiveness. The "lyrical model of socialism" gave way to a model whose only raison d'être was increase of consumption. Can, however, a political system regenerate legitimacy through effectiveness? Some think that Hungary did, but others take the view that the Communist Party of Hungary secured only passive obedience of the subjects through economic effectiveness. Tarkowski holds that effectiveness is a weak and incomplete substitute for legitimacy and that the system that relies too much on this substitute is easily caught up in a legitimacy crisis. Gierek's team treated economic effectiveness as virtually the only argument that proves their claim to power and legitimacy of the system. As a result, the sharp economic crisis instantly delegitimized the entire political system.[23]

Economic performance as a substitute for legitimacy inevitably politicizes the economy. The first and foremost task of the state becomes to improve the subsistence and consumption of the population. That means that paternalism determines the basic identity of the system. The most important element of this arrangement is a deal in which society gives up freedom in exchange for protection. A crisis mentality arises when the state becomes unable to carry out its paternalistic task. When the power elite maintains universal control of society and at the same time justifies its claim to power by economic effectiveness, the paternalistic "welfare state" is the only logical solution. The system cannot achieve a satisfactory level of economic effectiveness, however, unless it enjoys a minimum level of legitimacy. The expected cycle of effectiveness→legitimacy→effectiveness transforms itself into a vicious cycle of weak legitimacy→low effectiveness→weaker legitimacy.[24]

Every time the Polish government timidly tried to raise food prices, the people reacted violently and often forced the leadership to resign. They regarded price hikes as a violation of the unwritten contract between rulers and subjects—namely, the promise of constant improvement of the living standard. Any kind of legitimacy must be reinforced and periodically subjected to popular confirmation, but the system and the power elite that derive their mandate from economic performance must vindicate it almost every day. Even a significantly more efficient system than the Polish economic one could survive such constant pressure only with difficulty.[25]

Faithful to the tradition since Lipset, most Polish scholars locate the legitimacy problem in the sphere of values. Some, however, question the concept of a legitimating formula. Polish sociologist Miroslawa Marody criticizes the one-sided concentration on values: First, we cannot describe the sphere of social actions only with a knowledge of values, as people's actions do not always coincide with the values they believe. Second, concentration on values leads us to the so-called oppressive theory of society which describes the society in terms of enslavement. In the enslaved society legitimacy is neither enough nor needed to stabilize the system. On the other hand, the concept of "compliance" leaves aside the important field of values. Instead of the "oppressive theory" it introduces an "adaptational theory of individuals." Marody suggests a new concept of "collective sense". According to her, this concept makes it possible to describe stability and change of the social order and at the same time to take into consideration both the sphere of values and the sphere of social actions.[26]

By "collective sense" Marody means a value that gives an orientation to the collective effort of society and at the same time constitutes the basis of acceptance of authorities by society. It is a sphere of specific consensus between authorities and society and an effect of "negotiations": The authorities "commit themselves" to introduce and maintain the social order, and the society "commits itself" to submit to the authorities. In this sense it is a value that incorporates a dimension of community and a dimension of subordination.[27]

According to Marody, epochs of postwar Polish history had their own collective sense: *reconstruction of the country* (1945–49), *social and civilizational advance* (1949–56), and *economic development and democratization of public life* (1956–80). She makes the following qualifications. First, each version of the collective sense is not a complete negation of the preceding one. Second, though the social order is built as a result of actions by authorities as well as by the society, authorities control the institutional order, while the society controls the normative order. Third, at each stage somewhat different groups of the society become involved in the process of supporting the authorities, while somewhat different groups also remain outside of the pale of the existing consensus.[28]

Although it is related primarily to stability not legitimacy, Marody's concept of collective sense is even more convincing than the concept of a legitimating formula. But when we try to apply it to socialist countries other than Poland, problems arise. Revolutionary utopianism does not appear on Marody's list of collective senses for Poland, but it applies to other socialist countries, at least for a time (for instance, Russia in the 1920s and China in the 1950s). Moreover, collective senses that Marody detects in Poland are missing in other socialist countries. "Democratization of public life," for instance, is absent in most of the socialist countries with the exception of Czechoslovakia in the years immediately

preceding the Prague Spring in 1968. Yet a "quest for national sovereignty," which Marody does not mention for Poland, may be identified
as a collective sense in Yugoslavia, Romania, Albania, and North Korea.

DIVERSE SOURCES OF STABILITY

Let us turn now to sources of stability other than legitimacy. Communist
governments that claim to be legitimate on the basis of the country's
economic performance have already made the transition from legitimacy to quasi-legitimacy. Many other claims helped to stabilize the
system. Most of them, however, collide with the basic tenets of Marxism-
Leninism. They, therefore, stabilize the system at the same time that
they undermine the effect of the very formulas by which the system has
tried to justify itself. These claims have not been made with the same
force in all socialist countries and in all phases. Generally speaking,
communists hesitated to resort to those quasi-legitimacy claims in the
initial period of their power, but gradually came to depend on them, in
many cases until they believed they could not survive without them.

We now will consider four of those claims: the claim to be guardian
of national interests, the claim to be guardian of national values and
traditions, the claim to enjoy the trust of persons or institutions that are
supposed to command the genuine support of the population, and the
claim to enjoy recognition by foreign powers. I begin with the claim to
be guardian of national or state interests. From a Marxist point of view,
"national interests" are nothing but a phrase the bourgeoisie uses to
justify egoistic class interests in the name of nation; there are no abstract
interests that stand above concrete class interests. In the first years after
the revolution, the Bolsheviks never used the concept of national interests to justify their claim to power; for them class interests had absolute
priority. Even if there were something like national interests of Soviet
Russia, they should be surbordinated to the class interests of the international proletariat—namely, a world revolution. Stalin's new theory of
"socialism in one country" brought a fundamental change, but even
Stalin at that time seldom used the term "national interests." Only after
the onslaught of Nazi Germany on the Soviet Union did the Soviets
officially and frequently use terms such as "defense of state interests."

In countries where communist power emerged, or is supposed to have
emerged, from a national liberation struggle, the emphasis from the
very beginning was on national interests rather than class interests. Of
course, communists did not wage the national liberation struggle for its
own sake; they waged it for a communist revolution; here, too, class
interests were supposed to go before national interests. Emphasis on

national interests tended to fade away once communists achieved power. The concept of national interests, however, turned out to be too useful for them to abandon. Class or national interests are dependent variables of the enemy concept. If the enemy is perceived to be internal, class interests are emphasized, and if external, national interests. Very often both enemies converge; then the distinction between class and national interests blurs. Moreover, communists, like all power-holders, are prone to resort to the proven method of rallying the nation around their flag by concocting an external enemy. In that case national interests are a more useful argument than class interests.

The understanding of national interests varies. Countries with great-power ambitions have an offensive understanding of national interests. The best way to serve national interests is to acquire and maintain the ability to influence the conduct of other countries. But countries without great-power ambitions have a defensive understanding. They identify national interests mainly with defense of national sovereignty and integrity. The Soviet Union and China may be counted among the former. Vietnam, North Korea, Mongolia, and East European countries may be counted among the latter. Their understanding of national interests inevitably collides with that of the former. If they successfully defend independence against socialist great powers (Yugoslavia, Albania, and Romania against the Soviet Union; Vietnam against China; and North Korea against the Soviet Union and China), they may well make credible their claim to be defenders of national interests. The case of East European satellites is more complex. Let us consider Poland and the GDR.

"What instead of legitimacy?" asks Andrzej Rychard. "Of course, geopolitics above all. Its role is predominant. It stabilizes the system suffering a lack of legitimacy."[29] The concern about geopolitics is expressed with reference to *raison d'état*. Probably there is no other country in Europe where reference to *raison d'état* was made to justify the existing political order so frequently as in Poland. In other countries *raison d'état* is referred to only when those in power feel exposed to acute threats or internal or external conflicts—in other words, when they feel in a crisis. In the normal situation they prefer "the national interest."[30] The increasingly frequent reference to *raison d'état* in Poland may be indicative of the crisis of communism there since the mid-1950s. *Raison d'état* was originally used to justify Poland's alliance with the Soviet Union against Germany. Because the Communist Party was the only political force inside Poland that enjoyed the trust of the Soviet Union, the argument of *raison d'état* automatically helped to justify the claim to power of this force. The meaning of the argument underwent a subtle change with the passage of time. In later years one was reminded not so much of the German danger as of the danger of Soviet intervention. The argument went something like this: A Soviet military intervention would be a national catastrophe for Poland. The Soviets would not intervene so long as the Communists are in power. Therefore, those who are concerned about the fate of the state, regardless of their party affiliation, should do everything possible to leave the Communists in power. The Communist Party used the bogy of a Soviet military intervention to cling to power.[31]

What is important from my point of view is not that such propaganda was issued, but that it was widely believed. The threat of Soviet intervention seemed to be quite real in the light of events in the GDR, Hungary, Czechoslovakia, and the Soviet Union. The Soviets' behavior toward Poland in words and deeds strongly hinted at their intention to intervene. Since October 1956 independent Catholic groups (first of all the *Znak* group) had supported the communist government for no reason other than *raison d'état*. Maybe to reassure the Soviets Solidarity leaders (for instance, Tadeusz Mazowiecki and Bronislaw Geremek) continued to use the argument of *raison d'état* even after the Solidarity government came into being in 1989.[32] The concern about geopolitics certainly stabilized the communist political system, but it is doubtful that it strengthened its legitimacy. What the regime attained by using the argument of geopolitics was, at most, toleration by the population.

Poland occupies one extreme among the Soviet satellites in Eastern Europe. The other extreme is represented by the GDR. The GDR was perhaps the only former Soviet satellite where the communists strictly refrained from using *raison d'état* to justify their claim to power. They could not use it in the GDR because that country was built on the very denial of *raison d'état* of the German state. The GDR upheld a teleological formula up to the last moment of its existence. As late as August 1989, Otto Reinhold, president of the Academy of Social Sciences (which is attached to the Central Committee of the GDR's Communist Party), stated: "The GDR can exist only as an anti-fascist socialist state, a socialist state as opposed to the FRG. . . . If the GDR would adopt a Hungarian type of reform which introduces capitalist elements, there would be no reason for a capitalist GDR to exist."[33] The same emphasis on ideology rather than *raison d'état* may apply to other divided countries like North Korea or former North Vietnam, but neither Korea nor Vietnam was a defeated country like Germany, and the establishment of communist authorities could not be directly linked to the military occupation by a hostile foreign power. In these countries communists could assert with certain grounds that the other, capitalist half of the country was built on the denial of *raison d'état* of their state.

Second, consider the claim to be guardian of national values and traditions. "The working class has no fatherland" is a well-known motto of Marxists. They are internationalists and supposed to have no special interest in national values and traditions. As a matter of fact, communists were strongly opposed to all kinds of nationalism when they were in opposition. Sharp conflicts between nationalists and communists characterized most of the countries before the communists came to power. In Soviet Russia the Bolsheviks were opposed to all manifestations of nationalism long after the revolution.

Again it is only after the outbreak of the German-Soviet war that national values and traditions became part of the official policy in the Soviet Union. The Soviet authorities renamed the war the Great Patriotic War to inflame Russians' nationalistic hatred of foreign invaders. Nationalistic sentiments, exalted by the military victory, survived well into the postwar period and found outlet during the cold war in the praise of everything Russian. This assumed an almost ridiculous dimension. For instance, all important scientific inventions in modern history were attributed to Russians.

In other socialist countries communists reconciled themselves to national values and traditions in a more natural way. Most of them came to power in a war for national liberation rather than in a social revolution. From the beginning these communists emphasized their ability to promote national values and continuity with the national past. They even claimed to be a legitimate heir of sanctified national traditions, and they often consciously inflamed nationalistic sentiments against certain segments of society or against foreign countries. That communists in these countries tried to justify their claim to power by national symbolism rather than revolutionary symbolism is understandable. While they were confident of the teleological formula of legitimacy, they did not need national symbolism. Their current need of national symbolism to support their authority indicates their insecurity and sense of a legitimacy crisis.

This is true especially in countries where revolutionary impulses from within were weak and the communist regime had to be imported from outside. Consider the case of Poland. The Kosciuszko Division, a Polish army set up on Soviet soil in 1943 under the strict control of the communists, imitated symbols of the prewar Polish army in the smallest detail, such as uniforms, badges of rank, epaulets, decorations, military songs, etiquette, ceremonies of oath-taking, and even military priests. The effectiveness of this use of national symbols is another question. It was very hard for Polish communists to get rid of the odium of having taken the side of the Russians who annexed a half of prewar Polish territories. Notwithstanding all the failures, the Polish communists continued to appropriate national symbols. In the midst of the Solidarity crisis in 1981, a parliamentarian of the Communist Party made a motion to restore a crown on the eagle in the national emblem as it had been before the war.

Romania, like Poland and Hungary, had weak revolutionary impulses from within in 1945. It is by no means a coincidence that this country produced a very nationalistic communist leader, Nicolae Ceausescu. Ceausescu's reign resembled a tyrannical monarchy more than a communist dictatorship. History textbooks published during his rule are full of exaggerations of the national past. Ceausescu liked to be likened to Ion Antonescu, the nationalistic military dictator during the Second World War.

The GDR as a divided country had to be cautious about the national past. In the early 1970s, when the GDR was forced to open the country in the wake of détente, Erich Honecker adopted the policy of *Abgrenzung* (delimitation) because he feared that the GDR society would be contaminated by all-German nationalism. The East German communists systematically eliminated from official documents and institutions all symbols with any hint of the possibility of unification (*Entdeutschungspolitik*). But in the late 1970s, when it turned out that the influence of all-German nationalism was not as destabilizing as had been feared, Honecker decided to rehabilitate the German past, first of all the Prussian one. Heroes of German history who had been denounced as reactionaries (Martin Luther, Friedrich the Great, and even Otto Bismarck) began to reappear in history textbooks. Evidently, East German communists tried to legitimize themselves as the heir to glorious German and Prussian traditions.[34]

The communists often tried to mobilize popular antipathies against other nationalities to stabilize the system. This easy but dubious method to achieve quasi-legitimacy has been practiced in many socialist countries, especially in Eastern Europe.

The Poles suffered much at the hands of Germans during the war, and anti-German feelings were high in the immediate postwar years. The communists exploited these feelings for their political interest. After tenacious negotiations with the Russians in the last phase of the war, the Polish communists succeeded in committing them to a transfer to Poland of vast German territories about which even the most right-wing political parties in Poland had not dreamed before the war. This was political capital for the communists to start with after the war. They expelled from the area about 8 million Germans and encouraged Poles from other parts of the country, many from the parts annexed by the

Russians, to settle there. To the anti-German feelings was added a fear of German revanchism, a fear that the communists consciously kept alive through propaganda. The bogy of German revanchism was widely believed among the population, until Willy Brandt launched the *Ost-politik*. It is no coincidence that the popular uprising against price hikes of foods in December 1970 broke out just when the government concluded the Treaty of Normalization with the Federal Republic of Germany. After this, anti-German propaganda to support government authority no longer worked well, although repeated attempts were made to reactivate anti-German feelings.

In almost every East European country, communist authorities manipulated national feelings. Anti-German and anti-Hungarian feelings were encouraged among Czechs and Slovaks, anti-Hungarian feelings among Romanians, anti-Serb and anti-Turkish feelings among Bulgarians, anti-Serb feelings among Albanians, and so on.

Anti-Semitism has a long tradition in Russia and Eastern Europe. It is a feeling deeply rooted in the psychology of the mass. We are currently witnessing a powerful revival in Russia of a political movement that publicly professes anti-Semitism, namely, the *Pamiat'*. In Russia there are still many Jews, but anti-Semitism may be strong where Jews are few in number. Take Poland for instance. The Jewish community in Poland today is of negligible size as a result of the Nazi extermination policy during the war and the postwar exodus. Nevertheless, anti-Semitism there is strong.

It is well known that Stalin in his late years developed anti-Semitism and persecuted a lot of citizens of Jewish origin. Anti-Semitism spread to Eastern Europe in the late 1940s and early 1950s. Less than two years after smoke stopped rising from the last Nazi crematorium in Auschwitz, a pogrom took place in a small town in Southern Poland, called Kielce. The communist authorities did not combat it energetically enough, and the circumstances of the pogrom have never been clarified in a satisfactory way by the communist police. In Czechoslovakia, Hungary, and Romania a lot of communist activists of Jewish origin fell victim to the purge. Anti-Semitism was rampant in Poland in the 1960s when the so-called partisan group, headed by Gen. Mieczyslaw Moczar, wielded considerable power. The culmination was the student revolt in March 1968. A mass exodus of Jewish citizens followed.[35]

Official anti-Semitism was meant to emphasize the authorities' national character ("Polishness," for instance) and to legitimize them in the eyes of the public. Although such a policy was rather popular, it remains open to question whether stability, not to mention legitimacy, was achieved by it.

A third claim to stability is the claim to enjoy the trust of persons or institutions that command genuine support of the population. This may be called "borrowing legitimacy." Such a phenomenon may be observed more or less in every political system. Under the communist regime, however, it has a special meaning. According to the official doctrine, no persons or institutions outside the Communist Party can command genuine support of the population. Already the fact that such persons or institutions exist undermines the credibility of the doctrine. The communists make every effort, therefore, to destroy or eliminate such independent authorities. If they can completely suppress independent authorities yet maintain political stability (as in the Soviet Union of the 1930s), they have no need to "borrow legitimacy." Experience shows, however, that in such a case it is extremely difficult to control the situation. In some countries the communists prefer to allow certain independent authorities and to deal with them.

The Catholic Church enjoys enormous prestige in Poland. It is the country's most ancient institution, and it has always played a prominent role in politics. In Poland, as in other Christian countries during the Middle Ages, the church was one of the sources of legitimacy of the secular ruler. He could not be enthroned without the Church's blessing. Until the eighteenth century, the Primate of the Catholic Church in Poland acted for the king at the time of an interregnum. After the Second World War it was very hard for communists in Poland to compete for legitimacy with the Church, particularly because population transfers made the country almost purely Catholic.

After a brief attempt to combat the Church's influence, the communists switched tactics. They began to seek a workable compromise with the Church. Wladyslaw Gomulka struck such a compromise with Cardinal Stefan Wyszynski in 1956. That the Church tolerated, if not blessed, the atheist regime was an important gain for the communists and a stabilizing factor for the system. As social tensions grew in the 1970s, the party's dependence on the Church's authority increased. Gierek sought an audience with the Pope in the Vatican in 1977. The next year an unexpected event greatly strengthened the Church's authority: Karol Wojtyla, cardinal in Cracow, was elected Pope John Paul II. His triumphal pilgrimage to Poland in 1979 severely damaged the party's authority, but the Church did not want to destabilize the system. John Paul II granted an audience to the secular ruler Gierek. When the strikes broke out on the Baltic coast, Primate Wyszynski came to the help of the communists in the name of *raison d'état*. The Church played a role of mediator between the party and Solidarity.

In the 1980s the cooperation between the communist state and the Catholic Church was almost institutionalized. Wojciech Jaruzelski and Josef Glemp, the new primate, held regular meetings to discuss political questions.

The party and the Church no longer competed for legitimacy, but cooperated to strengthen the authority of the government. Obviously, the Church commanded much more authority among the population than did the Communist Party. Here we observe the party "borrowing legitimacy" from the Church. Surely this arrangement helped to stabilize the system, but it could not prevent ultimate disintegration.

Other socialist countries did not have institutions comparable to the Catholic Church in Poland that could compete for legitimacy with the communist authorities. No question arose, therefore, of the state's striking a compromise on a central level with another institution or "borrowing legitimacy" from it. Similar relationships could, however, exist on a smaller scale or in local context. When the power of the communist authorities declined, they had to seek a compromise with influential non-communist personalities or institutions even on a central level. A well-known example is how Soviet dissident leader Andrei Sakharov, exiled in Gorky, one day received a phone call from Gorbachev and was immediately released. From that time up to his death he cooperated with the Gorbachev administration, though in a critical way. Similarly, beginning in 1987 Gorbachev tried to reach a compromise with the Russian Orthodox Church.

Lastly, there is the claim to enjoy recognition by major foreign powers. For great powers, external recognition does not help unless the regime enjoys internal recognition. The same cannot be said of small powers: External recognition means something. The regime may survive even if it lacks internal recognition. The legitimacy of a government-in-exile, if something like that exists, stems solely from recognition by foreign powers. Of course, it must submit itself to confirmation by the population as soon as it returns home, but prior external recognition will greatly help the government-in-exile to obtain internal recognition because the population of a small power knows that it could do little against the combined will of major powers. Recognition by one foreign power or one group of foreign powers will not suffice; such a regime may be regarded as a marionette. But recognition by all major powers weighs heavily.

Most of the East European governments were formed at the end of the war at the initiative of local communists and under the pressure of the Soviet government. These governments then sought recognition by

Western powers. The Soviets were ready to make concessions (such as holding free elections or including Western exiles) to obtain Western recognition of those governments as soon as possible. From the communists' viewpoint, the Western recognition was a decisive moment for legitimation of the regime because they could now tell the people that opposition is futile since it is accepted by the entire world.

The only state in Eastern Europe that did not enjoy worldwide recognition was the GDR. For more than twenty years it was recognized only by bloc countries. All the efforts of GDR diplomats to obtain recognition of Third World countries were to little avail. The GDR leaders' intense insecurity about the future of their state did not lessen until the early 1970s. Worldwide recognition of the GDR came as a result of the *Ostpolitik* of the FRG. But international recognition did not prevent the GDR from being deserted by the population and collapsing as a state. Today North Korea seems to be following the path of the GDR. Whether international recognition will rescue Kim Il Sung's regime from its legitimacy crisis remains to be seen.

BETWEEN POLITICAL APATHY AND LEGAL LEGITIMATION OF AUTHORITY

What if the communist regime has spent all of its legitimating possibilities? Even if it has, it can survive for decades. The rulers simply act as if their legitimating formula were still believed by the ruled. One fine day, however, they will confront the truth. This day is dawning. But one communist regime faced the moment of truth ten years earlier than the others: the regime in Poland.

In many respects Poland was a precursor of the development of other socialist countries. When Gierek's policy of imported growth ended in a complete fiasco, it became obvious that economic effectiveness could no longer serve as a legitimating formula. The regime tried hard to find a credible formula to replace economic effectiveness, but failed. The imposition of martial law in 1981 was nothing but an admission of this failure. The martial law regime is a regime based on brute force. Its sole legitimating formula is that some kind of order is necessary. A very specific situation emerged: a communist regime that did not try to legitimate itself by ideology, but only by reference to order.

As to the basis of legitimacy for the martial law regime and its successor, Polish scholars are divided. Polish political scientist Wojciech Lamentowicz seems to suggest that the formation of a powerful class of functionaries contributed to stabilization. In Poland more than 10 percent of the employees in the state sector (more than 1 million people) are managing clerks (*kierownicy*). The class of functionaries is not closed, but open to outsiders. All those who are watchmen over the conformism or opportunism of other people can be functionaries without a managerial position at their place of work and, of course, without a position covered by the party nomenklatura. They are "teachers of helplessness and civic impossibility." They learn how to play roles assigned to them and how to assign roles to others. Control of roles takes place in three dimensions: (1) degree of frustrations and their distribution among various social strata, (2) degree of fears and hopes and their distribution, and (3) behavior and utterances in public.[36] Lamentowicz's thesis reminds us of the theory of "totalitarian society." It seems to describe not the basis of legitimacy, but rather technicalities of ruling. Lamentowicz suggests that the inflexibility of the system and adaptation of people to roles of "the system's functionary" are stabilizing. Rychard, however, objects. He states that flexibility and the possibility to modify inflexible requirements are stabilizing.[37]

According to Marody, refusal of the sociopolitical system takes place in the symbolical sphere (sphere of opinions and evaluations). Its acceptance (active or passive) takes place in the sphere of actions. Coercion is not an adequate explanation. We must look for values that constitute the basis of consensus. Thus, she identifies the collective sense of the fourth epoch of postwar history as public peace and social security.[38]

She substantiates her thesis with ample empirical data. The longing for public peace comes from a high level of anxiety. There are three fears: fear of war, fear of anarchy, and fear of punishment. In 1984, 85.5 percent of the respondents agreed with the following passage in Jaruzelski's speech—"We celebrate our 40th anniversary in a strained, dangerous international situation"—although only 12.2 percent stated that his speech as a whole is "in line with what I think." Respondents to the survey were asked to complete the following sentence: "What is most important for us is peace and quiet, quiet and work, or harmony in the country." Seventeen percent of the seventy-one respondents said "peace and quiet," 13 percent said "quiet and work," and 4 percent said "harmony in the country."[39]

In 1984, 55.7 percent regarded the imposition of martial law as correct. Of them, 11.7 percent thought that martial law was in the exclusive interest of society, 32.8 percent in the exclusive interest of the authorities, and 41.3 percent in the interest of authorities and society. Forty-one percent accepted the statement that martial law introduced law and order. Forty-five percent thought that a majority of citizens are obedient to authorities, and of them, 78.5 percent accepted the view that "they obey because it makes their life easier and solves a variety of problems."

This indicates that acceptance of the system has an instrumental character.[40]

Longing for social security is related to the feeling of helplessness that spread in the 1970s. Most of the citizens prefer socialism to capitalism, but socialism as a system that guarantees social security, not as a system based on a certain ideology. What are the merits of socialism? The respondents selected the following: a guarantee of work, a lack of unemployment, or job-security (41 percent), wide access to education (36 percent), health care, universal, free medical care, or access to hospitals and sanatoriums (25 percent), and social and judicial equality, equal start for all, or social justice (13 percent). What are the shortcomings of capitalism? The same answers appeared in reverse: unemployment or job insecurity (30 percent); social inequalities, class differences (13 percent), and social pathology, banditry, narcotism (13 percent).[41]

Poles favor a tutelar state (*panstwo opiekuncze*)—a state in which citizens are taken under tutelage by state authorities. According to a public opinion poll in 1985, 62 percent said yes to the model of a tutelar state, and only 29 percent to the model of a state in which everyone takes responsibility for his or her own fate. Lack of unemployment and freedom from responsibility for one's own fate become important values. In 1980–81 the social reality became incomprehensible to many Poles. "Universal helplessness" gave rise to the conviction: "Better to have any kind of order than to have none."[42]

Marody makes two qualifications. First, the collective sense in the 1980s was basically an "antisense." Nonaction became the main form of social activity. Second, all the trends and aspirations that are important for Polish society were left beyond the pale of "negotiated" collective sense. People had the feeling that the situation was provisional.[43]

The Polish situation in the 1980s is best described by the words "political apathy." Citizens lost interest in public affairs in general. Not only the authorities, but also the underground opposition were unable to involve citizens in a public action.[44]

Another Polish sociologist, Jadwiga Staniszkis, sees the problem from a different angle. She points out: Under socialism concrete groups have no economic interest in systemic changes. Conflicts are missing in the sphere of production. All demands in conflict situations are related to the sphere of distribution and the sphere of power. Demands in the sphere of distribution, however, only reproduce the system.[45] A radical stand on self-identification by no means reveals the ability to think about an alternative. People who refuse the system in general terms, when asked about a desirable system of ownership, often mention the same system under which they live. This is likely to promote political stability and the reproduction of the system.[46]

Rychard does not agree with the systemic hopelessness theory, although he also inclines to pessimism. He observes that in the 1980s the Polish society was dichotomically divided along political views or ways of life; a countersystem emerged that functioned mainly in private life or in the second economy and was tolerated by authorities. The relationship between authorities and the "public" (*spoleczenstwo*) is one of active mutual adaptation. Here Rychard arrives at a paradoxical conclusion: "The adaptation mechanism delegitimizes the system, but at the same time stabilizes it. Thus, the system is both more and more delegitimized and more and more stabilized."[47]

All prognoses of the Polish situation in the mid-1980s by intellectuals living inside the country were pessimistic, and their pessimism in a few years proved to be well founded. But we should not be misled by those prognoses or later developments. History is open at any moment to many possibilities. The situation could have unfolded differently. Let us take a look at an aspect of legitimation often overlooked by Polish intellectuals at that time—namely, legal legitimation of authority.

In the 1980s the Polish government made judicial organs more independent from government and party control. The Supreme Court of Administration was set up in January 1980. To this court citizens can bring a charge against abuses of the authorities. Lawsuits, even on censorship, were included in the court's jurisdiction in July 1981. The Supreme Control Chamber, a kind of board of audit, was restored to the Sejm in October 1980. Up to that time it had been placed under the government, which it was supposed to control. The State Tribunal was reestablished in March 1982. This special court judges high-ranking officials for their "constitutional responsibilities." The Constitutional Tribunal, established in April 1985, rules on the constitutionality of laws or government acts. Then in July 1987 the Spokesman of Civil Rights (an ombudsman position) was set up. The Sejm appointed nonparty lawyer Ewa Letowska as the first spokesman.[48]

Not all of these institutions were as effective as expected. For instance, the State Tribunal indicted only two communist high officials of the 1970s and could not prove the guilt of even these two. It could not bring a charge against Gierek because he held "only" a party post, not a government one. These institutions were not completely free from outside pressure because they were subjected to control by the parliament where communists still dominated. Communist organizations were not removed from the normal courts of justice. There were many other defects in the legal reforms, as Polish jurists assiduously pointed out.[49] The reforms were, however, unprecedented in socialist countries. They were credible and extremely popular. For instance, the Spokesman for Civil Rights received 46,000 complaints from citizens in the first nine months of its existence, and 60,000 in its first twelve months.[50] Judicial organs were now more or less autonomous, and neither government nor party could interfere with legal procedures so recklessly as they had before.

Legislative as well as judicial organs recovered some of their former prerogatives. The Sejm passed 42 acts in 1976–80 and 203 acts in 1980–85. The practice of taking a vote of confidence on each newly nominated minister (*absolutorium*) was reestablished. An opinion poll in 1984 revealed that the Sejm ranked third, after the Catholic Church and the army, in popular trust.[51] Legislative organs, however, were not representative because elections were not free. The government was very timid in election reforms, but there was some progress. A bold step forward was the November 1987 referendum on political and economic reforms. It was held under completely free conditions. The results were ambiguous: The government proposals won two-thirds of the votes, but not a majority of those who were entitled to vote as the law required.

Rigby's distinction between task-achieving bureaucracies and rule-applying bureaucracies may well apply to communist regimes in general, but an important change has occurred in some communist countries since he made this observation. The legitimation of authority in goal-rational terms exhausted all its possibilities in Poland and maybe also in Hungary. In these two countries serious, almost desperate attempts were undertaken in the 1980s to put legitimation of authority on a new basis: formal-legal rationality. Stanislaw Gebethner described the period since 1980 as "a time of endeavors to recreate a consensus, establish as wide a compliance as possible and even attempt to build a more complete and more solid legitimation of the political system."[52] In the rest of Eastern Europe, to say nothing of other socialist countries, no attempts were made to renew the basis of legitimacy.

BUILDING LEGITIMACY UNDER PLURALISTIC DEMOCRACY

In recent years most of the East European countries have firmly committed themselves to principles of pluralistic democracy, although it still remains to be seen whether they will become functioning democracies.

The communist parties that have survived here and elsewhere are now fully aware that old legitimating formulas have lost credibility. The party in Bulgaria, Romania, and Serbia adopted a new party name and a new party program. Only Asian communists, except for those in Mongolia, cling to old formulas as if they believed that these formulas were still believed by the ruled.

For all practical purposes, Eastern Europe has ceased to be communist. Even the Albanian communists have finally recognized the hopelessness of their situation and are introducing a fundamental reform. We can no longer discuss Eastern Europe in the framework of "comparative socialism." However, if we regard the political system as a continuum, there is sense in including the post-1989 Eastern Europe into our consideration particularly because, as a precursor, it may give a key to the understanding of the future development of other socialist countries.

Authority in Eastern Europe is now legitimized through democratic procedures. In Romania the continuity of authority broke down completely due to a popular uprising. In all other countries some continuity was maintained. Everywhere, however, a profound metamorphosis of the system took place. The new rules that govern formation of government authority thoroughly differ from the old ones, and they satisfy all the requirements of a democratic regime.

But democratic procedures alone cannot guarantee the viability of a political system. In Romania, Bulgaria, and Serbia, the communists won a clear victory in free elections, but they cannot stabilize the system. The same may be true of anticommunist forces that won elections. As I indicated earlier, elections were a plebiscite, but a negative one (that is, a poll on what the future constitution should not be and not on what it should be). An inevitable result of this is the ambiguity from the outset about the forces that won the elections. Those forces had never been a cohesive political group with a coherent political platform. They were united only so long as communists were in power. No sooner had the communists stepped down than they began to split. It is not even known whether they can govern since most of them are inexperienced in politics and administration.

In revolutionary upheavals such as those Eastern Europe is experiencing, a charismatic legitimation usually prevails. But charismatic leaders are conspicuously missing in Eastern Europe, with the sole exception of Poland's Lech Walesa. Czechoslovakia's Vaclav Havel might be considered charismatic, but his charisma seems to have been shaped by the events rather than the events by his charisma. The lack of charismatic leaders is partly explained by the suddenness of the transformation. The events in 1989 caught most East Europeans by surprise. The opposition, if there was any, was not prepared to take power. The main reason for the lack of promising leaders, however, seems to lie in the very nature of the communist regime: It monopolizes the process of elite recruitment and eliminates the potential counterelite as far as possible.

In the initial phase of East European revolutions in 1989–90 the legitimation of authority through elitist compromise prevailed. This is the phase of the Round Table. The example was made by Poles, and other East Europeans, except for Yugoslavs and Albanians, quickly followed suit. The Round Table, an elitist concept, was a body of self-appointed representatives without any mandate from the ruled. In Poland's case it was composed of two sides: the government-coalition side and the opposition-Solidarity side. In other words, it was a body where the elite of the government and the elite of the opposition met on an equal footing and deliberated on problems of mutual concern. This body made decisions of cardinal importance for the entire nation. Insofar as it meant a denial of the leading role of the party, it was a democratization of the public life, but the elitist nature of the arrangement could not be overlooked.

The indispensable prerequisite for success in such an arrangement is that a credible elite is formed both on the government and the opposition side. Such a condition existed only in Poland, one of the most remarkable developments after Solidarity came into being. In the rest of Eastern Europe, such a condition was missing, which partly explains why the Round Table did not achieve such a success as in Poland. Let us analyze the outcome of the elitist compromise, taking Poland as an example.

The Polish Round Table decided that the communists would remain in power for four more years (or six years if we take the term of the newly created presidential office). Solidarity gained a powerful means to check the government. It would be given up to one-third of the seats in the Sejm and a majority of seats in the newly created Senate. Thus, the phase of elitist compromise was supposed to last rather long, but the arrangement soon suffered a serious blow when free elections involved the masses in the political process.

Elections were held in June 1989, only two months after the Round Table was finished. The groups represented at the Round Table made haste to hold elections in order to demonstrate that they were not self-appointed but real representatives of the nation. For them the elections were both a great success and a disaster: a great success because the Round Table forces monopolized the seats, and a disaster because, contrary to expectations, the government-coalition forces and the opposition-Solidarity forces at the Round Table were not balanced. The latter won a landslide victory.

Solidarity's landslide victory was quite unexpected for both the government and Solidarity. It became impossible to put into practice the scenario envisaged by the Round Table. At this juncture the famous formula "Your President, Our Premier" was coined by Solidarity's publicist, Adam Michnik. While most of the Solidarity leaders were hesitating to take government responsibility, Lech Walesa cut the Gordian knot. Solidarity allied itself with two former satellite parties of the communists (the United Peasants' Party and the Democratic Party). The communists strongly resisted exclusion from the government. Thus, a grand coalition came into being with Solidarity's Tadeusz Mazowiecki as premier.

It is true that these moves were unleashed by the unexpected results of the popular elections, but the Mazowiecki government was not a direct product of popular elections. First, it came about in spite of elections. The election ordinance, theoretically and practically, precluded the possibility of victory for groupings other than the communists and their satellites. Of course, communists won in the districts reserved for them, and they obtained a majority of two-thirds in the Sejm, but their victory was only on paper. Because their morale was so badly shaken by Solidarity's landslide victory in free districts, they gave up the mission of forming a government. Most of the communist parliamentarians became loyal supporters of the Mazowiecki government. Second, the most important figures of the political scene—Jaruzelski, Walesa, and Mazowiecki—did not run in the elections. The most important decisions were taken outside the parliament.[53]

It is Walesa's charisma that brought about the Mazowiecki government. When his arbitrary action encountered criticisms among Solidarity parliamentarians, he declared:

> I made the choice on behalf of you because you are not able to do it. Please do not have a grudge against me that I single-handedly succeeded in what you 260 had not succeeded in. Indeed, I played this game knowing that you are not able to do it. But can you have a grudge against me because of this?"[54]

This revealed that Walesa's authority was much stronger than that of the elected parliamentarians.

Mazowiecki became premier through Walesa's grace, but he did not become his marionette. Elections spoiled the compromise barely reached at the Round Table. Mazowiecki, however, continued the strategy of elitist compromise. He was a true child of the Round Table. He did not regard the compromise as a tactical move. He sincerely believed in it. In his inaugural speech he declared that he did not intend to dismiss any official who remained loyal to the government.[55] Aware that it would be unpopular, he undauntedly supported the austerity program of Finance Minister Balcerowicz. The Balcerowicz plan suffocated the galloping inflation in a short period. Shops were flooded with commodities, and queues disappeared. But the real income dropped by 30 percent, and industrial production by even more. Unemployment soared. Surprisingly, however, Mazowiecki was very popular in the first months of his government. In many public opinion polls his popularity was as high as 85 percent in spite of all the hardships his policy caused.

When Mazowiecki's popularity started to decline, Walesa challenged his authority. It was a charismatic-populist challenge. When Jaruzelski's position became untenable as a result of political upheavals throughout Eastern Europe, he offered to resign. The next president was to be elected in a general election. Walesa immediately made a bid for it. He regarded the compromise of the Round Table as a tactical move, and he argued that the people no longer needed to feel bound by it now that they did not have to fear the Brezhnev doctrine. In the presidential election campaign he promised everything to everybody regardless of whether he could put it into practice. He propagated a wholesale dismissal of nomenklaturist officials in order to make room for Solidarity activists. He did not hesitate to resort to anti-Semitic phraseology.

In the last phase of the election campaign, a dark horse sprang into the race, Stanislaw Tyminski. He won 23.10 percent of the vote in the first ballot. Mazowiecki received only 18.08 percent. Tyminski challenged Walesa in the final ballot. He was completely unknown in the political map of Poland. He returned home only two months before the elections after twenty years of absence. At first his career as a businessman in Canada and Peru seemed to indicate that he was a candidate of Western-oriented, liberal-democratic circles. But the opposite was true. His supporters were inhabitants of small towns, youth, women, uneducated people, employees in the commercial and service sectors, and unskilled workers. People who cherished an unconscious nostalgia for a stable social order under communism voted for Tyminski. It was no coincidence that he won more votes than did any other candidate in Katowice, the traditional stronghold of communists. During the election campaign he spoke in the affirmative of martial law in 1981–83, and he publicly opposed the reprivatization of industries and the influx of foreign capital.[56]

Another candidate with a genuine communist background, Wlodzimierz Cimoszewicz, obtained a surprisingly large share of the vote, 9.21 percent. If those who voted for Cimoszewicz favored the reformist wing of the former Communist Party, those who voted for Tyminski favored the conservative wing. In any event, together they collected one-third of the total votes cast—telling evidence of how lasting the communists' longtime efforts to legitimize their power were.

With Walesa's election as president, the charismatic-populist legitimation of authority prevailed over the paternalistic and elitist ones. The prerogatives of the president have not yet been defined. The Poles elected a president before they established the constitution. How capable of governing the new president will be is unknown. In the meantime his charismatic appeal has declined. Contrary to his prediction of receiving 80 percent, he obtained only 39.96 percent in the first ballot.

The politics of elitist compromise failed, even in Poland where its chances looked good. Incipient political parties got involved in the mass politics of the election campaign. New forces were disorganized, while forces based on the paternalism of the communist past were at work everywhere in Eastern Europe. Given such conditions, it is no surprise that free elections have not brought forth a strong government. All the governments that emerged from free elections are rather weak, unless they are underpinned by charismatic leaders like Walesa or Havel. Persons or groups that were defeated in elections freely challenge the government authority in Hungary, Romania, Bulgaria, and Serbia. The government does not have enough means to control them. Even the police do not always listen to the government. One has the impression of an authority vacuum.

This is perhaps because public life in Eastern Europe is far from being rationalized in formal legal terms. According to Max Weber, one of the indicators of rationalization of public life is modern bureaucracy. In Eastern Europe modern bureacracy was underdeveloped even before the communists came to power. It was rather retarded under communism, because the communists introduced goal-achieving bureaucracy but not rule-applying bureaucracy. Although new authorities in Eastern Europe have legitimized themselves by democratic procedures, their legitimacy is far from legal in the Weberian sense. It will take quite some time until legal legitimacy has been established in Eastern Europe.

If elected governments cannot exercise authority relying solely on democratic procedures, they must seek other sources of authority. When the communist ideology ceased to be the official doctrine, quasi-legitimacy perhaps became legitimacy. To justify their claim to power, the new rulers can refer to substitutes for legitimacy under communism as their genuine legitimating formulas. They can refer also to completely new formulas, such as formulas of traditional legitimacy. Generally speaking, while paternalism is pleaded for by old forces, economic effectiveness is promised by new ones. The argument of national or state interests is accepted by almost all forces. Nationalism is rampant everywhere, but particularly among national minorities like Slovaks, Croats, Slovenes, and Macedonians. Anti-Semitism is a semiofficial slogan of the Democratic Forum in Hungary that won the election. Many groups compete to elicit support of influential nongovernmental institutions such as the Church. All groups boast of recognition by foreign governments or statesmen as if this could legitimate their position. Influential circles try to enlist traditional authorities like ex-monarchs or governments-in-exile. Fearing disturbances, the Romanian government refused the ex-monarch entry into the country. To use the paradox of Rychard in a reversed way, the political system in Eastern Europe today seems to be both more and more legitimized and more and more destabilized.[57]

NOTES

1. Max Weber, *Wirtschaft und Gesellschaft* (Koeln/Berlin: Kiepenheuer and Witsch, 1956), vol. 1, pp. 157–88.
2. Maruyama Masao, *Seiji no sekai* (Tokyo: Ochanomizu shobo, 1952), pp. 33–42.
3. Maria Hirszowicz, *The Bureaucratic Leviathan: A Study in the Sociology of Communism* (Oxford: M. Robertson, 1980).
4. T. H. Rigby, "Political Legitimacy, Weber and Communist Mono-organizational Systems," in T. H. Rigby & Ferenc Feher, eds., *Political Legitimation in Communist States* (London: Macmillan, 1982), pp. 10–14. For the criticism of Rigby's view, see Jan Pakulski, "Legitimacy and Mass Compliance: Reflections on Max Weber and Soviet-Type Societies," *British Journal of Political Science* 16 (1986): 44–45.
5. Stanislaw Gebethner, "Legitymizacja systemu politycznego a koncepcja ladu porozumien," in Andrzej Rychard and Antoni Sulek, eds., *Legitymacja. Klasyczne teorie i polskie doswiadczenia* (Warsaw: Polskie Towarzystwo Socjologiczne, 1988), pp. 99–100. The term "compliance" seems to derive not from Gebethner but from Andrzej Rychard.
6. Rigby, "Political Legitimacy," p. 15.
7. David Bachman, "Socialist Reform, State Capacity, Legitimacy, and Civil Society: Definitions, Relations, and Chinese and Soviet Examples," unpublished papers, Princeton University, 1990, p. 10.
8. Because of the complicated election ordinance, it is difficult to ascertain how many votes various political groups obtained. The figure is based on the estimation of *Gazeta Wyborcza*, June 13, 1989.
9. For Czechoslovakia, see Jaroslaw A. Piekalkiewicz, *Public Opinion Polling in Czechoslovakia, 1968–69. Results and Analysis of Surveys Conducted During the Dubcek Era* (New York: Praeger, 1972). For Poland, see David S. Mason, *Public Opinion and Political Change in Poland, 1980–82* (Cambridge: Cambridge University Press, 1985).
10. Gebethner, "Legitymizacja systemu politycznego," pp. 108–9. For Gebethner the type of "legitimation without compliance" is an artifical construction, since it means incoherence of political attitudes, which, however, he regards as quite possible.

11. Ibid., p. 109.
12. Cited in ibid., p. 110.
13. Ibid., pp. 110–11. Although Gebethner does not give figures concerning trust for public persons, we may find them in many Polish newspapers and journals.
14. Ibid.
15. Teresa Tonanska, *Oni: Stalin's Polish Puppets* (London: Collins Harvill, 1987). Gebethner, "Legitymizacja systemu politycznego," p. 114.
16. Miroslawa Marody, "Sens zbiorowy a stabilnosc i zmiana ladu spolecznego," in Rychard and Sulek, eds., *Legitymacja*, pp. 279–87.
17. Wojciech Lamentowicz, "Kulturowe aspekty legitymizacji monocentrycznych struktur politycznych," in Rychard and Sulek, eds., *Legitymacja*, pp. 74–76.
18. Jacek Tarkowski, "Sprawnosc gospodarcza jako substytut legitymacji w Polsce powojennej," in Rychard and Sulek, eds., *Legitymacja*, pp. 251–52.
19. Ibid., p. 255.
20. Lamentowicz, "Kulturowe aspekty," p. 76. See also Wojciech Lamentowicz, "Die Legitimation der politischen Herrschaft in Polen seit 1944," *Berichte des Bundesinstituts fuer ostwissenschatliche und internationale Studien*, 1986, No. 23, Koeln, pp. 54–61.
21. Seymour Martin Lipset, *Political Man: The Social Bases of Politics* (Garden City, N.Y.: Doubleday, 1960), p. 77.
22. Thomas Baylis, *The Technical Intelligentsia and the East German Elite: Legitimacy and Social Change in Mature Communism*, cited in Tarkowski, "Sprawnosc," p. 257.
23. Tarkowski, "Sprawnosc," pp. 257–59, 263. For the substitute for legitimacy or quasi-legitimacy, see Pakulski, "Legitimacy and Mass Compliance," pp. 45–47. For the crisis of self-legitimation within the elite, see Paul G. Lewis, "Legitimation and Crisis: East European Developments in the Post-Stalin Period," in Paul G. Lewis, ed., *Eastern Europe: Political Crisis and Legitimation* (London: Croom Helm, 1984), pp. 1–41. For Hungary's case, see Bill Lomax, "Hungary: The Quest for Legitimacy," in Lewis, *Eastern Europe*, pp. 90–101.
24. Tarkowski, "Sprawnosc," p. 259. See also Ferenc Feher, "Paternalism as a Mode of Legitimation in Soviet-type Societies," in Rigby and Feher, eds., *Political Legitimation*, pp. 64–81.
25. Tarkowski, "Sprawnosc," p. 261.
26. Marody, "Sens zbiorowy," pp. 269–73.
27. Ibid., pp. 273–74.
28. Ibid., pp. 277–79.
29. Andrzej Rychard, "Komu potrzebna jest legitymizacja?" in Rychard and Sulek, eds., *Legitymizacja*, p. 305.
30. Czeslaw Mojsiewicz, "Polska racja stanu," *Sprawy Miedzynarodowe*, 1989, no. 12, pp. 29–30.
31. See Ito Takayuki, "Sengo Pōrando no gaikō seisaku," in Momose Hiroshi, ed., *Yōroppa shōkoku no kokusai seiji* (Tokyo: University of Tokyo Press, 1990) pp. 89–122.
32. Zbigniew Domaranczyk, *100 dni Mazowieckiego* (Warszawa: Andrzej Bonarski, 1990), pp. 119, 151.
33. Cited in *Asahi shimbun*, morning edition, September 12, 1989.
34. See Ito Takayuki et al., *Doitsu gendaishi* (Tokyo: Yamakawa, 1987), pp. 365–73.
35. On official anti-Semitism in postwar Poland, see Michael Checinski, *Poland, Communism, Nationalism, Anti-Semitism* (New York: Karz-Cohl, 1982).
36. Lamentowicz, "Kulturowe aspekty," pp. 88–95.
37. Rychard, "Komu potrzebna," p. 306.
38. Marody, "Sens zbiorowy," p. 279–87.
39. Ibid.
40. Ibid.
41. Ibid.
42. Ibid.
43. Ibid.
44. David S. Mason, Daniel N. Nelson, and Bohdan M. Szklarski, "Apathy and the Birth of Democracy: The Polish Struggle," 1990 (unpublished paper).

45. Jadwiga Staniszkis, "Stabilizacja bez uprawomocnienia," in Rychard and Sulek, eds., *Legitymacja*, p. 216.
46. Ibid., p. 227.
47. Rychard, "Komu potrzebna," pp. 306–14.
48. See Ito Takayuki, "Shakaishugi koku ni okeru kenryoku bunryu: Pōrando no baai," *Hikakuhō kenkyū*, no. 52, January 1991.
49. See, for instance, Jerzy Stembrowicz, "Praemisse zur Gruendung des Verfassungsgerichtshofes," *Osteuropa. Recht*, 1986, no. 1, p. 29.
50. Anna Karnicka, "Rzecznik Praw Obywatelskich. Pierwsze doswiadczenia i perspektywy organizacyjne," *Panstwo i Prawo*, 1988, no. 12, p. 37.
51. Klaus Ziemer, "Auf dem Weg zum Systemwandel in Polen. I: Politische Reformen und Reformversuche 1980 bis 1988," *Osteuropa*, 1989, no. 9, p. 795.
52. Gebethner, "Legitymizacja systemu politycznego," p. 100.
53. For the political process until the birth of the Mazowiecki government, see Ito Takayuki, *Rentai 10 nen no kiseki* in *Shakaishugi no 20 seiki*, vol. 3 (Tokyo: NHK-Publishers, 1990), pp. 69–103.
54. Domaranczyk, *100 dni*, p. 85.
55. Ibid., p. 143.
56. Jacek Mlynarski, "Tyminski, czyli tesknoty nieuswiadomione," *Zycie Warszawy*, November 27, 1990; Witold Pawlowski, "Stan Swiadomosci. Fenomen Tyminskiego: idealnie wypelnil luke," *Polityka*, December 1, 1990 (No. 48), p. 7. See also ballot results in *Rzeczpospolita*, November 27, 1990.
57. Rychard, "Komu potrzebna," pp. 306–14.

IV

LINKAGES BETWEEN FOREIGN AND DOMESTIC POLICY

10

Soviet and East European Relations

Paul G. Lewis

The failure of strategies of reform in Eastern Europe and the Soviet Union during the 1980s was primarily due to political control of the economy and persistent attachment to administrative centralism. From the point of view of Eastern Europe, much of this problem was derived from the relationship with the Soviet Union and the institutions and processes that held it in place. Economic reform, in particular, was impeded by the enforced primacy of political processes and by the suppression of market forces. It was also impeded by obstacles to greater integration with the world economy and by a paradoxical insistence on principles of national autarchy within the Council for Mutual Economic Assistance. CMEA intensified existing tendencies to underspecialization.[1] Part of the cost of this relative failure was paid by the Soviet Union, which cushioned the economic impact of the higher energy prices introduced during the 1970s.

SOVIET INFLUENCE AND THE PATTERN OF REGIONAL LINKAGE

By the mid-1980s, this moderating influence had largely disappeared, and the countries receptive to reform initiatives (Hungary and Poland) found themselves squeezed by the consequences of their ill-judged enthusiasm for Western credits. The conditions imposed by the Soviet–East European relationship seemed to have made reform projects largely unrealizable and to an increasing extent, in the presence of the negative consequences of previous initiatives, economically unattractive. Conditions for reform in Eastern Europe during the 1980s were, then, not very favorable. For much of the period, Soviet leaders showed great reluctance to implement structural change. Even the acceptance by Mikhail Gorbachev between 1987 and 1991 of the need for accelerated political change and effective democratization was not accompanied by measures to promote thorough economic reform or to stimulate market relations.

The economic and political decay within the Soviet Union in the mid-1970s was masked by its strengthened global position and the apparent weakening of U.S. international influence.[2] But the basis of this Soviet preeminence was overwhelmingly military, which had further implications for Soviet economic problems and the process of relative decline. Within Soviet–East European relations the military aspect of regional integration had been greatly strengthened since the invasion of Czechoslovakia in 1968, while the military component in communist rule was highlighted by the imposition of a state of war in Poland and the continuing role played by the military in sustaining party dominance. Such conditions were hardly conducive to reform initiatives in terms either of domestic or regional change. For much of the 1980s, there were few signs that the Soviet leadership was ready to contemplate any major reform in the tenor of Soviet–East European relations or to loosen the ties that maintained regional coordination.

Nor was it clear for much of the decade that the Soviet Union saw any great advantage in changing this situation. Writing of Soviet–East European relations in the mid-1980s, Bunce expressed the view that Eastern Europe appeared to be "that rare example of an ideal colony, eminently worthy of, and highly amenable to, imperial exploitation."[3] The advantages to the Soviet Union of the postwar settlement in Eastern Europe had indeed been considerable. The primary gain was probably that of a buffer zone to minimize the geographical vulnerability of Russia. The need for such a zone had been drastically demonstrated in both world wars. The postwar settlement offered the prospect of regional stabilization and the establishment of allied socialist regimes that would help seal the Soviet border from Western influences and weaken the threat of cultural and ideological competition. They could also be a source of alternative conceptions and innovative ideas about the construction of socialism, while the acquisition of socialist allies amongst relatively developed European neighbors also reinforced the legitimacy of Soviet-style socialism.[4]

From this view of Soviet interests, Eastern Europe appeared to be an ideal colony—in Bunce's words: "easy to control, cheap to administer, and highly valuable in economic and geopolitical terms." Within a matter of years, however, this comfortable relationship had come to an end, its value to the Soviet Union apparently much diminished, its demise hastened by Gorbachev's dissatisfaction with the costs of excessive stability, and its fate sealed by his determination to set Soviet international relations on a radically different course. For the great majority of the postwar years, though, Soviet interests were clearly predominant in Eastern Europe, even if on occasion their achievement met with temporary resistance. These interests found clear institutional expression in the leading organizations of the region. Beginning in 1949 economic integration within the Soviet bloc was effected through the Council for Mutual Economic Assistance, an organization primarily composed of the Soviet Union and its six major European Allies, although Vietnam, Cuba, and Mongolia later became members.

CMEA developed in line with key Soviet preferences: an affinity for central planning, the ambition to behave as a superpower, and resolution to maintain a strong defense system.[5] The bargaining process with East European allies secured for the Soviet Union their allegiance expressed in terms of domestic stability and a range of economic, ideological, political, military, and other strategic benefits. The Soviets may have been able to use other means to extract some of these benefits, but they often chose to accept subsidization within the CMEA framework. Integration and supranational economic coordination were never strong points of CMEA. After the invasion of Czechoslovakia, steps were taken to strengthen coordination, but little effective change occurred. For one thing, growing economic problems meant that demands for reform had to be taken seriously, and the decentralization and marketization this implied did not accord with moves toward greater integration.[6]

Associated with this trend was the growth in East-West trade. In the medium term this, too, brought little improvement to the East European economies. By the mid-1980s change was clearly well overdue: Implicit subsidies appeared to be increasingly in evidence, the policy-making apparatus was becoming less effective, and growth rates in most CMEA countries were in decline. The other main formal institution of Soviet–East European integration was the Warsaw Treaty Organization, the military arm of international coordination made up of the Soviet Union and its six European allies. Founded in 1955, when the Federal Republic of Germany was admitted to NATO, it developed steadily and evolved more complex and effective agencies of integration. The date for its renewal fell only a few months after Gorbachev's accession to the Soviet leadership. Despite some reluctance by East European members, renewal and a strong commitment to mutual military coordination was achieved by Gorbachev.[7]

The military links of the Soviet Union with its allies and military control over the East European region were by no means exercised exclusively within the Warsaw Treaty Organization, as might be deduced from the date of its founding. There were originally the forces of direct military occupation. Bilateral military agreements between the

Soviet Union and individual allies were also important. Military influence over national economic and political developments and within CMEA organizations was strong from the early years.[8] Warsaw Pact advisers supplemented agents of Soviet military intelligence (GRU) who had long played a significant role in Eastern Europe. The role of Soviet state security (KGB) agents was, of course, not negligible either, and their influence was exercised in close association with the activities of East European party officials. The significance of the WTO was as much political as military, and it remained in military terms a largely paper organization until the 1960s.[9]

It was only with the Czechoslovak crisis of 1968 and the military means chosen to force a solution that the principles that underlay the original agreement took on a more developed organizational form.[10] One legacy of the invasion was the permanent garrisoning of Soviet armed forces in Czechoslovakia. In terms of supranational organization, WTO integration reached its highest level in the 1970s, and toward the end of that decade the Pact armies increasingly came under direct Soviet military control.[11] The political role played by the military in Poland during 1981 and in subsequent years indicates the more general profile the armed forces had developed in the region. The degree of Soviet control over the East European military meant that Kremlin preferences could be implemented without involving direct Soviet intervention. Military solutions to security problems within Eastern Europe became more prominent, and the question of Soviet control in that region, it was argued, became increasingly a matter of military integration.[12]

The military organization occupied a critical position in the maintenance of East European stability. From a Soviet viewpoint the independent East European national military forces were "inherently unreliable" and the essential purpose of the WTO structure, concluded Jones, was to "fragment national command over national armed forces."[13] The level to which the WTO evolved and the growing centrality of its role for the Soviet Union in Eastern Europe help explain Gorbachev's resolve to expedite the extension of the treaty in 1985. Rather than seeking to restructure the alliance, Gorbachev appeared at that stage to identify it as a model for interbloc relations and a secure basis on which to develop "new thinking."[14] The third main mechanism of Soviet–East European integration was that of interparty coordination and political cooperation between ruling party bodies and their key personnel. The dominant underlying principles were socialist internationalism, democratic centralism, and the leading role of the Communist Party.

The principles were operationalized through three central mechanisms that ensured parallelism between party and government bureaucracies, maintained the centralized *nomenklatura* system of appointments, and placed party committees in all social groups of any significance. As will be readily apparent, the three dimensions of Soviet–East European integration were closely connected. Socialist internationalism, for example, was far from being restricted to the arena of ideology or party activity, and in particular crisis situations it was sustained by military action. Both democratic centralism and the party's leading role were maintained and reinforced by the Jaruzelski coup in 1981 in Poland. Gorbachev's emphasis at the Twenty-Seventh Party Congress on the need for an overhaul of the mechanisms of CMEA integration reflected a reappraisal of implications of socialist internationalism under the conditions of contemporary economic life. Personal links were also important and reinforced the institutional mechanisms.

The initial contribution of Eastern Europe to the USSR was to help the imperial center achieve its central objectives of economic growth, national security, and domestic support and stability. According to some views, however, the value of this contribution rapidly went into a marked decline. To assess this claim it is first necessary to specify precisely how disadvantageous regional relations were for the Soviet Union and the extent to which Eastern Europe became a liability. During 1987–88, as Gorbachev's *perestroika* initiative accelerated (particularly in the Soviet Union itself), political conflict intensified in Hungary and Poland, although not to the levels reached in the Baltic, Transcaucasian, and Central Asian republics of the Soviet Union. Nevertheless, political instability increased in the countries of Eastern Europe most closely associated with reform initiatives.

The enforced departure of Janos Kadar from the Hungarian leadership, a figure long identified as the leading East European force in reform policy innovation, and the resignation of Polish Prime Minister Zbigniew Messner, in the wake of extensive strike action and the apparent resurgence of Solidarity as a national political force, were signs of this. Soviet ability to control the East European nomenklatura seemed to have declined; by 1985, it appeared, the erosion of Soviet authority in Eastern Europe had become a source of conflict and, perhaps, of helplessness in Moscow itself.[15] These could well be judged negative developments from the Soviet point of view, although the achievement of a new international status had come to be seen as a firmer guarantee of Soviet security than the preservation of the territorial *cordon sanitaire*. It was more the economic costs of the regional commitment that attracted Soviet attention in later years.

Different views were expressed about the benefits derived from Soviet–East European economic relations. In the absence of market prices or relatively unambiguous statistical indicators, it is far from easy to reach a conclusive judgment about the direction of economic benefits.

Nevertheless, talk of the empire "striking back" in economic terms and raising its costs to unassimilable levels was probably exaggerated. Much of the cost was not a direct one but a matter of relative advantage conditioned by the fact that Soviet exports (particularly raw materials and energy resources) were increasingly attractive on the world market. The economic burden of the East European connection may have been rather different from the opportunity costs that were incurred from commitment to a particular political and strategic situation.[16] Other accounts presented a different picture. Zimmerman suggested that "the issue of who was exploiting whom in Soviet–East European relations from 1956 to 1973 was at least an open question."[17] But after the OPEC price increases the situation changed significantly. The terms of trade shifted in favor of the Soviet Union, and its improved bargaining position allowed it to insist on better quality products from its East European suppliers.

Although Soviet oil prices for East European customers reached new peaks in the early 1980s, the double economic bind of the late 1970s on the East Europeans "had grown considerably more acute a decade later."[18] Account should be taken of the substantial deterioration during the first half of the 1980s in the terms of trade of the East European countries with the Soviet Union and the decline in real terms of Soviet exports to the region. At the same time the volume of Soviet imports from Eastern Europe in 1985 was 30 percent above the 1980 level. This casts a particular light on the Soviet trade surpluses with Eastern Europe in the 1981–85 period and the decline in those surpluses as the terms of trade began to be less favorable to Eastern Europe. Eastern Europe was less of an economic burden to the Soviet Union, concluded Marer and Poznanski, "than conventional wisdom in the West asserts. . . . [I]n fact, by the mid-1980s Soviet subsidization has ended."[19]

Another sharp decline in Soviet subsidies was reported following Gorbachev's accession to power in 1985.[20] The claim that the empire struck back in terms of costs and benefits must be viewed with considerable scepticism. The costs of empire to the Soviet Union declined overall after 1981. The weight of the East European component in those costs also was reduced as a separate item.[21] In rational choice terms, Bunce later concluded, the Soviet Union still gained from its position of regional hegemony.[22] This is not to say that the outcome of CMEA economic activity was satisfactory to the Soviet Union but rather that the disappointing economic outcome could not be solely attributed to Soviet–East European relations. The framework into which all communist economies were locked blocked the path of development by impeding processes of reform. As the problems of weak economic growth seemed to stem from the structures and systems common to all European communist systems, the shift in Soviet–East European economic relations placed the question of reform even more strongly on the East European policy agenda. The international context, however, provided them with less favorable conditions under which reform policies could be formulated and pursued.

THE IMPERIAL CONCEPT IN
SOVIET–EAST EUROPEAN RELATIONS

For the Soviet Union it was far less the military or economic costs involved in maintaining East European stability that imposed a burden on the system than the problems arising from global competition with the United States and the drive to maintain military and technological prestige on the supraregional level. While the economic drain on the Soviet Union deriving from its East European commitment was the subject of some debate, it was certainly not the more independent or unruly members of the East European alliance who caused the Soviets to disburse the most funds. Romania and Poland received less from CMEA exchanges than did other allies. Perhaps their problems provided an excuse for the Soviet Union to cut back support.[23] The problem, in any case, cannot be reduced to that of the costs of empire but also must involve consideration of the kind of system that the imperial connection created in Eastern Europe and its implications for socialist development.

The influence of the postwar Soviet state in Eastern Europe was soon understood to be exercised within an imperial framework. Following World War II, Stalin's territorial acquisitions in Eastern Europe quickly became referred to as satellites—an appropriate description for nation-states held in a strong gravitational pull by the continental power. Their social, political, and economic trajectories were fully determined by the central force.[24] The intensity of this control declined after the dictator's death in 1953, and a distinct wobbliness could be identified by 1956 in the political course of Poland and Hungary. The "Moscow-ruled satellite empire," in Korbonski's conception, "gave way in the late 1950s to a socialist commonwealth of nations."[25] By the 1960s it was possible to delineate a full pattern of "de-satellitization, de-Stalinization, and ideological nationalization" and to write of the transformation of "satellites into junior allies."[26]

Around the same time, Ionescu was discussing a similar process in terms of the breakup of the Soviet empire in Eastern Europe.[27] But developments in Czechoslovakia during 1968 and the Brezhnev doctrine put an end to the speculative extremes of this kind of reasoning. The East European satellites might well have evolved into junior allies, but they remained resolutely subordinate to the Soviet Union; the Soviet empire in Eastern Europe was certainly not going to be allowed to break up. The tension between the conceptions of Eastern Europe as a socialist commonwealth and imperial possession persisted in the minds of Soviet leaders.[28] This, however, is not to say that Soviet–East European relations did not change between the invasion of Czechoslovakia and the rise of Gorbachev. It was during this period, according to Bunce, that the empire "struck back" and became more of a burden to the Soviet Union.

Seventeen years after the invasion of Czechoslovakia, Gati asked whether the end of the Soviet empire was finally in prospect.[29] The persistence of strong Soviet–East European links, moreover, served neither to accelerate integrated growth patterns nor to facilitate the national economic development of individual CMEA members. Efforts to convert colonial empires into commonwealths failed, Krasner noted: "The Soviet effort to base relations in Eastern Europe on transnational functional agencies rather than state-to-state agreements has eroded over time."[30] Indeed, state and associated national interests were becoming more prominent in Eastern Europe. National diversity, increasingly expressed through the agency of the state, became a major feature of the East European scene in the 1980s.

Contributing to this process were factors like the persistence of autonomous social movements in Poland despite conditions of military rule, the looming breakdown of the moderate reformist consensus in Hungary, and the resurgence in Czechoslovakia of the national aspirations associated with the Prague Spring. But the issue was not a straightforward one. By the end of the 1970s, in Hough's view, Eastern Europe had begun to pose for the Soviet Union the fundamental problem of the maintenance of empire which, for Brezhnev and his close colleagues, was "undoubtedly the only issue." To support this situation, however, they also developed the somewhat paradoxical view that regional stability depended on the identification of the East European regimes with forms of local nationalism. This required some kind of independence from—"and even defiance of—the Soviet Union."[31] As Kuhns also concluded, the nature of East European nationalism could perhaps "help the Soviet leaders contain and control its effects before it gets entirely out of hand."[32]

Aspects of growing social autonomy and national tradition were incorporated within the Soviet imperial project in the attempt to counter its increasingly evident weaknesses. It was a process accompanying the intensification of Soviet and East European economic problems that could be seen to mitigate the otherwise stagnant political vision of the late Brezhnev period. The continuing presence of the imperial relationship, combined with the return to prominence of the state and growing social autonomy in Eastern Europe, suggests a need to sharpen the focus of attention on the Soviet–East European relationship. Differences between traditional empires and modern states in terms of economic capacity and strategy recall the distinctive characteristics of the contending postwar social systems—of East and West, the Soviet bloc, and contemporary capitalism.

Dominant principles of economic organization and development have been critical here: "The modern state, in contrast to premodern empires, tends toward intensive rather than extensive development. . . . [T]he economic function of the premodern state was primarily to facilitate exploitation of the masses by the elite and to protect society from being exploited by foreign conquerors."[33] It is, indeed, precisely the problems experienced by the Soviet economy in attempting to shift from an extensive mode of development (a crash industrialization program, the large-scale shift of resources from the rural to the urban economy, the favoring of heavy industry over consumer sectors) to an intensive path (technological innovation, qualitative rather than quantitative development, changing relative levels of capital and labor input) that underlay the terminal problems of the Soviet Union and critically influenced its relations with Eastern Europe.

In general, the Soviet imperial role can be seen as a factor legitimating backwardness; it served to enhance Soviet grandeur and its role as a systemic model, helping to dispel thoughts of alternative paths of development and consideration of modifying existing patterns of activity. The role of Eastern Europe could be understood to serve as a stimulus to the adoption of more conservative ideas in the Soviet Union, encouraging the dominant power to block rather than tolerate innovation and reform in Eastern Europe.[34] In a certain sense, it was the weakness of the communist state as much as the dominance of state structures that provided the greatest barrier to effective development.[35] The determinants of the outcomes of the different economic reform initiatives in Eastern Europe have been, it is argued, essentially political. What even the Hungarian example shows above all, in one view, is the political inability of communist systems to cope with even relatively simple crises.[36]

Much of this was later explicitly recognized in Soviet sources: "The old forms of cooperation took shape when there was a tendency to maintain the pace of development of 'extensive' methods' . . . By the late 1960s, however, many of these resources had been exhausted. But the task of all-round intensification had not yet been formulated." The Twenty-Seventh Party Congress had seen "frank admissions of . . . mistakes and failures in political and practical work."[37] The backwardness of the Soviet economy in combination with the rigidly enforced dominance of the development model it evolved had a particularly pernicious influence on the more developed East European economies as well as on intrabloc relations more generally: "Hegemony without efficiency tends to move towards imperial-type economies, as is the case in the Soviet bloc."[38] The dynamic of economic development has been muted and the intensification of productive processes seen to be restrained as the fact of empire militates "against the full impact of capitalism."[39]

In terms of the Soviet empire, an analogous process could be perceived in the consequences of Soviet influence as it militated particularly against development of the more advanced East European economies. A distinction has been made between Roman and English (or Greek) forms of empire. The first involves control over economies as advanced or more advanced than its own. It is the Roman model that "more aptly characterizes the Soviet role in Eastern Europe."[40] Apart from its economic position, this relationship involved psychological and cultural perceptions of the status of the Soviet Union relative to the more advanced nations of Eastern Europe, which had various effects on the psychology of the Soviet elite. A further comparison, this time with the role of the United States in Latin America, also suggests the critical role Eastern Europe performed for the Soviet Union.

The entire Latin American GNP was about one-quarter that of the Unites States, while that of Eastern Europe was calculated to be over half that of the Soviet Union. Twelve percent of U.S. foreign trade was with its Latin American hinterland, while 46 percent of that of the Soviet Union was within the European communist bloc in 1983.[41] The similarities of the Soviet Union and the United States with respect to neighboring subordinate states thus masked major differences in terms of underlying economic relations and relative socioeconomic status. Furthermore, the overall performance of the East European economies since 1960 was not much lower than that of the United States or the EEC countries. All lagged far behind the performance of Japan (see Table 10-1). Within the CMEA group, it was the less developed countries, including the Soviet Union, that achieved higher growth rates. Those already better off showed distinctly less impressive results.

This particularly concerned Czechoslovakia, which did not reap the same benefits as the GDR from the West German *Ostpolitik* and did not have the same preferential access to EEC economic benefits. From this point of view, the costs of empire should be calculated, not just from the hegemonic power, but also from that of the advanced colony. Trade

Table 10-1
ESTIMATED REAL GNP (BILLION US$)

Country	1960	1984	Increase from 1960 to 1984	Per capita GNP (1984)
Japan	237.9	1,233.5	418%	10.3 thousand
United States	1,647.2	3,662.8	122	15.5
EEC Countries	1,030	2,200	114	8.7
Eastern Europe	363	771	112	6.9
Romania	39.4	117.6	198	5.2
Bulgaria	22.7	56.4	148	8.3
Poland	104.8	228.5	118	6.3
Hungary	40.2	77	92	7.2
GDR	85.8	163.7	91	9.8
Czechoslovakia	69.9	127.9	83	8.3
USSR	821.7	1,957.6	138	7.1

Source: K. Dawisha, *Eastern Europe, Gorbachev, and Reform* (Cambridge: Cambridge University Press, 1988), pp. 138–39.

patterns, for example, froze the region "into an excessively energy- and raw material-intensive production structure."[42] The more general points about the economic impact of the imperial relationship find some support from these results. The historical failure of empires to secure the conditions for growth has been closely associated in some conceptions with factors underlying the cycle of their rise and decline. The rising burden of military obligations and the high cost of military deployment placed a critical burden on the capacity to increase the economic surplus from imperial territories: Under these conditions "the empire either fragmented or was forced to reduce its territorial control and financial burdens."[43]

In the likely event that this was not possible, the decline of empire followed, and an alternative cycle of imperial development could begin. Not just the cost of warfare determined the conditions of imperial survival. But this cost often played an important part in the rising public expenditures that have proved to be a critical factor in the decline of empires. Military spending in the Soviet Union clearly burdened its economic capacity and resources, although it was by no means the imperial commitment in terms of its East Europe vassals that played the largest part here. A major problem was posed by the Soviet attempt to maintain its imperial claim over the East European territories by relatively traditional means as well as trying to meet the demands of global superpower competition which involved different levels of technology and strategic approach.

Table 10-2
U.S. AND SOVIET DEFENSE EXPENDITURES, 1955–1985
(MILLIONS OF US$)

	1955	*1960*	*1965*	*1970*	*1975*	*1980*	*1985*
U.S. (1976 prices)	98.3	100.0	107.2	130.9	110.2		
U.S. (1980 prices)					139.3	144.0	204.9
USSR (1976 prices)	51.2	48.0	65.2	92.5	99.8		
USSR (1980 prices)					122.4	131.8	146.2
USSR as a percent of U.S. (1976 prices)	52%	48%	61%	71%	91%		
USSR as a percent of U.S. (1980 prices)					88%	92%	71%

Sources: *SIPRI Yearbooks* (London: Taylor and Francis, 1980 and 1985); *SIPRI Yearbook* (New York: Oxford University Press, 1986).
Note: Figures for 1976 and 1980 prices differ because assumptions on base costs are periodically changed.

Soviet GNP was about half that of the United States much of the postwar period; expenditure by both superpowers on defense and the military sector was not always greatly different. The difference between the levels of expenditure narrowed in the 1970s, contributing significantly to Gorbachev's problematic inheritance. In view of the difference in their economic base, the burden of military expenditure in the Soviet Union was considerably heavier than in the United States. Relatively modest direct contributions were made by the other members of the Warsaw Pact, whose military expenditure probably declined from 6.1 percent of GNP in the mid-1960s to 5.9 percent in the early 1980s.[44] Nevertheless, it was proposed in this respect that "the 'workers' states of the Soviet bloc appeared to have an advantage over the capitalist economies in that they can suppress the consumption of the masses in favor of defense and military-related investments."[45] Developments in the Soviet Union and the performance of its imperial role suggest, however, that there was not enough give in the consumer sector to underwrite the continuing growth of military production, that it did impose an increasingly significant burden, and that a policy of concerted modernization and reform was needed to satisfy contemporary demands.

DEVELOPMENTS IN THE SOVIET IMPERIAL PERSPECTIVE UNDER GORBACHEV

It is inaccurate to assume that the Soviet bloc was "just another empire."[46] It is certainly unhelpful in terms of understanding and responding in practical terms to the Soviet self-image. The form of its political influence added credibility to the idea of the Soviet empire as a socialist family of nations, the relations being not dissimilar to those in a traditional extended family led by a patriarchal figure.[47] This was a view in accordance with Mlynar's picture of Brezhnev's demeanor directly following the 1968 invasion of Czechoslovakia. The Soviet leader appeared to believe "it was entirely natural and proper that his position as head of the family entitled him to the unconditional subservience and obedience of all its members."[48] Personal ties, trust, and loyalty played a large part in maintaining the Soviet–East European relationship and "Sasha" (Alexander Dubcek), it was claimed, had let down the Russian patriarch by not keeping him informed of his intentions and ignoring specific advice offered by Brezhnev.

In political terms this quality was also reflected in the Soviet practice of appointing CPSU *obkom* (provincial) secretaries to head East European embassies. This did not, as Frank suggested, confirm the adage that foreign policy is an extension of domestic policy. The Soviets perceived the East European countries to be, not within the sphere of foreign policy, but within that of domestic relations, or at least of the extended household.[49] This understanding of the socialist community sheds light on the ideological underpinnings of the Soviet empire in Eastern Europe and on the ways in which the Soviets were able to avoid identifying the imperial nature of their influence. It also implied the exercise of strong Soviet control and of political links that went way beyond the relations characteristic of a more conventional sphere of influence. Accompanying this view, as Gati has suggested with striking relevance to the developments of 1989–91, was the conviction of Soviet leaders that control over Eastern Europe had become synonymous with control over the Soviet Union itself.[50]

Such conceptions continued to influence the evolution of Soviet–East European relations in the 1980s and conditioned Gorbachev's shifting view of the region's proper role. The "single most important factor" here was the close linkage between Soviet domestic politics and Moscow's relations with the East European allies.[51] An early priority was to harness the region's underused potential to further Soviet restructuring. In a generally positive report to the Twenty-Seventh Party Congress, Gorbachev called for major changes in the work of the "very headquarters of socialist integration—the Council for Mutual Economic Assistance."[52] According to Gorbachev's analysis, much of the future "prestige of socialism" depended on qualitative improvement in economic performance and in the mediocre levels of achievement of former years. Crucial assistance was needed from more developed European allies.

It was noted in 1987 that CMEA production potential would need to double by the year 2000 and reach an annual growth rate of 4 to 5 percent, some 50 percent more than had been achieved in recent years.[53] An important part in this was to be played by the Comprehensive Program for Scientific and Technological Progress for CMEA member countries (COMPSTEP) and "special demands on the CMEA integration effort."[54] "Immense efforts" would be required, in Gorbachev's words, to achieve this. It promised to enhance Soviet economic control through fundamental transformation of Soviet–East European relations and represented a critical step toward a pattern of complex integration contrasting strongly with the Stalinist approach, which entailed the reproduction of the Moscow model in its satellites rather than effective regional integration. But the underlying principles of Soviet–East European relations remained ambiguous for some time. In 1987 there was still a significant lack of clarity in Gorbachev's approach to Eastern Europe.

On the one hand, the new Soviet leader "seemed to favor some degree of economic and even political reform; on the other hand he was obviously at pains to strengthen 'coordination' (read Soviet control) in CMEA, the Warsaw Pact, and the affairs of the alliance generally."[55] Some light had been shed on intrabloc relations early in Gorbachev's leadership. A debate about the limits of "socialist internationalism" and the inviolability of the sovereignty of socialist states took place in the Soviet press in the period preceding the Twenty-Seventh Party Congress in early 1986. No resolution of the issue had been reached by the time the Congress opened and, while Gorbachev's speech appeared to promise quite radical change, a more circumspect discussion appeared in the new CPSU program approved by the Congress. Informal leadership contacts were reportedly used to assure East European elites in November 1986 that new principles of national independence were indeed in operation.

This, however, required the proof of experience to be fully convincing and was in any case by no means a source of comfort for incumbent leaders who had previously relied on the threat of Soviet intervention to retain control over national populations.[56] The extent and nature of the changes in regional relations remained a matter of some uncertainty and concern. The program of regional economic development promised a further weakening of the national authorities in the individual East European states. The COMPSTEP initiative, it was hoped, would reinvigorate CMEA production levels through technological innovation, target particular areas within the East European economies, and encourage direct dealings between research and development centers.

Cooperative production agreements and joint ventures between enterprises throughout the CMEA area were part of Gorbachev's favored path of economic development as a means of preserving and enhancing the prestige of socialism.

Regional agreements promised to bypass national elites and produce more complex forms of integration between the Soviet and East European economies. Polish scholar Jadwiga Staniszkis saw a "third stage of dependency" in regional relations beginning in 1981 prior to these developments and a Soviet Union that "consciously took advantage" of the anarchy and national weakness that had developed during the 1970s.[57] This development, moreover, enabled it to reassert the kind of pressure it had used in the 1950s and to strengthen the influence it exercised through East European political elites. The elites at issue, however, were not necessarily in the party-state leadership but those heading specialized sectors and representing subnational groups. In Poland, therefore, an "isolation of the political centre could be observed," and the progression of dependency took place outside the influence of the Jaruzelski leadership. Any greater moves toward state sovereignty in Eastern Europe were therefore initially envisaged as only temporary and something of a hollow shell as more effective forms of economic integration were developed.

To the extent that the Soviet Union maintained a commitment to socialist internationalism in anything like its traditional form and the essentials of the imperial relationship were not eroded, heightened integration spelled intensified dependency relations for the East European nations. Recognition of the implications of such views of Soviet–East European relations was well entrenched before the advent of Gorbachev to the leadership. The first summit of CMEA members for thirteen years was held in 1984, and disagreement between the Soviets and East European participants was clearly evident at that stage. Representatives of the GDR and Czechoslovakia, conservatives on reform issues, were at one with more reform-minded Hungary in the reluctance they showed toward the Soviet promotion of joint enterprises and the use of energy price formulas. East European governments commonly favored the increased marketization of intra-CMEA links. The trend of developments, indeed, seemed to favor the enhancement of national independence.

In his speech on the seventieth anniversary of the Russian Revolution, Gorbachev endorsed the independence of the national Communist parties, and on a visit to Belgrade in March 1988 he emphasized the importance of "the organic blend of the independence of every party and state and a respect for one another's interests."[58] But it was by no means clear whether the principle of noninterference had general applicability throughout the Warsaw Pact.[59] On a visit to Yugoslavia in 1955, Nikita Khrushchev had expressed similar sentiments, which clearly did not rule out the decision to invade Hungary the following year. In the Central Committee theses published prior to the special Conference of the Communist Party of the Soviet Union in June 1988, the issue was presented in the following terms: "In the priority area of relations with the socialist countries . . . we have linked the principles of equality, independence and non-interference with objective reality—the diversity of national forms of socialist society. Our internationalist links are built on the basis of mutual benefit, a balance of interests and common responsibility for the fate and prestige of socialism."[60]

A general orientation toward reform and reevaluation of international relations was on the agenda, but the nature of that reform and the parameters of equality and independence for the East European states were uncertain. The precise implications of the common responsibility for the fate and prestige of socialism were also unknown. In the event, it would seem that it was in the spring of 1988 that Gorbachev's approach to the East European situation really began to change.[61] While some reports of Gorbachev's statements during his visit to Warsaw in July 1988 appeared to assume a repudiation of the Brezhnev doctrine, others suggested a greater measure of reserve and continuing priority of the emphasis on the need to maintain the unity of the Eastern military alliance.[62] Vadim Medvedev, who had been in charge of East European relations from within the Central Committee Secretariat and who received promotion to full Politburo membership in September 1988, was reported to have endorsed the full sovereignty of the East European states and to have equated it with the sovereignty recognized in relation to Western nations.[63]

But this, too, was not necessarily as significant as it sounded. Lynch quotes Soviet sources from the 1970s: "Respect of state sovereignty, of all sovereign rights of the socialist state, is assumed as the very content of the principle of socialist internationalism."[64] While Gorbachev's views were very different from those that held sway during the Brezhnev period, the issue of sovereignty with respect to the East European states retained a significant measure of uncertainty, and it was not until June 1989 that noninterference was officially incorporated into Soviet policy.[65] Gorbachev's unwillingness to press hard and consistently on the question of reform in the East European states paralleled his hesitancy with regard to the public statement of socialist sovereignty. Ambiguity on the part of the Soviet leadership conditioned the response of East European leaders to Gorbachev's initiatives and was reflected in the contrasting stances they adopted in the face of a range of pressing social, political, and economic problems.

In the northern tier of East European states, the leaders of the German Democratic Republic and Czechoslovakia showed great caution in their response to perestroika and glasnost. Together they resisted aspects of the new Soviet policies. Poles and Hungarians, on the other hand, were more receptive to Soviet initiatives in keeping with their greater public commitment to economic and political reform. More widespread was the dissatisfaction that developed as the CMEA reinvigoration program failed to take off, and it became clear that its ambitious goals could not be transformed into a workable program. Sharp criticism was voiced not only by Hungarian Rezso Nyers but also by Czech Prime Minister Ladislav Adamec, who complained of CMEA's obsolescence.[66] Soviet reluctance to define the parameters of East European autonomy and to make a full break with Stalinist traditions meant that perestroika was able to operate only as a general impetus for change rather than as a concrete model of economic development.

The Soviet reform plan itself was contradictory and incomplete, comprised of a bundle of heterogeneous elements.[67] The established practice of Soviet hegemony thus continued to exert a pernicious influence on East European developments. The relationship that underlay the regional reform process was a symbiotic one, and this encouraged neither the formulation of a clear model for reform, nor the drawing up of a timetable for implementation. In 1987 Gorbachev expressed the hope that Eastern Europe would emulate Soviet reform plans, which in turn, were largely based on the experience of its allies. Indeed, much of the Soviet reform effort had been tried out (and sometimes criticized by Moscow) in East European countries.[68] To the extent that it is possible to generalize about economic reform and its lack of success, it would seem that the patchwork approach to policy formulation is one of the best guarantees of failure.

The attempt to retrace the steps taken by one or more East European countries produced an approach that has been described as "fruitless and ineffective in the USSR."[69] The relevance of a reform experience like that of Hungary, for example, should not be mistaken as an argument for transferability. Differences of scale mask social contrasts and cultural differences. A strong central authority is required in a sprawling territory like that of the Soviet Union; in Hungary an informal network can bear much of the burden of system integration.[70] In general, Gorbachev's approach to economic reform and the development of market forces was less adventurous than it was in domestic politics or East-West relations.

In the domestic arena he initially favored pursuing Yuri Andropov's policy of strengthening central control to firm up sluggish economic processes and counteract lax social discipline. But problems soon prompted him to adopt a more radical position. A different political emphasis emerged in early 1987 at the January Central Committee Plenum, followed some months later by the formulation of an economic reform policy. The positions Gorbachev took up in the sphere of international relations (particularly with regard to the developed Western powers) largely followed the path marked out by the evolving domestic perestroika policy. Disarmament initiatives with regard to the United States, planned withdrawal from Afghanistan, and reappraisal of the Soviet role in world affairs suggested a reduced emphasis on the exercise of power and military weight of the Soviet state.

The record of the Gorbachev administration in relation to its immediate European neighbors was more ambiguous. While showing no sign of having entered the leading position with a clearly developed policy for the East European area and apparently sharing the ambivalence of former Soviet leaders to their imperial possessions, Gorbachev was quick to formulate an approach similar to that he was taking toward the domestic Soviet situation. As in the domestic sphere, the brisk managerial style initially adopted produced very few early results, and by the end of 1986 Gorbachev had reappraised his position. Unlike his judgment on the internal Soviet situation, however, he appeared to conclude that the difficulties and dangers involved in promoting a vigorous implementation of reform principles and forcing through a more radical perestroika of the allies' bureaucracies were too great to merit the attempt and East European developments were dogged by uncertainty and ambiguities. When the great change occurred in Eastern Europe, then, it came as a considerable shock and in a situation in some countries of advanced economic and social crisis.

ECONOMIC REFORM AND STRATEGIES OF CHANGE

Reform was obstructed by the structures imposed by the close Soviet–East European relationship and made more difficult to implement by the conditions under which regional relations developed, particularly the stronger role played by military organization within them. Toward the end of the 1970s the realignment of regional economic and trade patterns made reform somewhat less imperative for the Soviet Union. In the context of the economic slowdown of the 1980s, then, reform was by no means the evident or immediately available solution to the increasingly serious problems that emerged.

The imperial aspect of the Soviet–East European relationship further diminished the prospects of reform. It was by no means the direct costs of domination or the growing military burden on the Soviet Union from this source, both features characteristic of the classic imperial cycle of expansion and decline, that played the critical role in strengthening any tendencies in this direction in the Soviet Union. Nevertheless, the need for radical change was perceived by Gorbachev. His initial response was to raise the productivity of regional economic processes by enhancing Soviet control rather than by embracing meaningful Soviet–East European relations. Although Gorbachev's rhetoric and diplomatic performance seemed to promise substantial change in this area, only limited reform measures were introduced and these were less than fully put into practice.

The ambiguities apparent in his major domestic initiatives—the apparently sincere desire to combine democracy with the continuing role of the Soviet Communist Party, the promotion of the idea of economic reform without relinquishing the major principles of administrative centralism—were in this area compounded by the largely unacknowledged imperialist practices that sustained the socialist commonwealth. Furthermore, the lengthy Soviet domination of Eastern Europe meant that international and domestic obstacles to reform were often inseparable. The restrictive influence of CMEA on the opportunities for foreign trade open to Hungary, the most successful example of reform in communist Eastern Europe, seemed to be important but was far from being the whole story.

Some of the critical impediments, it has been argued, were internal and not imposed by international arrangements.[71] The Hungarian New Economic Mechanism, for example, could be defined as a plan for all seasons: Passages on decentralization were accompanied by provisos for a return to decentralization or even its preservation.[72] Its synthesis of economic decentralization with centralized political power and its attempt to increase entrepreneurial activity by administrative means were obvious contradictions.[73] While not strictly derived from the operation of international relations, these characteristics were closely linked with the dominance of the Soviet model and the postwar institutionalization of Soviet power on a regional scale. These were not the only international influences.

IMF influence (by no means negligible in the 1980s when Hungary was deeply immersed in debt problems) did reinforce the impetus toward reform, but it also prompted greater resistance by raising the level of Soviet vigilance and ringing alarm bells in that quarter because of the linkage of reform with the operations of world capitalism. Other weaknesses of reform programs were that they were generally adopted in situations of crisis and adversity that did not provide appropriate conditions or time-scales necessary for their implementation. The programs were rarely given the chance to prove themselves, therefore.[74] The framework for reform was always difficult to install, and reform measures were relatively easy to cut back on.

"Natural" economic responses that made sense in terms of reform turbulence and existing structures were always at hand but fatal to the further pursuit of reform. Both in Hungary and Poland recentralization was an understandable response to inflation, indebtedness, shortages, uncontrolled investment, and poor liquidity. But they did not help the course of further reform.

As communist and postcommunist regimes faced the challenge of more concerted change and economic reconstruction, questions of consistency and leaders' decisiveness played no less a role. But the temptation not to adopt programs of radical change also remained strong. Gorbachev's actions during 1990 provide a good illustration of this. A critical dimension was the linkage of economic reform and decentralization with the territorial and political integrity of the Soviet Union. Because of the progressive disintegration of the Soviet economy, the leadership had a pressing need to take effective remedial action and adopt a program of thoroughgoing reform. A political climate for the introduction of initial reform measures had been prepared during the preceding years and necessary legislation had passed, but little practical implementation or effective reform of economic processes was in evidence.

The economic condition of East European allies was instructive during this period. Developments in the Polish economy toward the end of the decade showed the effects of the deepening crisis of the 1980s and the consequences of the unsolved problems carried over from Poland's problematic entry into the currents of world finance in the 1970s. The situation that came to a critical head in 1988 and 1989 required the installation of a noncommunist government to take the stringent measures that carried some hope of stabilizing the economy and creating the conditions for recovery. But from the Soviet point of view, the Polish remedial program during 1990, which restrained inflation, stabilized markets, and balanced the budget, offered equally compelling reasons for not taking similar radical action. In Poland industrial output declined by 30 percent, wage levels fell by 40 percent, and unemployment rose to over 0.5 million by midyear, all of which threatened popular turmoil and political upheaval.

The Soviet leadership fought shy of decisive action, and by mid-September 1990 had still failed to adopt the plan either of Prime Minister Nikolai Ryzhkov or of Yeltsin's adviser Stanislav Shatalin. Waffling, Gorbachev proposed the production of a synthesis of both plans. He made frequent references to the Polish case and to the likelihood of immediate political and economic instability if its example was followed. The Soviet regime, it was claimed, did not have the legitimacy now enjoyed by the postcommunist Polish government to take such steps. One of the ironies of this situation was that it had been the hesitant attitude of the Jaruzelski leadership throughout the 1980s to questions of economic policy that had helped bring the Polish economy to the critical state it faced at the end of the decade. The problems of seeking reform through the structures of a centralized bureaucracy had proved insoluble and eventually all notions of reform within the established socialist structures discredited, which played a large part in producing the conditions responsible for the downfall of the communist regime.

Polish leadership vacillation and half-hearted policy implementation played a significant part in decapitalizing industry, halting economic growth, running down infrastructure, and fueling inflation. Successive reform programs, like the "second stage" announced in 1987, were implemented only partially and finally abandoned—preparing the ground for the eventual adoption of the painful measures ultimately implemented in 1990. An important contribution to the failures of the 1980s was made by the elements of uncertainty introduced by the ambitious plans for CMEA development, which bore little relation to the economic realities of Eastern Europe. The restricted autonomy imposed on the East European states by the continuing influence of the Soviet Union made any national action tentative and unlikely to be successful. The course of Soviet–East European relations after 1945 and, particularly, the combination of continued dogmatism and vacillation during the 1980s did not provide favorable conditions for an effective economic program during Jaruzelski's leadership.

The parallel trajectory of Soviet and East European developments (at least in some countries) was highlighted in the report on the economic situation in the Soviet Union delivered to the U.S. president in December 1990 by the International Monetary Fund. Commissioned by the Group of Seven and drawn up in consultation with representatives of other leading international economic organizations, the report emphasized the need to prepare for the establishment of a liberal, decentralized economy in the Soviet Union. The methodology and type of reforms proposed reflected major elements of the model recently

implemented in Poland.[75] Ambiguity about the necessity and consequences of reform programs, hesitancy with regard to the adoption and
implementation of reform proposals, and the hypocritical embrace of
contradictory principles all contributed to the eventual need for commitment to a radical program of thoroughgoing reform. It was significant that the Soviet Union had continued to seek respite in the continuing but decreasingly effective enhancement of central powers and held
out longest against an effective commitment to reform, long sought but
obstructed in Eastern Europe by the lengthy period of Soviet dominance. When the Soviet stance changed, East European countries
started on a new path of development.

NOTES

1. J. S. Prybyla, "The Great Malaise: Economic Crisis in Eastern Europe," in N. N.
   Kittrie and I. Volgyes, eds., *The Uncertain Future: Gorbachev's Eastern Bloc* (New York:
   Paragon House, 1988).
2. F. Halliday, *The Making of the Second Cold War*, 2d ed. (London: Verso, 1986).
3. V. Bunce, "The Empire Strikes Back: The Transformation of the Eastern Bloc from
   a Soviet Asset to a Soviet Liability," *International Organization* 39 (1985):1–46.
4. K. Dawisha, *Eastern Europe, Gorbachev and Reform* (Cambridge: Cambridge University
   Press, 1988), pp. 160–62.
5. M. Marrese, "CMEA: Effective but Cumbersome Political Economy," *International
   Organization* 40 (1986): 287; see also J. C. Brada, "Interpreting the Soviet Subsidization of Eastern Europe," *International Organization* 42 (1988):639–58.
6. A. Korbonski, "CMEA, Economic Integration and *Perestroika*, 1949–1989," *Studies in
   Comparative Communism* 23 (1990):62.
7. R. L. Hutchings, *Soviet–East European Relations*, 2d ed. (Madison: University of Wis-
   consin Press, 1987), pp. xxii.
8. M. Checinski, "Warsaw Pact/CEMA Military-Economic Trends," *Problems of Communism* 36 (1987):15–28.
9. A. Ross Johnson, "The Warsaw Pact: Soviet Military Policy in Eastern Europe," in S.
   M. Terry, ed., *Soviet Policy in Eastern Europe* (New Haven: Yale University Press, 1984),
   p. 260.
10. H. Carrere d'Encausse, *Le Grand Frère: L'Union Soviétique et L'Europe Soviétisée* (Paris:
    Flammarion, 1983), p. 318.
11. I. Volgyes, "The Warsaw Pact: Changes in Structure and Functions," *Armed Forces and
    Society* 15 (1989):553.
12. "Introduction" to J. Simon and T. Gilberg, eds., *Security Implications of Nationalism in
    Eastern Europe* (Boulder: Westview Press, 1986), pp. 3 and 8.
13. C. D. Jones, "Agencies of the Alliance: Multinational in Form, Bilateral in Content,"
    in Simon and Gilberg, eds., *Security Implications*, p. 164.
14. C. Jones, "Gorbachev and the Warsaw Pact," *Eastern European Politics and Societies* 3
    (1989): 217, 230.
15. C. Gati, "The Unsettled Condition of Eastern Europe," in H. S. Rowen and C. Wolf,
    eds., *The Future of the Soviet Empire* (London: Macmillan, 1988), pp. 48–49.
16. J. F. Hough, "Attack on Protectionism in the Soviet Union," *International Organization*
    40 (1986): 490–91.
17. W. Zimmerman, "Soviet–East European Relations in the 1980s and the Changing
    International System," in M. Bornstein, Z. Gitelman, and W. Zimmerman, eds., *East–
    West Relations and the Future of Eastern Europe* (London: Allen and Unwin, 1981), p.
    94.

18. Hutchings, *Soviet–East European Relations*, p. xvii.
19. P. Marer and K. Z. Poznanski, "Costs of Domination, Benefits of Subordination," in J. F. Triska, ed., *Dominant Powers and Subordinate States: The United States in Latin America and the Soviet Union in Eastern Europe* (Durham, N.C.: Duke University Press, 1986), p. 398; see also K. Z. Poznanski, "Opportunity Cost in Soviet Trade with Eastern Europe: Discussion of Methodology and New Evidence," *Soviet Studies* 40 (1988): 290–307.
20. A. Lynch, "Changing Contours of Soviet–East European Relations," *Journal of International Affairs* 42 (1989): 429.
21. C. Wolf, "The Costs and Benefits of the Soviet Empire," in Rowen and Wolf, eds., *The Future of the Soviet Empire*, pp. 133–35.
22. V. Bunce, "Decline of a Regional Hegemon: The Gorbachev Regime and Reform in Eastern Europe," *Eastern European Politics and Societies* 3 (1989): 247.
23. Marrese, "CMEA"; see also K. Crane, "Soviet Economic Policy Towards Eastern Europe," in M. Carnovale and W. C. Potter, eds., *Continuity and Change in Soviet–East European Relations* (Boulder: Westview Press, 1989), p. 119.
24. For example, Y. Gluckstein, *Stalin's Satellites in Europe* (London: Allen and Unwin, 1952).
25. A. Korbonski, "Eastern Europe as an Internal Determinant of Soviet Foreign Policy," in S. Bialer, ed., *The Domestic Context of Soviet Foreign Policy* (Boulder: Westview Press, 1981), p. 313.
26. Z. K. Brzezinski, *The Soviet Bloc: Unity and Conflict* (Cambridge: Harvard University Press, 1967), pp. 433–34.
27. G. Ionescu, *The Break-Up of the Soviet Empire in Eastern Europe* (Harmondsworth: Penguin, 1965).
28. E. Moreton, "Foreign Policy Perspectives in Eastern Europe," in K. Dawisha and P. Hanson, eds., *Soviet–East European Dilemmas* (London: Heinemann, 1981), p. 178.
29. C. Gati, "The Soviet Empire: Alive But Not Well," *Problems of Communism* 34, no. 2 (1985): 73–86.
30. S. D. Krasner, "Sovereignty: An Institutional Perspective," *Comparative Political Studies* 21 (1988): 89.
31. Hough, "Attack on Protectionism," pp. 490–91.
32. W. J. Kuhns, "Political Nationalism in Contemporary Eastern Europe," in Simon and Gilberg, eds., *Security Implications*, p. 103.
33. R. Gilpin, *War and Change in World Politics* (Cambridge: Cambridge University Press, 1981), p. 122.
34. Z. Gitelman, "The Impact on the Soviet Union of the East European Experience in Modernization," in C. Gati, ed., *The Politics of Modernization in Eastern Europe* (New York: Praeger, 1974), p. 257.
35. P. G. Lewis, "Democratization in Eastern Europe," *Coexistence* 27 (1990): 252.
36. A. Korbonski, "The Politics of Economic Reforms in Eastern Europe: The Last Thirty Years," *Soviet Studies* 41 (1989): 17.
37. B. Ladygin, *CMEA: Achievements, Problems and Prospects* (Moscow: Novosti, 1987), pp. 4, 9, 7.
38. Gilpin, *War and Change*, p. 129.
39. J. A. Hall, *Powers and Liberties: The Causes and Consequences of the Rise of the West* (Harmondsworth: Penguin, 1986), p. 48.
40. J. L. Hughes, "On Bargaining," in Triska, ed., *Dominant Powers*, p. 195.
41. R. Wesson, "Historical Overview and Comparative Analysis," in Triska, ed., *Dominant Powers*, pp. 80–81.
42. Marer and Poznanski, "Costs of Domination," pp. 380–81.
43. Gilpin, *War and Change*, p. 115; see also P. Kennedy, *The Rise and Fall of the Great Powers* (London: Unwin Hyman, 1988). Kennedy's analysis closely follows Gilpin's.
44. Dawisha, *Eastern Europe*, p. 85.
45. Gilpin, *War and Change*, p. 164.
46. Dawisha, *Eastern Europe*, p. 204.

47. K. Jowitt, "Moscow Centre," *East European Politics and Societies* 1, no. 3 (1987), p. 299.
48. Z. Mlynar, *Night Frost in Prague* (London: Colin Hurst 1980), p. 239.
49. P. Frank, "The CPSU Local Apparat," in C. Keeble, ed., *The Soviet State: The Domestic Roots of Soviet Foreign Policy* (Aldershot: Gower, 1985), p. 167.
50. Gati, "Unsettled Condition," pp. 47–48.
51. S. M. Terry, "Gorbachev's East European Dilemma: Perestroika or Recurrent Crisis," in R. Weichhardt, ed., *The Economies of Eastern Europe Under Gorbachev's Influence* (Brussels: NATO, 1989), p. 295.
52. M. Gorbachev, *Political Report of the CPSU Central Committee to the 27th Party Congress* (Moscow: Novosti, 1986), p. 90.
53. Ladygin, *CMEA*, pp. 15–17.
54. Ibid.
55. J. F. Brown, "The East European Setting," in L. Gordon et al., *Eroding Empire: Western Relations with Eastern Europe* (Washington, D.C.: The Brookings Institution, 1987), p. 38.
56. T. Garton Ash, "Reform or Revolution?" *New York Review of Books,* October 27, 1988.
57. J. Staniszkis, "The Dynamics of Dependency," Wilson Center East European Program Occasional Paper no. 10 (Washington, D.C.: Woodrow Wilson International Center for Scholars, East European Program, 1987).
58. M. Gorbachev, *On the Basis of Full Equality, Independence and Mutual Respect* (Moscow: Novosti, 1988), pp. 4–5.
59. C. Gati, "Eastern Europe on Its Own," *Foreign Affairs* 68 (1989): 104.
60. *The Guardian,* June 20, 1988.
61. M. Kramer, "Beyond the Brezhnev Doctrine," *International Security* 14 (1989/90): 35.
62. *The Independent,* July 15, 1988; *Uncensored Poland News Bulletin,* August 18, 1988; and *The Guardian,* July 16, 1988.
63. *Polityka* (Warsaw), September 10, 1988.
64. A. Lynch, *The Soviet Study of International Relations* (Cambridge: Cambridge University Press, 1987), pp. 117–18.
65. R. de Nevers, "The Soviet Union and Eastern Europe: The End of an Era," *Adelphi Papers* 249 (1990): 23.
66. M. Svec, "East European Divides," *Foreign Policy* 77 (1989/90): 47.
67. H-H. Hohmann, "Soviet *Perestroika,* Economic Reform and Integration Problems in Eastern Europe," *Journal of Communist Studies* 5 (1989): 19–21.
68. D. S. Mason, "Glasnost, Perestroika and Eastern Europe," *International Affairs* 16 (1987): 432–33.
69. L. V. Palei and K. L. Radzivanovich, "How to Carry Out Economic Reform: Points of View and Reality," *Soviet Studies* 42 (1990): 34.
70. C. Gati, "Reforming Communist Systems: Lessons from the Hungarian Experience," in W. E. Griffith, ed., *Central and Eastern Europe: The Opening Curtain* (Boulder: Westview Press, 1989).
71. W. Brus, "The East European Reforms: What Happened to Them?" *Soviet Studies* 31 (1979): 266; W. Brus, "Economic Reforms as an Issue in Soviet–East European Relations," in Dawisha and Hanson, eds., *Soviet–East European Dilemmas;* and Gati, "Reforming Communist Systems," p. 228.
72. J. F. Brown, "Soviet Interests and Policies in Eastern Europe," in R. D. Vine, ed., *Soviet–East European Relations as a Problem for the West* (London: Croom Helm, 1987), p. 55.
73. E. Comisso and P. Marer, "The Economics and Politics of Reform in Hungary," *International Organization* 40 (1986): 444–47.
74. Brus, "East European Reforms," p. 264.
75. *Le Figaro* (Paris), December 21, 1990.

11

Openness: Linking Domestic and Foreign Policy Reform

Gerald Segal

As the catch words "glasnost" and "open door strategy" suggest, openness is a key component of the broad reform program in six Communist Party states: China, the Soviet Union, Vietnam, Hungary, the German Democratic Republic, and North Korea. This chapter focuses on the reform of foreign policy in these states and defines reform as openness. As Alex Pravda and I have developed earlier, closed policies are concerned with the conservation of the concentration of power within a few institutions.[1] Openness in foreign policy means more interdependence and less isolationism and autarky.

The chapter is divided in two large sections. The first looks at the impact of reform of foreign policy on domestic politics. The second assesses the impact of foreign policy reform on the international system. Both of these sections are divided into subsections on foreign economic policy and defense policy. Four general conclusions are made in the chapter. First, domestic and foreign policy reform are not necessarily linked. Although far-reaching reform of foreign policy tends to take place when major domestic reforms are under way, important foreign policy reforms have been accomplished without major domestic reforms. Second, there is no necessary link between reform of defense policy and reform of foreign economic policy. Third, the pattern of foreign policy reform varies from state to state. Although there are some commonalities in reforming states, the differences are sometimes far more helpful in explaining the pattern of reform. Finally, to understand the causes of foreign policy reform, one must assess the operation of both the internal and international systems.

Listed below are the major reforms of foreign policy discussed in the chapter. The core of the text attempts to explain why these reforms took place.

- States that attempt domestic economic reform change their view of the international economy. They see less class struggle and more of an international division of labor.
- In an age of attempts at domestic economic reforms, only China became a more important actor in the international economy.
- In an age of attempts at domestic economic reform, only China changed its type of trade by moving into more manufactured goods.
- Foreign direct investment has risen sharply in China and constitutes an important part of domestic growth. Similar trends were evident in the Soviet Union and perhaps in Vietnam.
- Hungary and China have been largely successful in joining international economic institutions. The Soviet Union found it harder to join them, as has Vietnam.
- In response to external and internal pressures in reforming states, the decision-making process on foreign economic relations was decentralized and opened to wider influences.
- The value of the currency was set at more realistic rates in response to external and internal pressures.
- The legal system governing foreign economic relations was brought more into line with the demands of the international market, especially in China, Vietnam, and the Soviet Union.
- Only China reformed its banking or securities system.
- The Soviet Union demilitarized its foreign policy by withdrawing from Afghanistan. Vietnam did the same in quitting Cambodia. China did the opposite in its Spratly operation in 1988.
- The Soviet Union demilitarized its defense policy by cutting back military operations beyond its home territory, especially in naval deployments. China did the opposite.
- The Soviet Union, the East Europeans, and even Vietnam cut their defense budgets. China has both increased and decreased its defense spending since 1979. But all these countries have cut the size of their armed forces.
- The Soviet Union took a more positive role in arms control negotiations. To a much lesser extent, Vietnam has demilitarized its defense policy by tacit arms controls in Indochina. Chinese policy has been more ambiguous.
- The Soviet Union became more willing than it was in the past to support U.N. involvement in the peaceful settlement of disputes. China and Vietnam moved far less in this direction.
- The Soviet Union increased contacts between its military professionals and those in Western countries. China did the same, and Vietnam is beginning this process. In general, the Soviet Union,

and to some extent China and Vietnam, were willing to accept more transparency on military matters.

- The Soviet Union and China eventually reduced their arms transfers, after having initially increased them. The changes were primarily due to changing market conditions.
- The Soviet Union sought less tight alliance unity in confrontation with military rivals. The East Europeans took advantage of such demilitarization.
- The Soviet Union's armed forces stressed greater professionalism. China's People's Liberation Army (PLA) did the same and Vietnam's People's Army of Vietnam may be following such a policy.

THE DOMESTIC DIMENSION

Foreign Economic Policy

Foreign economic reform and domestic institutions are obviously linked, but the linkage is far from clear if only because import-led modernization is often adopted as an alternative to economic reform. For example, by the early 1980s the share of foreign trade in national income in resolutely unreformed Czechoslovakia was roughly the same as in reforming Hungary (43 percent). Moreover, if calculated on the basis of realistic exchange rates, the relative proportions of socialist and nonsocialist trade (50-50) seem to be the same.

Similarly, the propensity to undertake large hard-currency borrowing does not seem to be related to the introduction of economic reforms. To be sure, the biggest debtors, Poland and Hungary, were the reformers in Eastern Europe, but the GDR was also a big debtor by the early 1980s. Czechoslovakia, with an economic system very similar to that of the GDR, borrowed fairly little, and after 1981 it was able to keep borrowing to a minimum. Thus, what seems to have happened in many parts of Eastern Europe was an ill-thought-out increase in economic exposure to the West, without any of the internal adjustments in economic structure that are an essential condition of effective economic integration into the world market. Although the quantitative openness of Hungary increased in the 1970s and 1980s, the basic import-substituting assumptions continued to dominate economic policy making.

In Hungary the import-substituting mentality was a product of the same powerful coalition of ideological, bureaucratic, and domestic monopoly-producer interests that had blocked economic reforms. Its response to the world market changes in the 1970s was to turn inward, resort to protectionism, and pretend that growth could continue as before. This unwise strategy resulted in an uncontrollable surge in debt, and it undermined economic reform. In the late 1980s the proclaimed strategy of increasing openness seemed to be part of a basically old pattern: The task of improving efficiency was subordinated to the immediate goal of reducing debt. Turning to the outside world was merely a way of obtaining capital—a substitute for the introduction of nonstate production in the internal economy. In effect, openness was really a substitute for reform.[2]

In some countries, however, the increased contact with the noncommunist world influenced the institutions of government. In China institutional changes were made during the decade of reform albeit not to the extent of an abandonment of communist power. Decision making was often taken away from the party as political reform came to mean greater professionalism. What is more, decision making was devolved to lower and often more specialist levels. Barbara Krug describes this as an evolving "bargaining economy" rather than a real market economy.[3]

Enterprises were allowed to raise foreign capital and send personnel abroad to experiment with new ideas of management and production. Even foreign trade monopolies were shattered and a "responsibility system" was implemented. Chambers of commerce were established in 1987; they assumed some of the functions formerly fulfilled by local bureaucracies. The service sector was especially open to such reforms, and direct contacts were established with foreigners that made some organizations far more independent of domestic guidance. Western procedures like the German standardization system (DIN) were accepted in China, as were World Bank and OECD systems for accounting. Even Vietnam rapidly discovered some benefits of openness: The Ministry of Fishery and Water was reorganized to allow more efficient contacts with the outside world. Certainly, joint ventures shaped the way business was run. To be sure, the changes were often insufficient and halting, but they were evident.[4]

The key to reform in China was the notion of professionalism—the drift from "red" to "expert" in managing the economy. Every contact with Western business reinforced this trend. Contact with international organizations, such as the International Monetary Fund and the World Bank, was not as unsettling for China as it was for smaller economies in the developing world. These foreign institutions did help reinforce those parts of the Chinese system pushing for reforms.

Reform of foreign economic policy in the Soviet Union did not go as far as it had in China before 1989, but then the Soviet Union's economy was much worse than China's. Even before the death of Leonid Brezhnev, decentralizing measures had been introduced in the Soviet Union.

For example, a Council of Ministers resolution on July 9, 1981, granted branch ministries and their subordinate production associations and enterprises the right to establish direct contacts with counterparts in the countries belonging to the Council for Mutual Economic Assistance (CMEA), but this was far from the root-and-branch approach that was required.

A far more sweeping reform began in 1986.[5] A joint resolution of the CPSU Central Committee and the Council of Ministers on August 19 effectively broke the monopoly of the Ministry of Foreign Trade by granting the right to engage directly in foreign trade to twenty-one other ministries, sixty-six enterprises, and a few other bodies including the Union republics. By the end of 1987, about nine hundred economic bodies at various levels were engaged in direct foreign economic relations.

The pattern of this reform included a reorganization of the central management structure. A superministry was created with the aim of streamlining coordination. Thus, power was not genuinely devolved to independent actors. The creation of joint ventures and the granting of the right to conduct foreign trade to cooperatives did move somewhat in the direction of more autonomy, despite opposition from the Ministry of Foreign Trade. By April 1990 some 2,500 cooperatives were registered to conduct foreign trade. But in March and December 1989 the government had restricted foreign economic activity to trade in those goods used or produced directly by the firm. Export licenses were introduced in response to growing shortages on the domestic market. In the confusion of a wide range of economic and political changes, none of the participants in Soviet foreign economic relations seemed to know where the ground was firm.

In neither Hungary nor the GDR did foreign economic relations change very much. Although Hungary's New Economic Mechanism led to an increase in the number of enterprises with foreign trade rights, the central state enterprises retained their vital role.[6] The real turning point was the Ministry of Trade's Decree No. 1 of 1987. It established foreign trade as a statutory right of economic organizations, including joint ventures. Thus, permission was no longer required from the Ministry of Trade, only formal registration. The number of firms engaged in foreign trade rose from about 350 in December 1987 to about 1,000 in mid-1989 with the number of private firms reaching 300. Yet some 40 percent of convertible currency exports were not included in these reforms, and CMEA trade was still closely controlled by the ministry.

In the GDR the Kombinat reform of 1979 created 132 foreign trade firms under central direction and 93 under regional authorities.[7] By

1986 some sixty-four foreign trade enterprises were operating, and they all were supervised by the Ministry of Foreign Trade. Although there was some decentralization of decision making, the essential power remained with the center.

In stark contrast, Vietnam followed the Chinese route to a more radical decentralization to local levels.[8] Some enterprises can conduct their own export policy and import of materials, machinery, and spare parts. Decentralization since 1986 has gone too far in some areas. In the rice trade Hanoi has established an Association of Rice Exporters to control competition and keep a minimum export price. The association also helps provinces find export markets, and it mediates conflicts.[9]

As the Chinese experience makes plain, the widening of reforms in foreign economic policy helps change the regional and sectoral state of the country. There is good evidence that China can be treated as more than one country for vast parts of its foreign trade.[10] By opening several doors to the outside world, the tendency toward regionalism in China was allowed to develop. Some provinces, most notably Guangdong, have managed to resist new orders from the center during times of retrenchment. They are able to grow their way out of inflationary problems that afflict the rest of the country. Indeed, by demonstrating their independence they encourage the outside world to regard the province as a special part of China relatively immune to shifts evident in Beijing and other regions.[11]

Not all regionalism depends on openness to the West. Guangdong depends on Hong Kong, Fujian depends on Taiwan, and Hainan Island seems tied to a range of investors. Shandong is building bridges with South Korea. Dongbei as well as Xinjiang are opening crossborder contacts with the Soviet Union. Once the open door policy was adopted, it became impossible to go back to old ways except at a terrible cost few seem prepared to pay, as events after June 1989 make clear.

In the post-1989 China, Shanghai has staked a claim to return to its former status as the leading cosmopolitan city in China. Rival Guangdong province struggles to recover from the recent retrenchment. Guangdong found some of its wings clipped (high rates of tax on foreign currency earnings paid to the center and control of Shenzhen taken by the center). Shanghai and other parts of China still look for opportunities. This competition stimulates the creation of better conditions for foreign investment.[12]

The Soviet Union, unlike the East European countries, was big enough to benefit as well as suffer from such centrifugal tendencies. Indeed, it seems that as the Union of the Soviet Socialist Republics became less Soviet and socialist, they also became less united republics.

Even before the doors were fully opened to outside economic influence, parts of the Soviet Union were already heading for the exit. In the Baltic republics, the expected economic benefits from independence and integration with the European economy helped to feed nationalism. It was certainly not evident that there was much immediate economic logic to rapid separation from the Soviet Union, but the expectation of medium-term gains did seem reasonable.

In Moldavia and Central Asia the calculations of nationalists seemed far less sound, at least in economic terms. Unlike the Baltics or the Chinese Gold Coast, these regions were not able to get a better deal from the international economy than they already had from the Soviet Union. Yet the problems of repressed nationalism suddenly uncapped and unnatural political frontiers seemed to defy economic logic. In the Soviet Far East foreign interest was expected to reshape local politics. Various voices in the Soviet Pacific, despite the absence of a formal regional structure of government, demanded greater local autonomy in setting wage rates and tax policies. This was done in part because the foreign partners wanted special deals and in part because of longstanding resentment over neglect by the center. When outside economic forces combine with powerful local voices changes can be made in the communist system. But, as the case of the Far East suggests, it is insufficient to merely change regulations if the basic structure of the economy is not ready for reform. The bewildering disarray in the Soviet Union in 1990 caused by conflicting demands for regional autonomy, including within the Russian Republic, coupled with basic problems of distribution and confused lines of policy implementation, meant that hurried reform was leading to disintegration, especially in a country the size of the Soviet Union.

In smaller states the problems and opportunities of regionalism were obviously different than in China and the Soviet Union. South Vietnam seems to have more people willing to take up the opportunities provided by the new incentives in agriculture, and because of contacts with the United States during the Vietnam War there is far more of a base for doing business with the Western economy. The change of political system after 1975 did not entirely demolish the structure of South Vietnam's ties to the capitalist economy outside. The siting of joint ventures in the South is yet another manifestation of the new opportunities. Because local authorities were allowed to establish direct contacts with the outside world, they began to obtain the producer and consumer goods they needed. This facilitated technological retooling. The changes were most clearly seen around Ho Chi Minh City. Of course, it is still too early to tell if the same sorts of centrifugal forces that operated in China will pull Vietnam in different directions. In smaller states, and especially ones with such bitter legacies of division, the risks seem much higher than they are in China or were in the Soviet Union.

In sum, openness at home and abroad does reshape domestic decision making. Reform does not necessarily buy stability for the regime, but failure to reform seems to lead to crisis. But it is still not clear that foreign economic policy reform must fail if there is no sweeping political reform at home. The Chinese and Vietnamese cases suggest there is much that can be done that is more reform than revolution. The key, at least in the Chinese case, is producing enough economic goods to ensure legitimacy for the ruling regime. Because of its size, China may be able to go in different directions at the same time. At least for the medium term, it may continue to be ruled by the Communist Party and yet retain some reforms.

Defense Policy Reform

In the Soviet Union, China, Vietnam, and to a very limited extent even North Korea, the armed forces of the Communist Party were crucial participants in the revolution. Although the civil war in the Soviet Union and to some extent in North Korea and Vietnam took place after the revolutionary state was proclaimed, the reality was that without successful armed forces, the party would have lost power. Both Vietnam and North Korea also benefited from "fraternal assistance" from China and the Soviet Union. As a result, the relationship between party and army was complex; many officials wore more than one cap at a time.[13]

The armed forces of the Soviet Union were professionalized under Nikita Khrushchev, and they grew more remote from society. The Soviet military was transformed into a natural participant in politics, with new freedom to determine defense policy on its own.[14] Lack of information necessary for making sensible defense policy excluded other political actors from the process. Soviet SALT negotiators from the Ministry of Foreign Affairs allegedly obtained information on Soviet deployments from their Western counterparts and not from their colleagues in the Soviet armed forces.[15]

The People's Liberation Army of China was far less professional, and far more open because of the stress on political accountability. Vietnam and Korea, through the 1980s still in a certain state of war, were under heavy political control and were highly militarized societies. In Hungary, and especially the GDR, the armed forces were so heavily penetrated by the Soviet Union that they were a major feature of the Soviet control mechanism in Eastern Europe.

In the 1970s the militarization of Soviet defense policy reached its peak with the narrowly based decision to invade Afghanistan.[16] In China Mao's part of the Chinese Communist Party called on the PLA to intervene in politics in order to seize control from radical Red Guards and restore order. The gradual disengagement of the armed forces depended on the establishment of stable civil rule in China. With the purge of the Gang of Four in 1976 and the emergence of Deng Xiaoping as the dominant leader in 1978, the retreat of the PLA from civilian politics was made possible.[17] Vietnam and North Korea remained heavily involved in military confrontations and their civil-military relations underwent little change.[18] Following China's de facto defeat in the war against Vietnam in 1979, the PLA was slimmed down and encouraged to focus on narrow professional interests. As part of the general attempt to distinguish party and state roles, the PLA was encouraged to think less about politics.

China failed to achieve its objectives in its brief border war with Vietnam. China had to increase its defense budget to cover the costs, but it was also interested in moving forward with the strategy of Four Modernizations, only one of which was in defense policy. Thus, the armed forces could not simply continue to obtain a great share for the defense budget, even though the PLA had not sought a war in Vietnam and was shoved into the conflict by the civilian leaders.[19]

It seems that an explicit deal was struck between senior PLA officials and Deng Xiaoping. If the PLA allowed modernization of the economy to take priority for a few years, then the overall state budget would grow quickly enough to finance increased defense spending.[20] It was thought that military professionals would soon find they were getting more "wreckage for the yuan" and a greater say on how the funds were allocated than in the days of more political control. Defense spending as a percentage of government spending fell for much of the 1980s, although the absolute total of spending began increasing in the late 1980s, and the spending-per-soldier increased very clearly after the PLA was slimmed down by 1 million men in 1985–87.[21]

There was evidence that the drop in the PLA's percentage of the budget was halted. But late 1988 was also a time of economic crisis with inflation bursting out of control and a subsequent decision on economic retrenchment. In 1989 the PLA was called in to save the majority of the party from protestors in Beijing, and allow the civilians to deal with the serious economic crisis in China. The PLA's share of the state budget again appeared to increase. The debates and indications in 1988 suggest that the decision to satisfy the PLA's financial demands was taken before the Beijing massacre.

Vietnam is a special case because it has more or less been at war since the foundation of communist rule. The need to fight the French, the Americans, the Cambodians, and the Chinese left no room for a major domestic economic modernization program. But by 1986 and the gradual consolidation of power in Cambodia, Vietnam began to look more seriously at domestic economic priorities. As in China, the armed forces had to be cut in size and defense spending reduced. As we shall see, "friends," such as the Soviet Union, encouraged these readjustments in priorities.

So far Vietnam has not reached the stage that China did in 1986 when the armed forces began to draw the line against the cuts.[22] As in China, the armed forces did not like all aspects of the new policy, but they recognized it was correct in principle. The Vietnamese economy had reached such a pathetic state by the mid-1980s, and the security environment had improved sufficiently, that some cuts in defense spending were possible.[23]

The armed forces were already much further down the road of professionalism in the Soviet Union than in China and Vietnam. Although not the highest in the world, Soviet defense spending was well above the percentages common in the developed world. The Soviet economy was simply not efficient enough to continue draining the system to serve the armed forces. Neither were the reforms working fast enough to convince hard-core military professionals that modernization would bring them new technology in the near future. As the Soviet economy staggered into ever deeper crisis, the tension over money between civil and military forces was bound to worsen. The economy was in such bad shape that most people recognized that the priority was to get some growth back in the economy.[24]

North Korea spends heavily on defense. It has failed to adopt any serious reforms. Among the Warsaw Pact countries the GDR was one of the biggest spenders on defense, although there is some evidence that earlier in the decade, the East Germans, like other East Europeans, were reluctant to increase spending when asked to do so by Moscow. But in the era of Gorbachev, the GDR was not asked to make military cuts, and it was only after the revolutions in 1989 that such matters came to the fore. Although Hungary was always less penetrated by the Soviet high command than was the GDR, it, too, saw little change in defense spending until the 1989 revolutions.

One distinctive feature of defense policy reform in China and the Soviet Union was the conversion of the defense economy to civilian production. In these centrally planned economies, defense policies epitomized the irrationalities of the old system. The defense sector badly distorted the whole economy by siphoning off resources and skills. The Soviet Union became a superpower on this basis, but a one-legged superpower because of the crippling effects on its economic leg. China never sought to divert so many resources in its civilian economy, but it also suffered from the wartime mentality of a command economy. Decentralization and demilitarization in China and the Soviet Union helped sever the link between military and industry in both countries, but the process was extremely complicated.[25]

China's defense industries have always been famous for turning out bicycles as well as bombs, but the conversion to civilian production went much further in the decade of reform.[26] Yet in the Chinese case, not to mention the Soviet case, the basic centralization of defense procurement remains in place. The Chinese experience suggests that there is no direct link between reform and the number of institutions created.[27]

Conversion of the defense industry was less well developed in the Soviet Union than in China.[28] Of course, the task of producing high technology was greater for the Soviets, especially considering the tougher COCOM regulations. The Chinese armed forces have been able to benefit from high-technology imports in the wider civilian economy, but the Soviet Union was only developing such possibilities in the late 1980s. Of course, the Soviet "defense complex" was always more integrated than many analysts had suggested, but the stress of the reforms was to make the new technological innovation outside of the defense complex.[29] Joint ventures in particular were seen as a way to ease the flow of technology around residual barriers of concern about Soviet military plans. The hope was that these would be obvious gains when the defense sector released the expertise it controlled in order to aid the civilian modernization.[30]

Demilitarization of society in Vietnam has only just begun. The South has had far fewer years of militarization than has the North. American occupation was of a chaotic kind that even encouraged thinking of ways around military authority. To be sure, South Vietnam has little experience with law-governed society, but it does seem to be accepting the importance of an easier social life and better ways to make a living. As a result, coping with demobilized soldiers in the new conditions has been especially difficult in the South. In the North it can be said that the shock of the new policy seems a bigger change with the past. The Vietnamese press is full of stories of the hardships being suffered by soldiers who lose their sense of purpose and whose living conditions are being hit harder than are those of the population at large. The army press reported that only 35 percent of those who left the army had found full-time jobs. Special job-training schemes have been established for the mass of demobilized soldiers.[31]

In China demilitarization of society is nothing new. Indeed, traditional China was well known for its poor treatment of military professionals. Society seems to be far less militarized than it is in Vietnam and especially North Korea. The Chinese took to economic reforms with glee, especially in the countryside. Immediately, the PLA ran into social problems. Peasants wanted to stay out of the armed forces and make more money.[32] Some skills, such as driving or electronics, could be learned in the PLA, but the opportunities in the civilian market seemed to be opening up rapidly. Families did not want their children to become soldiers when they could be used far more effectively in the liberalized rural economy.

In comparison to the pampered state of the PLA, the Soviet armed forces had even further to fall in terms of privilege and perhaps social status. China never had the massive military parades so beloved of the Soviet armed forces. Neither did the Chinese armed forces control the civilian economy as did the Soviet military. Since the high point of the defeat of Nazi Germany, the Soviet military's reputation in society had been coasting downhill. The soldiers' honor had not been tested for decades until the invasion of Afghanistan. The displaced conflict of such exploits as the space program was no substitute for battle scars in defense of the state.

Yet the Afghan experience demonstrated that the new armed forces were not worthy of high social standing.[33] Although individual soldiers fought bravely, they were soon seen as not fighting for the Soviet Union as much as for the folly of doddery leaders.[34] Drugs and violence returned with the homecoming soldiers, and social problems in the country as a whole were seen as directly linked to military adventure. Needless to say, trainloads of coffins of war dead, in a war with no end that cost over $60 billion, led to reassessments of the military.

None of the states under consideration in this chapter is under military rule. But demilitarization of defense policy in these states might involve a greater role for civilian leaders and indeed even public opinion at large. Yet in few of the cases of reform has there been any such apparent change, although the reasons for the relative lack of change seem to be different.

In China, at the peak of military power in the early 1970s, more than half the Politburo could be defined as military men. But by the time the reforms got under way in the early 1980s, military representation was down to some 20 percent as it had been in the 1950s. With stability in the provinces, military authority was also scaled back. Regular rotations of regional commanders ensured loyalty to the party and the absence of "independent kingdoms." Even following the leadership changes in 1989–90, the military did not increase its representation in top bodies of the party or state.[35]

Policies that required the use of force, either at home or abroad, were not particularly affected by the military's demands. The war against Vietnam is a striking case in point. If anything, the professional high command was lukewarm about the war. The decision to send troops to suppress protestors in Beijing in 1989 was also taken without a dominant military voice, although consultations with military men affected the timing and the use of force.[36]

This nondominance of Chinese military men in top decision making suggests that a "natural" level of military representation was found. But the military participated in decisions, especially those affecting their direct interests, in China in the 1980s. Indeed, it seemed to be part of the new professionalism in the armed forces: Professionals participated in professional decisions but otherwise tended to stay out of politics. In China, as in the Soviet Union, some senior military leaders spent so long in the top echelons of power that they became more politicized, and developed different interests from more professional officers. Similarly, some civilian leaders developed such close working relations with the armed forces that they "went native" and defended military positions.[37]

The changes are best seen in the light of a general decommunization rather than a depoliticization of decision making on military matters. As the role of the Communist Party diminishes in decision making, party control of the military decreases as well and the power of political commissars fades. Under such circumstances it became much harder to talk of the Soviet Union as a Communist Party state with control of its communist armed forces. But such a conclusion also suggested that although some parts of the Soviet armed forces resisted the pace and direction of these changes, it was not a civil-military split as much as one between orthodox and liberal forces in the society at large.

Vietnam, like China, is nowhere near that type of openness. Military voices are still heard loud and clear in top decision-making bodies, in part as a confidence-building measure to ensure the top brass that the changes are under control. But with far less time having passed since the revolutionary wars, the tendency of Vietnamese leaders to wear both civil and military hats is still far greater than in China and the Soviet Union. The passing of such leaders is therefore far more a matter for the actuarial tables.[38] But if China and the Soviet Union are anything to go by, Vietnam will find a natural level of military representation as a more professional body seeks its rightful place at the top table.

Especially in large countries such as China and the Soviet Union, there is always a risk decentralization of decision making will lead to regionalism and perhaps even separatism. Since one of the major tasks of the armed forces is to ensure the territorial integrity of the state, regionalism may well lead to an enhanced role for the military. Indeed, such tension between reform and the integrity of the state is already evident in the Soviet Union and to some extent in China.

Of course, both China and the Soviet Union were empires, each having grabbed land and people for centuries, well before the coming of communism. Yet China remains far more ethnically coherent, with a 94 percent Han population as opposed to the 50 percent Russian population in the Soviet Union. More than half of Chinese territory was acquired less than three hundred years ago; much of the Russian empire was two-thirds newer. Clearly, the Soviet Union was always likely to face a far more pressing problem of regional disintegration than China.[39]

In the decade of Chinese reforms, decentralization of policy has involved the granting of relatively more autonomy on some matters to such poor areas as Tibet and Xinjiang, and such rich areas as the different parts of the coastal regions.[40] While the rich regions have found satisfaction in economic interdependence, the poor regions have released their anger on the occupying Chinese power. More liberal policies toward local religion and culture led some to believe that even more independence could be obtained. Greater freedom to contact the outside world led to wider knowledge about successful kin or even just other independence movements. In Tibet martial law had to be imposed by the PLA when the public security apparatus proved incapable of controlling riots in 1989. In Xinjiang in 1990, unrest flared, apparently encouraged by similar uprisings across the border in the Soviet Union.

The PLA, under the instructions of the central leadership, demonstrated the limits of reform. Under no circumstances was decentralization to mean independence. So long as no outside power did anything to assist the rebels, China was able to draw such a line, although blood had to be shed to maintain it. Yet China was also clear that as the Soviet empire proved less solid, then China might find itself with a far more serious problem, especially in Central Asia.

Central Asian regionalism was not the most important threat to the territorial integrity of the Soviet Union. The peoples of the Baltics and the Caucasus posed the most imminent threat to the leadership in Moscow. As in the case of China, greater openness and talk of demilitarized politics encouraged people in the regions to believe they could take their future into their own hands. In the Baltics in particular, the memory of Soviet oppression was still very painful, and thus there was active hope for freedom. The fact that the Soviet armed forces had failed to subdue the Afghan people, even under the tougher Brezhnev administration, led some to believe that they could break away from Kremlin rule. Freedom in Eastern Europe, without bloodshed, fed the fount of hope.

It was unclear at what point the Soviet Union would call on its armed forces to defend the empire. The outer empire in Eastern Europe had gone, and yet force was used in the Caucasus, Central Asia, and the Baltics, at least in part to keep the Soviet Union from disintegrating. Military voices were prominent among those calling for a fight for the union, although there was little evidence of the military acting on its own to remilitarize a situation that Moscow wanted demilitarized.[41] The growing opposition to military service in some republics only added to the anger in the armed forces and polarized the debate.

When the cautious reformers failed to hold the inner empire, they were eventually removed from power.[42] Knowledge of such a possibility drove those favoring reform to remilitarize the issue, and as in the case of any country where the basic stability of society was under threat, it was always likely that the armed forces would play a major part in determining the new political order. The result was the failed coup of August 1991.

I have suggested that professionalism of the armed forces can be considered a reform of defense policy. But as has already been indicated, this is a difficult judgment to sustain in all circumstances. If professionalism is defined as a concern with skills necessary to carrying out the task of ensuring territorial integrity and independence, then it should become clear that demilitarization has its limits. Most obviously, demilitarization does not apply to the military as a profession. Indeed, the logic of demilitarization is that while the military influence is removed from civilian sectors of the economy, society, and foreign relations, it should be strengthened in the narrower confines of professional pursuits.

The problem with such a formulation is that the confines of narrower professional pursuits are far from precise. The military's responsibility for territorial integrity might well lead it to sound a klaxon of alarm about regional unrest well before a civilian leader anxious to support decentralization of decision making. Is it unprofessional for a regional commander to argue, as was done in the Soviet Union, that demands for regional independence should be swiftly suppressed with military force? It is a professional matter, even though it is also a sensitive political question. On the other hand, in China in 1989 there was evidence that some military commanders were less than anxious to send in the troops to quell unrest that the party leadership saw as stimulated in part by foreign agitators.[43] In both cases, professional military judgments were part of politics.

In Vietnam the massive transition from a war economy to a more open reform pattern poses major threats to social order. Naturally, military men will voice their opinions and soldiers will complain about the effects on their lives.[44] There is no way in which they can be expected to hold in their anger, and the hope must be that letting off steam in the expectation that policies can be amended will keep the armed forces from doing something as unprofessional as seizing power.

Yet there are other areas of more specific professional concern that are also touched by military reforms. For example, interservice rivalry can be affected by demilitarization and changes in contacts with the outside world. Giving the armed forces less control over industry and a less powerful voice in procurement policy in general forces them to think about the impact of markets on their spending patterns. The old-style stress on massive numbers of weapons in place of quality is harder to sustain when the economy has other priorities for steel and scarce qualified personnel. When the economy is encouraged to focus on higher technology, then the air force, navy, and even nuclear forces stand to gain.

Such debate between "steel-eaters" and "electronics" had been a feature of prereform interservice rivalry. Reform tends to support the electronics school. Young officers interested in enhancing their skills and professional self-esteem will support a stress on high technology.[45] Foreign engagements become more costly for all concerned, and weapons are far more for prestige than use when they become too costly to replace.

This is not the simple cynicism of a civilian observer. These indeed have been the trends in the two countries able to decide such basic aspects of their defense policy—China and the Soviet Union. Chinese reforms, including the removal of 1 million men from the rolls of the PLA, have been specifically achieved by hitting the ground forces hardest. The navy has actually improved its position and seems to be the leading benefactor of the reform program.[46] The expansion to a more blue-water naval strategy has been matched by a reduction of tension along the frontier with the Soviet Union. Although all services have received new equipment in the past decade, the most striking improvements have been in the navy. When matched by a stress on more rapid economic development of the coastal regions, China becomes more of a complete maritime power and less obsessed about traditional threats from neighbors on land. As China also looks to the global and regional East Asian economy, the maritime orientation takes on greater importance and Central Asia becomes less important.

Reforms in the Soviet Union were far less clear. The disengagement from the outer empire hurt the ground forces, as the withdrawal from out-of-area operations damaged the prestige of the navy. The penetration of Soviet airspace by foreign aircraft was taken as an opportunity to reform air defenses.[47] Only the nuclear program escaped virtually untouched, but then it was always the part of the defense budget that provided the most rubble for the ruble.

But as in the case of China, the general policy of demilitarization supported those stressing higher technology services. It was part of the appeal to younger officers that only wholesale reform of society and the economy would provide the newer technology necessary for modern defense and professional self-esteem. Guard duty in the GDR or combat in Afghan hills was less preferable to these young professionals than service at home and practice on modern weaponry. If these professionals merely came home to internal guard duty and poor living conditions, then all services were more likely to unite in opposition to civil authority. Unlike the Chinese case where new professional satisfaction was being delivered by a growing defense budget, Soviet soldiers had far less to look forward to.

With demilitarization there must be changes in military doctrine. In the three countries where some demilitarization has taken place—China, the Soviet Union and Vietnam—military doctrine evolved with the new economic constraints in very different ways. China has now had at least a decade of modern military doctrine under the slogan of "people's war under modern conditions."[48] Analysts do not agree on the full meaning of the new doctrine, but it seems to combine the old "people's war" stress on the poverty and populousness of China with the modern conditions of mobility and high technology. Combined arms operations have been developed and professional skills honed. Despite the upset of 1989, these new components seem to have been retained and the PLA is resisting efforts of the politically conscious to return to greater stress on the political component of the old Maoist notion of a people's war.[49]

Professionalism in this new doctrine also means more stress on military education in academies and on training fields. More foreign contact is encouraged in order to get a better measure of China's ranking and learn about new ideas and technologies. Some foreign weapons are purchased as short-cuts to modernization. Arms are sold abroad in order to get money to pay for new hardware at home and in some cases even to obtain evidence on the performance of weapons. Less money is now spent on soldiers and more on research and development since 1 million men were cut from the Chinese armed forces. Thus, demilitarization in defense policy as a whole means enhanced military professionalism in the armed services themselves. China's armed forces have become leaner and fitter than ever before, and at a time when defense policy reform has made China more secure than at any point in the past several hundred years.

Vietnamese doctrinal reform is neither as developed nor as obviously successful.[50] Of course, China has been successfully deterred and the Vietnamese-supported regime clung to power in Phnom Penh. But the pressing need for economic growth made the Vietnamese armed forces far less happy about adopting a new military doctrine. They, too, retain an affection for a people's war, but PAVN is in dire need of modernization. While it defended itself against China by use of people's war tactics, it used more set-piece offensive tactics against the Khmer Rouge in Cambodia. But neither strategy will do against perhaps the most pressing military threat, Chinese encroachment in the South China Sea. The loss of some islands in the Spratlys in 1988, and the apparent recapture of some in June 1989, suggests it can stand and fight for its interests, but only if China is otherwise distracted or deterred. Vietnam looks likely to pay far more attention to naval aspects of its defense doctrine.

Yet the most sweeping doctrinal changes were still to come in the dying days of the Soviet Union.[51] Of course, even under Brezhnev significant changes were made to Soviet military doctrine without being part of a broader demilitarization of defense policy. The stress on nuclear war as an unusable instrument of military policy was the product of much earlier debates. Under Gorbachev this became a more clearly accepted notion, and was joined by a new stress on sufficiency of military equipment rather than the more open-ended need to keep up with every revision in the technology arms race. As a consequence, Soviet officials began discussing and indeed even implementing asymmetrical cuts in weapons as part of an arms control process. Discussion of defensive defense doctrine was part of debates about the role of higher technology in new defense strategy and the need to focus on conventional weapons rather than nuclear weapons.[52]

For all the importance of theoretical debates about future strategy, the most far-reaching doctrinal revisions came as part of the package of ideas behind the abandonment of control of the outer empire in Eastern Europe. Needless to say, Soviet foreign policy was not the same after the second half of 1989 when the basic policy priorities were changed.

Demilitarization was so recent that a new coherent military doctrine did not emerge.[53] Nuclear weapons policy remained virtually unchanged, and the armed forces continued to argue about the potential threat to Soviet security. This slowness in revising formal doctrine suggested that doctrine was more a response to defense policy and less a shaper of it. So much depended on whether the inner empire held together and what cost would be paid in that struggle. So much depended on the economic and social reforms, and so much seemed uncertain in those respects. China's defense policy is more successful than it has been for centuries. The Soviet Union, however, had never been weaker since the dark days of the Second World War, and, in the end, the empire and the ideology collapsed in the end of 1991. A more complete picture of these differing reforms emerges when looking at the impact on the international system.

THE INTERNATIONAL SYSTEM

Foreign Economic Policy Reform

One of the most important reforms in foreign economic policy is the willingness to create the conditions conducive to foreign direct investment (FDI). In the communist world China has led the way in attracting foreign investment. By the end of 1988, China had entered into nearly 16,000 FDI contracts, more than 6,000 of which were already in operation. Some $28 billion in commitments were attracted, of which $11 billion had been utilized. China not only led the communist world in attracting FDI, it was also one of the leaders in the developing world.[54] This FDI made a major contribution to China's own modernization program despite the fact that investment was often erratic and confronted major socioeconomic problems in China's domestic economy.

Indeed, China's ability to attract investment has ebbed and flowed. Pragmatism, or the strategy of "feeling the stones while crossing the river," meant that there were identifiable phases when FDI flowed more freely. From 1979 to 1982, major efforts were made to obtain funds for the four special economic zones (SEZs). No serious effort was made to attract funds outside the zones, and investors could not hold more than 49 percent of ventures. In 1983–85 FDI was sought for the SEZs but also for fourteen coastal cities and three deltas along the east coast. Decision making was decentralized, and most FDI decisions no longer required central approval. But tension soon followed as China's search for capital and technology was met by investors' complaints about problems in obtaining local credit, energy, raw materials, and skilled labor. Because of the lack of skilled Chinese administrators, there were numerous redundancies in projects, and some operated in less essential areas.

The retrenchment period of 1986–87 involved a sharp reduction in the amount of FDI. The Gold Coast strategy begun in the spring of 1988 was meant to be accompanied by comprehensive price reform. But massive inflation alarmed the leadership and led to a further cooling of the ardor for FDI.[55] The reform effort of 1988 did result in more areas being opened to FDI, including Hainan Island. China stressed its cheap labor and the fact that wholly-owned foreign ventures could be opened. Some foreigners were attracted by these reforms, especially those wishing to shift from increasingly expensive, labor-intensive operations elsewhere in the booming East Asian economy.[56] Some partial selling into the vast Chinese market was allowed, thereby increasing hopes that the huge potential of China might be opened to foreign investors.

Although the events of 1989 helped cool the fever for FDI in China, it was already clear before the events of June that there were economic problems in continuing the rapid pace of FDI growth. Inflation, the bidding of the cost of scarce labor, rising social discontent, and differences between the Gold Coast and the interior were all reasons to slow the pace of FDI. But most Chinese leaders recognized that they had benefited from FDI and wanted it to continue. FDI constituted only 2 percent of total gross investment in the decade from 1978. Its impact was much greater in the coastal regions where it was concentrated. Over 60 percent of the gross investment in the SEZs and 13 percent in the fifteen open coastal cities in the first half of 1988 was FDI.[57] Most investment went into the service sector, which was essential for building future investment. The energy sector was the second largest FDI benefactor. In all cases the government's tax revenue from FDI gradually increased. Needless to say, the greater access to technology from abroad and the positive impact on the trade balance were all major benefits from the openness to FDI. Some regions, such as Guangdong, benefited far more than others, such as Shanghai ($2.37 billion compared with $360 million in 1989). The gains were still clear to see.[58] The FDI also resulted in increased employment. For example, Guangdong found that by 1988 Hong Kong capital employed more than 1.5 million workers, far more than in Hong Kong's own industrial sector.[59]

In the Soviet Union the legislation for joint ventures with nonsocialist partners was amended several times after it first appeared in mid-1986. Thus, by December 1988 the permission to establish joint ventures no longer had to come from the Council of Ministers and could be granted by state enterprises. By December 1988 the permitted share of foreign ownership was raised to 99 percent and the transfer of shares to a third party no longer required permission from the government. Most crucially, joint ventures were no longer bound by Soviet labor laws or rates of pay. In September 1987 the joint ventures were no longer banned from selling to the local market for hard currency, and their purchases did not have to be through Soviet foreign trade enterprises. In a world of unconvertible rubles, the joint ventures were allowed to export goods other than their own products and to import goods other than for their own needs. This right was withdrawn in March 1989 when goods became so scarce on the domestic market.[60]

The total number of joint ventures increased in the Soviet Union, although nothing like on the Chinese scale. By June 1990, 1,600 were registered, although there was serious doubt about how many were actually in operation. Total foundation capital exceeded $5 billion.[61] There was a clear connection between the loosening of legal restrictions and the number of joint ventures registered, but the comparisons to China still suggested the Soviet Union was not as attractive a place to do business.[62] Leading investors came from the EC and the vast majority were in manufacturing. But basic problems remained, including the uncertain politics and legal regimes, not to mention the absence of skilled labor, of proper infrastructure, and of a convertible ruble. A Soviet economist wrote in June 1987 that "according to the most patriotic evaluation, only 17–18% of our manufacturing industry conforms to world standards."[63] The creation of SEZs was less rapid. It was planned to set up zones at Vyborg near the Finnish border, the districts of the Maritime Territory adjoining Nakhodka, and Armenia and the Crimea in the South. But major debates surrounding the nature of these SEZs were not resolved by the time of the August 1991 revolution.

Vietnam is the only other country where FDI has been taken very seriously as part of a reform program. Foreign investment legislation in Vietnam in 1987 attempted to provide a framework for FDI, but the continuing American boycott has hampered the process. Nevertheless, in 1988–90 Vietnam granted FDI permits of more than $1 billion to some 130 projects, including six vital contracts on oil and natural gas exploration. Some 80 percent of the FDI was concentrated in the South, which was seen as more economically dynamic.[64]

The terms governing joint ventures in Vietnam compare favorably with those in the Soviet Union or China. Tax rates are the lowest of the three.[65] Yet the legal structure is the least developed and causes the most concern among foreign investors. Infrastructure also is the least developed and the bureaucracy the most arcane.[66] The American restraint on financing is a major problem that affects lending from international institutions. Overseas Chinese have been able to prosper as investors in small-scale enterprises because of their ability to operate local networks and their experience of dealing in the communist Chinese system.[67] The overseas Vietnamese community looks set to join this process, an advantage Vietnam and China have but the Soviet Union seems to lack.[68] Yet the Soviet Union has been an important joint venture partner in the most productive sector—the oil industry. The deal with Vietsovpetro in the White Tiger field involves exports to Japan, France, and Singapore.[69]

The authorities in Saigon have established a Zone of Fabrication and Exportation where foreign companies would be free to import commodities, assemble products with low-cost local labor, and re-export the products.[70] But despite the obvious potential to repeat the Chinese success, Vietnam has yet to develop the potential for SEZs based on low-cost labor plugged into the East Asian market.

Compared with Hungary and the GDR, Vietnam has been successful in attracting FDI and joint ventures. Hungary has allowed joint ventures since 1972, but the terms have not been attractive to Western firms. New regulations in January 1986 and 1987 liberalized the conditions of operation; Hungarian taxes for foreign holdings were reduced.[71] By mid-1988 there were some 250 joint ventures bringing in some $300 million. Legislation in December 1988 gave foreigners full protection against nationalization, and the number of joint ventures rose to 870 with FDI of $450 million, mostly in trade, tourism, and the service sector.

In October 1988 the Hungarian Parliament passed a new law that created the possibility of joint stock companies and 100 percent foreign ownership. It opened the way for a stock market, but foreigners would be confined to special "named" stocks that involved considerable red tape.[72] In 1989 companies were sold to Western firms, but by the time of the democratic revolution later in the year, the scene was set for far more sweeping reforms. There had been insufficient time to see if the latest round of reforms regarding FDI would have much effect.

Compared with the GDR and North Korea, where there has been no significant FDI, Hungary must be counted, along with Vietnam, as a country that did take the prospects of FDI seriously. But only in China has there been sufficient time to see the evolution of policy toward FDI and, despite ebbs and flows, the general picture is of real reform. The Soviet Union seemed set on the same course, although with even more problems than in China, and in 1992 its successor states are in earnest.

A crucial feature of all approaches to FDI is the attitude to the value of currency. As China abolished many aspects of guaranteed price stability at home, budget deficits appeared and inflation ensued. Thus, exchange rates had to be adjusted in order to maintain a competitive edge in attracting mobile international capital. China chose the strategy of regular currency devaluations in lieu of a fully convertible currency, although it evolved special currencies for foreign use as a concession to the international market economy. Unofficially, the renminbi yuan remains linked to the U.S. dollar.

No other country was as flexible as China when it came to manipulation of its currency. The Vietnamese dong and the ruble remained officially unconvertible, although both currencies were effectively devalued to provide a more realistic rate of exchange. The Soviet Union held foreign currency auctions to test the real value of the currency and to learn about the operations of the international money markets.[73] Both China and the Soviet Union investigated commodities markets with foreign advice.[74] Nevertheless, the Chinese case suggests just how far reform of foreign economic policy can go without establishing a fully convertible currency. While a fully capitalist banking and security system might be seen as useful parts of a full marketized economy, there is still much that Communist Party states can do short of sweeping domestic reform if their objective is to become more a part of the international economy. There is no necessary link between full domestic reform and major reforms of foreign policy.

It is almost a requirement of our definition of foreign policy reform that the range of trade partners increases. This is not the same as saying that the ratio of foreign trade to GDP should rise, for China in the Soviet Model period in the 1950s was heavily dependent on a few trade partners. East European ratios were higher than those in Western Europe, but that merely showed forced integration of a narrow range of partners. Although the slogans spoke of mitigating the problem of "capitalist encirclement" and avoiding the "anarchic market forces," these states were not able to minimize the impact of the outside world if that was understood to include other socialist allies. Foreign trade was never merely fulfilling a residual role for the East Europeans, if only because trade policy was in part a tool of the Soviet policy of maintaining the cohesion of the bloc. The elimination of most market mechanisms ensured that the trade that was carried out could be fixed at unreal levels. As the quip has it, "we sell them two dead cats and they sell us one dead dog."

The resulting bloc autarky was every bit as unreal as that for an individual state. The CMEA framework tried to create such absurdities as a Hungary producing iron and steel despite the virtual absence of iron ore or coking coal.[75] Not surprisingly, the East Europeans were dragged kicking, screaming, and sabotaging into the CMEA system. The results were arbitrary trade relations not based on world-market competitiveness, technological achievement, or up-to-date-standards.

Reforms in the 1970s that involved extensive borrowing by the East Europeans from the West were unhappily sanctioned by the Soviet Union on both political and economic grounds.[76] When the West foolishly made dubious loans to unstable economies, the Soviet Union contained its concern as long as it knew they would remain within the Soviet sphere. When the debt burden grew heavy and economic crises deepened, Western banks pulled out or imposed heavy terms. The East Europeans became even more dependent on the Soviet Union, and the domestic reforms stalled. Poland even collapsed into crisis and martial law. The Soviet Union could have done without such crises, but its more conservative leaders could feel satisfied that the East Europeans knew they had to get on with the Soviet Union because the West would not bail them out.[77] It was not until 1989, when the Soviet Union allowed the East European regimes to stand or, more properly, fall on their own, that fundamental change in external economic relations became possible. Only when Communist Party rule was gone did the West promise real aid, finance, and the opportunities for radically reoriented trade patterns. To be sure, none of these changes would happen as fast as those in the GDR, but real change in trade ties did in fact depend on revolution rather than on reform.

Yet the same can hardly be said in East Asia, and perhaps not even in the Soviet Union. China demonstrated that real domestic reforms could lead to a real change in trade patterns. China's open door policy developed more distinctly after 1978 as the number of trade partners expanded and the ratio of trade to GDP tripled to a level higher than that in Japan.[78] By the mid-1980s China rose from thirty-second to fourteenth place among world exporters. By the late 1980s China had become the fifth largest trader in the Pacific basin, and it was closing in on South Korea. Exports in China, unlike in most developing states, do not depend on food and primary goods. In 1988, 69 percent of exports were manufactured goods. The speed of China's adjustment to the halving of its oil export earnings suggests the benefits of a command economy, at least in some respects. The import structure was also adjusted by, for example, using joint ventures to build cars in China and thereby satisfying 80 percent of its domestic car needs by 1988. These changes in trends were the direct result of an avowedly experimental approach to foreign trade. Small case studies were expanded by central fiat to the country as a whole. International organizations played a vital part in this experimentation, especially in helping establish feasibility studies and managing foreign debt.

China became Japan's third largest trade partner and was attracting investment from all over the booming region.[79] The Special Economic Zones along the coast were attracting heavy investment from Hong Kong and overseas Chinese and in general China's entry into the lower wage end of the regional economy was encouraging the "hollowing out" process in a number of East Asian states. If only by virtue of its size, China's entry into the international economy was a significant consequence of its domestic reforms.

In contrast with the first thirty years of communist China, modernization was being defined by international standards and the international market. This is illustrated by China's bias toward trade with the West and its willingness to accept Western procedures (for example, the German standardization system for goods and the World Bank and OECD systems for accounting and foreign trade statistics).[80] Hong Kong in particular played a vital role in drawing the Guangdong region into the international system. Some even describe the region as a proto-NIC (newly industrialized country).[81]

No other country in our survey has found its trade policy changed quite as dramatically as has China. Although the Soviet Union made many noises about similar reforms, the reality was very slow in catching up. In East Asia, the Soviet Union found some marginal changes in its trade patterns. Sino-Soviet trade grew rapidly, and China became the Soviet Union's second most important trade partner in the Pacific (after Japan). The Soviet Union moved to fourth among all China's trade partners by the late 1980s. But the Soviet Union also began to practice pragmatic politics and opened trade links with South Korea and Taiwan. Diplomatic relations with South Korea were established in September 1990.

In Europe, where the vast majority of Soviet trade was concentrated, there were less obvious reforms. The overall Soviet share of world trade fell from 4.6 percent in 1983 to 3 percent in 1989. In 1983 the Soviet Union ranked sixth in world trade tables but by 1989 it had slipped to twelfth place. The share of East-West trade in world trade actually fell from 1.8 percent in 1970 to 1.6 percent in 1982.[82] Despite its size, the Soviet Union was clearly poorer for its autarkic approach to trade.

The main reason for this decline relates to the Soviet Union's vast exports of raw materials and the falling prices for such goods. Between 1972 and 1983, the total hard currency earnings from energy exports increased from 29 percent to 80 percent.[83] This windfall reduced domestic pressures for reforms. According to Soviet Finance Minister Boris Gostev, the Soviet Union lost 40 billion rubles in 1985–88 because of the sharp drop in world oil prices.[84] Changes in currency values meant the value of other Soviet exports also fell in this period. Without a major switch to industrial production that could be measured against international standards, there was unlikely to ever have been any real improvement in the structure of Soviet trade unless energy prices changed.

Without "hard budget constraints," exporters were unlikely to produce competitive goods. Joint ventures would not thrive if they were merely grafted on to this inefficient economy where real prices were unknown.[85] Import bias and export aversion continued in the Soviet economy. The ad hoc but still powerful intervention from above on micro issues made any real reform in export policy hard to imagine. Far more than the matter of convertible currency, these micro-level problems hampered reform.

The share of industrialized Western countries in Soviet trade was 33 percent in 1980 and fell to some 22–26 percent in the Gorbachev era. Comparable figures for China's trade with OECD states are three times higher. The Soviet trade deficit also grew in these years. A surplus was run with CMEA states until 1987, when falling energy prices also sent this aspect of trade into deficit. In 1991 Soviet trade with CMEA members began to be conducted using world prices and hard currency settlements.

Pressure for reform in foreign economic policy existed. The real limit was the slow pace of economic reform in the Soviet Union and the related fear of instability in the Soviet system. Developed OECD states' trade with the Soviet Union was a relatively low percentage of their total trade, with the notable exception of West Germany. But OECD states often registered real rates of growth in their trade with China in the 1980s.

Vietnam also showed the link between changing trade patterns and domestic reform. The pre-reform policy of close and unnatural reliance on CMEA trade was rapidly jettisoned in favor of closer integration with Vietnam's Indochinese neighbors and the more developed states of East Asia. Trade patterns grew more diversified in the late 1980s, and airline links proliferated as foreigners flooded into Vietnam, particularly in the South, to look for the next untapped economy of the Pacific region.

The Soviet Union accounted for 60 percent of Vietnamese trade during the CMEA era. Today reforms in Eastern Europe, as well as domestic pressures in Vietnam, are leading to major changes in the direction of trade. More than two hundred thousand Vietnamese workers in

Eastern Europe were sent back to Vietnam. The country had to move quickly to finance its foreign trade.[86] The export of boat people to other parts of East Asia declined as Vietnam assumed a more constructive part in the regional economy of East Asia.[87] Japan was emerging as the major capitalist trading partner, and trade links with Taiwan and South Korea were also being developed.[88] Because of domestic reforms there was a sharp increase in agricultural and marine product exports, and Vietnam's deficit in trade with the convertible currency states has dropped.[89] Plans were even being laid for a reform of the banking sector in order to invite some foreign banks in to help deal with the shortage of FDI and expertise on the international economy. Remittances from overseas Chinese are believed to be about $200 million per year, which hardly makes a dent in Vietnam's large foreign debt. But major progress as a rice exporter suggests domestic reforms can have a swift impact. Foreign trade and rice exports accounted for 20 percent of foreign currency earnings in 1989.[90]

Vietnam's progress in reforming its foreign trade pattern is in contrast to Hungary's stalemate. At first Hungary achieved success, but then it seemed to stall. Hungarian trade with the West increased throughout the 1970s at a rapid pace. By 1980 exports reached 1334 percent of their 1970 level, while imports rose even more rapidly. Trade deficits were recorded each year. Trade with CMEA countries expanded at roughly half the rate, and trade deficits were also recorded in most years.

By contrast in the 1980s, Hungary was constantly in surplus with the CMEA mainly due to the fall in the oil price. Trade with the West was virtually stagnant with imports rising only 16 percent by 1987 over the 1980 level. Exports were up 167 percent, reflecting emergency efforts to cope with high levels of debt.

The commodity composition of trade shifted during the 1980s, symptomatic of the crises at home and in the CMEA. The share of industrial machinery exports to the CMEA grew to 55 percent from 48 percent in 1980, but these exports to the OECD barely increased from 12 percent to 12.8 percent. A key export item in this period was fuel, which was re-exported from the Soviet Union, but falling prices also hurt Hungarian trade. Thus, despite periodic attempts at reform at home, the pattern of Hungarian trade seems to have shown no real reform.

The GDR, which had no real reform at home, also showed little change in foreign economic policy. During the 1970s the GDR built up trade deficits with both CMEA and the OECD states. By the early 1980s it had become one of the most indebted countries of the bloc, but its highly advantageous arrangements with the Federal Republic allowed it to weather the debt problem caused by the Polish crisis with relatively little destabilization of the domestic economy. The slowdown in growth was markedly less acute, and the standard of living was protected. The centralism of the economic system proved an advantage in the early 1980s in retaining control of the basic economic processes that in Hungary were mismanaged or inadequately controlled. Imports were effectively controlled, and trade with the West was in surplus after 1981.

This does not indicate success in running the economy, except in the narrowest terms. A degree of balance was restored in the short term but at the cost of further isolating the country from the world economy. The GDR and Czechoslovakia enjoyed the dubious distinction of being the two countries in the CMEA which, despite being the most developed, had by the mid-1980s a much smaller share of CMEA trade with the West than they had in the mid-1960s. In 1965 the GDR accounted for 14.7 percent of CMEA exports to the West and 17.2 percent of imports. By 1983 the respective shares had fallen to 12.2 percent and 12.3 percent. In most respects, the GDR appeared to have become a more closed economy than it was before the 1980s. This was the result of a conscious policy, unlike in Hungary, where an unmanageable economic crisis forced the government to take emergency measures.

Thus, the patterns of trade and investment of reforming communist states seem relatively clear. Without reform, little sustained increase in trade, finance, or aid is possible. Chaotic or unsustained reform only leads to brief and erratic increases in economic relations with the capitalist world. Now that the East Europeans have had their revolution and seem determined to explore new economic relations, it is likely that trade patterns will undergo major changes. Chinese reforms have already transformed bilateral relations in the region to the extent that Japan and the NICs seem anxious to minimize the economic impact from the political unrest in 1989. China has developed a vital need for an open door, and the East Asian region seems to be developing a vital stake in a stable Chinese economy.

Multilateral Economic Relations

The most striking feature of the international economy is the extent to which it is dominated by the global market economy. Only one regional economic organization, the European Community, has proven able to transform trade relations among its partners and as a result has attracted additional members. By contrast, in Eastern Europe, as I have already noted, the CMEA was an artificial creation made no more stable by the forcible trade relations. The prime focus of the CMEA was on imports. The demand for imports was set by the rate and pattern of growth as defined in the national economic plan of each member. With persistent political pressure to set high growth rate targets, the demand for imports was insatiable. On the other hand, each state had an interest in limiting exports to the minimum necessary to cover the import bill because of the pressures of domestic demand generated by the forced pace of growth. This was always an artificial system that prevented an open approach to foreign economic relations. Although it was recognized eventually that some trade with the OECD states was inevitable, it was assumed that this could be restricted to about 20 percent of total trade turnover.

By the end of the 1970s, the pattern of trade of CMEA states had come under considerable pressure. The cost to the Soviet Union of subsidizing its allies' energy consumption was a major problem. The resulting pressures on the CMEA forced individual states onto world markets. This further weakened CMEA linkages. Powerful domestic producers were often strong supporters of the CMEA system, which made far less demands on the quality of their products.

But the East Europeans were also experiencing increasing problems in trade with the West. A far too large increase in imports led to debt, while exports stagnated. Drastic cuts in imports produced a sharp economic downturn at home, which in turn further restricted exports. More borrowing was impossible because of high levels of debt, and major domestic reforms were impossible because of the perceived political costs of austerity. The revolutions of 1989 were built on the basis of these dilemmas.

It was always likely that real economic reforms in Eastern Europe would lead to the demise of the CMEA structure, even if certain important trade links between its former members were retained for some time. Yet a number of East European states intend to make their way as swiftly as possible into the EC-dominated world. The GDR has the quickest route via a takeover by West Germany.

The Soviet Union had a large domestic economy that could not be closely integrated into the global economy for decades, and then only if there was sweeping and successful reform at home. Having lost its dependent trade partners as export markets for second-rate machinery, the Soviet trade structure became even more dependent on raw material exports. As for Australia or Canada, there was a niche in international interdependence for such an economy, but it was a necessarily uncomfortable place when the price of primary products fluctuates as it does. With its vast frontiers, the Soviet Union had the prospect of being involved as an actor in the global economy, serving as at least a notional land-bridge between Europe and East Asia. But the basic architecture of the international economy remained the three-legged structure of Europe, North America, and East Asia with very little else likely to intrude. The international economy did very well without the Soviet Union, and thus it has little need to make major adjustments to fit it in. After the London G-7 summit in July 1991, Mikhail Gorbachev made his case for major assistance from the world's richest nations, but it was made clear to the Soviet leader that no "Grand Bargain" was possible, especially if it involved major Western funds, unless there was evidence that real economic reforms were under way and there was an agreement on relations between the republics and the Union.

The Soviet Union recognized its difficult position and took a far more positive approach to the international institutions of the global market economy. Eduard Shevardnadze reportedly regarded IMF membership for the Soviet Union as "a logical continuation of its policy of wider involvement in global economic cooperation."[91] IMF membership was some way off, but the Soviet Union made progress in finding a seat in the GATT. On May 16, 1990, the Soviet Union was admitted as an observer. The Soviet Union's intention was to further its own foreign economic relations and to help bring some of the methods of the international market economy into the Soviet Union.[92] Similar calculations were at work in the Soviet participation as observers in the Asian Development Bank (since 1987).[93] But membership in the IMF was a much trickier proposition because of the dominating role of the United States. The IMF represented the hard-line approach to the international market economy, and Soviet membership would have required a full commitment on Moscow's part to an open foreign economic policy. The credits from the IMF would obviously have been welcome, but not at the cost of a restructuring determined in the capitals of the G-7. Membership would have meant participation as a medium-sized state without a seat on the executive board. Recognition of this lowly status was hard for a former superpower to accept.

China and Vietnam, like the Soviet Union, are much more likely to be changed by the international economy than able to reshape it in their own image. China joined the IMF in April 1980 and the World Bank a month later. It became part of the multifiber agreement in 1984, and it joined the African Development Bank in 1986. China made its GATT application in the same year, but its prospects are mixed up with the application from Taiwan, and the Western restrictions on economic relations with China after the Beijing massacre in June 1989.

The World Bank has played an important role as adviser and provider of funds for China's domestic reforms. While China joined the international economic community, the community also entered into the heart of the Chinese economy. Advice from the Bank has helped shape the reforms, and China has also become more forthcoming with the provision of data in accordance with World Bank and IMF rules. The size of China's debt has been monitored by the IMF and despite the boycotts after June 1989, contacts have been maintained as China got over the debt hurdle of the early 1990s.[94]

Of the countries discussed in this chapter, China is the most integrated into the international economy and its institutions. Vietnam is still struggling to overcome diplomatic barriers held in place by the United States. As the United States began to ease its attitude toward Vietnam over Cambodia in July 1990, there were prospects for Vietnam to follow China into a closer relationship with the institutions of the international economy. Vietnam also holds out some hope of growing closer to the Association of Southeast Asian Nations (ASEAN), even though the association remains a less than successful body in terms of economic integration.

Hungary has been a signatory of the GATT since 1973 (Poland joined in 1967 and Romania in 1971). Hungary's main motive for joining the GATT was to get key trade partners in the EC to end discriminatory quotas and it was so disappointed that regular complaints were lodged. Hungary concluded that only direct talks with the EC would resolve its problems.[95]

In November 1981 Hungary applied for membership in the IMF and the World Bank. Some observers interpreted this as a declaration of independence from Moscow.[96] Hungary was also searching for a solution to its debt crisis and the approval on May 6, 1982 to join the IMF and on July 7th to join the World Bank was fortunately timed. Loans soon followed that allowed Hungary to weather the immediate crisis while retaining the confidence of the West. Western bank lending resumed in August 1982 when a syndicated loan was obtained on the eurocurrency market.

Thus, Hungary managed to be the only communist state in all three of the major institutions of the market economy. But as the very different cases of Hungary, Vietnam, the Soviet Union, and China show, membership is not enough to change foreign trade or reform domestic policy. The experience of Vietnam suggests that membership in these bodies is somewhat more than useless in these regards, but the case of Hungary suggests it is something less than a cause of reform.

In sum, China—more than the Soviet Union, Vietnam, Hungary, the GDR, and North Korea—has demonstrated that it is possible to have real reform of foreign economic policy. The international system can have an important impact in shaping the reforms, and yet this impact is most evident when domestic politics are moving in the same direction. What is perhaps most remarkable is the range of policies that can be pursued by a country such as China and the extent to which it can respond to pressures from the international system without complete reform at home. Certainly, in comparison to the East European cases, the Chinese determination and ability to find a solution short of total collapse of the Communist Party state is striking.

Defense Policy Reform

Reforming defense policy requires some confidence that common security is preferable to narrow national security. But only an extremely irresponsible leader would pursue common security if no one else in the international environment was willing to cooperate. Thus, it is essential to appreciate the extent to which the international system has helped or even stimulated the reform of defense policy.

The Threat of War. Vietnam was in an almost continuous state of war for forty years. So long as the Vietnamese communists wished to bring a communist variant of independence to their country, they had to fight various great powers who were intent on stopping the spread of the rival ideology, or rival variants of a supposedly shared ideology. The fact that Vietnamese communists were successful in defeating France and the United States made it all the more likely that despite the heavy costs of war, the Vietnamese would feel that war was a useful instrument of policy.

Yet the intracommunist conflict with Cambodia was different. Communists were in power in Phnom Penh when war broke out with Vietnam.[97] This war was a complex mix of traditional rivalries, an ambitious and often ruthless regime in Cambodia, and an overlay of Sino-Soviet rivalry supporting different communist factions. Indeed it was the latter factor that led China to attack Vietnam in February 1979 after Vietnamese troops established a favorable regime in Phnom Penh.[98] As far as Vietnam was concerned, victory (or at least the absence of defeat) meant that it would stagger on sustaining the occupation of Cambodia, despite the heavy costs in terms of delayed domestic reform. In the ensuing years Vietnamese troops were able to consolidate control over most of Cambodia, and they could therefore begin to relax about external threats. Chinese attacks along the frontier with Vietnam became more ritual as Beijing also began to seek less confrontation along its borders.[99]

Relaxation of tension was perhaps the most challenging kind of development for Vietnam because it then suggested that heavy militarization of defense policy might be reduced. Thus, the basic stimulus for reform came from a mix of domestic needs and success on the battlefield. But pressure was added by its main ally, the Soviet Union. By 1986 Moscow was reassessing its own defense policy. Heavy support for distant allies was perceived as a drain on Soviet interests and the exchequer.[100] Soviet visitors to Vietnam began making it plain that Soviet aid would be reduced from $2 billion per year and Vietnam would be expected to engage in its own domestic reforms in order to get any subsequent assistance. China indicated to the Soviet Union that Sino-Soviet relations could be normalized if the Vietnamese left Cambodia. Moscow then began pushing Vietnam to leave. Soviet pressure was undoubtedly important, but if the Vietnamese economy had not been in such a perilous state, it might have resisted such pressure as it had in earlier phases of conflict in Indochina. Vietnam withdrew from Cambodia in September 1989 for various reasons, but this basic reform in defense policy seemed to be based on domestic problems.

The Soviet invasion of Afghanistan in December 1979 is comparable to the Vietnamese occupation of Cambodia. Indeed, the withdrawal of Soviet troops in February 1989 showed some of the same features that affected the much smaller and weaker Vietnam. In Vietnam, however, the decision to enter Cambodia was made by mostly the same people who decided it was time to leave. In the Soviet Union a new leadership was required to decide to change policy. If the fundamental motive in Vietnam withdrawing was the need to begin reform at home, the Soviet calculation was similarly based on the priority of domestic reform.[101] It is true that Vietnam was less advanced in its reform program than was the Soviet Union when it decided to pull out of foreign wars, but the sense of foreign engagements as a drain was similar.

Of course, pressures from the international system were different. The Soviet Union had no Soviet "ally" exerting pressure, although it did have a China anxious to see a withdrawal in order to pursue a larger foreign policy détente. The Soviet Union also had pressure from the Islamic and Western worlds either threatening more problems or promising more favors if the Kremlin decided to withdraw from Afghanistan.[102] The point was the same: Withdrawal was encouraged by the international system with a mix of carrots and sticks. And, of course, the Soviet Union faced a greater problem in subduing the local population in Afghanistan. But as in Cambodia after the withdrawal of Vietnam, the favored regime remained in place in Afghanistan, even if not in total control of the country. Thus, unlike the United States' withdrawal from Vietnam, where defeat was complete, Vietnam and the

Soviet Union could leave with some sense of success. Would Vietnam have left Cambodia and the Soviet Union quit Afghanistan without external pressure? More than Vietnam, the Soviet Union made up its own mind—as one might expect of a so-called superpower. In both cases, however, the basic decision was an internal one shaped by battle-field problems and encouraged by external factors.

In contrast to these examples of reformed defense policy is the vexing problem of China. China invaded Vietnam in a punitive war lasting a few weeks. It apparently never had any intention of staying longer, even if it did hope to be more successful and devastating in its attack. But the real problem is that this war, and the more successful seizure of islands in the Spratly group in March 1988, was launched by a reforming leadership. For China at least, a reformed foreign policy left room for the use of force to settle territorial claims.[103] Whether ruled by reformers or radicals, China will try and satisfy its territorial claims, as it has done ever since the communists came to power.[104] The Chinese action suggests that, at least in its case, there are distinct limits to the demilitarization of defense policy. Indeed, professionalism, which we have defined as a part of general demilitarization, can be turned into an offensive force that militarizes international relations. As in the case of the Soviet military reforms of the early 1960s, or of the 1970s in the era of détente, there is no necessary link between all aspects of demilitarization of defense policy, let alone between reform of defense policy and foreign economic policy. Especially in the realm of defense policy, some aspects of common security can be sought, while some elements of nationally defined national security are pursued.

This is not to suggest that China is prepared to use its military power whenever possible. As in the Soviet Union in the 1960s, defense modernization in China has involved a reassessment of the role of nuclear weapons and of the "inevitability of war." As early as 1980, China was arguing that war was no longer inevitable. Therefore, China could find the breathing space in which to modernize and reform. Cynics will note that this change in doctrine came despite the recent spate of wars on China's periphery and suggested a change of heart rather than the emergence of a new reality. China wanted a breathing space so it was determined to see one.[105]

Chinese doctrine evolved in the 1980s. Although large wars did not appear likely, small ones were. Indeed, China was likely to be involved in limited conflicts. Chinese defense modernization stressed air power and especially naval power, not the massed ranks of ground troops that would be useful in a general war.[106] Although China did modernize its nuclear arsenal in this period, the most striking change was the shift to a more SLBM-based deterrent. Despite a greater capacity to deploy large numbers of weapons in each category of a nuclear arsenal, China kept to its strategy of minimum deterrence across a range of weapons.[107]

The Soviet Union had long thought that war could be prevented. Thus, for Moscow there was no need to reform this aspect of its defense policy, and the fact that China did so merely became another strand in the Sino-Soviet détente of the 1980s. Optimists might argue that China is just catching up with modern military doctrine and that its use of force in the past decade is an anachronism unlikely to be repeated once the defense reforms take hold. The events of March 1988 suggest otherwise, as do China's policies toward arms transfers.

A reformed defense policy might be expected to include less "displaced conflict" or even profiting from the conflicts of others. If instead of direct involvement in conflict, a country gives the tools of war to others to wage war in its stead, serious reform is not taking place. Thus, it was argued during East-West détente in the 1970s that rising levels of Soviet arms sales to the developing world indicated a "proxy war" serving Soviet interests.

Although the GDR and Hungary have never been significant players in the arms transfer business, North Korea does have a significant indigenous arms industry, at least by the standards of small and developing states. Vietnam, China, and the Soviet Union all have played important roles in fueling regional conflict through arms transfers.[108]

Vietnam was a major supporter of other communists in their common struggle against the United States and its allies. Vietnam organized the transfer of Soviet and Chinese weapons to allies in Laos, Cambodia, and southern Vietnam. By 1975 Vietnam had taken over all of its own country and installed a favorable regime in Laos. Cambodia was far from friendly, and eventually it was invaded. The subsequent Heng Samrin regime was supported by Vietnam so that when Hanoi's troops pulled out in 1989, the Phnom Penh government could more or less hold its own against the Chinese-supported Khmer Rouge. Thus, while Vietnam withdrew from Cambodia, arms transfers increased.

The Soviet Union did precisely the same thing with Afghanistan as a way of easing its withdrawal. In such cases, arms transfers were part of a demilitarization of defense policy, but they also indicated its very distinct limits. Indeed, ambiguity surrounds the entire issue of arms transfers in a time of a more open defense policy. On the one hand there were initial signs that the Soviet Union was reducing its arms transfers. Soviet sales to the developing world fell by 66 percent according to some estimates in 1987–88, although this was part of a contract-

ing market because of economic problems in the developing world.[109]
But it seems that the Soviet Union's share of the market for exports to
developing states actually rose, and in 1989 was higher than in 1985.
Yet with the collapse of markets in Eastern Europe and Iraq, the Soviet
share of a shrinking market fell back sharply in 1990.[110]

Arms transfer statistics are notoriously complicated, but there is some
evidence to suggest that the desire to make money from arms transfers
may become more acceptable at a time of greater openness to the international market as a whole, and arms sales may become more a part of
international economic policy than of defense policy. Clearly, openness
of defense policy would suggest a reduction in arms transfers as a useful
instrument of policy, but in an age when reform seems dominated by
economic calculations, the profit motive may well lead to an increase in
arms sales. Needless to say, the potential for disarray in defense policy
and for conflict at home and abroad is likely to increase. As Soviet
military officials in the age of reform made clear, the civilian reformers
had to choose whether the Soviet Union wanted to give up the benefits
from arms sales or make transfers at "friendship prices." But the decline
in the demand for arms proved a more powerful cause of reform, and
Soviet arms transfers were cut in the post–cold war world.

The decision not to sell at friendship prices any more was part of
China's reforms in foreign policy. By 1990, however, China also found
that shrinking markets meant arms sales were reduced.[111] But this did
not mean China had decided to reduce arms sales for profit. In fact,
before the slump in the market, China had emerged as a major player
in the international arms market. Economic reform seems to be a key
limit on this aspect of defense policy reform. China's armed forces seek
profits to plough back into the defense budget. Foreign policy pragmatism has led China to sell to both sides of the Iran-Iraq War and in some
cases to become leading suppliers of heavy equipment. China sold tanks
to Iraq and antitank weapons to Iran. While trying in the Security
Council to arrange an end to the conflict, China sold antiship missiles
that sank Western-flagged tankers. China acquired modern military
technology from Israel, but sold some of its newer missiles to Israeli
adversaries in the Persian Gulf.[112] China also acquired modern technology from Western states in Europe and the United States, only to
sell to Iran other technology that sank Western ships. The basic motive
was money, but there was also a hope of finding friends in the region
when the war was over.

China became a far more credible superpower in the 1980s as its
defense policy embraced arms sales as a tool of policy. It was not so
much that China sought to influence the outcome of the war as the

superpowers used to do (for example, in Angola in the mid-1970s). Rather China, much more like France or Britain, wanted to make money. This was not a reformed defense policy, although it is true that it could have been more militarized if China had supported one ally to change the balance of power in the Middle East.

Peaceful Settlement of Disputes. Another characteristic of reformed defense policy is a positive approach to the settlement of international disputes. Vietnam, once it had withdrawn from Cambodia, became a key actor in determining whether a solution could be found to the Cambodian conflict.[113] Vietnam, as a source of refugees, was also involved in disputes with ASEAN states, Hong Kong, and various Western states concerned with settling refugees. In both cases Vietnam took a positive role in achieving a peaceful settlement. This cautiously accommodating position is in keeping with the tentative nature of many of Vietnam's reforms and the steady pressure from the Soviet Union.

The Soviet Union found that its more accommodating line on the peaceful settlement of disputes was met by conciliation on the part of its adversaries. Observers of the pre-Gorbachev era will recall only too well how Soviet support for national liberation movements around the globe fueled East-West conflict and helped destroy earlier phases of détente. Although the signs of change in Moscow's policy toward national liberation movements were apparent to astute observers before the Gorbachev era, it is clear that only under Yuri Andropov did the Soviet Union seriously reconsider its policy.[114]

Perhaps the most striking evidence of the change in the Soviet policy was its new attitude toward the United Nations.[115] The settlement in Namibia could not have been possible without Soviet pressure on Cuba and Angola and a matching American pressure to force South Africa to reach agreement.[116] Moscow also cut back assistance to Ethiopia in an effort to reduce burdens on the Soviet Union, but with the consequence that the regional conflict on the Horn of Africa worked toward a resolution.[117] In Central America the message to Cuba and Nicaragua was similar. Most important of all, the Soviet Union worked closely with the United States in the Security Council to formulate a dozen resolutions against Iraq, following Iraq's invasion of Kuwait in August 1990, culminating in one approving the use of force against the former Soviet ally, Iraq.

Unlike earlier phases of détente when there were arms control agreements but no deals on regional conflicts, the Gorbachev era included comprehensive reform of defense policy. The linkage between all kinds of conflict was recognized. While earlier détente had been damaged by the absence of any such linkage, the Soviet Union's recognition of the need for more comprehensive approaches to genuinely interdependent security smoothed the way to wide-ranging cooperation.[118]

Yet again China stands out as a relatively old thinker when it comes to interdependent security. While the Soviet Union helped shove Vietnam and Cambodia to a more moderate position on the Indochina conflict, China did far less to push the Khmer Rouge to serious talks.[119] China has shown in the past that it is prepared to turn off the taps of support to revolutionary movements in Southeast Asia in order to improve relations in the region. But Beijing still retains its support for the Khmer Rouge as a way to press Vietnam into a more submissive position and even to get a more favorable regime in Cambodia. There is some evidence that China does see the need for a settlement, especially in the wake of Western criticism after the events of June 1989, but Beijing is far less willing to demilitarize the Indochinese conflicts.

Yet China's policies are patchy. Perhaps its most positive approach to regional security has been its pressure on North Korea to desist from destabilizing the booming northeast Asian economy.[120] When China decided to open economic contacts with South Korea, it had to ensure that the North did not disrupt the new lucrative relations. China had traditionally been more a supporter of Kim Il Sung's harder line on negotiations with South Korea, and the Soviet Union always feared that if it pushed Kim too hard to the negotiating table, he might take China's side in the Sino-Soviet split. But with growing détente in Sino-Soviet relations, it was far easier for both China and the Soviet Union to tacitly cooperate in limiting the risks of conflict on the Korean peninsula. This arrangement was apparently not negotiated, but it evolved as China demonstrated by deeds that communist states could do business with South Korea and need not bother much with North Korea. Moscow joined in the new strategy and encouraged the Hungarians to be the first to establish formal diplomatic relations with South Korea. All states, except North Korea, wanted to attend the Seoul Olympiad in 1988. Therefore, Pyongyang was told by China and the Soviet Union to refrain from dangerous military action. Considering the growing importance of the northeast Asian region for the global economy, this was particularly important evidence of a positive approach to regional security.

Indeed, China's attitude to other conflicts in Asia, including that between India and Pakistan, or in Namibia, the Horn of Africa, or the Gulf crisis in 1990–91, has been, like the Soviet Union, that of a constructive member of the U.N. Security Council.[121] China has sent observers to the Middle East truce supervisory units, and it has loosened its ban on contacts with Israel in order to prepare for future negotiations. By contrast, China's attitude toward the Iran-Iraq war undermined international efforts to resolve the conflict. During the Kuwait crisis in November 1990, China abstained from voting on the Security Council resolution sanctioning the use of force against Iraq.

It used to be said that China was merely a great power and not a superpower because its ability to influence distant conflicts was limited. Its rhetorical support for factions in the Angolan civil war could not be translated into active military support; nor could its backing of the PLO mean anything unless the Soviet Union agreed. Now that China can deliver weapons anywhere, and in large quantities, it has demonstrated key features of being a superpower. To that extent, China is militarizing its defense policy, and at a time when others, such as the Soviet Union, have demilitarized their attitude to regional conflict.

Arms Control and Disarmament. Is arms control an element of defense policy reform? The answer depends more on whether arms control contributes to international security than on whether there is an absolute reduction in forces. Vietnamese troop reductions certainly demonstrated this point, for cuts in the armed forces only followed a more general sense that Cambodia had been stabilized, China had been deterred and there was a pressing domestic need to engage in reform. Vietnam had the third largest armed forces in the communist world. Its decision to cut five hundred thousand off the rolls was a unilateral effort, albeit encouraged by the Soviet Union. Vietnam negotiated with no one and determined the extent of the cuts. Indeed there has never been a formal arms control agreement in Asia that limits forces.[122]

Nevertheless, as reductions along the Sino-Soviet frontier have made clear, there is real arms control in Asia. In fact, the Euro-Atlantic obsession with de jure arms control has never been accepted in the East Asian context of more pragmatic politics. De facto arms control along the Sino-Soviet frontier was far more impressive than anything seen in the pre-1990 European theater. China began the process in the early stages of its reforms by unilaterally pulling back its forces from the frontier to allow for a more mobile defense doctrine to be put into operation.[123] The Soviet Union, in the unreformed old days of Brezhnev, decided that the deployments in the Soviet Far East were sufficient to deter a Chinese threat. Divisions were unofficially "thinned out" by reducing the category of readiness. More than eighty thousand troops were taken off the frontier before Gorbachev came to power. China responded, albeit tacitly, by reducing its armed forces by some 1 million men in 1985–87. About ninety thousand troops were removed from the Sino-Soviet frontier.

The virtuous cycle of détente continued with Gorbachev's announcement at the United Nations in December 1988 that some five hundred thousand Soviet troops would be taken off the battle rolls. Fifty-two percent of the cuts were to come from Soviet forces in Asia, 40 percent from the frontier facing China. In 1989 China and the Soviet Union finally began formal negotiations on confidence-building measures along the frontier. Although not all the promised cuts have yet been achieved on the Soviet side, the trend is clear. Real arms control and disarmament could be achieved by unilateral means, and indeed informally interlocked unilateral disarmament was much faster than the juridical nit-picking that so slowed European and superpower arms control. The key was the decision by China and the Soviet Union that they both needed a more peaceful international environment in which to pursue modernization. So long as they saw their rival was prepared to reciprocate in kind, cuts in troops could be made without obtaining perfect parity. Military sufficiency was part of a more comprehensive sense of national security.

Of course, none of these cuts was formally agreed to, and thus no provision was made for formal verification. Confidence building through formal arms control did appear to follow the informal accord and may well be designed to help get over future instability that might arise from unforeseen challenges to the new status quo. But in the meantime both countries can benefit from the peace dividend. Crossborder contacts such as trade can flourish without waiting for the lawyers to agree. Swift agreement that shows immediate success also allows less time for political back-chat that might undermine a deal.

A general reform in defense policy in China helped start the process of arms control. It is interesting that the Soviet Union, not otherwise seen to be in a mood for defense reform, followed suit. But as was evident in the 1970s during superpower nuclear arms control, there is no necessary link between arms control and a general strategy of reform.[124] If the reductions can be viewed in the national interest as well as the international interest, then an agreement is possible. A greater concern with the interdependence of security would undoubtedly make the virtuous circle even stronger, as indeed was demonstrated by the reinforcement given by the Gorbachev priorities after 1985.

Although the earliest cuts in Soviet conventional forces took place in Asia, reductions were later made in the European theater. Indeed, it was a vital part of the détente in Europe that the Soviet Union was prepared to make disproportionately larger cuts in its forces.[125] Although progress was made in conventional arms control talks in Europe before the second half of 1989, the decommunizing revolutions of the second half of the year once again showed that politics is a better means than law to achieve real reductions.[126] It was the Soviet decision to allow the East Europeans to dispose of communist rulers that led to the most rapid demilitarization since the end of the Second World War. New governments in Eastern Europe soon demanded Soviet troop withdrawals from Europe far in excess of what the negotiators had agreed. As the Warsaw Pact collapsed, arms controllers had to retreat to their word processors to turn out radical new proposals for restructuring forces in Europe. Clearly, the comical efforts to update the conventional forces in Europe (CFE) agenda were frustrated by a fast-moving political agenda. By the time the accord was ready to be signed, the political momentum in Europe had ensured that troops were already well on their way to being withdrawn before the observers could count them properly. And yet the growing crisis in the Soviet Union in 1991 and the return of more conservative forces, including the armed forces, led to a reassessment of the CFE accord. Confusion caused by the war in the Gulf in 1990–91 and Soviet violations of the CFE accord made it seem for a time that the treaty would not be formally ratified. Yet the strengthening of the reformers in the Soviet Union meant a deal could be hammered out on CFE, suggesting that, at least in this respect, the linkage of domestic and foreign policies was close.

The coming to Europe of the East Asian style of arms control was frustrating for those wishing to see a formal accord. Yet the reality was real cuts in conventional forces derived from Soviet reforms. To be sure, we had earlier CSCE (Conference on Security and Cooperation in Europe) accords before such sweeping reforms, for reasons already suggested. Where national security and international security coincided, some accords were always possible. But when national security concepts were fundamentally reassessed, and it was decided that real security for the Soviet Union required allowing more of Western Europe into the Soviet Union—the true meaning of a Common European Home—then defense policy reform reached new levels.

The first consequence of the decision was that hegemonic control over Eastern Europe could not be maintained. The decision was taken in Moscow, but the pressure had come from the East Europeans. They demonstrated a determined unwillingness to serve Soviet interests.[127] The burden of imperial overstretch grew too heavy to carry. Gorbachev gambled that the Soviet Union would benefit more from a cooperative attitude to all of Europe. By stressing the notion of a Common European Home, Gorbachev hoped to persuade Europeans that the Soviet Union could contribute to the greater good of the continent. He wished to give Europeans a stake in reform of the Soviet Union because this would help him overcome conservative opposition.[128]

But it was an astounding gamble to take. The former East European allies seized their independence with hardly a thank you to Moscow once the tanks had departed. Worried about German imperialism, the

Poles would seek some Soviet support, but it was only the developed West Europeans who could really help Gorbachev out with domestic reform.

The key to building confidence will be less a matter of the number of troops deployed and more a matter of the transparency of the new security order. Soviet reformers made clear that transparency was vital. Indeed, it was more possible in the present atmosphere of demilitarization of Soviet society.[129] Of course, CSCE-type transparency was negotiated during the Brezhnev and Reagan presidencies, and it was not necessarily reliant on contemporary reforms. But as was evident from the sharply increased level and range of military-to-military contacts, there was a new meaning to modern transparency. The Soviet Union negotiated detailed exchanges of high-level military personnel with its adversaries, including the dispatch of ships for "friendly" port calls and the exchange of military college staff. When the CFE accord was called into doubt in early 1991, many of these elements of transparency also became questionable. The rise of the military voice in a more conservative Kremlin in 1991 clearly meant some reduction in defense policy reform. Defense policy reform tends to follow other reforms and is often best seen as a manifestation rather than a basic cause of détente.

The most important reason for thinking about military security in terms of common security is the threat that nuclear weapons pose to civilization as a whole. The earliest major agreements between the great powers concerned ways of limiting the risk of nuclear war or even nuclear fallout from tests. The "spirit of Camp David" in the 1950s and the détente of the 1970s were the result of this concern about common security. Of course, great power agreements on nuclear issues were reached without any general reform in defense policy. This suggests there is no clear link between domestic and foreign policy reform.

The nuclear issue is distinctive because of the strange esoterica of nuclear weapons strategy. The doctrine of deterrence, especially in its variant of Mutual Assured Destruction, requires a peculiar mix of certainty and uncertainty: certainty about the destructiveness of weapons and uncertainty about the conditions under which they would be used. Thus, if defense policy reform means openness, it will tend to run up against a doctrinal desire to leave some uncertainty about the where abouts of weapons and the chances that they might be used. Confidence about a secure second-strike potential as a guarantee of deterrence positively requires that the adversary not be able to find and destroy SLBMs, bombers, or even mobile-land-based weapons. The paradox of nuclear strategy is clear. Nuclear weapons are a basic reason for seeking common security and a more open discussion of nuclear strategy. Yet stable deterrence requires secrecy and some uncertainty, thereby limiting any possible openness in nuclear strategy.

Only two of the states discussed in this chapter have nuclear weapons, the Commonwealth of Independent States and China, although rumors persist about North Korea's intention to join the nuclear club. Yet there was no significant nuclear demilitarization in the age of reform, apart from the 1987 Intermediate-range Nuclear Force (INF) accord, until the July 1991 Strategic Arms Reduction Talks (START) accord. Until the START deal, the most successful nuclear arms control took place in 1972 under Brezhnev and Nixon, hardly a time that could be described as one of domestic reform in the Soviet Union. For most of its period of reform, China was engaged in no nuclear arms control talks apart from the ritual of the United Nations Disarmament Committee. But in August 1991, after years of refusing to sign the Non-Proliferation Treaty of 1968, China suddenly found itself the only great-power holdout. (France had signed in June 1991.) Thus China finally signed a major arms control accord, but more because of changes in the international system than because of any linkage to domestic politics. China has still not signed the Partial Test Ban pact of 1963, and it refuses any invitation to discuss tighter bans. It has acceded to the protocols of the South Pacific Nuclear Free Zone treaty, although it poses no limits on Chinese forces.

Nevertheless, China has not exported nuclear weapons, even to Pakistan. Nor has China been a conspicuously dirty tester of nuclear weapons. It switched to underground tests when the technology became available. Free of any constraint except cost, technology, and doctrine, China has continued to modernize its arsenal. The decision to retain minimum levels of nuclear weapons in most categories does not especially aggravate international security, although it certainly does not help build confidence in a nuclear free world. India obtained nuclear weapons in large measure because China did, and Pakistan seems to be trying to follow the Indian course.

Although this proliferation seems controlled, far less confidence might be expressed about a nuclear standoff between North and South Korea. Persistent reports since 1989 of North Korean attempts to obtain nuclear weapons make the Soviet and Chinese efforts to keep Pyongyang under control more important than ever before. Neither great power has an interest in encouraging Korean proliferation, and yet it is also clear from the Soviet Union's vain attempts to prevent China from becoming a nuclear power in the 1960s that the acquisition of the technology is not beyond the reach of developing states.

If the superpowers reduce their arsenals to the levels of the medium nuclear powers, Beijing has said it will contemplate joining the arms control process. Like France and Britain, China sees no sense in making proportional cuts in an arsenal that would suffer far more damage than would the superpowers' arsenal with so much overkill.[130] Indeed, the stability of the Chinese deterrent would be degraded if China made such cuts, given its minimum deterrence capability.

The Soviet Union is another matter entirely. Its arsenal, like that of the United States, was way beyond anything needed for minimum deterrence. Yet Gorbachev's reform of defense policy barely affected this nuclear capability.[131] The INF accord of December 1987 was the only significant nuclear arms control agreement in the first five years of the Gorbachev era. It was achieved after major concessions by the Soviet Union broke the negotiating deadlock left by Konstantin Chernenko, and once again it was a gamble that unilateral concessions would provoke a faster paced détente.[132] In this case the INF accord banning all land-based intermediate-range nuclear missiles was militarily insignificant but politically farsighted.

Of far more importance were the negotiations on START. The United States and the Soviet Union demonstrated that nuclear weapons were a vital part of defense policy reform when they signed a full START accord in July 1991. They also demonstrated that the nuclear issue remained a peculiar case of common security. In fact, it was the Soviet Union that declined to provide full information about its mobile-land-based missiles because it would compromise its second-strike capability.[133] The sophisticated and necessarily secret game of cat-and-mouse at sea focused on SLBMs became the main type of second-strike deterrent force. In 1992 Russia became the nuclear power, but weapons remained in three other Soviet successors.

Members of the armed forces were part of the negotiating teams for both superpowers. There was little sense that defense policy reform would mean the elimination of the military from negotiations. Reductions in nuclear weapons will certainly be a very different process from conventional demilitarization. The costs of maintaining nuclear forces are small—no small consideration in an age of economic priorities.

CONCLUSION

Let us return to the foreign policy reforms listed in the introduction. What follows are tentative explanations of why these reforms took place.

- Only four states (Vietnam, Hungary, the Soviet Union, and China) reformed their official position with respect to the international economy and the international division of labor. In each case these reforms took place after reforms at home were under way, and after a search began for assistance from the outside world. But acceptance of the features of the international economy did not necessarily lead to an abandonment of the basically command economy at home, even though features of a market economy were introduced.

- Only China became a much more important actor in the international economy. The Soviet Union actually lost ground during the time of reform, as did the East Europeans. China did so well because it was able to make use of its low-wage economy and export light manufactured goods to the global economy. Debt was always kept within manageable levels. When inflation grew, the center reasserted control for a time, but the essential market reforms remained in place to take up the growth rates when the restraints were removed. Regional variations in reform made for a far more flexible system.

- The patterns of FDI also suggest that China has led the communist world in reforms. China developed a range of ways to attract FDI and a willingness to change its practices when necessary. The presence of Chinese overseas and Hong Kong played a crucial role in attracting FDI. Successful reforms at home were important in both China and Vietnam in convincing the outside world that FDI made sense. The absence of effective reforms in the Soviet Union was a major problem in attracting large-scale FDI and support for membership in international organizations.

- Membership in international economic institutions is seen by the reforming state as part of its reforms. But the simple act of joining these bodies does not in itself solve any deep-seated problems. Advice and aid are helpful in the reform process but they cannot overcome internal obstacles.

- Real decentralization of decision making took place only in China. The Soviet reforms were not properly developed, but it did appear that the larger countries saw giving greater power to regional bodies as an essential feature of reform. Smaller and more ethnically homogeneous states like Hungary found it less necessary to decentralize and therefore basic reforms were avoided. The case of a divided Vietnam suggested regionalism of some sort has also operated as part of the reforms.

- Setting a more realistic value for the currency was a vital reform. China made frequent efforts in this regard, and the Soviet Union and Vietnam began to undertake similar action. Changes in currency are caused by a mix of internal and external factors.

- Reforms in the legal system were essential to encouraging FDI and even trade. China, Vietnam, and the Soviet Union were most responsive to the needs of the international market economy because they wanted continued FDI and an expansion of trade.
- Reform in banking and securities seems to be among the last of the domestic reforms. Much reform in foreign economic policy can be undertaken without these specialized reforms. But both sectors can be useful as additional ways of encouraging FDI and enhancing integration in the international economy.

In sum, to 1990 foreign economic policy was really reformed only in one state—China. Other countries shared either signs of reform (the Soviet Union, Vietnam, pre-1989 Hungary) or no signs of reform (the GDR and North Korea). China's success is easy to prove but hard to explain. Certainly prolonged domestic reforms set the proper atmosphere for reform of foreign economic policy. As a nonrival of the United States, China avoided political problems blocking Vietnam and the Soviet Union. Because of the overseas Chinese, China's regional differences, and the special role of Hong Kong, FDI was always easier to come by. Its large size broadened the scope for experimentation. Sadly, China's success in reforming its foreign economic policy has few features that can be replicated in other reforming communist states.

The reform of defense policy is summarized below.

- The main reason the Soviet Union and Vietnam withdrew from their foreign military engagements was to focus on domestic reforms. The Soviet decision was tougher because it was less obviously successful in its foreign war. Yet the Chinese experience in the Spratlys, as well as continued Soviet and Vietnamese support for allies, suggests that domestic and foreign policy aspects of defense reform are not necessarily linked.
- Reductions in military operations in the Soviet Union beyond its frontiers could be attributed to the desire to focus on domestic reforms. But as China's opposite trends suggest, there was little inherent in the international system that made such changes inevitable.
- Cuts in the size of defense forces and defense budgets are related to economic priorities. Soviet cuts came despite U.S. increases. Increases in China's defense budget came at the same time as rising military budgets in Japan and India. The link to the changes in the international system is unclear.

- Arms control has followed broader changes in foreign and domestic policy. Major reforms seem to mean much more unilateral and informal arms control. Nuclear arms control remains a special case. It limits how open defense policy can be.
- The role of international institutions, such as the United Nations, is enhanced by the new search for a peaceful settlement of disputes.
- Increased transparency and contacts between military professionals are more an effect than a cause of defense policy reform. The lower the perception of threat, the more such transparency and contacts become possible.
- A change in arms transfer policy may not lead to a cut because of the countervailing desire to make money by arms sales. This suggests the limits of defense policy reform and the complexity of its connection to other foreign policy reforms. By far the most important reason for changes in arms trade policies is changes in the international market.
- The loosening of alliance ties came largely because of opposition to such limits from smaller partners, and a sense that the burdens of alliance were greater than the benefits. Burdens are measured in economic was well as political and military terms.
- The stress on military professionalism as part of defense policy reforms is natural because the rest of society is also stressing professionalism. But it also makes possible a more aggressive defense policy in the future and seems to aggravate tensions within the armed forces about new directions for the new professionals.

This book has attempted to identify common features of reform in Communist Party states. Yet it is clear from the analysis of foreign policy reform in this chapter that this is a difficult task. The more one tries to compare more than two states, and the more one attempts to link reforms of domestic and foreign policies, the more difficult it is to identify common features of reform. There is little evidence, especially in terms of foreign policy reform, that China or Vietnam will follow the East European route. China has had remarkable success in reforming its foreign economic policy. This success has demonstrated that major reforms of domestic and foreign policy are not always linked. Nor is there a necessary link between reform of foreign economic policy and defense policy. Of course, it has been useful to search for common features of reform, but with a result that stresses the uniqueness of each case, this author believes that one should have the courage to admit that there is no theory broad enough to encompass a far more complex reality.

NOTES

This chapter is part of a wider project at the Royal Institute of International Affairs assessing the connection between the reform of domestic and foreign policy in communist states. Subsequent publications will include material on reform of ideology, culture, and communication.

This project is a cooperative effort, and the material used in this chapter has benefited from a series of study groups at the RIIA. Earlier papers, parts of which have been incorporated in this chapter, were contributed by Judy Batt and John Phipps. Other members of the core group include Peter Ferdinand, Neil Malcolm, and Alex Pravda.

This chapter is concerned with reform of foreign policy in Communist Party states. Thus, material on China, North Korea, and Vietnam is as up-to-date as possible. The Soviet Union ceased to be a Communist Party state in August 1991. The East European cases are the GDR and Hungary, both of which ceased to be Communist Party states in the last half of 1989.

1. Alex Pravda, "Introduction," in Tsuyoshi Hasegawa and Alex Pravda, eds., *Perestroika: Soviet Domestic and Foreign Policies* (London: Sage for the Royal Institute of International Affairs, 1990):1–24; and Gerald Segal, "Introduction," in Gerald Segal, ed., *Chinese Politics and Foreign Policy Reform* (London: Kegan Paul International for the Royal Institute of International Affairs, 1990):1–16.
2. R. E. Ericson, "Soviet Economic Reforms," *Journal of International Affairs* 2 (1989).
3. Barbara Krug, "Economic Reform," in Gerald Segal, ed., *Chinese Politics and Foreign Policy Reform* (London: Kegan Paul International for the RIIA, 1990):61–76.
4. Jim Mann, *Beijing Jeep* (London: Simon and Schuster, 1989).
5. Arguments developed from Leonard Geron, *Soviet Foreign Economic Policy Under Perestroika* (London: Frances Pinter for the RIIA, 1990).
6. This section draws heavily on P. Naray, "The End of the Foreign Trade Monopoly: The Case of Hungary," *Journal of World Trade* 23 (December 1989):85–97. See also I. Salgo, "Economic Mechanism and Foreign Trade Organisation in Hungary," *Acta Oeconomica* 36 (1986):271–87; and I. Berend, *The Hungarian Economic Reforms* (Cambridge: Cambridge University Press, 1990).
7. H. D. Jacobson, "The Foreign Trade and Payments of the GDR in a Changing World Economy," in I. Jeffries and M. Melzer, eds., *The East German Economy* (London: Croom Helm, 1987).
8. "A Guide for the British Businessman," British Embassy, Hanoi, January 1990.
9. *Far Eastern Economic Review*, 10 May 1990, p. 32.
10. Peter Ferdinand, "Regionalism," in Segal, ed., *Chinese Politics*:135–158; and Stafan Landsberger, *China's Provincial Foreign Trade* (London: RIIA Special Papers, 1989).
11. Ezra Vogel, *One Step Ahead in China: Guangdong under Reform* (Cambridge: Harvard University Press, 1989).
12. *Far Eastern Economic Review*, 15 March 1990, pp. 38–39.
13. For historical detail see Thomas Hammond, *The Anatomy of Communist Takeovers* (New Haven: Yale University Press, 1975). See also Geoffrey Stern, *The Rise and Decline of International Communism* (London: Edward Elgar, 1990).
14. Timothy Colton, *Commissars, Commanders* (Cambridge: Harvard University Press, 1979).
15. John Baylis and Gerald Segal, eds., *Soviet Strategy* (London: Croom Helm, 1981).
16. Michael MccGwire, *Military Objectives in Soviet Foreign Policy* (Washington: Brookings, 1987).
17. Ellis Joffe, *The Chinese Army After Mao* (London: Weidenfeld, 1987).
18. On these cases see Douglas Pike, *PAVN: People's Army of Vietnam* (Novato, Calif.: Presidio Press, 1989); and Young C. Kim, "The Political Role of the Military in North Korea," in Robert Scalapino and Jun-Yop Kim, eds., *North Korea Today* (Berkeley: Center for Korean Studies, University of California, 1983).
19. Gerald Segal, *Defending China* (Oxford: Oxford University Press, 1985).

20. Joffe, *Chinese Army;* and Yitzhak Shichor, "Defence Policy Reform," in Segal, ed., *Chinese Politics*, pp. 77–99.
21. Chwen-chi Liu, "A Preliminary Study on the Defense Economy of the PRC," in Richard Yang, ed., *SCPS Yearbook on PLA Affairs* (Kaohsiung: Sun Yatsen Center for Policy Studies, 1990).
22. Defense Minister on 5 December 1989 in BBC, *SWB,* FE/0633/B/2–5 and 0634/B/3–4.
23. *Far Eastern Economic Review,* 28 September and 19 October 1989.
24. Yuri Kirshin in *New Times,* no. 12, March 1990:30–31.
25. For a Soviet view of the Chinese experience, see Boris Gusev, "Conversion of War Industry: China's Experience," in *Far Eastern Affairs* (1990):231–39.
26. Richard Latham, "China's Defense Industrial Policy," in Richard Yang, ed., *SCPS Yearbook on PLA Affairs.*
27. Well covered in *China News Analysis,* 15 May 1990.
28. Julian Cooper, "Soviet Resource Options: Civil and Military Priorities," in Hasegawa and Pravda, eds., *Perestroika,* pp. 141–54.
29. Yevgeni Adamov, "The Economic Reform and Conversion," in *International Affairs* (Moscow) no. 1, 1990:112–22.
30. See Cooper, "Resource Options" and Edwina Moreton, "Comrade Colossus," in Curtis Keeble, ed., *The Soviet State* (London: Gower for the RIIA, 1985):125–39.
31. Hanoi Home Service, 12 March 1990, in FE/0719/B/3 and *Far Eastern Economic Review* 19 October 1989.
32. Joffe, *Chinese Army.*
33. Daria Fame, "After Afghanistan: The Decline of Soviet Military Prestige," *The Washington Quarterly* (Spring 1990):5–16.
34. Shevardnaze in *Vestnik,* April 1990, p. 16.
35. Ellis Joffe and Gerald Segal, "The Chinese Army and Professionalism," in *Problems of Communism,* November 1978:1–19; and Gerald Segal, "The Future of the PLA," in David S. G. Goodman and Gerald Segal, eds., *China at Forty: Mid-Life Crisis* (London: Jane's, 1989):37–40.
36. Tai Ming Cheung, "The PLA and the Tiananmen Crisis," in *SCPS Yearbook on PLA Affairs, 1989–90* (Kaohsiung: SCPS, 1990).
37. Harlan Jencks, *From Muskets to Missiles* (Boulder: Westview, 1982).
38. For some sense of these potential changes, see Quan Doi Nhan Dan on 6 June 1990 in FE/0791/B/2.
39. Bohdan Nahaylo and Victor Swoboda, *Soviet Disunion* (London: Hamish Hamilton, 1990).
40. David Goodman, ed., *China's Regional Development* (London: 1989).
41. Fame, "After Afghanistan."
42. Peter Frank, "The End of Perestroika," *The World Today,* May 1990:87–89.
43. Tai Ming Cheung, "The PLA."
44. Hanoi Home Service, 14 March 1990 in FE/0719/B/2; and Hanoi Home Service, 26 December 1989 in FE/0651/B/3–5.
45. David Holloway, *The Soviet Union and the Arms Race* (New Haven: Yale University Press, 1984); Stephen Meyer, "The Sources and Prospects of Gorbachev's New Thinking on Security," in *International Security* (Fall 1988):124–63; and Raymond Garthoff, "New Thinking in Soviet Military Doctrine," *The Washington Quarterly* (Summer 1988).
46. Shichor, "Defence Policy."
47. For a general discussion of the Soviet case, see Christoph Bluth, *New Thinking in Soviet Military Policy* (London: RIIA Printer Publishers, 1990).
48. Ellis Joffe and Gerald Segal, "The PLA Under Modern Conditions," *Survival* (July 1985):146–57.
49. Gerald Segal, "The Chances of a Coup," in *SCPS Yearbook on PLA Affairs, 1990–91* (Kaohsiung: SCPS, 1990).
50. Defense Minister Le Duc Anh in December 1989, FE/0633 and 0634/B/2.

51. Bluth, *New Thinking,* chap. 2:9–21.
52. William Odom, "The Soviet Military in Transition," *Problems of Communism* (May-June 1990); and Pal Dunay, *Military Doctrine: Change in the East* (New York: Institute for East-West Security Studies, Occasional Paper No. 15, 1990).
53. *Izvestiia,* 11 April 1990 in FBIS/Sov/90-072, pp. 54–55.
54. Shen Xiaofang, "A Decade of Direct Foreign Investment in China," *Problems of Communism* (March-April 1990).
55. Jan Prybyla, "China's Economic Experiment," *Problems of Communism* (January-February 1989).
56. *The Economist,* 19 August 1989.
57. Shen, "A Decade," p. 65.
58. *Far Eastern Economic Review,* 15 March 1990, pp. 38–39.
59. Ezra Vogel, *One Step Ahead in China* (Cambridge: Harvard University Press, 1989), p. 383.
60. Geron, *Soviet Foreign Economic Policy,* Chap. 4:39–53.
61. *Vestnik,* April 1990, p. 79.
62. Geron, *Soviet Foreign Economic Policy,* Chap. 4:39–53.
63. Ibid.
64. *International Herald Tribune,* 20 June 1990; and *Far Eastern Economic Review,* 24 May 1990, pp. 72–73.
65. *Far Eastern Affairs,* no. 1, 1990, p. 45.
66. *The Economist,* 7 April 1990, pp. 111–12.
67. *The Economist,* 19 May 1990, pp. 113–14.
68. *Far Eastern Economic Review,* 27 April 1989.
69. *Far Eastern Economic Review,* 11 May 1990.
70. R. J. Cima, "Vietnam's Economic Reform," *Asian Survey* 8 (August 1989):786–99.
71. E. Kerpel and D. Young, *Hungary to 1993* (London: EIU Economic Prospects Series, Report No. 1153, 1988).
72. T. Sarkozy, ed., *Foreign Investment in Hungary* (Budapest: Lang Kiado, 1989).
73. *The Economist,* 31 March 1990; and a survey in 28 April 1990.
74. *International Herald Tribune,* 4 June 1990.
75. Nagy, "Why Does It Not Work," *Acta Oeconomica* 39, no. 1-2 (1988).
76. Karen Dawisha, *Eastern Europe, Gorbachev and Reform* (Cambridge: Cambridge University Press, 1988).
77. William V. Wallace and Roger A. Clarke, *Comecon Trade and the West* (London: Frances Pinter, 1986).
78. Michele Ledic, "Foreign Economic Policy," in Segal, ed., *Chinese Politics,* pp. 230–55.
79. Gerald Segal, *Rethinking the Pacific* (Oxford: Oxford University Press, 1990).
80. Barbara Krug, "Economic Reform," p. 25.
81. Vogel, *One Step.*
82. Geron, *Soviet Foreign Economic Policy.*
83. Jonathan Stern, *Soviet Oil and Gas Exports to the West* (London: RIIA, Energy Papers, no. 21, 1987), p. 123.
84. Cited in Geron, *Soviet Foreign Economic Policy.*
85. Philip Hanson, "The Internationalization of the Soviet Economy," unpublished manuscript, October 1989.
86. *The Economist,* 24 February 1990, p. 68.
87. Frederick Brown, *Second Chance* (New York: Council on Foreign Relations, 1989), Chap. 9.
88. *Far Eastern Economic Review,* 27 April 1989, p. 73; and 24 May 1990, pp. 72–73. See also *SWB,* FE/Wo/118, A/6 and 0667/A3/7.
89. *International Herald Tribune,* 21 April 1990, p. 17; and *Far Eastern Economic Review,* 10 May 1990, pp. 32–33.
90. *Far Eastern Economic Review,* 10 May 1990, pp. 32–33.
91. *The Times* (London), 30 July 1990.
92. Phil Hanson, "The Internationalization of the Soviet Economy," mimeo, 1990.

93. Ed Hewett, "The Foreign Economic Factor in Perestroika," in Paul Lerner, ed., *The Soviet Union 1988* (New York: Crane Russak, 1989):123–39.
94. Krug, "Economic Reform."
95. A.M. Van den Bossche, "GATT: The Indispensable Link Between the EEC and Hungary," *Journal of World Trade* 23 (June 1989):141–55.
96. Peter Hardi, "Détente in Retrospect and Prospect" (Paper presented to a RIIA study group, October 1989).
97. Nayan Chanda, *Brother Enemy* (N.Y.: Harcourt Brace Jovanovich, 1986); and Gary Klintworth, *Vietnam's Intervention in Cambodia in International Law* (Canberra: Australian Government Publication Service, 1989).
98. Robert Ross, *Indochina Tangle* (New York: Columbia University Press, 1988).
99. Simon Long, "China and Kampuchea," *The Pacific Review* 2 (1989):151–57.
100. Gerald Segal, *The Soviet Union and the Pacific* (Boston: Unwin/Hyman for the RIIA, 1990).
101. Shevardnadze in *Vestnik*, April 1990.
102. George Arney, *Afghanistan* (London: Mandarin Books, 1990), chap. 13–14.
103. Gerald Segal, "Introduction," in Segal, ed., *Chinese Politics* :1–16.
104. Gerald Segal, *Defending China* (Oxford: Oxford University Press, 1985).
105. Shichor, "Defence Policy Reform."
106. Xu Shuming, "Perspectives on Maritime Security in the Asia-Pacific Region," in *International Strategic Studies* (Peking), no. 1, 1990.
107. Chong Pin-lin, *China's Nuclear Weapons Strategy;* and Gerald Segal, "China; The Maverick Nuclear Power," in Regina Cowen-Karp, ed., *Security with Nuclear Weapons* (Oxford: Oxford University Press for SIPRI, 1990):189–205.
108. Data from Stockholm International Peace Research Institute Yearbooks and Arms Control and Disarmament Agency's World Military Expenditure and Arms Trade.
109. Stephanie Neuman, "The Arms Market: Who's on Top?" in *Orbis* (Fall 1989):509–29; and O. Shevtov in *Komsomolskaya Pravda*, 12 June 1990.
110. For running data, see SIPRI yearbooks for 1990 and 1991.
111. Yitzhak Shichor, "Unfolded Arms," *Pacific Review*, no. 3, 1988.
112. Gerald Segal, "China and Israel," *SAIS Review* 2 (1987):195–210.
113. Gary Klintworth, "The Outlook for Cambodia," *The Pacific Review* 1 (1990):70–72.
114. Galia Golan, *The Soviet Union and the National Liberation Movements in the Third World* (London: Unwin/Hyman, 1988).
115. Jonathan Haslam, "The UN and the Soviet Union," *International Affairs* (Autumn 1989):677–85; and Aleksander Beloruga, "Soviet Peacekeeping Prospects," *Survival* (May 1990).
116. Geoffrey Berridge, "Diplomacy and the Angola/Namibia Accords," *International Affairs* (Summer 1989):463–79; and Chester Cricker, "Southern African Peacemaking," *Survival* (May 1990):221–232.
117. Bogdan Szajowski, "Ethiopia: A Weakening Soviet Connection," *The World Today* (August 1989):153–56.
118. Shevardnadze in *Vestnik*, April 1990.
119. Long, "China and Kampuchea."
120. Gerald Segal, "East Asia: The New Balances of Power," *World Policy Journal* (Fall 1989):731–57; and "All Aboard the Détente Train," *The World Today* (March 1990):49–53.
121. Alyson Bailes, "Settlement and Survival: China's Foreign Policy 1989–90," in *RUSI Yearbook* (London: RUSI, 1990).
122. Gerald Segal, "Introduction," in Gerald Segal, ed., *Arms Control in Asia* (London: Macmillan, 1987):1–17.
123. Discussed in Segal, *Soviet Pacific*.
124. A spirited discussion of this point can be found in Elgiz Pozdnyakov, "Foreign Policy and Home Policy: Paradoxes of Interconnection," in *International Affairs* (Moscow), November 1989:38–48.
125. Dale Herspring, "The Soviet Military and Change," *Survival* 4 (1989):321–38.

126. Lawrence Freedman, "The Politics of Conventional Arms Control," *Survival* 5 (1989):387–96.
127. Rene de Nevers, *The Soviet Union and Eastern Europe* (London: IISS Adelphi Papers, no. 249, 1990).
128. Neil Malcolm, "The Common European Home," *International Affairs* (Autumn 1989):659–76.
129. Shevardnadze, "Open Thinking Open the Skies," in *Vestnik,* April 1990:60-61.
130. Gerald Segal, "China as a Maverick Nuclear Power," in Regina Cowen-Karp, Ed., *Security without Nuclear Weapons* (Oxford: Oxford University Press for the Stockholm International Peace Research Institute, 1990).
131. Bluth, *New Thinking,* chap. 4:36–49.
132. Lawrence Freedman, "Europe Between the Superpowers," in Gerald Segal et al., *Nuclear War and Nuclear Peace* (London: Macmillan, 1988):81–124.
133. *International Herald Tribune,* 22 May 1990; and *The Independent,* 21 May 1990.

CONTRIBUTORS

The Editors

Gilbert Rozman, professor of sociology at Princeton University, compares China, Japan, and Russia and examines their mutual perceptions. His most recent book is *Japan's Response to the Gorbachev Era: A Rising Superpower Views a Declining One.*

Seizaburo Sato is professor of political science at the University of Tokyo and acting executive director of the International Institute for Global Peace in Tokyo. Sato plays an active role in Japanese political circles in discussions about Japan's role in the world and U.S.-Japanese relations. He has published widely in the fields of global security, international economic issues, and future international trends.

Gerald Segal, senior fellow in the International Institute for Strategic Studies and editor of the *Pacific Review,* London, is the author of several recent books on international relations along the Pacific rim. He takes a global approach to politics in the region, as in his 1990 book, *Rethinking the Pacific.*

Other Contributors

Judy Batt is professor at the Center for Russian and East European Studies at the University of Birmingham, U.K.

Shigeki Hakamada is professor in the International Politics and Economics Department, Aoyama Gakuin University, Tokyo, and a visiting faculty fellow at Princeton University.

Tsuyoshi Hasegawa was professor at the Slavic Research Center, Hokkaido University, Sapporo, Japan, and is now at the University of California, Santa Barbara.

Takayuki Ito was professor at the Slavic Research Center, Hokkaido University, Sapporo, Japan.

Nicholas R. Lardy is professor at the Center for Chinese Studies, Henry M. Jackson School of International Studies, University of Washington.

Paul G. Lewis is professor at the Faculty of Social Sciences, the Open University, Milton Keyes, U.K.

Tatsumi Okabe is professor at the Faculty of Law, Tokyo Metropolitan University.

Thomas F. Remington is professor of political science, Emory University.

Akihiko Tanaka is associate professor of international politics at the Institute of Oriental Culture, University of Tokyo.

INDEX